国家级精品课配套教材

21 世纪高等职业教育创新型精品规划教材

进出口单证实训教程

Practice of Import & Export Documentation

主　编　杨金玲

主　审　马卫民

天津大学出版社

TIANJIN UNIVERSITY PRESS

内 容 简 介

《进出口单证实训教程》是与国家级精品课配套的实训教材。教材的编写以刚刚毕业的王芳小姐受聘泰佛贸易公司后的职业生涯为主线，从初入单证部对单证的认知开始，到出于业务需要调入业务部具体负责来料加工，再到最后的安全收汇，实训内容就是在这样的模拟任务情境中展开的。本教程将进口与出口业务所涉及的单证工作有机地结合起来，紧贴业务实际，保证学生在校所学与实际工作的一致性。

教材分为六大模块十五项操作性强的任务，每项任务下均有业务背景介绍，使学生在一定的背景下从事具体的单证操作，减少上岗后的陌生感，尽快适应岗位要求，以及具备完成每项任务所需的知识、技能和贯穿始终的职业素质。

本书可用作经贸类应用文科院校的实训教材和在职人员的培训教材。

图书在版编目(CIP)数据

进出口单证实训教程/杨金玲主编. —天津:天津大学出版社,2009. 8

21世纪高等职业教育创新型精品规划教材

ISBN 978-7-5618-3095-6

Ⅰ. 进…　Ⅱ. 杨…　Ⅲ. 进出口贸易－原始凭证－高等学校－教材　Ⅳ. F740. 44

中国版本图书馆CIP数据核字(2009)第126268号

出版发行　天津大学出版社
出 版 人　杨欢
地　　址　天津市卫津路92号天津大学内(邮编:300072)
电　　话　发行部:022-27403647　邮购部:022-27402742
网　　址　www. tjup. com
印　　刷　昌黎太阳红彩色印刷有限责任公司
经　　销　全国各地新华书店
开　　本　169mm×239mm
印　　张　19. 75
字　　数　463千
版　　次　2009年8月第1版
印　　次　2009年8月第1次
印　　数　1－3 000
定　　价　35. 00元

前　言

随着我国加入 WTO，特别是自 2004 年 7 月 1 日起新的对外贸易法实施以来，我国进出口经营权由原来的审批制变为备案制，对外贸易的经营主体扩大到了自然人，外经贸企业如雨后春笋般蓬勃发展。在这种形势下，社会急需大量的国际贸易基础型人才——国际商务单证员。

《进出口单证实训教程》直接对应外经贸企业单证员岗位，教材的编写充分体现了以单证员实际岗位为基本、以具体工作过程为核心内容的课程设计理念，打造了融学习过程于工作过程中的职业情境。本书以真实工作任务为载体，按照进出口单证在实际业务中所处环节，序化教学内容。如图 0.1 所示，在整个教学过程中，坚持以学生为中心、以能力为本位，学中做、做中学，凸显工学结合的高职教育特色，体现教学过程的实践性、开放性

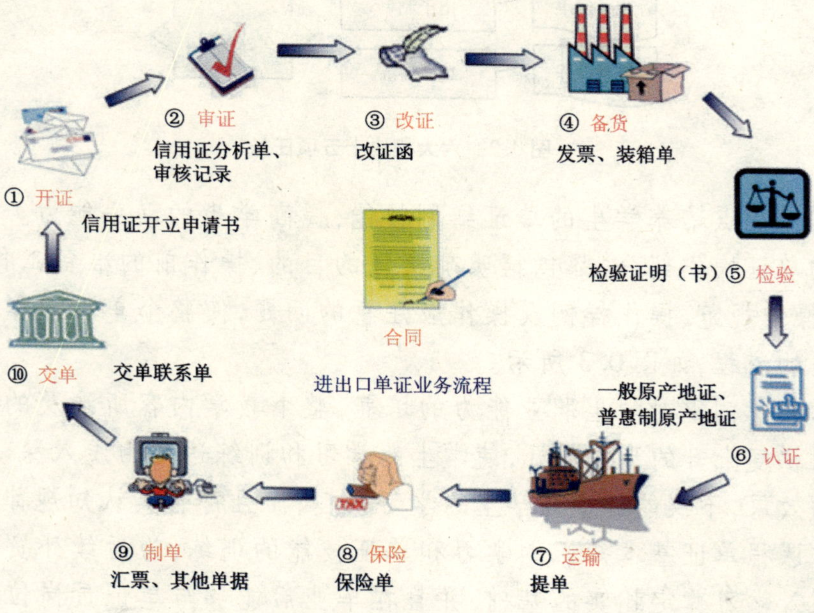

图 0.1　进出口单证业务流程

及职业性。

教材的编写是以刚刚毕业的王芳小姐受聘泰佛贸易公司后的职业生涯为主线，从最初进入单证部认知单证开始，到由于业务需要调入业务部具体负责来料加工业务，再到最后的安全收汇。整个教材围绕这样的业务背景展开，将进口与出口业务所涉及的单证工作有机地结合起来，紧贴实际，保证学生在校所学与在岗工作的一致性。

整个教材分为六大模块十五项操作性强的任务，如图0.2所示。在每项任务下，都有相应的业务背景介绍，使学生在一定的背景下从事具体的单证操作，减少上岗后的陌生感，尽快适应岗位要求，并使之具备完成每项实际工作所需的知识、技能和贯穿始终的职业素质。

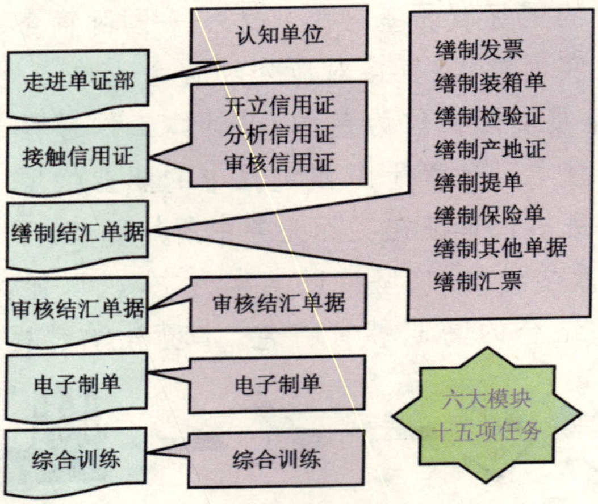

图0.2　六大模块十五项任务

本书重点培养学生的单证缮制技能，提高学生的动手能力。在每项具体的单证操作部分，都包括明确实训的目的、操作前的准备工作、操作程序、操作规范、操作样例及操作应注意的问题，使整个单证操作形成一个闭合的流程，如图0.3所示。

本教材侧重对学生职业能力的培养，整个教学内容所涉及的六大模块采用梯度上升的形式展开，使学生的学习和训练达到由浅入深、渐进式上升的效果，不仅能够提高学生的学习兴趣，而且符合其认知规律。学生通过本课程单证基本知识的学习和单证技能的训练，为后续外贸相关课程的深入学习奠定扎实的基础，并且在毕业后能够与单证员岗位零距离对接，为自身职业生涯打开一个良好开端。

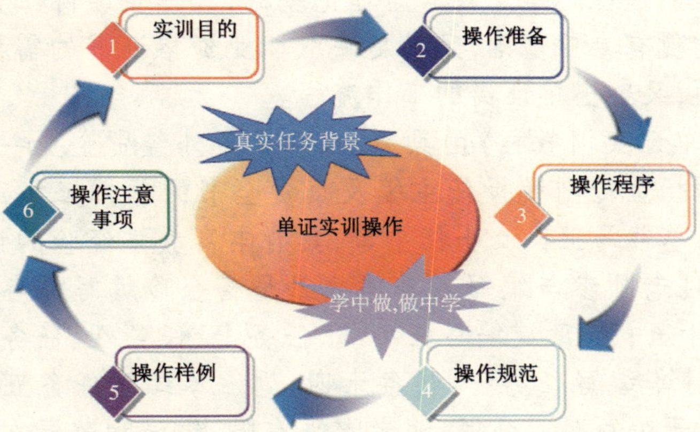

图 0.3　单证实训操作流程

本教材的编写贯彻了如下原则。

1. 实用性与真实性相统一

编写者具有丰富的外贸企业一线实战经验,对本教材的设计完全按照外经贸企业单证员岗位的业务流程进行,紧贴单证岗的工作实际,突出了教材的实用性、适用性和真实性,实现知识技能与实际业务的零距离结合。

2. 基础性与可操作性相统一

国际贸易所涉及的环节多,每个环节都有与之相对应的单证,但与安全收汇关系最为密切的是各种结汇单证。我们在使学生充分了解和掌握单证知识的同时,结合具体的业务背景,注重对学生的信用证审核能力、结汇单证缮制能力及结汇单证审核能力的培养。进而使学生了解国际商务单证今后的发展趋势,掌握电子制单等单证的缮制技巧,力争做到能真正通过学习适应今后单证岗位要求的零距离就业。

3. 针对性与广泛性相统一

本教材主要针对高职院校国际贸易实务专业及相关专业致力于从事国际商务单证岗的学生,又兼顾外经贸企业各类在职人员,针对性和广泛性相统一,是其工作中的好助手、好参谋。

4. 学历教育与证书教育相统一

本教材难易适中,既考虑高职在校生的现有专业基础,又基本满足单证员资格证书考试的需要,使学历教育与获取职业资格证书相结合。

总之,本教材设计力求开拓学生的视野,启发学生在国际贸易大环境中的开放性和创造性思维。既考虑理论基础,又注重实际工作技能;既考虑在校学生的现有专业基础,又满足获取职业资格证书的需要;既考虑应涵盖的知识面,又突出单证岗的工作流程。

《进出口单证实训教程》由具有长达15年外经贸企业一线实战经验的双师型教师杨金玲副教授任主编及负责全书的总撰工作,天服三悦服装进出口公司总裁马卫民女士任主审,具有丰富教学经验的许彦斌、张建华、周海琴三位老师参与编写。具体分工是杨金玲编写任务三、任务四、任务六、任务十五;许彦斌编写任务二、任务七、任务八、任务九、任务十、任务十一;张建华编写任务一、任务十四;周海琴编写任务五、任务十二、任务十三。由于编写时间仓促,编者水平有限,错误和疏漏在所难免。恳请教育界专家、同行企业家和广大学子不吝赐教。

编　者

2009年6月

目　录

1 走进单证部

任务一 认知单证

任务背景

王芳小姐毕业于天津外经贸学院,现受聘于天津泰佛(TIFERT)贸易公司。该公司是一家中型的专业进出口公司,主营纺织品、服装、工艺品、轻工产品、玩具及食品等进出口贸易。该公司的市场主要集中在欧美、日韩和中东地区。

作为一名新员工,王芳小姐首先被安排到公司的单证部,以熟悉有关单证方面的知识,进一步提高单证处理的技能和技巧,为今后从事具体业务奠定基础。王芳小姐从认知单据的概念、种类、作用,以及制单的依据、程序等主要内容开始,向公司的老员工们虚心学习。

【背景分析】

国际贸易买卖双方相距遥远,买卖双方不能做到一手交钱一手交货。在实际业务中,大多采用象征性交货方式,即卖方以交单代替交货,买方见单付款,因此国际贸易实质上是一种典型的单据买卖,进出口单证在国际贸易中处于一个非常重要的地位。王芳小姐作为公司的一名新员工,应该掌握和具备如下知识、技能及素质。

知识目标

①了解单证的基本概念和作用。

②熟悉单证的种类。

③掌握单证的工作环节。

技能目标

①看懂并识别不同的单证。

②熟悉并掌握常用的制单软件。

素质目标

①养成耐心细致的工作作风。

②真正理解单证工作在国际贸易中的重要性。

一、认知单证的基础知识

【单证的概念】

单证(Documents)是指在进出口业务过程中所使用的各种单据、证书及信用证。在国际贸易中,由于买卖双方所处的地理位置相对遥远,商品的买卖往往表现为单据的买卖,即买卖双方凭借单证来处理商品的交付、运输、商检、保险、报关及结汇等。进出口单证贯穿于进出口业务的成交、货源、运输、收汇的全过程,它的专业性和时间性强,工作量大,涉及面广,除了外经贸企业内部的协调配合外,还要与货物的生产单位、运输部门、银行、保险公司、海关、检验检疫机构及有关的行政管理机关等方面协调配合。对外经贸企业来说,在完成了货物的交付后,单证工作能否正确、完整、及时地完成,是决定能否顺利结汇的关键,直接关系到外经贸企业的经济利益。因此,单证工作是进出口业务中的一项非常重要的工作。

【单证的种类】

1. 根据进出口单证的性质划分

①金融单据:是指汇票、本票、支票及其他用于取得款项的凭证。

②商业单据:是指发票、装箱单、运输单证及其他与进出口业务有关的非金融单据。

2. 根据进出口单证的用途划分

①资金单据:如汇票、本票及支票等。

②商业单据:如商业发票、装箱单、重量单及规格单等。

③运输单据:如至少包括两种不同运输方式的运输单据、提单、非转让海运单、租船合约提单、快递收据、邮政收据或投邮证明,以及空运、公路、铁路或内陆水运单据等。

④保险单据:如保险单、保险凭证及预保单等。

⑤公务单据:如原产地证书、检验检疫证书及配额许可证等。

⑥附属单据:如寄单证明、寄样证明、航程证明及装运通知等。

3. 根据进出口商品的流向划分

①进口单据:如进口许可证、进口报关单、进口检验检疫单及保险单等。

②出口单据:如出口许可证、出口报关单、商业发票、装箱单、运输单据、汇票、出口检验检疫证、原产地证书及保险单等。

4. 根据单证签发的单位划分

①出口商自制的单据:如汇票、商业发票、装箱单及重量单等。

②协作单位签发的单据:如运输单据、保险单据、品质证书及有关证明函等。

③政府机构、民间机构签发的单据:如许可证书、检验检疫证书及原产地证书等。

【单证的作用】

在某种意义上说,国际贸易就是单据买卖,几乎所有贸易环节的具体操作都与单据的交换密切相关。在计算机技术高度发展的今天,单据同样扮演着相当重要的角色(如 EDI 无纸贸易和电子单据的运用)。不熟悉和不了解单证知识就意味着不懂贸易,无法与业务部门的相关人员进行正确沟通和交流,同时也意味着所进行的交易不可能顺利达成,其结果很可能会是旷日持久的官司,永远无法取得的货款或一辈子都收不到的货物。进出口单证工作的重要性具体表现在以下几个方面。

1. 履行买卖合同的证明

买卖合同的履行,一般是通过商品和货币的交换来实现的。但在国际贸易中,买卖双方分处于不同国家,在绝大多数情况下,商品和货币不能进行简单的直接交换,而必须以单证作为交换的媒介。在国际贸易合同履行过程中的单证,大致可分为两类:一类具有商品的属性,它们有的代表商品,有的表示商品的交换价值,有的说明商品的包装内容,有的保证商品的质和量,有的为商品输入国提供必要的证明;另一类具有货币的属性,它们有的直接代表货币,有的为货币的支付作出承诺或作出有条件的保证。各种单证都具有特定的功能,它们的缮制、签发、流转、交换等具体的应用反映了合同履行的进程,也反映了买卖双方权责的发生、转移和中止。由此可见,进出口单证是完成国际贸易程序不可缺少的工具,是履行买卖合同的证明。

2. 结汇的必要工具

国际贸易结算起初是以黄金、白银或铸币的交付来清偿货款,实行“现金结算”,15 世纪以后发展为以票据(光票)的授受来进行结算的“非现金结算”方式。随着航海运输和保险等行业的发展,海运提单从一般的货物收据演变为可以转让的货物所有权凭证,承担运输风险的保险单也变成可以背书转让的有价证券。这些单据在一定时间内可以作为一种抵押品,于是出现了跟单汇票付款的方式。在国际贸易中,货物的单据化使得商品买卖通过单据买卖来实现。卖方交给单据,代表交给货物;买方付款赎取单据,代表买到货物。在国际贸易结算中,不论采用哪一种支付方式,买卖双方之间都要发生单据的交接。单据代表着货物,掌握了单据就等于掌握了货物,单据转移达到了货物转移的目的,并使得货物的转移合法化。国际贸易中货物的单据化大大地便利了货物买卖时货权的让渡或转移,因此,在国际贸易中,全套正确、完整的单据，是卖方安全、迅速结汇的必要工具，同时也是买方取得物权证明的保证。

3. 避免和解决争端的依据

国际贸易就是单据贸易，所以在合同订立的前、中和后期都要对相关单据严格把关，不然就可能因单据的不规范、不确切或存在可授人以柄的漏洞，而引发麻烦或在发生有关争议后无法利用合法的手段（出示合格的单据）保护自己，更谈不上对对方的不合理要求据理力争、成竹在胸地说“不”。国际商务单证不但是收汇的依据，当发生纠纷时，它也是处理争议的依据。因此，它必须严格符合有关国家的法律、规则和惯例等要求。例如，货物在运输途中受损，货方向保险公司提出索赔，保险单就是赔偿的凭证；如关系到赔偿额的计算问题，发票又是赔偿的依据；如属于承运人的责任，向承运人索赔，提单或其他运输单据就是处理索赔的依据；如货物品质发生争执，品质检验证书又是处理纠纷的依据。

4. 外经贸企业经营管理水平的重要标志

进出口单证工作是外经贸企业经营管理的重要组成部分，是为国际贸易全过程服务的。单证工作的质量直接反映了企业管理水平的高低，单证工作在进出口业务中能起到“把关”的作用。如果在履行买卖合同的某个环节不能正确、及时地缮制或流转有关的单证，就会影响整个合同履行的进程。同样，进出口业务管理中的问题也会在单证工作中体现出来。因此，单证工作不能简单地等同于单证的缮制、复核和流转，而是能否围绕单证及时、妥善处理好进出口业务中的各项工作，能否协调和解决进出口业务中的各种矛盾，能否确保顺利结汇及维护企业的信誉，能否不断提高企业经营管理水平的重要标志。

加强单证工作并提高单证的缮制质量，不仅可以有效地制止差错事故的发生，弥补经营管理上的缺陷，加快对外交货的效率，还可以增收节支，加速资金周转，为国家创造大量外汇，并能提高企业信誉，促进进出口贸易的发展。所以，业内专家们说：“单证就是外汇。”

【单据缮制程序】

当买卖双方经过友好洽商按照 CIF 贸易术语达成一笔交易时，若合同中规定采用信用证支付方式，其单证流程如图 1.1 所示。

①为执行合同，买方首先到银行申请开立信用证。

②卖方收到买方通过银行开立的信用证后，要依据合同条款对信用证进行逐条审核。

③若信用证中的某些条款与合同中的条款不符且不能接受，卖方要求买方联系开证行办理修改信用证手续。

④待收到银行正式的改证通知后，卖方按照合同中约定的品质要求开始备货，随之产生发票和装箱单等单据。

⑤货物备妥后是否符合合同中的品质要求，最好委托第三方如出入境检验检疫局对货物施检，随之产生检验证书。

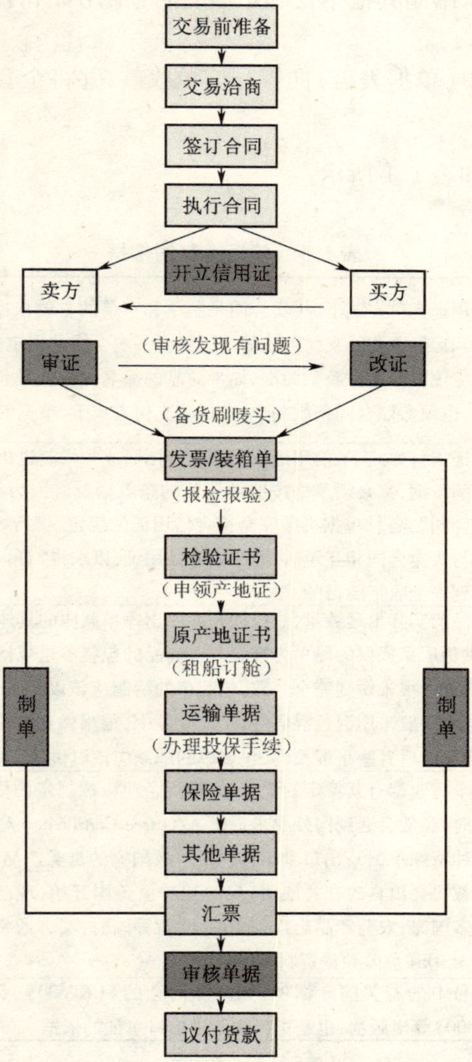

图 1.1 进出口单证流程图

⑥货物出口前，按照有些国家的规定要对货物的国籍进行认定，以便进口国按照不同的原产地征收不同的进口关税，卖方需要向贸促会或出入境检验检疫局申领原产地证书或办理有关发票的认证手续。

⑦委托船运公司或货代公司将货物装运出境，需要办理租船订舱手续，随之产生运输单据。

⑧国际贸易买卖双方相距甚远，运输途中会遭遇各种风险，为了转移风险需要与保险公司办理投保手续，随之产生保险单据。

⑨根据信用证要求缮制其他单据和汇票,按照信用证和合同要求备妥全套结汇单据。

⑩填写交单联系单(单据表盖)向银行交单收款,并将全套副本单据存档备查。

【单据缮制依据】

单据缮制的依据如表 1.1 所示。

表 1.1　单据缮制的依据

买卖合同	在非信用证支付方式下,买卖合同是制单和审单的首要依据,从商品名称、数量、规格、价格条件到运输方式及支付方式等均应符合买卖合同的规定;而在信用证支付方式下,单据的缮制应该以信用证条款为准,如果商品的品名、规格、单价及佣金等在信用证中没有明确规定,也须参照合同条款制单;在托收支付方式下,单据的缮制更需要以合同为基础
信用证	在信用证支付方式下,信用证取代买卖合同而成为缮制进出口单证的主要依据,凡是信用证项下的单据,都必须严格按照信用证的条款缮制。因为银行付款原则是“只凭信用证而不问合同”,各种单据必须完全符合信用证的规定,银行才能承担付款责任。如果信用证条款与买卖合同相互矛盾,除非修改信用证,以求得“证同一致”,否则应以信用证为准才能达到安全收汇的目的
仓库的出库单/供货厂家的码单	有关商品的实际出运数量,一般以仓库的出库单载明的具体数量、重量、规格、尺码等为准,或以供货厂家提供的码单为准。有些商品的包装不是规格统一,如棉花一般采用机压包,每包的重量很难做到完全一致,包装单的缮制应该以供货厂家提供的磅码单为准;再如服装、鞋帽一般采用混色混码装,实际业务中,很难做到所有的货物都严格按照搭配要求装箱,往往最后有些是混箱的,包装单的缮制应该以供货厂家提供的码单为准
业务上的特殊要求	由于每个行业都有其特定的要求,外经贸企业应按规定的格式和要求缮制单据。如出口纺织品时,经常会遇到国外要求提供 AZO free Certificate(无偶氮证明,这是与人类健康有关的一种特殊单据);出口到信仰伊斯兰教国家的禽类产品,进口商会要求提供由出口地伊斯兰教协会出具的有关证明;AMS 舱单由美国开始,现已扩展到加拿大、澳大利亚、欧洲等许多国家;农药产品出口到美国、欧盟等国时,买方通常要求卖方提供所出口的农药产品的 MSDS(危险数据资料卡)等
有关国际惯例	国际贸易中的有关国际惯例,如国际商会的《UCP600》、《托收统一规则》及《INCOTERMS 2000》等出版物,也是正确缮制进出口单证的依据

二、认知单证的基本技能

【实训目的】

通过本项任务的实训,应掌握的基本技能如下。

①看懂并识别不同的单证。

②熟悉常用的世格外贸单证教学(训练)系统。

【操作前准备】

进行本项任务的实训前，应准备的内容如下。

①登录“进出口单证实务”精品课网站（http://222.30.8.5:100 教育网入口；http://218.68.0.220:100 公网入口），进入教学资源中的单证全库，查看并熟悉常用的结汇单据的样例。

②登录南京世格外贸单证教学系统，熟悉操作步骤。

③登录全国国际商务单证考试中心（www.icd.net.cn），了解和熟悉单证员考试有关信息并查看历年考试真题。

【操作程序】

①进入外贸单证教学系统，建立个人信息。

②查看操作任务，作好操作前准备。

③进行操作并提交操作结果。

④查看操作成绩、参考答案和教师评语。

【操作规范】

外贸单证教学系统的功能及使用步骤如下。

1. 进入系统

①点击“世格单证”图标，进入世格外贸单证教学系统主页，如图 1.2 所示。

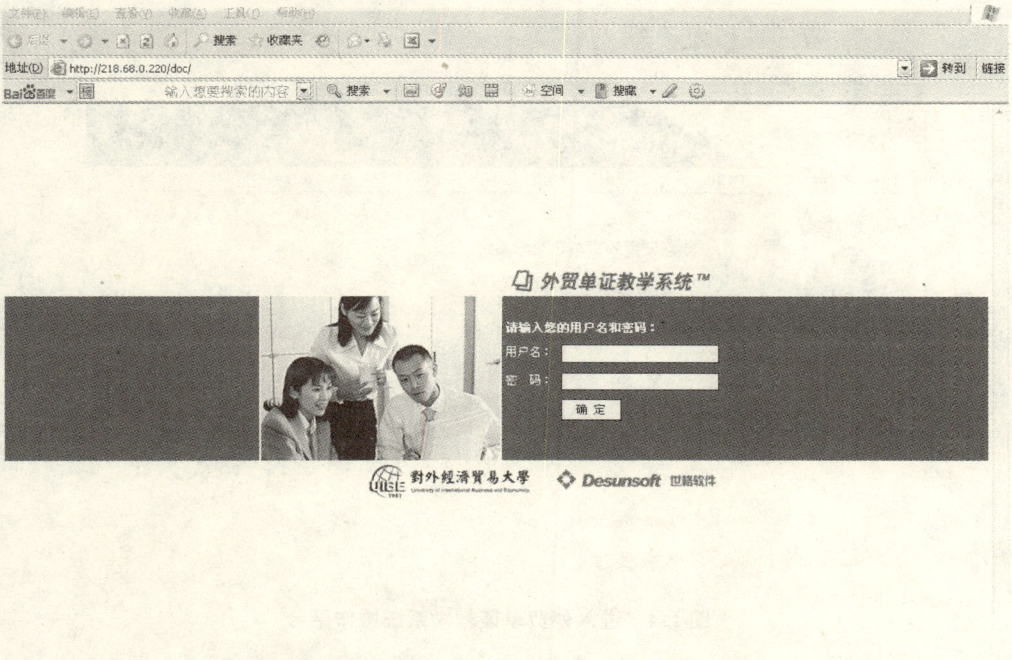

图 1.2 世格外贸单证教学系统主页

②输入用户名(由指导教师提供)、密码(初次使用无须密码),点击“确定”,进入外贸单证教学系统操作平台,如图 1.3 和 1.4 所示。

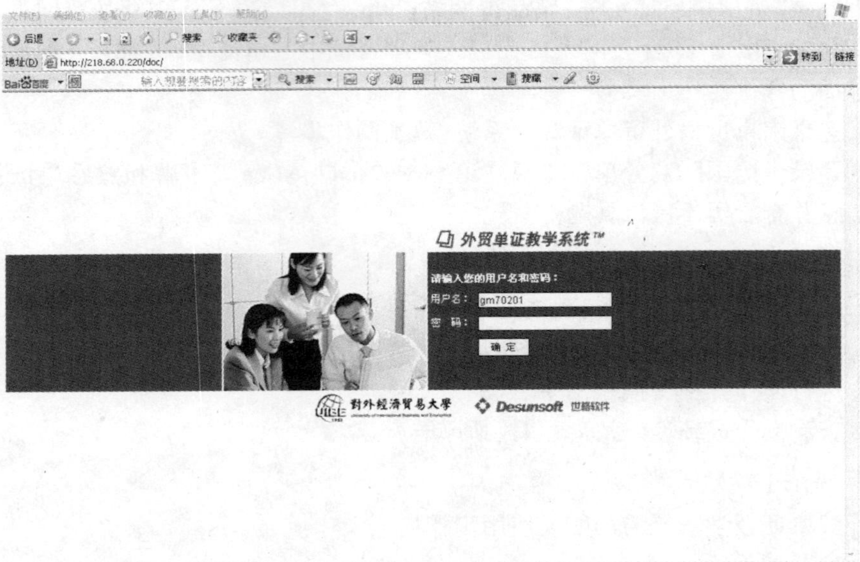

图 1.3　输入用户名和密码

图 1.4　进入外贸单证教学系统操作平台

③点击“个人信息”,在打开的对话框中输入自己的真实姓名、密码,点击“修

改”,如图 1.5 和图 1.6 所示。

图 1.5　输入个人信息

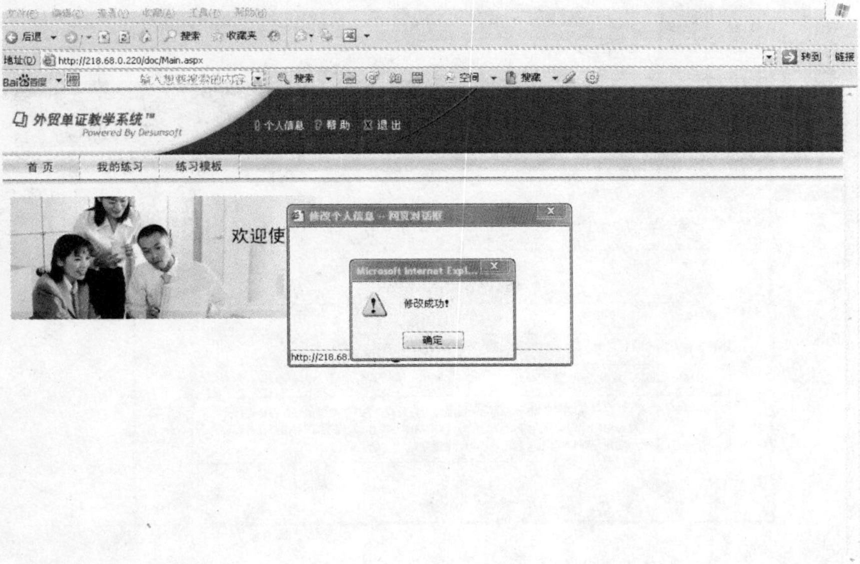

图 1.6　确定个人信息

2. 查看任务

①点击操作平台上“我的练习”图标,打开我的练习首页,查看练习任务,如图

1.7 所示;点击查看按钮,如图 1.8 所示。

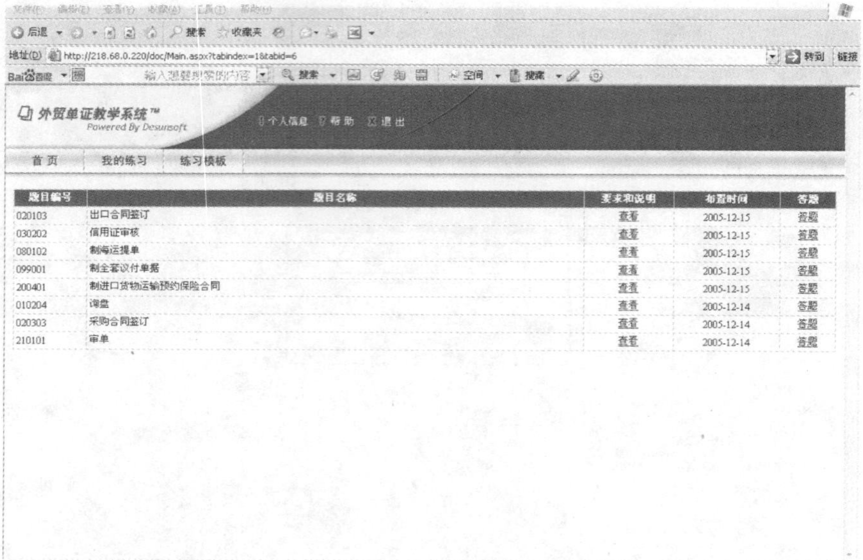

图 1.7 查看练习任务

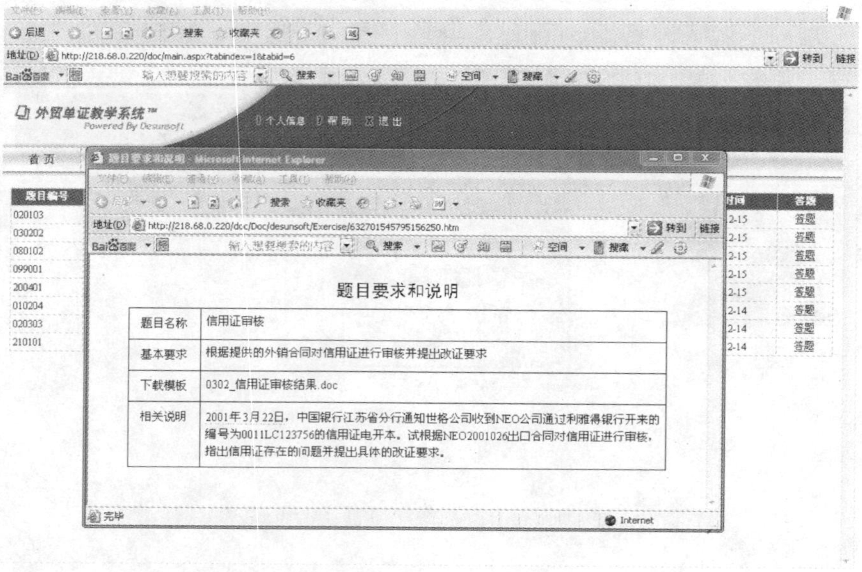

图 1.8 确认查看

②点击拟训练任务(单据)对应的“答题”按钮,进入“答题”界面,如图 1.9 所示。

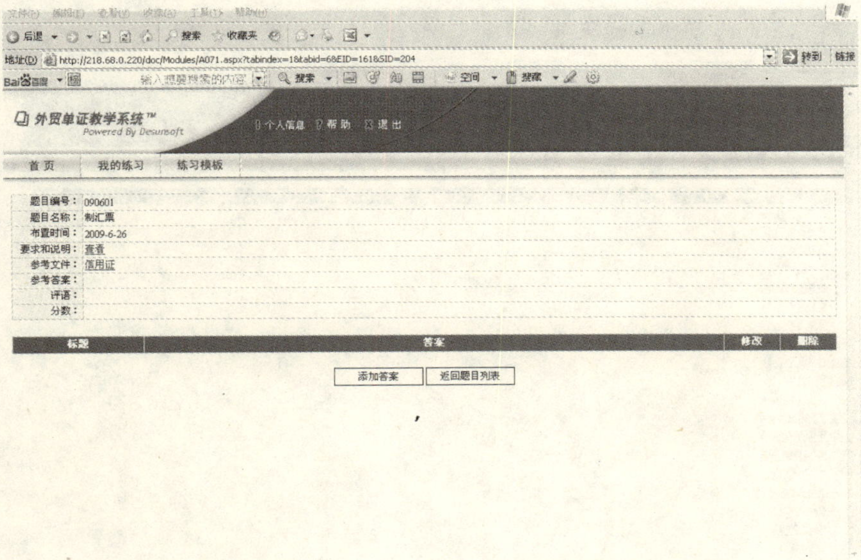

图 1.9　进入答题界面

③点击“参考文件”中所给单据名称按钮，查看所给单据信息，如图 1.10 所示。

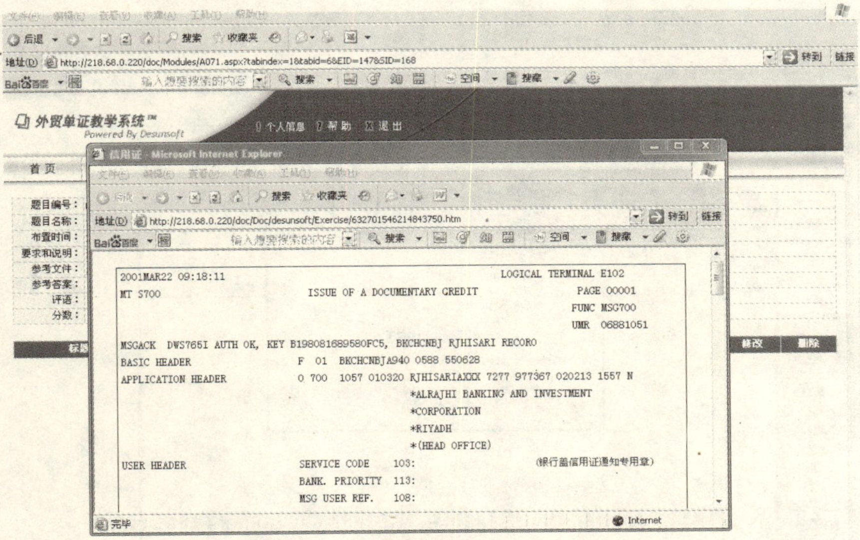

图 1.10　查看单据信息

④点击操作平台上“练习模板”，查找操作单据，如图 1.11 所示。

图 1.11　查找操作单据

⑤点击操作单据名称(如汇票),下载单据模板,准备操作,如图 1.12 和图 1.13 所示。

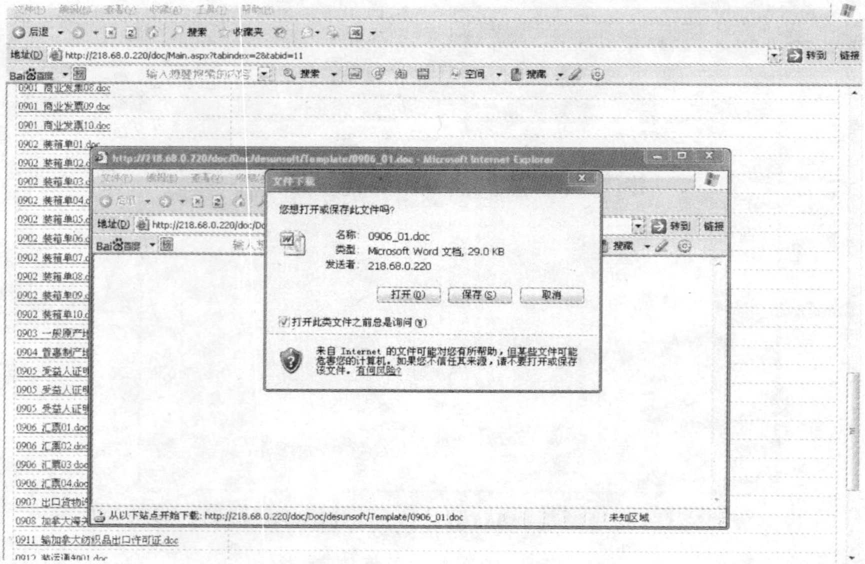

图 1.12　点击操作单据名称

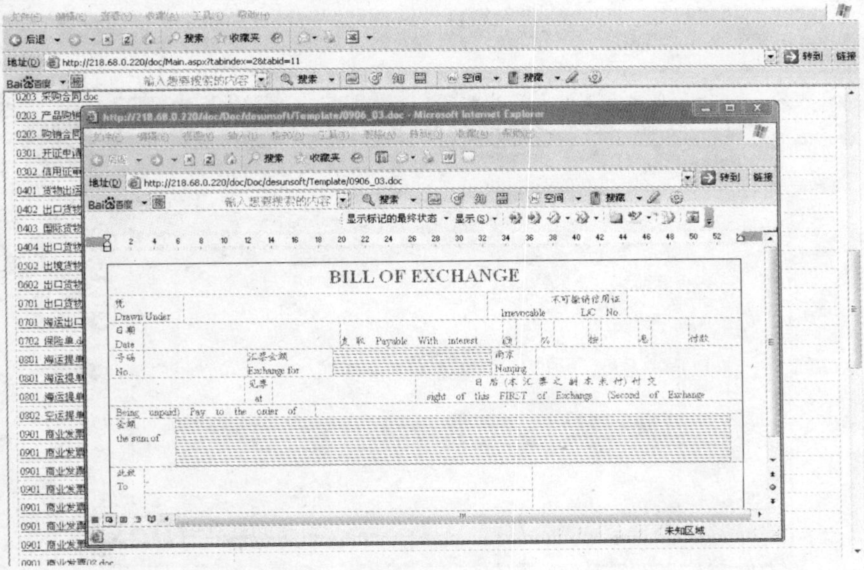

图 1.13 下载单据模板

3. 操作及提交

①根据所给信息，在下载模板上进行相关信息操作、缮制，并将其保存到适当位置，如图 1.14 和图 1.15 所示。

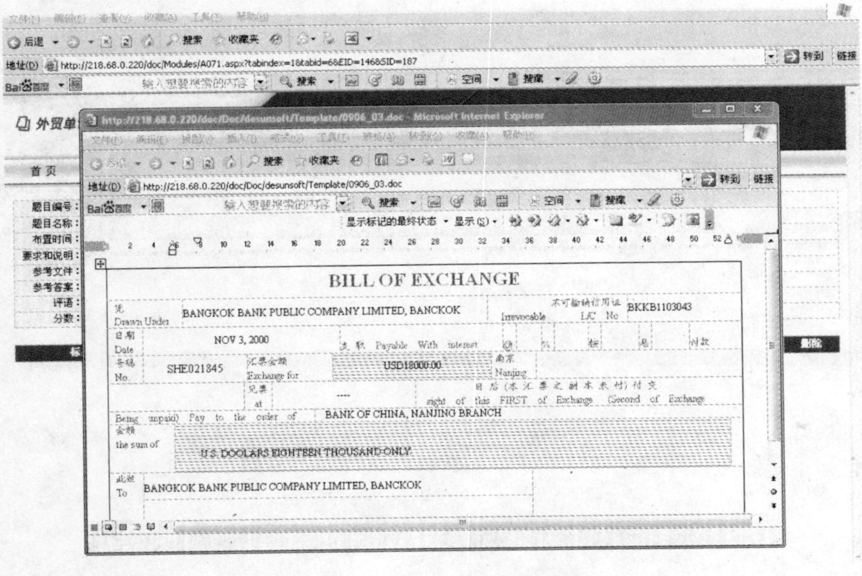

图 1.14 缮制单据

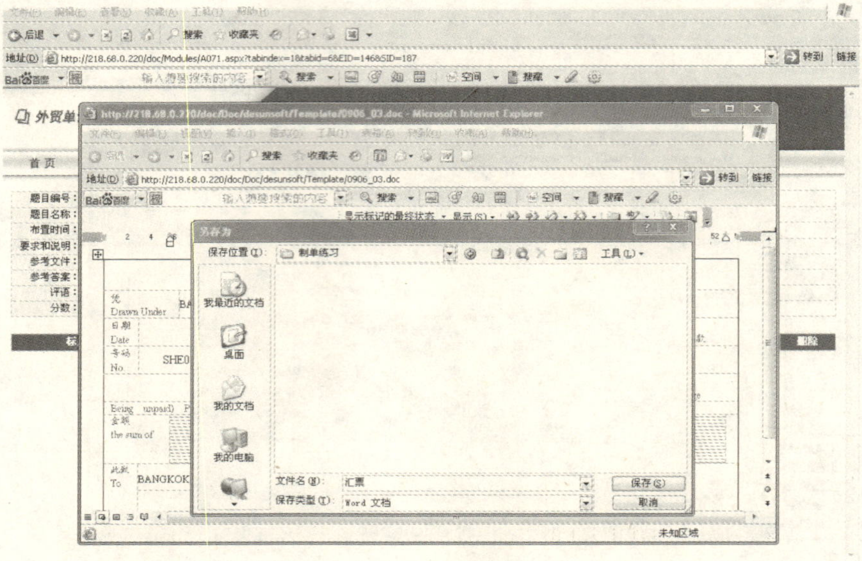

图 1.15　保存到“我的电脑”

②点击操作平台上“添加答案”按钮，在出现的对话框（标题栏）内，输入要提交答案的文件名（如姓名＋单据名称），点击浏览按钮，选择要提交的文件，并将其“打开”如图 1.16 和图 1.17 所示。

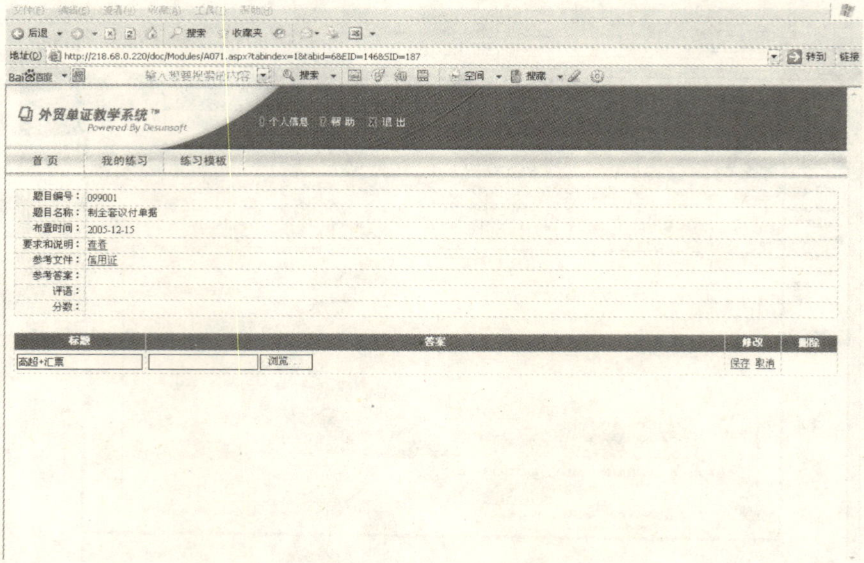

图 1.16　输入要提交答案的文件名

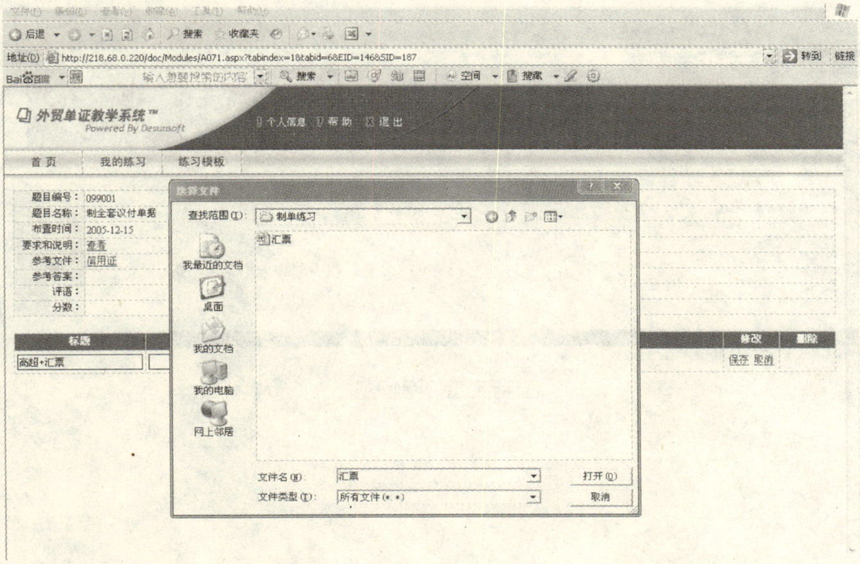

图 1.17 选择要提交的文件

③浏览栏目中出现提交文件路径、名称后，点击保存，如图 1.18 所示；完成作业提交任务，如图 1.19 所示。

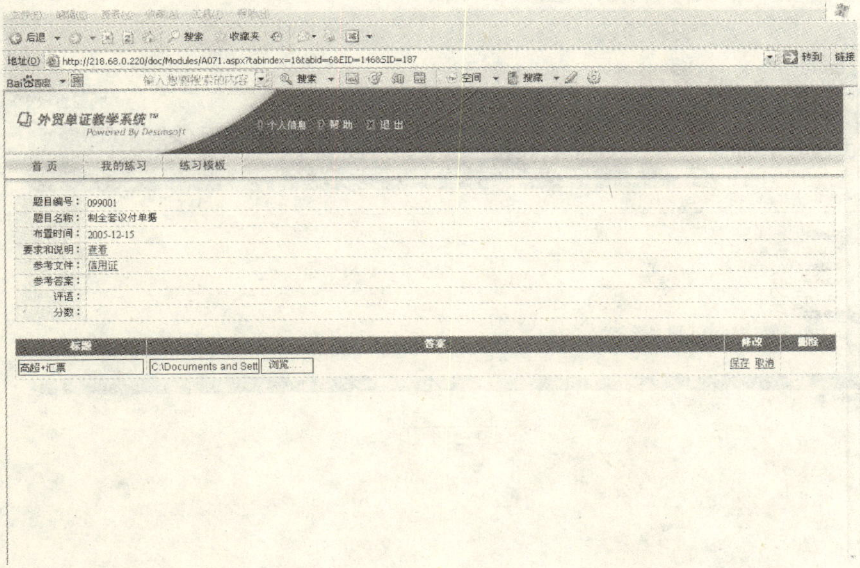

图 1.18 点击保存

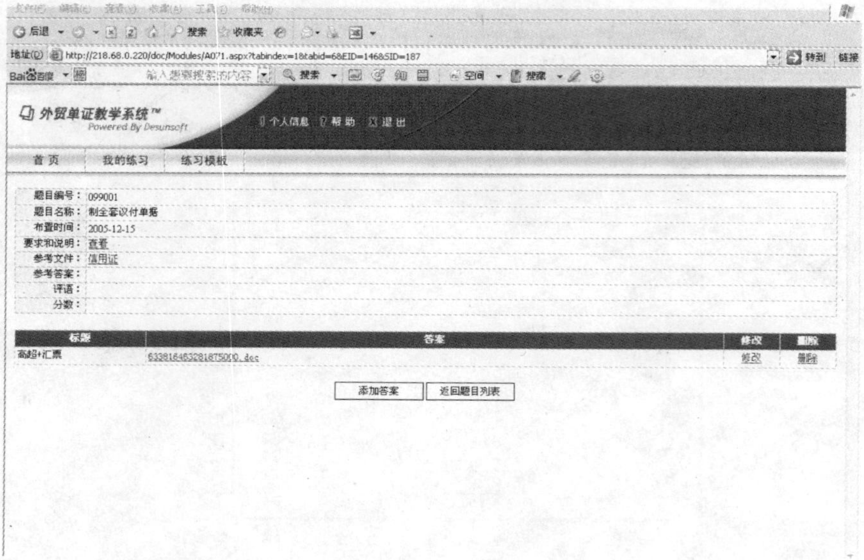

图 1.19　完成作业提交任务

4. 查看反馈

①指导教师评阅学生作业并打分、写出评语后，学生即可在"我的练习"中看到自己的作业成绩和教师评语，如图 1.20 所示。

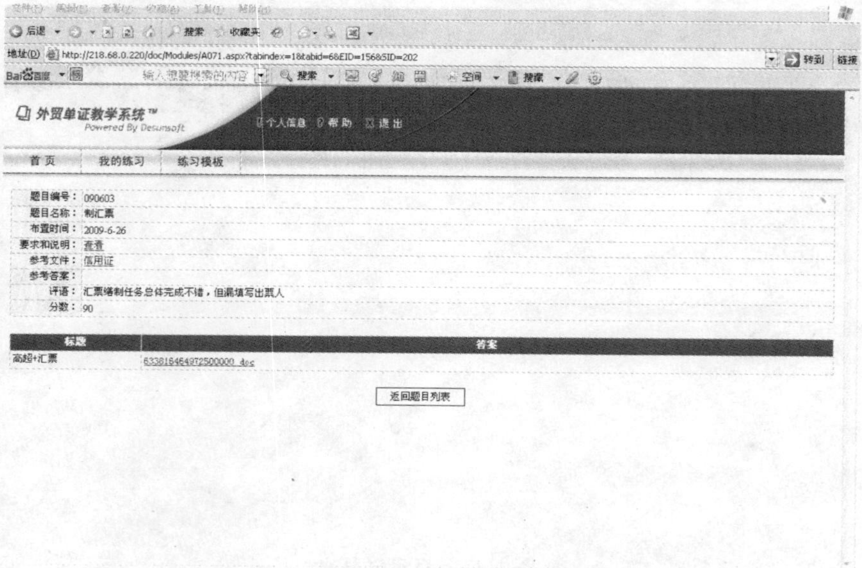

图 1.20　查看作业成绩和教师评语

②如果指导教师公布了参考答案，学生可在“我的练习”中“参考答案”栏内点击相关单据名称（如汇票），查看有关参考答案，如图 1.21 所示。

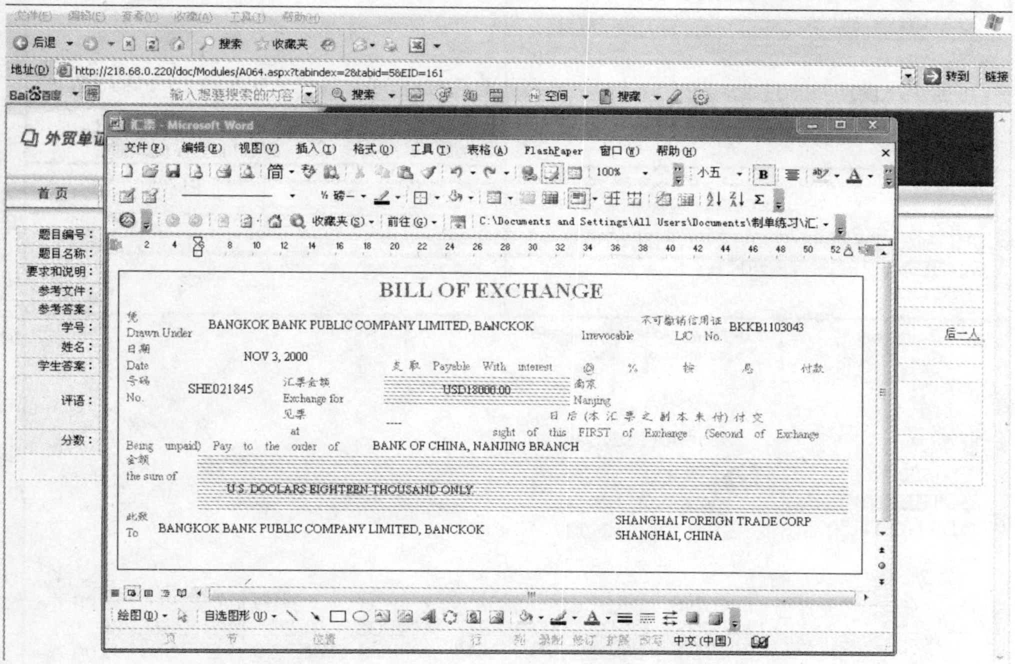

图 1.21 查看参考答案

【单证样例】

基于外经贸实际工作的洗衣袋出口业务所缮制的全套结汇单据样例包括发票、装箱单、检验证书、普惠制原产地证书、一般原产地证书、海运提单、保险单、证明函及汇票，分别如图 1.22 ~ 1.30 所示。

【操作注意事项】

①注意进入世格外贸制单教学系统时，用户名是由教师提供的，一般是专业名称的缩写、所在班级及本人的学号，切记勿填本人的姓名，否则无法成功登录该系统。

②成功登录系统后要及时建立个人信息，并牢记自己设定的密码，忘记密码同样也无法成功登录该系统。

③点击操作平台上“添加答案”按钮，在出现的对话框“标题”栏内，一定写入要提交答案的文件名称，如：姓名 + 单据，否则作业无法被成功提交。

④提交作业后一定要确认“答案”下面有列表后，才表明作业已成功提交，否则要重新提交。

Issuer TIANJIN GARMENT I/E INC NO.1 YOU YI ROAD, HE XI DISTRICT, TIANJIN, CHINA	商 业 发 票 COMMERCIAL INVOICE
To H_M TRADING SWEDEN AB KORSGATAN 15 SE 412 18 SWEDEN	No. G2008S/A16001 Date OCT 18, 2008
	S/C No. YD16008 L/C No. FM0809378
Trans Detail SHIPMENT FROM TIANJIN, CHINA TO GOTHENBURG SWEDEN BY SEA	Terms of payment BY L/C AT SIGHT

Marks & numbers	Number and kind of packages; description of goods	Quantity	Unit Price	Amount
H_M YD16008 GOTHERNBURG CTN NO.1-180	180 CARTONS = 5400PCS LAUNDRYBAG 100% POLYESTER SIZE 72 x 110CM			
	30CTNS ORDER NO.080816	900PCS	USD1.95/PC	USD1755.00
	120CTNS ORDER NO.080817	3600PCS	USD2.05/PC	USD7380.00
	30CTNS ORDER NO.080818	900PCS	USD2.00/PC	USD1800.00
	180CTNS	5400PCS		USD10935.00

TOTAL: GROSS WEIGHT 4500.00KGS
NET WEIGHT4320.00KGS
MEASUREMENT 4.726M3

天津服装进出口股份有限公司
TIANJIN GARMENTS IMPORT & EXPORT INCORPORATION

图 1.22 发票

Issuer:

TIANJIN GARMENT I/E INC
NO.1 YOU YI ROAD, HE XI DISTRICT,
TIANJIN, CHINA

To

H_M TRADING SWEDEN AB
KORSGATAN 15 SE 412 18 SWEDEN

装 箱 单

PACKING LIST

Invoice No. G2008S/A16001 Date OCT 18, 2008

Marks and numbers | Number and kind of packages Description of goods

H_M
YD16008
GOTHERNBURG
CTN NO.1-180

LAUNDRYBAG
100% POLYESTER
SIZE 72 x 110CM

ORDER NO.	QTY	CTN NO.	G.W.	N.W.	MEAS
ORDER NO.080816	900PCS	30CTNS	750KGS	720KGS	0.788M3
ORDER NO.080817	3600PCS	120CTNS	3000KGS	2880KGS	3.150M3
ORDER NO.080818	900PCS	30CTNS	750KGS	720KGS	0.788M3
TOTAL:	5400PCS	180CTNS	4500KGS	4320KGS	4.726M3

L/C NO. FM0809378

TOTAL: GROSS WEIGHT 4500KGS
NET WEIGHT 4320KGS
MEASUREMENT 4.726M3

图 1.23 装箱单

中华人民共和国出入境检验检疫　　　　正　本

ENTRY-EXIT INSPECTION AND QUARANTITE　　ORIGINAL

OF THE PEOPLE'S REPUBLIC OF CHINA

编号 No.: 120600209026897

QUALITY CERTIFICATE

发货人
Consignor TIANJIN GARMENT I/E INC

收货人
Cosignee * * * *

品名 Description of Goods LAUNDRYBAG 报检数量/重量 Quantity/Weight Declared 5400PCS 包装种类及数量 Number and Type of Packages 180 CARTONS 运输工具 Means of Conveyance HENGHE RIVER V.385	标记及号码 Mark & No. H & M YD16008 GOTHERNBURG CTN NO. 1-180

检验结果

Result of inspection

SAMPLES WERE DRAWN AT RANDOM FROM THE WHOLE LOT OF GOODS AND INSPECTED STRICTLY ACCORDING TO THE S/C NO. YD16008

ORDER NO. 080816　900PCS　30CARTONS
ORDER NO. 080817　3600PCS　120CARTONS
ORDER NO.080818　900PCS　30CARTONS

THE ABOVE RESULTS OF INSPCTION ARE IN CONFORMITY WITH THE REQUIREMENTS IN THE SAID CONTRACT.　　L/C NO. FM0809378

印章：　　签证地点 Place of Issue 天津　　签证日期 Date of Issue OCT 26, 2008

Official Stamp

天津

授权签字人 Authorized Officer ZHANG MING　　签名 Signature 张明

我们已尽所知和最大能力实施上述检验，不能因我们签发本证书而免除卖方或其他方面根据合同和法律所承担的产品质量责任和其他责任。

All inspection are carried out conscientiously to the best of our knowledge and ability. This certificate dose not in any respect absolve the seller and other related parties from his contractual and legal obligations especially when product quality is concerned.

图 1.24　检验证书

ORIGINAL

1. Goods consigned from (Exporter's business name, address, country) TIANJIN GARMENT I/E INC NO. 1 YOU YI ROAD, HE XI DISTRICT, TIANJIN, CHINA	Reference No. G091206100070200 **GENERALIZED SYSTEM OF PREFERENCES** **CERTIFICATE OF ORIGIN** **(Combined declaration and certificate)** **FORM A** Issued in THE PEOPLE'S REPUBLIC OF CHINA (country) See Notes, overleaf
2. Goods consigned to (Consignee's name, address, country) H _M TRADING SWEDEN AB KORSGATAN 15 SE 412 18 SWEDEN	
3. Means of transport and route (as far as known) SHIPMENT FROM TIANJIN, CHINA TO GOTHENBURG SWEDEN BY SEA	4. For official use

5. Item number	6. Marks and numbers of packages	7. Number and kind of packages; description of goods	8. Origin criterion (see Notes overleaf)	9. Gross weight or other quantity	10. Number and date of invoices
1	H _M YD16008 GOTHERNBURG CTN NO. 1-180	180 (ONE HUNDERD AND EIGHTY) CARTONS OF LAUNDRYBAG L/C NO. FM0809378 * * * * *	"P"	4500KGS	INV NO. G2008S/ A16001 OCT 18, 2008

11. Certification It is hereby certified, on the basis of control carried out, that the declaration by the exporter is correct. TIANJIN CHINA, OCT 18, 2008 Place and date, signature and stamp of certifying authority	12. Declaration by the exporter The undersigned hereby declares that the above details and statements are correct; that all the goods were produced in CHINA (country) and that they comply with the origin requirements specified for those goods in the Generalized System of Preferences for goods exported to SWEDEN (importing country) TIANJIN CHINA, OCT 18, 2008 Place and date, signature of authorized signatory

S065500265

图 1.25 普惠制原产地证书

ORIGINAL

1. Exporter
TIANJIN GARMENT I/E INC
NO.1 YOU YI ROAD, HE XI DISTRICT,
TIAJIN, CHINA

Certificate No. CCPIT 083711879
08C1200A0018/00175

CERTIFICATE OF ORIGIN
OF
THE PEOPLE' S REPUBLIC OF CHINA

2. Consignee
H_M TRADING SWEDEN AB
KORSGATAN 15 SE 412 18 SWEDEN

3. Means of transport and route
SHIPMENT FROM TIANJIN, CHINA TO
GOTHENBURG SWEDEN BY SEA

4. Country / region of destination
SWEDEN

5. For certifying authority use only

6. Marks and numbers	7. Number and kind of packages; description of goods	8. H.S.Code	9. Quantity	10. Number and date of invoices
H_M YD16008 GOTHERNBURG CTN NO.1-180	180(ONE HUNDERD AND EIGHTY) CARTONS OF LAUNDRYBAG L/C NO. FM0809378 * * * * *	6305	4500.00KGS	INV NO. G2008S/ A16001 OCT 18, 2008

11. Declaration by the exporter
The undersigned hereby declares that the above details and statements are correct, that all the goods were produced in China and that they comply with the Rules of Origin of the People's Republic of China.

TIANJIN OCT 18, 2008 陈晓宏
Place and date, signature and stamp of authorized signatory

12. Certification
It is hereby certified that the declaration by the exporter is correct

中国国际贸易促进委员会 单据证明专用章 (津) CHINA COUNCIL FOR THE PROMOTION OF INTERNATIONAL TRADE (TIANJIN)

TIANJIN OCT 18, 2008
Place and date, signature and stamp of certifying authority

图 1.26 一般原产地证书

Shipper
托運人

TIANJIN GARMENT I/E INC
NO. 1 YOU YI ROAD, HE XI DISTRICT,
TIAJIN, CHINA

B/L No. EASL089021186

EAS LINE
大通航運有限公司
EAS EXPRESS SHIPPING LTD.
联　运　提　单
COMBINED TRANSPORT BILL OF LADING

Consignee or order
收貨人或指示

TO ORDER

Notify party
通知地址

H _M TRADING SWEDEN AB
KORSGATAN 15 SE 412 18 SWEDEN

RECEIVED the goods in apparant good order and condition as specified below unless otherwise stated herein.
The carrier in accordance with the provisions contained in this document,
1) undertakes to perform or to procure the performance of the entire transport from the place at which the goods are taken in charge to the place designated for delivery in this document, and
2) assumes liability as prescribed in this document for such transport.
One of the Bills of Lading must be surrendered duly indorsed in exchange for the goods or delivery order.

Pre-carriage by 首段運輸	Place of receipt 收貨地點
Ocean vessel 海運船隻	**Port of loading 裝貨港**
HENGHE RIVER V. 385	TIANJIN, CHINA

Port of discharge 卸貨港	Place of delivery 交貨地點	Freight payable at 運費支付地	Number of original Bs/L 正本提單份數
GOTHENBURG, SWEDEN			THREE

Marks and Nos. 標志和號碼	Number and Kind of packages 件數和包裝種類	Description of goods 貨名	Gross weight (kgs.) 毛重(公斤)	Measurement (m^3) 尺碼(立方米)
H _M YD16008 GOTHERNBURG CTN NO. 1-180	180CARTONS	LAUNDRYBAG FREIGHT PREPAID SHIPPER'S LOAD, COUNT AND SEAL L/C NO. FM0809378	4500. 00KGS	4. 726M3

Original

ON BOARD
OCT 28, 2008

EASL4789321/11568/180/CFS/CFS

TOTAL: ONE HUNDRED AND EIGHTY CARTONS ONLY

以上細目由托運人提供
ABOVE PARTICULARS FURNISHED BY SHIPPER

Freight and charges
運費和費用

IN WITNESS whereof the number of original Bills of Lading stated above have been signed, one of which being accomplished, the other (s) to be void.

Place and date of issue
簽單地點和日期　TIANJIN　OCT 28, 2008

Signed for or on behalf of the carrier
代表承運人簽字

EAS EXPRESS SHIPPING LTD.
韩　伟
As agent

图 1.27　海运提单

PICC 中国人民财产保险股份有限公司
PICC Property and Casualty Company Limited

货物运输保险单 CARGO TRANSPORTATION INSURANCE POLICY

印刷号 (Printed Number) N 001572　　保险单号(Policy No.) TT08/1201071198404542
合同号 (Contract No.) YD16008
发票号 (Invoice No.) G2008S/A16001
信用证号(L/C No.) FM0809378
被保险人(Insured): TIANJIN GARMENT I/E INC

中国人民财产保险股份有限公司（以下简称本公司）根据被保险人要求，以被保险人向本公司缴付约定的保险费为对价，按照本保险单列明条款承保下述货物运输保险，特订立本保险单。
THIS POLICY OF INSURANCE WITNESSES THAT PICC PROPERTY AND CASUALTY COMPANY LIMITED (HEREINAFTER CALLED "THE COMPANY") AT THE REQUEST OF THE INSURED AND IN CONSIDERATION OF THE AGREED PREMIUM PAID TO THE COMPANY BY THE INSURED, UNDERTAKES TO INSURE THE UNDERMENTIONED GOODS IN TRANSPORTATION SUBJECT TO THE CONDITIONS OF THIS POLICY AS PER THE CLAUSES PRINTED BELOW.

标记 MARKS & NOS.	包装及数量 QUANTITY	保险货物项目 GOODS	保险金额 AMOUNT INSURED
AS PER INV. NO. G2008S/A16001	180 CARTONS	LAUNDRYBAG L/C NO. FM0809378	USD12029.00

总保险金额:
Total Amount Insured: TWELVEN THOUSAND AND TWENY-NINE ONLY

保费(Premium): AS ARRANGED　　启运日期(Date of Commencement): AS PER B/L

装载运输工具(Per Conveyance): HENCHE RIVER V.385

自: From TIANJIN, CHINA　　经: Via　　至: To GOTHENBURG, SWEDEN

承保险别(Conditions):

COVERING ALL RISKS AND WAR RISK AS PER OCEAN MARINE CARGO CLAUSES OF PICC DATED 1/1/1981 INCLUDING WAREHOUSE TO WAREHOUSE

所保货物如发生保险单项下可能引起索赔的损失，应立即通知本公司或下述代理人查勘。如有索赔，应向本公司提交正本保险单（本保险单共有 2 份正本）及有关文件。如一份正本已用于索赔，其余正本自动失效。
IN THE EVENT OF LOSS OR DAMAGE WHICH MAY RESULT IN A CLAIM UNDER THIS POLICY, IMMEDIATE NOTICE MUST BE GIVEN TO THE COMPANY OR AGENT AS MENTIONED. CLAIMS, IF ANY, ONE OF THE ORIGINAL POLICY WHICH HAS BEEN ISSUED IN TWO ORIGINAL(S) TOGETHER WITH THE RELEVANT DOCUMENTS SHALL BE SURRENDERED TO THE COMPANY. IF ONE OF THE ORIGINAL POLICY HAS BEEN ACCOMPLISHED, THE OTHERS TO BE VOID.

THE INSURANCE COMPANY OF SWEDEN, LTD
KORSGATAN 18, SE 416 12 GOTHENBURG, SWEDEN
TEL: 0046 3 8756354

保险人:
Underwriter: PICC Property and Casualty Company Limited
Tianjin Branch
电话(TEL): (022)23317855 23315367
传真(FAX): (022)23301297
地址(ADD): No.2 Qu Fu Road, Heping District, Tianjin China 300042

赔款偿付地点
Claim Payable at GOTHENBURG IN USD
签单日期(Issuing Date) OCT 25, 2008　　授权人签字: Authorized Signature

核保人:　　制单人:　　经办人:

www.piccnet.com.cn

图 1.28 保险单

TIANJIN GARMENT IMPORT AND EXPORT INC

NO.1 YOU YI ROAD, HE XI DISTRICT, TIAJIN, CHINA

CERTIFICATE

INV. NO. G2008S/A16001
DATE: OCT 30, 2008

WE HEREBY CERTIFY THAT ONE ORIGINAL GSP FORM A AND ONE SET OF NON-NEGOTIABLE OF SHIPPING DOCUMENTS INCLUDING COMMCERICAL INVOICE, PACKING LIST, INSPECTION CERTIFICATE, INSURANCE POLICY AND BILL OF LADING HAVE BEEN SENT TO H _M TRADING SWEDEN AB DIRECTLY WITHIN 3DAYS AFTER SHIPMENT.

天津服装进出口有限公司(20)
TIANJIN GARMENTS IMPORT & EXPORT INCORPORATION

(此章仅供进出口单据专用)

图 1.29　证明函

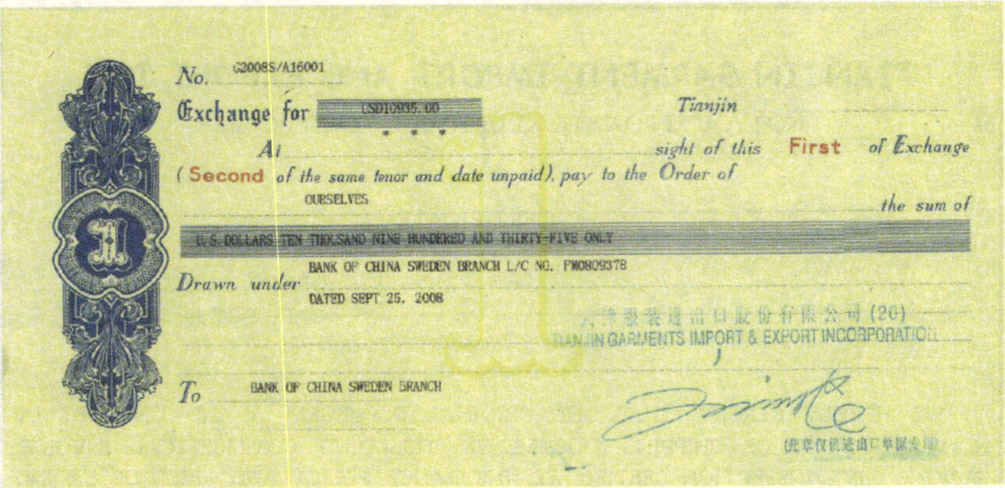

No. G2008S/A16001

Exchange for USD10935.00 Tianjin

At * * * sight of this First of Exchange

(Second of the same tenor and date unpaid), pay to the Order of OURSELVES the sum of

U.S. DOLLARS TEN THOUSAND NINE HUNDERED AND THIRTY-FIVE ONLY

Drawn under BANK OF CHINA SWEDEN BRANCH L/C NO. FM0809378

DATED SEPT 25. 2008

天津服装进出口股份有限公司 (20)

TIANJIN GARMENTS IMPORT & EXPORT INCORPORATION

To BANK OF CHINA SWEDEN BRANCH

(此章仅供进出口单据专用)

图 1.30　汇票

三、认知单证的操作训练

【翻译语句】

①purchase contract　②sales contract

③sales confirmation　④purchase confirmation

⑤more or less　⑥description of the commodity

⑦shipment clause　⑧insurance clause

⑨payment terms　⑩arbitration & claim

⑪S324 15 cm Christmas Bear with cap and gloves, as per the sample dispatched by the seller on 20 Oct. 2008.

⑫CHINESE PEANUT 500 metric tons, gross for net, 5% more or less at seller's option at contract price.

⑬To be packed in poly bags, 25 pounds in a bag, 4 bags in a sealed wooden case which is lined with metal. The cost of packing is for seller's account.

⑭Shipment to be effected within 20 days after receipt of L/C. The relevant L/C must reach the seller not later than 30 days before shipment.

⑮Insurance to be effected by the seller on behalf of the buyer for 110% of invoice value against all risks, premium to be for buyer's account.

【动脑思考】

①我国某进出口公司出口德国一批涤棉漂白棉床单，信用证规定面料的纱支密度为 30s ×30s 78 ×65，该公司实际交付的床单符合该规格。但缮制商业发票时，该

公司的单证员误将每平方英寸密度 78 ×65 打成 78 ×56，单据到国外后遭到开证行拒付。此前进口商在收到该批船前样时，认为床单面料的手感较硬，白度不好，不易销售，早有毁约意图，正苦于没有借口，恰巧发现发票上的一字之差，借故拒付货款。最后几经周折我进出口公司不得不以低价转卖其他客户，损失惨重。作为公司的单证员，你从中应吸取什么教训？

②我国某大型生产企业出口一批机床到埃及，机床型号为“BIZ-12”，数量 10 台，每台单价为 5 500 美元 CIF 亚历山大港，合同总金额为 55 000 美元。货物出口后，我方企业顺利地制单结汇。可一个月后我方企业突然收到进口商的传真，被告知该批货物已经抵达亚历山大港，在报关时被海关查出我方单据上的机床型号与机床上实际的型号不符，海关已扣留该批货物。若要提货则每台机床要被罚款 500 美元，要求我方企业立即电汇该笔罚款否则向我方提出更大的索赔。后来经过多次交涉，最后由我方企业电汇 4 000 美元罚款才了结此案。作为公司的单证员，你从中体会到什么？

③某公司生产的产品商标为“黄河牌”，习惯意译为“Yellow River Brand”，而日本客户开来的信用证却音译为“Huang He Brand”，单证员在缮制单据时仍按习惯打成“Yellow River Brand”，单据缮制完毕审单时发现了信用证音译为“Huang He Brand”，由于临近交单期匆匆修改单据，但遗漏产地证中货物描述部分的“Yellow River Brand”没有更改，最后单据到日本开证行因单单不符遭拒付。鉴于该产品当时市场销路很好，最后进口商要求降价 10% 结束此案。作为公司的单证员，你从中悟出了什么？今后工作又该如何改进？

④香港某银行于 2008 年 4 月 12 日开来 L/C 一份，金额为 540 000 美元，装期为 8 月 15 日，效期为 8 月 30 日。该证所引用贸易合约号为“CN1830325”。8 月 9 日受益人交来议付单据，所有单据中的贸易合约号均列为“CNI830325”，据受益人称，他们历来的合约号均为 CNI 为字首，开证行的来证肯定搞错了。因此，受益人坚持以该公司正式编号为准，把单据中的合约号均写为“CNI830325”。议付行对此未认真对待，认为进口方易于查清，遂接受议付寄单，并向偿付行索汇。单据到开证行后遭拒付，不久，受益人收到开证行的拒付电，你认为开证行拒付理由是否成立？

⑤开证行收到金额为 447 160 美元的单据，汇票大写金额描述成“U. S. Dollars Four Hundred Forty Seventy Thousand One Hundred And Sixty Only”。作为单证员，你预测一下该公司能否安全收回货款？为什么？

【动手操练】

实训操作一

泰佛贸易公司（Tifert Trading Co., Ltd., No. 86, Zhujiang Road, Tianjin, China）与英国盛行服装有限公司（Current Garment Company Ltd., No. 108 Tower Bridge Building, London, England）经过友好洽商就全棉女童夹克 GJ234 达成一出口合同。合同具体条款如下，请按照这些条款用空白销售合同（见样例 1.1）草拟一份出口合同，合同号为 S/C 08TF0858。

品名及货号:全棉女童夹克 GJ234

面料(SHELL):梭织全棉斜纹(WOVEN TWILL 100% COTTON)

里料(LINING):梭织100%涤纶(WOVEN 100% POLYESTER)

单价:10.50 美元/件,CIF LONDON 含5%佣金

数量:5 000 件

金额:52 500 美元

数量和金额都允许有5%的增减

包装:每件装一塑料袋,20 件装一个出口纸箱

正唛:CURRENT

S/C 08TF0858

LONDON

CTN 1-UP

付款方式:采用见票后60天付款的议付信用证,要求在2008年8月15日前开抵卖方

装运:收到信用证后60天装运,从天津至伦敦,允许转运不允许分批装运

保险:由卖方按照发票金额的110%投保一切险和战争险

检验:出运前由天津出入境检验检疫局对货物进行检验,检验合格后方可出运

SALES CONTRACT

No.:

Date:

The seller:

Add.:

The buyer:

Add.:

We hereby confirm having sold to you the following goods on the terms and conditions as specified below:

(1) 货物名称及规格 Name of commodity and specifications	(2)数量 Quantity	(3)单价 Unit price	(4)总值 Total amount

(5) Packing:

(6) Shipping mark:

(7) Time of shipment:

(8) Port of shipment: Destination:

(9) Payment terms:

(10) Insurance:

(11) Inspection:

Remarks:

(1) % more or less in quantity and amount is allowed

(2) Quality/quantity discrepancy: In case of quality discrepancy, claim should be filed by the buyer within 2 months after the arrival of the goods at the port of destination while for quantity discrepancy claim should be filed by the buyer within 15 days after the arrival of the goods at the port of destination. It is understood that seller shall not be liable for any discrepancy of the goods shipped due to causes for which the insurance company, shipping company and other transportation organization are liable

(3) The seller shall not be held liable for failure or delay in delivery of the entire lot or portion of the goods under this sales contract in consequence of any force majeure incidents.

Confirmed by

CURRENT GARMENT COMPANY LTD. TIFERT TRADING CO., LTD.

Bonnie 王宏

买方(the buyer) 卖方(the seller)

样例 1.1 销售合同

实训操作二

买卖双方经过友好洽商签订了一份出口合同。若合同规定采用非信用证方式支付,卖方应该按照合同约定的品质和数量备妥货物,并根据合同的有关要求缮制单据;如合同规定采用信用证支付方式,为执行合同,买方应及时申请开立信用证,收到信用证经审核无误后,卖方即进行办理托运、缮制单据、交单结汇等后续工作。缮制单据,一般有以下几个步骤。顺序若与实际单证操作业务不符,可根据实际情况重新排序。

1.“制”

制单可以从发票和装箱单着手,因为发票记载的内容比较全面,它是一切单据的中心,装箱单又是发票的补充。把发票和装箱单制妥后,便可参照发票和装箱单着手缮制其他单据。

单证员必须熟悉各种单据的用途,单证中每一栏应该缮制的内容及哪些是必要事项,哪些是一般事项。例如,不同国家、地区的海关发票都有各自专门的格式,不能错用。各种格式自上而下,从正面到背面,栏目繁多,都要按照规定填制。错填或漏填会直接影响买方收取货物和办理进口清关手续。

2.“配”

根据合同或信用证规定,将本批货物所需的各种空白单据或空白单据模板,按照需要的份数配置在操作夹内或文件夹内,这样做既可以防止某一单据的遗漏,又能提高单据缮制的工作效率。

3.“核”

将货物的出库资料(出仓单或提货单)与合同或信用证核对,弄清货同是否相符、货证是否相符,如有问题,必须联系有关环节解决。

4.“审”

单据制妥后,单证员应自行审核一遍,如有差错立即更正,这样可以收到事半功倍的效果。如事后经数道环节发现差错再更改或重新返工,不仅费时、费事,更改的内容牵涉到协作单位签发的单据的话,还有可能造成不良影响或酿成巨大损失。

5.“算”

单据中往往涉及很多数字应该计算,如货物的件数、毛重、净重、尺码、单价及金额等。某些商品根据行业习惯或客户需要还须提供具体的详细码单要求,逐码核对和计算累计数量。这些都必须在缮制单据前完成。

6.“交”

单据经仔细审核如无问题,应尽早交到银行议付货款,早一天交单就意味着能早一天把款收回,加速资金周转,提高企业的经济效益。

请将你认为通常制单的正确工作流程填入图1.31。

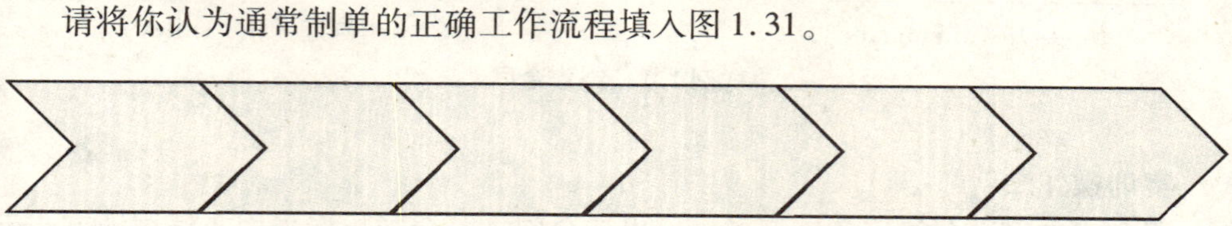

图1.31 单据缮制流程

2 接触信用证

任务二　开立信用证

任务背景

王芳小姐在单证部工作一段时间后，以认真、细致的工作态度和不辞辛苦的作风赢得了纺织品部部门经理的赏识。由于业务需要，王芳小姐被正式调入纺织品部，成为纺织品部的一名员工。纺织品部完全采取一条龙操作流程。近来，除了一般贸易外，进料加工业务也随之增多，于是王芳小姐被安排负责进料加工业务。

纺织品部与日本丸红株式会社成交一批夹克衫，规定面料从日本进口，里料和所有辅料在国内采购。为履行该合同，纺织品部在天津海关办妥进料加工备案手续后，安排王芳小姐到中行天津分行办理面料进口的开证手续。

【背景分析】

买卖双方签订合同，若规定采用信用证付款方式，为履行合同，买方应及时到银行办理开证手续，这是双方履行合同的一个前提条件。买方开证必须填写开证申请书，提交开证保证金、交纳开证手续费。银行应买方的请求开出信用证，通知行将该证转递给受益人。开证是一个非常关键的环节，在此环节中，王芳小姐应该掌握和具备如下知识、技能及素质。

知识目标

①了解开证申请书概念及开立信用证的程序。

②看懂合同中有关支付条款的内容。

技能目标

①准确翻译合同中的支付条款。

②独立、正确填写开证申请书。

素质目标

①发扬重合同、守信用的传统美德,及时开出信用证。

②工作上要精益求精,严格依据合同条款开立信用证。

一、开立信用证的基础知识

【开证申请书的概念】

开证申请书(Documentary Credit Application)是银行开立信用证的依据,是申请人与开证行之间明确彼此权利与义务关系的契约。申请书包括两部分:第一部分是请求银行开出信用证的内容;第二部分是进口企业对开证行的承诺书,用以明确双方的责任。

【开立信用证的基本程序】

进口商应该在合同规定的开证时间内向出口商可接受的本地银行申请开立信用证。如合同规定开证日期,进口商应在规定期限内开立信用证;如合同只规定了装运期的起止日,则应保证受益人在装运期开始前收到信用证;如合同只规定最迟装运日期,则应在合理时间内开证,以使出口商有足够时间备妥货物并予出运。开证日期通常控制在交货期前一个月至一个半月左右。开立信用证的基本程序如图 2.1 所示。

1. 填写开证申请书

进口商办理开证手续时,除了要递交有关合同的副本及附件,还应填写开证申请书。特别注意开证申请书中所列内容应与买卖合同条款一致,不得将与信用证无关的内容和合同中过细的条款填写到开证申请书中,不能将模糊的、模棱两可的、可作弹性解释的或有争议的内容填写到申请书中。

2. 开证申请人提交保证金或抵押品

开证行首先对开证申请书的内容进行审核,看其各类项目是否齐全、有无矛盾等。在此基础上,对开证申请人的资信(包括开证申请人的经营状况、资金实力及经营作风等)作仔细的调查,根据不同开证申请人的资信情况给予不同的授信额度。若开证申请人申请开证的金额小于授信额度,则不须交付保证金或抵押品;若开证金额大于授信额度,则对超额部分向开证申请人收取保证金或抵押品。保证金和抵押品可以是如下几类。

①现金作押,即向开证行交付一定的现金,或者从存款账户中扣存。

②开证申请人也可提供抵押品。

③开证申请人还可以向开证行提交由其他银行或金融机构出立的保函。

3. 开证申请人向开证行支付开证费用

申请人须按开证金额的一定比例向开证行支付开证手续费,在开证当日按当天牌价(中间价)折算成人民币支付,其他费用则按实报实销的原则处理。

4. 开证行开立信用证

①开证要求:开证行应该严格按照开证申请书开立信用证。开证申请书是开证行开证的基础。

②审核并签发信用证:开立信用证后,开证行的有关人员须认真审证。审证无误后,由相应级别的有权签字人签发信用证。

③根据开证申请书的要求,选择开证方法:电开或信开。

5. 通知行通知信用证

通知行收到开证行开立的信用证后,首先从宏观上审核信用证,在辨别信用证真实无误的前提下及时将信用证通知出口商。

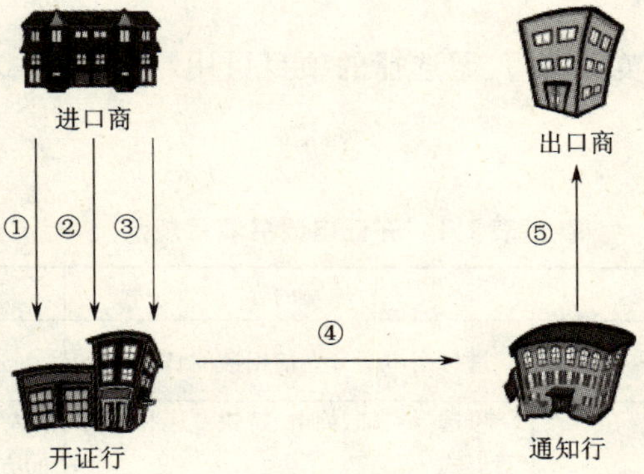

图 2.1 开立信用证流程图

二、开立信用证的基本技能

【实训目的】

通过本项任务的实训,应掌握的基本技能如下。

①熟悉并看懂不同银行开证申请书格式中的各项条款。

②掌握主要银行开证申请书的填写规范和技巧。

③学会独立填写开证申请书。

【操作前准备】

进行本项任务的实训前,应准备的内容如下。

①买卖双方签署的购货合同。

②首次办理开立信用证业务还须提供经营进出口业务的批文和工商营业执照等,办理保证金账户的开立手续。

③进口业务批文(如进口配额许可类证明、机电产品进口登记证明等)。

④外管部门规定的有关文件(如购汇申请书、进口付汇核销单、进口付汇备案表等)。

⑤空白银行开证申请书。

【操作程序】

①详细分析进口合同的各项条款。

②了解银行开证申请书标准格式的内容。

③填写开证申请书。

④交纳保证金。

⑤支付开证费用。

【操作规范】

开证申请书应以英文填写,需选择的项目可用"×"标记,填写规范如表 2.1 所示。

表 2.1 开证申请书填写规范

项目顺序号	填写内容	要点提示
(1)申请日期 Date	进口商申请开立信用证的日期	按英文习惯填写
(2)开立方式 Credit to be issued by	可选择空邮、简电、特快专递和电传等形式	尽量选择贸易双方均可接受的方式
(3)有效期及到期地点 Date and place of expiry	根据业务情况如实填写	有效期一般较最迟装运期晚 10~15 天,到期地点一般在受益人所在国
(4)通知行 Advising bank	通知行名称	此部分一般由银行填写
(5)受益人 Beneficiary	填写受益人名称及地址	应与合同中的卖方名称地址一致
(6)开证申请人 Applicant	填写开证申请人名称及地址	应与合同中的买方名称地址一致
(7)总值 Currency code and amount	根据合同填写小写金额和大写金额	应保持大小写的一致
(8)分批装运和转船 Partial shipments & transshipment	是否允许	应与合同约定一致

续表

项目顺序号	填写内容	要点提示
(9)装运港、目的港和装运期 From... to... latest date of shipment	填写装运港、目的港名称及装运期	根据合同约定填写
(10)具体兑付方式及兑付时间 Credit available with	需选择即期付款、承兑付款、议付或延期付款,是否使用受益人汇票,填写汇票金额、付款期和付款人	此部分应按照信用证付款惯例填写
(11)贸易术语 Trade term	选择贸易术语	根据合同约定进行选择
(12)信用证种类 Form of L/C	选择是否可转让	根据合同约定进行选择
(13)保兑 Confirmation	选择是否加保兑	根据合同约定进行选择
(14)单据条款 Documents required	选择并填写所需要的单据种类、份数、具体要求等	根据实际进口要求,填写并选择需要由出口商提供的单据
(15)货描 Description of the goods	填写商品名称、规格、数量、单价、包装等内容	根据合同约定进行填写
(16)额外指示条款 Additional conditions	填写其他需要的条款或指示	可根据贸易惯例和业务情况合理填写
(17)开证人签字盖章 Signature and seal of the applicant	开证人签字	
(18)银行使用 For bank user only	银行填写栏	

【开证申请书样例】

购　货　合　同

PURCHASE CONTRACT

合同编号：　　签订日期：　　签订地点：

Contract No.：08MC1568　　Date：NOV. 5, 2008　　Signed at：TIANJIN

1. 买方：

The buyers：TIFERT TRADING CO., LTD.

地址：

Address：NO. 86, ZHUJIANG ROAD, TIANJIN, CHINA

2. 卖方：

The sellers：MARUBENI CORP.

地址：

Address：5－7, HOMMACHI, 2－CHOME, CHUO-KU, OSAKA, JAPAN

经买卖双方确认根据下列条款订立本合同：

The undersigned sellers and buyers have confirmed this contract in accordance with the terms and conditions stipulated below：

3. 商品名称及规格 Name of commodity & specification	4. 数量 Quantity	5. 单价 Unit price	6. 总金额 Amount
WOVEN TWILL 100% COTTON	10000METERS	USD2.80/METER FOB TOKYO	USD28000.00

7. 总值(大写)

Total value (in words): U.S. DOLLARS TWENTY-EIGHT THOUSAND ONLY

8. 允许数量和金额溢短____%。

10 % more or less in quantity and value is allowed.

9. 成交价格术语:

Price terms:

☒ FOB ☐CFR ☐CIF ☐DDU

11. 包装

Packing: IN ROLLS OF 50METERS EACH

12. 运输唛头

Shipping mark:

TIFERT

08MC1568

TIANJIN

NO.1 – UP

13. 运输起讫:由______________(装运港)到______________(目的港)。

Shipment from TOKYO (Port of shipment) to TIANJIN (Port of destination).

14. 转运:☐允许 ☐不允许; 分批:☐允许 ☐不允许

Transshipment: ☒ allowed ☐not allowed

Partial shipment: ☒ allowed ☐not allowed

运输时间:

Shipment time: WITHIN 20 DAYS AFTER RECEIPT OF IRREVOCABLE SIGHT L/C.

15. 保险:

☐由卖方按发票金额的______%投保______,加保______从______到______。

☐Insurance: to be covered by the for % of the invoice value covering additional from to .

☐由买方投保。

☒ Insurance to be covered by the buyer.

16. 付款条件:

Terms of payment:

☐买方应不迟于______年____月____日前将100%货款用即期汇票/电汇支付给卖方。

The buyers shall pay 100% of the sales proceeds through sight (demand) draft/by T/T remittance to the sellers not later than / .

☒买方应于______年____月____日前通过__________银行开立以卖方为受益人的____天不可撤销信用证,有效期至装运后____天在中国议付,并注明合同号。

The buyers shall issue an irrevocable L/C at * * * sight through BANK OF CHINA in favor of the sellers prior to NOV. 10, 2008 indicating L/C shall be valid in China through negotiation within 15 days after the shipment effected, the L/C must mention the Contract Number.

☐付款交单:买方应凭卖方开立给买方的____期跟单汇票付款,付款时交单。

Documents against payment (D/P): the buyers shall duly make the payment against documentary draft made out to the buyers at / sight by the sellers.

□承兑交单:买方应凭卖方开立给买方的____期跟单汇票付款,承兑时交单。

Documents against acceptance (D/A): the buyers shall duly accept the documentary draft made out to the buyers at / days by the sellers.

17. 装运通知:一旦装运完毕,卖方应立即电告买方合同号、品名、已装载数量、发票总金额、毛重、运输工具名称及启运日期等。

Shipping advice: the sellers shall immediately, upon the completion of the loading of the goods, advise the buyers of the Contract No., names of commodity, loaded quantity, invoice value, gross weight, names of vessel and shipment date by FAX/MAIL.

19. 检验与索赔:

Inspection and claims:

①卖方在发货前由__________检验机构对货物的品质、规格和数量进行检验,并出具检验证明。

The buyer shall have the qualities, specifications, quantities of the goods carefully inspected by the SGS Inspection Authority, which shall issue Inspection Certificate before shipment.

②货物到达目的口岸后,买方可委托当地的商品检验机构对货物进行复检。如果发现货物有损坏、残缺或规格、数量与合同规定不符,买方须于货物到达目的口岸的_______天内凭______________检验机构出具的检验证明书向卖方索赔。

The buyers have right to have the goods inspected by CIQ the local commodity inspection authority after the arrival of the goods at the port of destination. If the goods are found damaged/short/their specifications and quantities not in compliance with that specified in the contract, the buyers shall lodge claims against the sellers based on the Inspection Certificate issued by the Commodity Inspection Authority within 30 days after the goods arrived at the destination.

③如买方提出索赔,凡属品质异议须于货物到达目的口岸之日起______天内提出;凡属数量异议须于货物到达目的口岸之日起______天内提出。对所装货物所提任何异议应由保险公司、运输公司或邮递机构负责的,卖方不负任何责任。

The claims, if any regarding to the quality of the goods, shall be lodged within 30 days after arrival of the goods at the destination, if any regarding to the quantities of the goods, shall be lodged within 60 days after arrival of the goods at the destination. The sellers shall not take any responsibility if any claims concerning the shipping goods in up to the responsibility of Insurance Company/Transportation Company/Post Office.

21. 不可抗力:如因人力不可抗拒的原因造成本合同全部或部分不能履约,卖方概不负责,但卖方应将上述发生的情况及时通知买方。

Force majeure: the sellers shall not hold any responsibility for partial or total non-performance of this contract due to force majeure. But the sellers shall advise the buyers on time of such occurrence.

22. 争议的解决方式:

任何因本合同而发生或与本合同有关的争议,应提交中国国际经济贸易仲裁委员会,按该会的规则进行仲裁。仲裁裁决是终局的,对双方均有约束力。

Disputes settlement: All disputes arising out of the contract or in connection with the contract, shall be submitted to the China International Economic and Trade Arbitration Commission for arbitration in accordance with its Rules of Arbitration. The arbitral award is final and binding upon both parties.

23. 法律适用:本合同的签订地,或发生争议时货物所在地在中华人民共和国境内或被诉人为中国法人的,适用于中华人民共和国法律,除此规定外,适用《联合国国际货物销售合同公约》。

Law applications: it will be governed by the law of the People's Republic of China under the circumstances that the contract is signed or the goods while the disputes arising are in the People's Republic of China or the defendant is Chinese legal person, otherwise it is governed by *United Nations Convention on Contract for the International Sale of Goods.*

24. 术语：本合同使用的贸易术语系根据国际商会《INCOTERMS 2000》。

Price terms: The terms in the contract are based on *INCOTERMS 2000* of the International Chamber of Commerce.

25. 文字：本合同中、英文两种文字具有同等法律效力，在文字解释上，若有异议，以中文解释为准。

Versions: This contract is made out in both Chinese and English of which version is equally effective. Conflicts between these two languages arising therefrom, if any, shall be subject to Chinese version.

26. 附加条款：本合同上述条款与本附加条款有抵触时，以本附加条款为准。

Additional Clauses: Conflicts between contract clause here above and this additional clause, if any, shall be subject to this additional clause.

27. 本合同共____份，自双方代表签字/盖章之日起生效。

This contract is in TWO copies, effective since being signed/sealed by both parties.

买方代表人：	卖方代表人：
Representative of the buyers:	Representative of the sellers:
签字	签字
Authorized signature:	Authorized signature:
TIFERT TRADING CO., LTD.	MARUBENI CORP.
王宏	小泉太郎

样例 2.1 面料进口合同

IRREVOCABLE DOCUMENTARY CREDIT APPLICATION

(Please mark × in appropriate boxes)

TO: Bank of China Tianjin Branch (1) Date: NOV. 10, 2008

(2) Credit to be issued by ☒ Full Teletransmission ☐ Airmail ☐ With a Preliminary Advice by Teletransmission	Irrevocable documentary Credit No. (3) Date and place of expiry Date: JAN. 15, 2009 Place: JAPAN
(4) Advising bank	(5) Beneficiary (name and address) MARUBENI CORP. 5-7, HOMMACHI, 2-CHOME, CHUO-KU, OSAKA, JAPAN
(6) Applicant (name and address) TIFERT TRADING CO., LTD. NO. 86, ZHUJIANG ROAD, TIANJIN, CHINA	(7) Currency code and amount In figures USD28000.00 In words SAY US DOLLARS TWENTY EIGHT THOUSAND ONLY

<table>
<tr><td>(8) Partial shipments
☒allowed ☐not allowed</td><td>Transshipment
☒allowed ☐ot allowed</td><td rowspan="2">(10) Credit available with
☒any bank ☐Issuing Bank
☐by sight payment ☐by acceptance ☒by negotiation
☐by deferred payment
against presentation of the documents detailed herein and ☒beneficiary's draft for 100 % of invoice value at ☒sight ☐days sight ☐days after date of shipment drawn on ☒Issuing Bank</td></tr>
<tr><td colspan="2">(9) Loading on board/dispatch/taking in charge
at /from TOKYO
For transportation to TIANJIN
Latest date of shipment DEC. 30, 2008</td></tr>
<tr><td colspan="2">(11) Trade term:
☒FOB ☐CFR ☐CIF
☐other term (please specify):</td><td>(12) Form of L/C
☐Transferable
☒Not Transferable

(13) Confirmation
☐Confirm
☒Without</td></tr>
</table>

(14) Documents required: (marked with ×)

1. ☒ Signed Commercial Invoice in 2 originals and 2 copies indicating L/C No. and Contract No. 08MC1568

2. ☒Full set ☐2/3 set (including 3 originals and 3 non-negotiable copies) of clean on board ocean Bills of Lading made out to order and blank endorsed, marked Freight ☒Collect ☐Prepaid ☒ notifying Applicant with full name and address

3. ☐Airway Bill consigned to ☐Applicant ☐Issuing Bank and notify ☐Applicant ☐Issuing Bank, marked Freight ☐Collect ☐Prepaid and indicating actual flight date

4. ☐Railway Bill showing Freight ☐Collect ☐Prepaid and consigned to

5. ☐Full set (including __originals and __copies) of Insurance Policy/Certificate for at least 110% of the invoice value showing claims payable in China in currency of the draft, blank endorsed, covering ☐ocean marine transportation ☐air transportation ☐overland transportation all risks, war risks and

6. ☒Packing List/Weight Memo in 2 originals and 1 copies indicating GROSS/NET WEIGHT AND MEASUREMENT OF EACH CARTON

7. ☐Certificate of Quantity in ____originals and ____copies issued by ____ indicating ____

8. ☐Certificate of Origin in 1 original and 2 copies issued by CHAMBER OF INTERNATIONAL COMMERCE

9. ☒ Certificate of Quality in 1 originals and 1 copies issued by SGS indicating L/C No.

10. ☒Beneficiary's Certified Copy of Fax/E-mail dispatched to the applicant within 24 hours after shipment advising name of vessel /~~flight No./wagon No.~~, B/L No., loading port /~~airport of departure~~, date of shipment, contract No., L/C No., commodity, quantity, weight and value of shipment

11. ☐Beneficiary's Certificate certifying that extra copies of all documents required in this Credit have been sent to the Applicant within ____days after shipment

12. ☐Other documents:

(15) Description of the goods:

10000 METERS OF WOVEN TWILL 100% COTTON

@ USD2. 80/METER FOB TOKYO

PACKING: IN ROLL OF 50 METER EACH

(16) Additional conditions	
1. ☒All Banking charges and interest, if any, outside Issuing Bank and our reimbursement charge are for account of the beneficiary. 2. ☒Documents to be presented within 15 days after the date of shipment but within the validity of the Credit. 3. □Third party as shipper/consignor in transport documents is not acceptable. 4. ☒Short form/blank back B/L is not acceptable. 5. ☒Both quantity and amount 10 % more or less are allowed. 6. ☒All documents should be forwarded to the Issuing Bank in one lot by courier. 7. ☒All documents must be issued in English. 8. □Other terms:	
(17) Signature and seal of the applicant Contact person: 王伟 Tel. No. 0086 22 85665678 Fax No. 0086 22 85665679	(18) For bank user only

样例 2.2 面料开证申请书

【操作注意事项】

①申请开立信用证前，对于国家管制商品、限制商品一定要落实进口批准手续及作好购汇准备。

②开证时间的掌握应以确保出口商收到信用证后能在合同约定的装运期内出运为原则。

③开证申请书填写完毕，为节省费用，避免日后改证，最好把开证申请书先传真给出口商，与受益人事先进行沟通，待双方对开证申请书中的所有条款达成一致意见以后，再开立信用证。

④开证要求“证同一致”，必须以对外签订的正本合同为依据。若货物描述过多、过长，可以注明“详情参照××合同”的字样，但不能将有关合同附件附在信用证后，因信用证是一个独立的文件，不依附于任何贸易合同。

⑤汇票的付款期限要与买卖合同的付款期限相吻合，如为远期，要明确汇票期限以及起算日期，价格条款必须与相应的单据要求、费用负担及表示方法相吻合。

⑥由于银行是凭单付款，不论货物质量如何，均不受合同约束，所以为使货物质量符合规定，可在开证时作出规定，要求出口商提供检验检疫证书以明确货物的规格品质，并指定检验检疫机构。

⑦单据条款要明确。开证时必须列明需要出口商提供的各种单据的种类、份数，规定各单据表述的内容及签发机构。特别是对运输单据、保险单据、商业发票以外的单据，开证申请中更应明确出单人及单据措辞等内容。

⑧合同约定的条款应转化在信用证相应的条款中并单据化，因为在信用证支付方式下，只要单据表面与信用证条款相符合，开证行就必须按规定付款。如信用证申

请书中含有某些条件而未列明应提交与之相应的单据，银行将认为此条件未列，而不予理睬。

⑨国外通知行由开证行指定。如果进出口商在订立合同时，坚持指定通知行，可供开证行在选择通知行时作参考。

⑩在信用证中规定是否允许分批装运、转运及是否接受第三者装运单据等条款。

⑪如果采用空运，不应在申请书中要求受益人提交一张以上的正本空运单据，更不能要求提供全套的正本空运单据，因为只有第三张正本空运单是提供给发货人的。

⑫各银行事先印制的固定格式开证申请书中凡涉及选择的项目，一律在有关项目前打"×"表示选中。

⑬除非有特殊要求和规定，信用证申请书原则上应以英文开立。

⑭我国银行一般不接受开立他行保兑的信用证及带电索条款的信用证，对可转让信用证也持谨慎态度。

⑮开证申请书的文字应力求规范、完整、明确。进口商要求银行在信用证上载明的事项必须完整、明确，不能使用含糊不清的文字，避免使用"约"、"近似"或类似的词语。这样一方面可使银行处理信用证和出口商履行信用证的条款时有据可循，另一方面也可以此保护自身权益。

三、开立信用证的操作训练

【翻译语句】

①payment

②acceptance

③negotiation

④airway bill

⑤cargo receipt

⑥weight memo

⑦price terms

⑧banking charges

⑨short form B/L

⑩courier

⑪date and place of expiry

⑫signed commercial invoice

⑬credit available with any bank by negotiation

⑭Third party as shipper is not acceptable, short form B/L is not acceptable.

⑮Documents must be presented within 10 days after the shipment date but within the validity of this credit.

【动脑思考】

①泰佛贸易公司与美国 ABC 公司签订了一项进口废纸的贸易合同，根据贸易合同需向中国银行申请开立信用证，请说明业务员应做好哪些准备工作。

②泰佛贸易公司应完成哪些信用证开立的程序？

③泰佛贸易公司应如何填写信用证开证申请书中的单据条款?

④泰佛贸易公司应如何填写信用证开证申请书中的附加指示条款?

⑤泰佛贸易公司应如何填写信用证开证申请书中的付款方式条款?

【动手操练】

实训操作一

2008 年 5 月,主要从事包装产品、造纸原材料等产品进出口业务的泰佛贸易公司与德国哈罗德有限公司签订了购买 150 吨废纸的进口合同,并于 6 月 3 日向天津中信银行提出开立信用证的申请,请根据下列信息及相关合同(见样例 2.3),填写信用证开立申请书(见样例 2.4)。

1. 买方

中文名称:泰佛贸易公司

英文名称:TIFERT TRADING COMPANY LTD.

地址:天津市珠江道 86 号(NO. 86, ZHUJIANG ROAD, TIANJIN, CHINA)

传真 FAX:0086 22 85665678

电话 TEL:0086 22 85665679

2. 卖方

中文名称:德国哈罗德有限公司

英文名称:HAROLD COMPANY LIMITED, GERMANY

地址:NO. 28, HAROLD STREET, HAMBURG, GERMANY

传真 FAX:0049 2 4245656

电话 TEL:0049 2 4245658

3. 商品情况

商品名称:废纸

英文名称:WASTE PAPER

商品数量:150 公吨,允许增减 10%

商品包装:6 个 40′集装箱

HS 编码:47043000

4. 购货合同

PURCHASE CONTRACT

No. TIFERT080515

Date: MAY 15, 2008

The buyer: TIFERT TRADING COMPANY LTD.

NO. 86, ZHUJIANG ROAD, TIANJIN, CHINA

Fax: 00862285665678 Tele: 00862285665679 Email: TIFERT@ trade. com

The seller: HAROLD COMPANY LIMITED, GERMANY

NO. 28, HAROLD STREET, HAMBURG, GERMANY

Fax: 004924245656 Tele: 004924245658 Email: HAROLD@ trade. net

1. Commodity: WASTE PAPER
2. Quality: PROHIBITIVE MATERIALS≤2%
   MOISTURE≤12%
   OUT-THROWS≤1%
3. Quantity: 150MTS(+/ -10%)
4. Unit price: USD70/MT CFR XINGANG, CHINA
5. Total value: USD10500. 00 (SAY US DOLLARS TEN THOUSAND FIVE HUNDRED ONLY)
6. Packing: EXPORT STANDARD PACKING IN CONTAINER SHIPMENT

The seller shall be liable for any damage of the commodity and expenses incurred on account of improper packing or inadequate and improper protective measures taken by the seller in regard to the packing, shipping marks are as follows: N/M

7. Time of shipment: BEFORE JUNE 20, 2008
8. Port of shipment: EUROPEAN MAIN PORT
9. Port of destination: XINGANG, CHINA
10. Insurance: TO BE COVERED BY THE BUYER
11. Payment: BY L/C 90 DAYS AFTER SIGHT

Sellers Buyers

RONALD 王宏

样例 2.3 购货合同

IRREVOCABLE DOCUMENTARY CREDIT APPLICATION

(Please mark × in appropriate boxes)

TO: China CITIC Bank TIANJIN Branch Date:

Credit to be issued by □Full Teletransmission □Airmail □With a Preliminary Advice by Teletransmission	Irrevocable documentary Credit No. Date and place of expiry Date: Place:
Advising bank	Beneficiary (name and address)
Applicant (name and address)	Currency code and amount In figures In words
Partial shipments □allowed □not allowed Transshipment □allowed □not allowed Loading on board/dispatch/taking in charge at /from For transportation to Latest date of shipment	Credit available with □any bank □Issuing Bank □by sight payment □by acceptance □by negotiation □by deferred payment against presentation of the documents detailed herein and □beneficiary's draft for % of invoice value at □sight □ days sight □ days after date of shipment drawn on □Issuing Bank
Trade term: □FOB □CFR □CIF □other term (please specify):	Form of L/C □Transferable □Not Transferable Confirmation □Confirm □Without

Documents required: (marked with ×)

1. □Signed Commercial Invoice in originals and copies indicating L/C No. and Contract No.

2. □Full set □2/3 set (including originals and non-negotiable copies) of clean on board ocean Bills of Lading made out to order and blank endorsed, marked Freight □Collect □Prepaid □notifying Applicant with full name and address

3. □Airway Bill consigned to □Applicant □Issuing Bank and notify □Applicant □Issuing Bank, marked Freight □Collect □Prepaid and indicating actual flight date

4. □Railway Bill showing Freight □Collect □Prepaid and consigned to

5. □Full set (including originals and copies) of Insurance Policy/Certificate for at least 110% of the invoice value showing claims payable in China in currency of the draft, blank endorsed, covering □ocean marine transportation □air transportation □overland transportation all risks, war risks and

6. □Packing List/Weight Memo in originals and copies indicating

7. □Certificate of Quantity in originals and copies issued by indicating

8. □Certificate of Origin in originals and copies issued by

9. □Certificate of Quality in originals and copies issued by indicating

10. □Beneficiary's Certified Copy of Fax /E-mail dispatched to the applicant within hours after shipment advising name of vessel /flight No. /wagon No., B/L No., loading port /airport of departure, date of shipment, contract No., L/C No., commodity, quantity, weight and value of shipment

11. □Beneficiary's Certificate certifying that extra copies of all documents required in this Credit have been sent to the Applicant within days after shipment

12. □Other documents:

____

Description of the goods:

Additional conditions

1. □All Banking charges and interest, if any, outside Issuing Bank and our reimbursement charge are for account of the beneficiary.

2. □Documents to be presented within days after the date of shipment but within the validity of the Credit.

3. □Third party as shipper/consignor in transport documents not acceptable.

4. □ Short form/blank back B/L not acceptable.

5. □Both quantity and amount % more or less are allowed.

6. □All documents should be forwarded to the Issuing Bank in one lot by courier.

7. □All documents must be issued in English.

8. □Other terms:

Signature and seal of the applicant Contact person: Tel. No. Fax No.	For bank user only

样例2.4 空白开证申请书

实训操作二

泰佛贸易公司与英国 J. C. B 公司就进口针织机械设备达成一订购合同,你作为公司的单证员依据下面的订购合同(见样例 2.5)填写开证申请书(见样例 2.6),并与招商银行联系开立信用证事宜。

<table>
<tr><td colspan="2" align="center">泰 佛 贸 易 公 司
TIFERT TRADING CO. , LTD.
NO. 86, ZHUJIANG ROAD, TIANJIN, CHINA
订 购 合 同
PURCHASE CONTRACT</td></tr>
<tr><td>卖方:
The sellers:
J. C. B SALES LIMITED
ROCESTER, STAFFORDSHIRE, ENGLAND ST 14 5JP</td><td>合同号码:
Contract No. : 08TJ198
地点 日期
Place: TIANJIN Date: MAY 18, 2008</td></tr>
<tr><td colspan="2">经同意按照下列条款由卖方出售,买方购进下列货物:
The seller agrees to sell and the buyer agrees to buy the undermentioned commodity according to the terms and conditions stated below:</td></tr>
<tr><td colspan="2">1. 商品名称及规格
Name of commodity, specification:
1000SETS KNITTING MACHINES NO. KM - 205
2. 单价及总值
Unit price: GBP349. 17/SET FOB LONDON
Total value: GBP349, 170. 00
3. 包装
Packing: IN STRONG WOODEN CASES OF ONE SET EACH
4. 生产国别及制造厂商
Country or origin and/or Manufactured: ENGLAND
5. 付款条件
Terms of payment: BY L/C AT 45 DAYS SIGHT
6. 保险
Insurance: TO BE COVERED BY THE BUYER
7. 装运时间
Time of shipment: WITHIN 60 DAYS AFTER RECEIPT OF THE RELATIVE L/C
8. 装运唛头
Shipping mark: TIFERT
KM - 205
TIANJIN
CTN NO 1 - 1000
9. 装运口岸
Port of loading: LONDON
10. 目的口岸
Port of destination: TIANJIN</td></tr>
<tr><td>卖方(The sellers)
J. C. B SALES LTD.
JOHN SMITH</td><td>买方(The buyers)
TIFERT TRADING CO. , LTD.
王 宏</td></tr>
</table>

样例 2.5 订购合同

APPLICATION FOR DOCUMENTARY CREDIT

Mark "×" in appropriate boxes

致:招商银行

To:China Merchants Bank

Please issue by □Teletransmission □Brief teletransmission □Airmail an IRREVOCABLE CREDIT as follows:	Expiry date: Place for presentation:
Applicant (name and address)	Beneficiary(name and address)
Advising bank	Amount in figures: Amount in words:

Credit available with nominated bank:

□by payment at sight

□by deferred payment at:

□by acceptance of drafts at:

□by negotiation

against the following documents □and beneficiary's drafts drawn on for % invoice value accompanied by the following documents.

Partial shipments	Transshipments	Transferable	Confirmation of credit
□allowed □not allowed	□allowed □not allowed	□transferable □not transferable	□requested □authorized if requested by beneficiary

Shipment from for transportation to via not later than

Goods description in brief

Price Terms: □CIF □FOB □CFR □CIP □others as per INCOTERMS

– All banking charges including relative reimbursement/payment charges, outside/inside issuing bank are for account of beneficiary.

– Documents to be presented within days after shipment date but within the validity of the credit.

– Please debit our account for your commission, charges and usance interest (the interest rate is LIBOR + ( ) BPs), if any. Our account No. :

This page is an integral part of the application which consists of the first page, the second page and attachment(s), if any.

CONTRACT NO. : CONTRACT AMT:

To be continued on the second page

APPLICATION FOR DOCUMENTARY CREDIT

致:招商银行

To:China Merchants Bank

Documents required:

□Signed commercial invoice in   original(s) and   copy(ies) indicating this L/C No. and Contract No.

□Packing list in   original(s) and   copy(ies).

□Full set of clean on board marine Bill of Lading marked □"Freight Prepaid" □"Freight to collect" made out to order and blank endorsed notifying the applicant with full name and address.

□2/3 set of clean on board marine Bill of Lading marked □"Freight Prepaid" □"Freight to collect" made out to order and blank endorsed notifying the applicant with full name and address.

□Full set of clean on board multimodal transport document marked □"Freight Prepaid" □"Freight to collect" made out to order and blank endorsed notifying the applicant with full name and address.

□2/3 set of clean on board multimodal transport document marked □"Freight Prepaid" □"Freight to collect" made out to order and blank endorsed notifying the applicant with full name and address.

□Clean Air Waybill indicating actual flight date consigned to __________ and notifying __________ marked □"Freight Prepaid" □"Freight to collect".

□Clean Rail Waybill indicating actual departure date consigned to __________ and notifying __________ marked □"Freight Prepaid" □"Freight to collect".

□Forwarding agent cargo receipt consigned to __________ and notifying __________ marked □"Freight Prepaid" □"Freight to collect".

□Full set of insurance policy /certificate blank endorsed for full CIF value plus 10pct with claims if any, payable at destination in the currency of this credit covering. □Institute Cargo Clauses A □Institute War Clauses □Institute Strikes Clause from warehouse to warehouse included.

□Certificate of origin in   original(s) and   copy(ies) issued by chamber of commerce in ____.

□Certificate of quality in   original(s) and   copy(ies) issued by chamber of commerce in ____.

□Certificate of quantity in   original(s) and   copy(ies) issued by chamber of commerce in ____.

□Beneficiary's certificate certifying that one set of non-negotiable documents including 1/3 set of original B/L has been sent to the applicant directly by courier/speed post and the postal receipt is required for negotiation.

Special terms and conditions:

□percent more or less are allowed on both credit amount and quantity.

□Third party as shipper is acceptable.

□Third party as shipper is not acceptable.

We hereby instruct you or any third party authorized by you to pay the usance draft(s) on sight basis, the relevant interest and charges will be for account of us.(申请开立假远期信用证时,需选择此项)

This page is an integral part of the application which consists of the first page, the second page and attachment(s), if any.

样例 2.6 空白开证申请书

任务三　分析信用证

任务背景

王芳小姐在办理夹克衫面料进口手续的同时,也在进行女童夹克衫成衣出口的各项工作。就女童夹克衫成衣出口与日本丸红株式会社签订出口合同后,王芳小姐催促日本丸红株式会社开立成衣出口信用证,不久收到中国银行东京分行开立的第 A-08-0058 号信用证,接下来,王芳小姐开始进入分析信用证的工作环节。

【背景分析】

信用证是国际贸易中买卖双方采用较多的一种付款方式,也是相对比较安全的付款方式。在实际业务中,特别是对新客户的业务大多采用信用证付款方式。因此王芳小姐应该掌握和具备如下知识、技能及素质。

知识目标

①了解信用证的概念、当事人及种类。

②看懂不同地区、不同开立方式的信用证的内容。

技能目标

①准确翻译信用证中的主要条款。

②正确填写信用证分析单。

素质目标

①养成扎实的工作作风。

②对待工作要精益求精。

一、分析信用证的基础知识

【信用证的概念】

国际商会在《跟单信用证统一惯例(2007 年修订本)》即国际商会第 600 号出版物(以下简称 UCP600)中对信用证定义为:信用证指一项不可撤销的安排,无论其名称或描述如何,该项安排构成开证行对相符交单予以承付的确定承诺(Credit means any arrangement, however named or described, that is irrevocable and thereby constitutes a definite undertaking of the issuing bank to honor a complying presentation)。

【信用证的当事人】

①申请人:指要求开立信用证的一方。

②受益人:指接受信用证并享受其利益的一方。

③开证行:指应申请人要求或者代表自己开出信用证的银行。

④通知行:指应开证行的要求通知信用证的银行。

⑤议付行:指向受益人预付或者同意预付款项而购买相符交单的汇票及/或单据的银行。

⑥付款行:指向议付行进行偿付的银行。

⑦保兑行:指根据开证行的授权或要求对信用证加具保兑的银行。

⑧指定银行:指信用证可在其处兑用的银行,如果信用证可在任一银行兑用,则任何银行均为指定银行。

【信用证的种类】

1. 跟单信用证与光票信用证

(1)跟单信用证(Documentary L/C)

这是指开证行凭跟单汇票或仅凭装运单据付款的信用证。实际业务中使用的信用证绝大部分是跟单信用证。

(2)光票信用证(Clean L/C)

这是指开证行仅凭不附单据的汇票(光票)付款的信用证。

2. 即期信用证与远期信用证

(1)即期信用证(Sight L/C)

这是指开证行或付款行收到符合信用证条款的跟单汇票或装运单据后,立即付款的信用证。

(2)远期信用证(Usance L/C)

这是指开证行或付款行收到符合信用证规定的单据后,不立即付款,而是待信用证规定的到期日再付款的信用证。

3. 保兑信用证与非保兑信用证

(1)保兑信用证(Confirmed L/C)

这是指开证行开出的信用证,由另一家银行保证对符合信用证条款规定的单据履行付款义务。保兑是指开证行以外的银行对信用证承担付款责任。保兑信用证不仅有开证行的付款保证,而且又有保兑行的兑付保证,保兑行与开证行一样负第一性付款责任,这种有双重保证的信用证对出口商最为有利。

(2)非保兑信用证(Unconfirmed L/C)

这是指开证行开出的信用证没有经另一家银行保兑。

4. 可转让信用证与不可转让信用证

(1)可转让信用证(Transferable L/C)

这是指信用证规定受益人(第一受益人)可将使用信用证的权利转让给其他人

(第二受益人)的信用证。

信用证只有注有“可转让”的字样时才允许转让并且只能转让一次,但第二受益人重新将信用证转让给第一受益人不在此限制内。卖方在合同项下的交货义务不随信用证的转让而转移。

(2)不可转让信用证(Non-transferable L/C)

这是指受益人不能将信用证的权利转让给他人,未注明“可转让”者,即为不可转让信用证。

5. 议付信用证、承兑信用证和付款信用证

(1)议付信用证(Negotiation L/C)

这是指允许受益人向某一指定银行或任何银行交单议付的信用证。议付信用证又分为限制议付信用证(规定了议付行)和公开议付信用证(可在任何银行进行议付)两种。

(2)承兑信用证(Acceptance L/C)

这是指银行将受益人提交的汇票和/或单据审核无误后,承兑汇票并发承兑电,到期后再付款,经银行承兑的汇票可以到金融市场进行贴现提前收回资金。

(3)付款信用证(Payment L/C)

这是指信用证指定的付款行凭受益人提交的符合信用证条款的单据付款的信用证。它又分即期付款和迟期付款信用证,无论是即期付款信用证还是迟期付款信用证,受益人无须开立汇票,开证行或指定的付款行凭相符单据付款,故无法在金融市场进行融资。

6. 对背信用证

对背信用证(Back to back L/C)是指受益人要求原证的通知行或其他银行以原证为基础,另开一张内容相似的新证。对背信用证的内容除开证申请人、受益人、金额、单价、装运期限及有效期限等可有变动外,其他条款一般与原证相同。对背信用证的条款修改上,新证的开证人需得到原证开证人的同意,修改较困难,且需时较长。

7. 对开信用证

对开信用证(Reciprocal L/C)是指两张信用证的开证申请人互以对方为受益人而开立的信用证。第一张信用证的受益人和开证人是第二张回头信用证的开证人和受益人,第一张信用证的开证行和通知行分别是第二张信用证的通知行和开证行。两张信用证的金额可以相等,也可以不等。两张证可以同时互开、同时生效,也可以先后开立、先后生效。

8. 循环信用证

循环信用证(Revolving L/C)是指在一定时间内信用证被全部或部分使用后,能够重新恢复信用证原金额并再度使用,周而复始,直至达到该证规定的次数或累计总金额用完为止。循环信用证又可分为按时间循环信用证和按金额循环信用证,按金额循环信用证又可进一步分为自动循环、非自动循环和半自动循环等。

9. 预支信用证

预支信用证(Anticipatory L/C)是指开证行授权通知行,允许受益人在装运交单前预支全部或部分货款的信用证,由开证行保证偿付并负担利息,它是进口商通过银行开立给出口商的一种以出口贸易融资为目的的信用证。

10. 备用信用证

备用信用证(Standby L/C)是指开证行根据开证申请人的请求向受益人开立的承担某项义务的凭证。即当开证申请人未能按时偿还借款、预收款或支付货款,或未能履约时,开证行保证付款。因此,如果开证申请人按期履行合同义务,受益人就无须要求开证行在备用信用证项下支付任何货款或赔偿,这便是其称为“备用”的由来。

二、分析信用证的基本技能

【实训目的】

通过本项目实训,应掌握的基本技能如下。

①熟悉不同地区、不同开立方式信用证的框架结构。

②熟悉并看懂信用证内容并能准确翻译信用证的主要条款。

③学会正确填写信用证分析单。

【操作前准备】

进行本项任务的实训前,应准备的内容如下。

①预习信用证有关基础知识。

②铅笔、水笔、橡皮等工具。

③空白的纸质的信用证分析单或空白的电子版的信用证分析单。

【操作程序】

①总体浏览信用证。

②逐部仔细阅读信用证的条款,对认为有问题或看不懂的地方用铅笔作出标注。

③填写信用证分析单。

④对照信用证检查分析单填写是否正确。

【操作规范】

表 3.1 信用证、信开证的主要内容及其常用表示方式

	信用证具体内容	信开/电开证常用表示方法	SWIFT 信用证常用表示方法
信用证本身说明	信用证页次	PAGES	SEQUENCE OF TOTAL
	信用证种类	KINDS OF CREDIT	FORM OF DOCUMENTARY CREDIT
	信用证证号	CREDIT NO.	DOCUMENTARY CREDIT NUMBER
	金额	AMOUNT/TO THE EXTENT OF	CURRENCY CODE, AMOUNT
	开证日期和地点	DATE AND PLACE OF ISSUE	DATE OF ISSUE
	装运期	DATE OF SHIPMENT	LATEST DATE OF SHIPMENT
	有效期和到期地点	DATE AND PLACE OF EXPIRY/ VALIDITY	DATE AND PLACE OF EXPIRY
	交单期	PERIOD FOR PRESENTATION	PERIOD FOR PRESENTATION
	兑用方式		AVAILABLE WITH... BY...
信用证当事人	开证申请人	APPLICANT/OPENER	APPLICANT
	受益人	BENEFICIARY/IN YOUR FAVOR	BENEFICIARY
	开证行	OPENING BANK	APPLICANT BANK
	通知行	ADVISING/NOTIFYING BANK	ADVISE THROUGH BANK
	议付行	NEGOTIATING BANK	NEGOTIATING BANK
	付款行	PAYING BANK	DRAWEE
汇票条款	出票人	DRAWER	DRAWER
	收款人	PAYEE	PAYEE
	付款人	DRAWN ON	DRAWEE
	付款期限	SIGHT /TIME DRAFT	DRAFTS AT...
	金额	FOR TOTAL INVOICE AMOUNT	FOR FULL INVOICE VALUE
	出票依据	DRAWN UNDER	
	跟单条款	ACCOMPANIED BY FOLLOWING DOCUMENTS	DOCUMENTS REQUIRED
货物描述	商品名称	COMMODITY	DESCRIPTION OF GOODS AND/ OR SERVICES
	规格/货号	SPECIFICATION/ART NO.	SPECIFICATION/ART NO.
	数量	QUANTITY	QUANTITY
	单价	UNIT PRICE	UNIT PRICE
	唛头	SHIPPING MARKS	SHIPPING MARKS
	详细资料参照	DETAILS AS PER....	OTHERS AS PER....

续表

	信用证具体内容	信开/电开证常用表示方法	SWIFT 信用证常用表示方法
装运条款	装运港	PORT OF LOADING	PORT OF LOADING/AIRPORT OF DEPARTURE
	目的港	PORT OF DESTINATION	PORT OF DISCHARGE / AIRPORT OF DESTINATION
	分批	PARTIAL SHIPMENT	PARTIAL SHIPMENTS
	转运	TRANSSHIPMENT	TRANSSHIPMENT
单据条款	发票	COMMERCIAL INVOICE	COMMERCIAL INVOICE
	装箱单	PACKING LIST	PACKING LIST
	提单	BILL OF LADING	BILL OF LADING
	保险单/凭证	INSURANCE POLICY OR CERTIFICATE	INSURANCE POLICY OR CERTIFICATE
	原产地证	CERTIFICATE OF ORIGIN	CERTIFICATE OF ORIGIN
	检验证书	INSPECTION CERTIFICATE	INSPECTION CERTIFICATE
	其他证明	OTHER CERTIFICATE	OTHER CERTIFICATE
	特殊条款	SPECIAL/ADDITIONAL CONDITION	ADDITIONAL CONDITIONS
付款承诺	开证行保证付款责任文句	THE GUARANTEE OF THE OPENING BANK	
适用惯例	信用证所适用惯例	THIS CREDIT IS SUBJECT TO... UCP 600	APPLICABLE RULES

【信用证样例】

信开证样例和分析单如样例 3.1 和样例 3.2 所示，SWIFT 信用证样例和分析单如样例 3.3 和样例 3.4 所示。

中国银行 BANK OF CHINA 东京分行

PAGE:1/1

	IRREVOCABLE DOCUMENTARY CREDIT NO. A－08－0058
DATE AND PLACE OF ISSUE 08/2/15	DATE AND PLACE OF EXPIRY 08/5/15 JAPAN
APPLICANT MARUBENI CORP. 5－7, HOMMACHI, 2－CHOME, CHUO-KU, OSAKA, JAPAN	BENEFICIARY TIFERT TRADING CO., LTD. NO. 86, ZHUJIANG STREET, TIANJIN, CHINA
ADVISING BANK	BANK OF CHINA, TIANJIN BRANCH

AMOUNT：USD52500. 00	SAY：U. S. DOLLARS FIFTY-TWO THOUSAND FIVE HUNDRED ONLY
LATEST SHIPMENT DATE 08/4/30 SHIPMENT FROM TIANJIN TO TOKYO PARTIAL SHIPMENT NOT ALLOWED TRANSHIPMENT NOT ALLOWED	CREDIT AVAILABLE BY NEGOTIATION AGAINST PRESENTATION OF THE DOC. DETAILED HEREIN AND YOUR DRAFT AT 30 DAYS SIGHT DRAWN ON APPLICANT FOR FULL INVOICE VALUE BEARING DRAWN UNDER L/C NO. A－08－0058 ISSUED BY BANK OF CHINA TOKYO BRACH DATED 08/2/15
LIST OF DOCUMENTS TO BE PRESENTED 1. SIGNED COMMERCIAL INVOICE IN TRIPLICATE COUNTERSIGNED BY APPLICANT 2. 2/3 SET OF CLEAN ON BOARD OCEAN BILL OF LADING MADE OUT TO ORDER AND BLANK ENDORSED NOTIFY APPLICANT WITH FULL NAME, ADDRESS AND TEL NO. 8745 9986 AND INDICATING THE NAME OF CARRYING VESSEL'S NAME AND TEL NO. AT THE PORT OF DESTINATION MARKED FREIGHT TO COLLECT. 3. PACKING LIST IN DUPLICATE SHOWING THE GOODS HAVE BEEN PACKED IN CARTONS OF 20PCS EACH. 4. INSURANCE POLICY OR CERTIFICATE IN THE NAME OF APPLICANT FOR 120% OF INVOICE VALUE AGAINST ALL RISKS AND WAR RISK AS PER ICC DATED 1/1/1982 CLAIM, IF ANY, PAYABLE AT PORT OF DESTINATION. 5. CERTIFICATE OF ORIGIN ISSED BY CCPIT SHOWING THE NAME OF MANUFACTURER. 6. BENEFICIARY'S CERTIFICATE CERTIFYING THAT 1/3 ORIGINAL B/L AND ONE SET OF NON-NEGOTIABLE SHIPPING DOCUMENTS TO BE SENT TO APPLICANT WITHIN 48 HOURS AFTER SHIPMENT. 7. INSPECTION CERTIFICATE IN DUPLICATE ISSUED AND SIGNED BY AUTHORIZED PERSON OF APPLICANT WHOSE SIGNATURE MUST COMPLY WITH THAT HELD IN OUR BANK'S RECORD.	
COVERING SHIPMENT OF 5000PCS OF GIRL JACKET STYLE NO. GJ234 SHELL：WOVEN TWILL 100% COTTON, LINING：WOVEN 100% POLYESTER PACKING：1PC TO A PLASTIC BAG, 20BAGS TO A CARTON UNIT PRICE：USD10. 50/PC CIF TOKYO DETAILS AS PER S/C 08TF0858	
OTHER TERMS AND CONDITIONS	

1. SHIPPING MARKS: MARUBENI
S/C 08TF0858
TOKYO
CTN 1 – UP

信用证通知费已收
津　中　行

2. ALL BANKING CHARGES ARE FOR BENEFICIARY'S ACCOUNT.
3. DOCUMENTS MUST BE PRESENTED TO THE NEGOTIATING BANK WITHIN 7DAYS AFTER SHIPMENT BUT WITHIN THE VALIDITY OF THE CREDIT.
4. SHIPMENT MUST BE EFFECTED BY CONTAINER ONLY AND B/L SHOWING THE SAME.
5. NEGOTIATION AND PRESENTATION OF THE DOCUMENTS UNDER THIS CREDIT IS RESTRICTED TO BANK OF CHINA TIANJIN BRANCH.
6. NEGOTIATING BANK IS KINDLY FORWARD ALL DOCUMENTS IN ONE LOT BY REGISTERED AIRMAIL IMMEDIATELY AFTER NEGOTIATION.
7. 10% MORE OR LESS BOTH IN QUANTITY AND AMOUNT ALLOWED.
8. THE CREDIT WILL BECOME EFFECTIVE AFTER RECEIPT OF APPROVAL OF PRE-SHIPMENT SAMPLE FROM THE APPLICANT.

WE HEREBY ENGAGE WITH DRAWERS, ENDORSERS AND/OR BONA FIDE HOLDERS THAT DRAFTS DRAWN AND NEGOTIATED ON PRESENTATION AND THAT DRAFTS ACCEPTED WITHIN THE TERMS OF THIS CREDIT WILL BE DULY HONORED AT MATURITY.
THIS CREDIT IS SUBJECT TO UNIFORM AND CUSTOMARY PRACTICE 2007 REVERSION PUBLICATION NO. UCP600

YOURS FAITHFULLY,
FOR BANK OF CHINA HONGKONG BRANCH

周秀仪　麦德强

印鉴核符

样例 3.1　信开信用证

信开/电开证分析单

信用证本身说明	信用证种类	IRREVOCABLE DOCUMENTARY CREDIT	是否生效	□是 ☒否	密押/印鉴是否相符	☒是 □否	是否保兑	□是 ☒否
	信用证号码	A – 08 – 0058	金额	USD 52500. 00	到期地点	JAPAN	兑用方式	BY NEGOTIATION
	开证日期	08/2/15	装运日期	08/4/30	有效期	08/5/15	交单期	7 DAYS
当事人	开证行	BANK OF CHINA TOKYO BRANCH		通知行	BANK OF CHINA TIANJIN BRANCH			
	开证人	MARUBENI CORP. 5 – 7, HOMMACHI, 2 – CHOME, CHUO-KU, OSAKA, JAPAN		受益人	TIFERT TRADING CO., LTD. No. 86, ZHUJIANG STREET, TIANJIN, CHINA			
	付款行			议付行	BANK OF CHINA TIANJIN BRANCH			

<table>
<tr><td rowspan="4">汇票条款</td><td rowspan="2">出票人</td><td colspan="3" rowspan="2">TIFERT TRADING CO., LTD.</td><td>付款期限</td><td colspan="3">☐即期 ☒远期</td></tr>
<tr><td>付款金额</td><td colspan="3">☒发票全额 ☐发票的百分之几</td></tr>
<tr><td>收款人</td><td colspan="3">TIFERT TRADING CO., LTD.</td><td rowspan="2">出票依据</td><td colspan="3" rowspan="2">L/C NO. A-08-0058 ISSUED BY BANK OF CHINA TOKYO BRACH DATED 08/2/15</td></tr>
<tr><td>付款人</td><td colspan="3">MARUBENI CORP.</td></tr>
<tr><td rowspan="3">货物描述</td><td>品名</td><td>GIRL JACKET</td><td>规格/货号</td><td>STYLE NO. GJ234</td><td>贸易术语</td><td>CIF TOKYO</td><td rowspan="3">唛头</td><td rowspan="3">MARUBENI
S/C 08TF0858
TOKYO
CTN 1-UP</td></tr>
<tr><td>数量</td><td>5000PCS</td><td>包装/件数</td><td>250 CARTONS</td><td>单价</td><td>USD10.50/PC</td></tr>
<tr><td>合同/订单号</td><td>08TF0858</td><td>溢短装条款</td><td>10% MORE OR LESS</td><td>包装方式</td><td>CARTONS</td></tr>
<tr><td rowspan="2">装运条款</td><td>装运港</td><td>TIANJIN</td><td>目的港</td><td>TOKYO</td><td>分批</td><td>NOT ALLOWED</td><td>转运</td><td>NOT ALLOWED</td></tr>
<tr><td>运输方式</td><td colspan="3">☒海运 ☐空运 ☐陆运 ☐其他</td><td>装运日期</td><td colspan="3">最早
最晚08/4/30</td></tr>
<tr><td rowspan="13">单据条款</td><td>种类</td><td>份数</td><td colspan="2">签字</td><td colspan="4">主要内容/特别加注</td></tr>
<tr><td>发票</td><td>3</td><td colspan="2">☒盖章 ☐手签</td><td colspan="4">COUNTERSIGNED BY APPLICANT</td></tr>
<tr><td>装箱单</td><td>2</td><td colspan="2">☐盖章 ☐手签</td><td colspan="4">SHOWING THE GOODS HAVE BEEN PACKED CARTONS OF 20PCS EACH</td></tr>
<tr><td rowspan="3">提单</td><td>托运人</td><td colspan="2">TIFERT TRADING CO., LTD.</td><td colspan="2">运费支付</td><td colspan="2">FREIGHT TO COLLECT</td></tr>
<tr><td>抬头人</td><td colspan="2">TO ORDER</td><td colspan="2">份数</td><td colspan="2">3</td></tr>
<tr><td>通知人</td><td colspan="2">APPLICANT</td><td colspan="2">特别加注</td><td colspan="2">INDICATING THE NAME OF CARRYING VESSEL'S NAME AND TEL NO. AT THE PORT OF DESTINATION</td></tr>
<tr><td rowspan="3">保险单</td><td>抬头人</td><td colspan="2">APPLICANT</td><td colspan="2">份数</td><td colspan="2">2</td></tr>
<tr><td>保险险别</td><td colspan="2">ALL RISKS AND WAR RISK</td><td colspan="2">赔付地点/币种</td><td colspan="2">PORT OF DESTINATION</td></tr>
<tr><td>依据条款</td><td colspan="2">ICC</td><td colspan="2">保险加成</td><td colspan="2">120%</td></tr>
<tr><td>产地证</td><td>种类</td><td colspan="2">☒一般原产地证 ☐普惠制原产地证</td><td colspan="2">签发机构</td><td>CCPIT</td><td>份数</td><td>2</td></tr>
<tr><td>检验证</td><td>种类</td><td colspan="2">☒品质证 ☐重量证 ☐其他证书</td><td colspan="2">签发机构</td><td>AUTHORIZED PERSON OF APPLICANT</td><td>份数</td><td>2</td></tr>
<tr><td>其他单据</td><td colspan="7">BENEFICIARY'S CERTIFICATE</td></tr>
<tr><td>特殊条款</td><td colspan="8">SHIPMENT MUST BE EFFECTED BY CONTAINER ONLY AND B/L SHOWING THE SAME.</td></tr>
</table>

样例3.2 信开/电开证分析单

08 NOV. 15 12:09:47
LOGICAL TERMINALPA11
MSGACK DWS7651 AUTHENTICATION SUCCESSFUL WITH PRIMARY KEY
BASIC HEADER F 01BKCHCNBJAXXX0205090946
APPLICATION HEADER
07051725911114MIDLGB22BXXXD146251 5499111151037 N
* MIDLAND BANK PLC
* LONDON

USER HEADER	BANK PRIORITY 113:	
MSG USER REF	108:	
SEQUENCE OF TOTAL	27:	1/1
FORM OF DOC. CREDIT	40A:	IRREVOCABLE TRANSFERABLE
DOC. CREDIT NUMBER	20:	MF3075989
DATE OF ISSUE	31C:	081115
APPLICABLE RULES	40E:	UCP LATEST VERSION
EXPIRY	31D:	DATE 090115 PLACE CHINA
APPLICANT	50:	W W TEXTILES P O BOX 9 CEMEERY ROAD PUDSET WEST YORKS LS28 7XD
BENEFICIARY	59:	TIFERT TRADING CO., LTD NO. 86, ZHUJIANG ROAD, TIANJIN, CHINA
AMOUNT	32B:	CURRENCY GBP AMONT 3180, 00
MAX. CREDIT AMOUNT	39B:	MAXIMUM
AVAILABLE WITH/BY	41D:	FREELY NEGOTIABLE AT ANY BANK IN CHINA
DRAFT	42C:	AT SIGHT
DRAWEE:	42A:	MIDLAND BANK PLC, LONDON
PARTIAL SHIPMENTS	43P:	ALLOWED
TRANSSHIPMENT	43T:	PROHIBITED
PORT OF LOADING	44E:	CHINA MAIN PORTS
PORT OF DISCHARGE	44F:	SOUTHAMPTON IN TRANSIT TO LEEDS
LATEST DATE OF SHIP.	44C:	081225
DESCRIPT. OF GOODS	45A:	

信用证通知费已收
津 中 行

10000 DOZEN COTTON TEA TOWELS
AT GBP0. 318 PER DZ CFR SOUTHAMPTON
COLOUR ASSORTMENT AS PER CONTRACT NO. 081131
DOCUMENTS REQUIRED 46A:
+ FULL SET OF CLEAN ON BOARD OCEAN BILL OF LADING, MADE OUT TO THE ORDER OF MIDLAND BANK PLC, LONDON MARKED FREIGHT PREPAID NOTIFY ACCOUNTEE
+ INSURANCE IS TO BE EFFECTED BY BUYER.
+ SIGNED COMMERCIAL INVOICE IN TRIPLICATE SHOWING ORDER NO. WW65 – 3
+ PACKING LIST IN DUPLICATE SHOWING THE TOTAL GROSS WEIGHT, NET WEIGHT AND MEASURE-

MENT.

+ GSP CERTIFICATE OF ORIGIN FORM A IN ONE ORIGINAL AND ONE COPY

ADDITIONAL CONDITIONS 47A:

ALL DOCUMENTS MUST BEAR CREDIT NO.

PERIOD FOR PRESENTATION 48:

WITHIN 15DAYS AFTER DATE OF SHIPMENT

CONFIRMATION INSTRUCTIONS 49: WITHOUT

CHARGES 71B:

ALL BANKING CHARGES OUTSIDE LONDON ARE FOR ACCOUNT OF BENEFICIARY.

INSTRUCTIONS TO PAY/ACCOUNT/NEG BK 78:

+ THE AMOUNT OF EACH DRAFT MUST BE ENDORSED ON THE REVERSE OF THIS CREDIT

+ ALL DOCUMENTS MUST BE FORWARDED TO US BY COURIER SERVICE IN ONE LOT ADDRESSED TO MIDLAND BANK PLC 456, EASTCHEP TST., LONDON, UK

样例 3.3 SWIFT 信用证

SWIFT 信用证分析单

	项目	项目性质(英文)	项目性质(中文)	具体内容
信用证本身说明	27	SEQUENCE OF TOTAL	电文页次	1/1
	40A	FORM OF DOCUMENTARY CREDIT	跟单信用证形式	Irrevocable Transferable
	40E	APPLICABLE RULES	适用规则	UCP Latest Version
	20	DOCUMENTARY CREDIT NUMBER	信用证号码	MF3075989
	31C	DATE OF ISSUE	开证日期	081115
	31D	DATE AND PLACE OF EXPIRY	信用证有效期和有效地点	Date 090115 Place China
当事人	51A	APPLICANT BANK	信用证开证的银行	Midland Bank Plc, London
	57A	ADVISE THROUGH BANK	通知行	Bank Of China Tianjin Branch
	50	APPLICANT	信用证开证申请人	W W Textiles
	59	BENEFICIARY	信用证的受益人	Tifert Trading Co., Ltd.
金额	32B	CURRENCY CODE, AMOUNT	结算的货币和金额	GBP3180.00
兑用	41D	AVAILABLE WITH... BY...	指定的有关银行及信用证兑付的方式	Freely negotiable at any Bank in China
汇票	42C	DRAFTS AT...	汇票付款日期	At sight
	42D	DRAWEE	汇票付款人	Midland Bank Plc, London

	项目	项目性质(英文)	项目性质(中文)	具体内容
装运条款	43P	PARTIAL SHIPMENTS	分装条款	Allowed
	43T	TRANSSHIPMENT	转运条款	Prohibited
	44E	PORT OF LOADING/AIRPORT OF DEPARTURE	装运港/出发机场	China main ports
	44F	PORT OF DISCHARGE/AIRPORT OF DESTINATION	卸货港/目的地机场	Southampton in transit to Leeds
	44C	LATEST DATE OF SHIPMENT	最后装船期	081225
货物描述	45A	DESCRIPTION OF GOODS AND / OR SERVICES	货物描述	10000 Dozen Cotton Tea Towels at GBP0.318 per dz CFR Southampton Colour assortment as per contract No. 081131
单据条款	46A	DOCUMENTS REQUIRED	单据要求	+Bill of Lading +Commercial Invoice +Packing List +GSP Form A
特殊条款	47A	ADDITIONAL CONDITIONS	附加条款	All documents must bear Credit No.
交单	48	PERIOD FOR PRESENTATION	交单期限	Within 15days after date of shipment
保兑	49	CONFIRMATION INSTRUCTIONS	保兑指示	Without
费用	71B	CHARGES	费用情况	All banking charges outside London are for account of beneficiary.

样例 3.4 SWIFT 信用证分析单

【操作注意事项】

①注意查看信用证的页次是否齐全,检查信用证是否完整。

②查看信用证是否有重复的现象,如果怀疑有重复问题一定及时通过通知行和国外开证行核实。

③阅读信用证必须从头至尾都要看到,认真细致,对于不清楚的条款一定作标记,并及时与国外进口商核实。

④对于信开证特别要注意信用证空白处、边缘处用打字机或橡皮戳记加注的文字,这些往往是对信用证内容的重要补充或新的修改,不能大意。

三、分析信用证的操作训练

【翻译语句】

①beneficiary ②applicant

③advising bank ④negotiating bank

⑤opening bank ⑥paying bank

⑦irrevocable L/C ⑧confirmed L/C

⑨transferable L/C ⑩accompanied by following documents

⑪payment by letter of credit at sight

⑫The buyer shall pay against documentary draft drawn by the seller at 30 days after date of B/L. The shipping documents are to be delivered against payment only.

⑬We are authorized to pay the face amount of your drafts upon presentation, discount charges being for account of applicant.

⑭This credit available with any bank by negotiation of beneficiary drafts at 60 days after sight drawn on us.

⑮We hereby issue irrevocable documentary credit in your favor which is available by negotiation of your draft at sight drawn on issuing bank.

【动脑思考】

①天津针织品进出口公司与香港中间商 HM 公司有长期业务关系,双方一直采用背对背信用证结算货款,但最近 HM 公司提议改用可转让信用证结算货款。作为公司的业务员,你接受 HM 公司的建议吗?如果接受该建议,对你公司安全收汇是否感到有隐患?

②国外客户开来信用证一份,在 27:SEQUENCE OF TOTAL 一栏标明 1/2,但你却仅收到一页信用证,你作为单证员该如何处理此问题?

③英国某大型采购商每月从泰佛贸易公司进口两个 40 尺高柜的玻璃器皿,客户要求礼品包装,货到后直接上架出售。为了免去进口商开证手续和节省开证的费用,作为业务员你建议进口商采用哪种信用证付款比较合适?为什么?这样做对你公司有何便利?

④通过双方友好洽商,泰佛贸易公司最近与非洲一新客户就印花棉布达成一出口合同,金额 56 000 美金。为了保证能安全及时地收汇,作为业务员,你在签订合同时采用哪种信用证为好?并阐明你的理由。

⑤如信用证列有以下几种远期付款期限,请分析哪种对出口商最有利,哪种对进口商最有利。

a. credit available by your draft at 30 days after sight

b. credit available by your draft at 30 days after date

c. credit available by your draft at 30 days after B/L date

d. credit available by your draft at 30 days after invoice date

【动手操练】

实训操作一

泰佛贸易公司与科威特 SAMIEH 纺织品公司经过友好洽商就涤棉面料达成一份出口合同，数量 6 000 码，金额 7 200 美金，付款方式即期信用证（Sight L/C）。随后科威特 SAMIEH 纺织品公司及时通过科威特银行开出第 609/23262 号信用证（见样例 3.5），作为单证员，你首先分析一下该信用证，并填写电开信用证分析单（见样例 3.6），为下一步审证做好基础性工作。

BANK OF KUWAIT

IRREVOCABLE LETTER OF CREDIT NO. 609/23262

KUWAIT, DATE: 5 MAY 2008

BENEFICIARY:

TIFERT TRADING CO., LTD.

NO. 86, ZHUJIANG ROAD, TIANJIN, CHINA

ADVISING BANK:

BANK OF CHINA, TIANJIN BRANCH

AMOUNT:

ABOUT USD7200.00 (ABOUT US DOLLARS SEVEN THOUSAND TWO HUNDRED)

APPLICANT:

SAMIEH TEXTLE CO. LTD.

P. O. BOX 299934, SAFAT,

KUWAIT

VALID IN: CHINA AVAILABLE AT: SIGHT

VALID UNTIL 15 JULY, 2008 TRADE TERMS : CFR KUWAIT

PLEASE ADVISE OUR ABOVE IRREVOCABLE LETTER OF CREDIT AVAILABLE BY BENEFICIARIES DRAFTS, WITHOUT RECOURSE DRAWN ON US FOR THE FULL INVOICE VALUE AND ACCOMPANIED BY THE FOLLOWING DOCUMENTS:

+SIGNED COMMERCIAL INVOICE IN QUINTUPLICATES CERTIFYING THAT EACH PIECE CARTON/ CASE OF THE GOODS CARRIES THE NAME OF COUNTRY OF ORIGIN IN NON - DETACHABLE OR NON - ALTERABLE WAY.

+CERTIFICATE OF ORIGIN IN ORIGINAL AND AT LEAST ONE COPY SHOWING BENEFICIARIES AS MANUFACTURERS

+PACKING LIST IN TRIPLICATE SHOWING DESCRIPTION OF GOODS ITEM NO. AS PER HARMONIC SYSTEM NO. NUMBER AND KIND OF PACKAGES, CONTENTS OF PACKAGE, GROSS WEIGHT, NET WEIGHT AND TOTAL COST OF EACH ITEM.

+COMPLETE SET OF AT LEAST 3/3 (OF WHICH TWO TO ACCOMPANY THE ORIGINAL SET AND ONE WITH DUPLICATE SET OF DOCUMENTS) CLEAN "ON BOARD" MARINE BILLS OF LADING ISSUED TO THE ORDER OF BANK OF KUWAIT NOTIFYING OPENER AND EVIDENCING "FREIGHT PREPAID".

SHIPPING DOCUMENTS TO EVIDENCE SHIPMENT FROM CHINA TO KUWAIT NOT LATER THAN 30 JUNE, 2008 BY VESSEL (SS/MV).

COVERING
ABOUT 6000 YARDS ART 032, 65% POLYESTER 35% VISCOSE MIXED SUITING FABRICS WEIGHT: ABT. 250 GRAMS PER YARD SIZE: 58″ X ABT. 25 YARDS PRICE @ USD1.20 PER YARD.
CERTIFIED ON INVOICES THAT ALL OTHER DETAILS OF THE GOODS SHIPPED ARE AS PER INDENT NO. CTT/CH – 33/93 S/C: 08APR30.
SPECIAL CONDITIONS:
+ CERTIFICATE OF ORIGIN MUST SHOW NAME AND ADDRESSES OF MANUFACTURERS AND NAME OF EXPORTING COUNTRY/IES
+ AT THE TIME OF NEGOTIATION, PLEASE DEDUCT FROM YOUR PAYMENTS TO THE BENEFICIARIES 3% OF INVOICE VALUE OUT OF WHICH 1% DUE TO SAMIEH BASHEER NESWETH KUWAIT AND THE BALANCE 2% DUE TO ACHIM TEXTILES CO. LTD. KUWAIT AS COMMISSION WHICH WILL BE PAID BY US LOCALLY.

TRANSHIPMENT: PERMITTED. IN THIS CASE, THROUGH BILLS OF LADING ARE REQUIRED.
TRANSHIPMENT AT ISRAEL IS PROHIBITED.
PARTIAL SHIPMENT: PERMITTED.
NEGOTIATION RESTRICTED TO ADVISING BANK/S ONLY
SHIPPING MARKS: ABUZIAD – KUWAIT/CTT/CH – 33/93/MADE IN CHINA

REIMBURSEMENT INSTRUCTIONS:
DRAW ON OUR ACCOUNT WITH THE BANK OF NEW YORK U S A CERTIFYING TO THEM AND TO US THAT THE CREDIT TERMS HAVE BEEN COMPLIED WITH.

ALL DRAFTS TO BE MARKED "DRAWN UNDER ALAHLI BANK OF KUWAIT (KSC) L/C NO. 609/23262 DATED 5 MAY 2008" WE UNDERTAKE TO HONOUR ALL DRAFTS DRAWN IN STRICT COMPLIANCE WITH THE TERMS OF THIS CREDIT.

PLEASE CLAIM YOUR CHARGES, IF ANY, DIRECTLY FROM THE REIMBURSING BANK AT THE TIME OF NEGOTIATION OR ON EXPIRY OF THE CREDIT

PLEASE FORWARD TO US THE ORIGINAL SET OF DOCUMENTS BY REGISTERED AIRMAIL AND THE DUPLICATES BY SUBSEQUENT AIRMAIL.

THIS CREDIT IS SUBJECT TO THE UNIFORM CUSTOMS AND PRACTICE FOR DOCUMENTARY CREDITS (2007 REVISION) INTERNATIONAL CHAMBER OF COMMERCE PUBLICATION NO. 600

样例 3.5 电开信用证

信开/电开证分析单

<table>
<tr><td rowspan="3">信用证本身说明</td><td>信用证种类</td><td></td><td>是否生效</td><td>□是
□否</td><td>密押/印鉴是否相符</td><td>□是
□否</td><td>是否保兑</td><td>□是
□否</td></tr>
<tr><td>信用证号码</td><td></td><td>金额</td><td></td><td>到期地点</td><td></td><td>兑用方式</td><td></td></tr>
<tr><td>开证日期</td><td></td><td>装运日期</td><td></td><td>有效期</td><td></td><td>交单期</td><td></td></tr>
<tr><td rowspan="3">当事人</td><td>开证行</td><td colspan="2"></td><td>通知行</td><td colspan="4"></td></tr>
<tr><td>开证人</td><td colspan="2"></td><td>受益人</td><td colspan="4"></td></tr>
<tr><td>付款行</td><td colspan="2"></td><td>议付行</td><td colspan="4"></td></tr>
<tr><td rowspan="4">汇票条款</td><td rowspan="2">出票人</td><td colspan="2" rowspan="2"></td><td>付款期限</td><td colspan="4">□即期 □远期</td></tr>
<tr><td>付款金额</td><td colspan="4">□发票全额 □发票的百分之几</td></tr>
<tr><td>收款人</td><td colspan="2"></td><td rowspan="2">出票依据</td><td colspan="4" rowspan="2"></td></tr>
<tr><td>付款人</td><td colspan="2"></td></tr>
<tr><td rowspan="3">货物描述</td><td>品名</td><td></td><td>规格/货号</td><td></td><td>贸易术语</td><td></td><td rowspan="3">唛头</td><td rowspan="3"></td></tr>
<tr><td>数量</td><td></td><td>包装/件数</td><td></td><td>单价</td><td></td></tr>
<tr><td>合同/订单号</td><td></td><td>溢短装条款</td><td></td><td>总额</td><td></td></tr>
<tr><td rowspan="2">装运条款</td><td>装运港</td><td></td><td>目的港</td><td></td><td>分批</td><td></td><td>转运</td><td></td></tr>
<tr><td colspan="3">运输方式 □海运 □空运 □陆运 □其他</td><td>装运日期</td><td colspan="4">最早
最晚</td></tr>
<tr><td rowspan="13">单据条款</td><td>种类</td><td>份数</td><td>签字</td><td colspan="5">主要内容/特别加注</td></tr>
<tr><td>发票</td><td></td><td>□盖章 □手签</td><td colspan="5"></td></tr>
<tr><td>装箱单</td><td></td><td>□盖章 □手签</td><td colspan="5"></td></tr>
<tr><td rowspan="3">提单</td><td>托运人</td><td colspan="2"></td><td>运费支付</td><td colspan="3"></td></tr>
<tr><td>抬头人</td><td colspan="2"></td><td>份数</td><td colspan="3"></td></tr>
<tr><td>通知人</td><td colspan="2"></td><td>特别加注</td><td colspan="3"></td></tr>
<tr><td rowspan="3">保险单</td><td>抬头人</td><td colspan="2"></td><td>份数</td><td colspan="3"></td></tr>
<tr><td>保险险别</td><td colspan="2"></td><td>赔付地点/币种</td><td colspan="3"></td></tr>
<tr><td>依据条款</td><td colspan="2"></td><td>保险加成</td><td colspan="3"></td></tr>
<tr><td>产地证</td><td>种类</td><td colspan="2">□一般原产地证
□普惠制原产地证</td><td>签发机构</td><td></td><td>份数</td><td></td></tr>
<tr><td>检验证</td><td>种类</td><td colspan="2">□品质证 □重量证 □其他证书</td><td>签发机构</td><td></td><td>份数</td><td></td></tr>
<tr><td>其他单据</td><td colspan="7"></td></tr>
<tr><td colspan="8"></td></tr>
<tr><td>特殊条款</td><td colspan="8"></td></tr>
</table>

样例 3.6 空白信开/电开证分析单

实训操作二

2008年6月，主要从事纺织品、食品的泰佛贸易公司与加拿大WENSCO食品公司签订了销售950箱蘑菇罐头的出口合同，金额10 380美金，付款方式装运后45天远期信用证。随后加拿大WENSCO食品公司及时通过多伦多NOVA SCOTIA银行开出第101800/146791号信用证（见样例3.7），作为制单员，你首先分析一下信用证，并填写SWIFT信用证分析单（见样例3.8），为下一步审证做好基础性工作。

BASIC HEADER F 01 BKCHCNBJA5XX 9828 707783

APPL. HEADER 0 700 1917000731 NOSCCATTAXXX 3775 931472 0008010718 N

+ BANK OF NOVA SCOTIA. TORONTO, CANADA

(BANK NO. :8015000) + TORONTO, ONTARIO, CANADA

MT:700-------------ISSUE OF A DOCUMENTARY CREDIT-----------------------------------

SEQUENCE OF TOTAL	27:	1/1
FORM OF DOCUMENTARY CREDIT	40A:	IRREVOCABLE TRANSFERABLE
DOCUMENTARY CREDIT NUMBER	20:	101800/146791
DATE OF ISSUE	31C:	080731
APPLICABLE RULES	40E:	UCP LATEST VERSION
DATE AND PLACE OF EXPIRY	31D:	080915 CHINA
APPLICANT	50:	WENSCO FOODS LTD., 1191 GREEN LAND STREET, WELLD. COQUITLAM, B. C., CANADA, V3K 5Z1
BENEFICIARY	59:	TIFERT TRADING CO., LTD NO. 86, ZHUJIANG ROAD, TIANJIN, CHINA
CURRENCY CODE, AMOUNT	32B:	USD10830,00
MAXIUM CREDIT AMOUNT	39B:	NOT EXCEEDING
AVAILABLE WITH ... BY ...	41D:	ANY BANK BY NEGOTIATION
DRAFTS AT	42C:	DRAFTS AT 45 DAYS AFTER BILL OF LADING DATE FOR 100 PERCENT OF INVOICE VALUE
DRAWEE	42D:	THE BANK OF NOVA SCOTIA, 650 WEST GEORGIA ST., PO BOX 11502, VANCOUVER, B. C., CANADA V6B 4P6
PARTIAL SHIPMENT	43P:	ALLOWED
TRANSSHIPMENT	43T:	ALLOWED
PORT OF LOADING	44E:	CHINESE MAIN PORT
PORT OF DISCHARGE	44F:	VANCOUVER, B. C., CANADA
LATEST DATE OF SHIPMENT	44C:	080831
DESCRPT OF GOODS/SERVICES	45A:	
EVIDENCING SHIPMENT OF		

P. O. NO. 2027

950 CARTONS CANNED MUSHROOM PIECES & STEMS EVERGREEN BRAND 24 TINS X 425 GRAMS NET WEIGHT AT USD11. 40 PER CARTON.

FREE ON BOARD TIANJIN, CHINA.

DOCUMENTS REQUIRED　　46A:

+ SIGNED COMMERCIAL INVOICE IN TRIPLICATE.

+ CANADA CUSTOMS INVOICE IN QUADRUPLICATE FULLY COMPLETED.

+ CERTIFICATE OF ORIGIN FORM A IN TRIPLICATE.

+ BENEFICIARY'S LETTER OF GUARANTEE STATING THEY WILL REIMBURSE ALL EXPENSES IN CASE OF REJECTION BY CANADIAN FOOD INSPECTION AGENCY IN TRIPLICATE.

+ BENEFICIARY CERTIFICATE IN TRIPLICATE STATING

1. THE SHIPMENT DOES NOT INCLUDE NON-MANUFACTURED WOOD DUNNAGE, PALLETS, CRATING OR OTHER PACKAGING MATERIALS.

2. THE SHIPMENT IS COMPLETELY FREE OF WOOD BARK, VISIBLE PESTS AND SIGNS OF LIVING PESTS.

+ FULL SET OF CLEAN ON BOARD OCEAN BILL OF LADING MADE OUT TO THE ORDER OF THE BANK OF NOVA SCOTIA MARKED FREIGHT COLLECT AND NOTIFY WENSCO FOODS LTD., 1191 GREEN LAND STREET, WELL D. COQUITLAM, B. C., CANADA, V3K5Z1.

ADDITIONAL CONDITIONS　　47A:

+ INSURANCE COVERED BY APPLICANT.

+ THIS LETTER OF CREDIT IS TRANSFERABLE. IF TRANSFERRED, THE DRAFT MUST BE ACCOMPANIED BY A LETTER BY THE BANK EFFECTING THE TRANSFER STATING THE NAME OF THE TRANSFEREE AND THAT THIS CREDIT HAS BEEN TRANSFERRED.

+ THE ADVISING BANK IS THE DESIGNATED TRANSFERRING BANK.

+ THIRD PARTY DOCUMENTS ARE ACCEPTABLE ONLY IF L/C IS TRANSFERRED.

+ AMENDMENT CHARGES (IF ANY) WILL BE FOR THE BENEFICIARY'S ACCOUNT IF THE CAUSE OF A-MENDMENT OCCURRED FROM THE BENEFICIARY'S SIDE.

+ IT IS A CONDITION OF THIS LETTER OF CREDIT THAT PAYMENT WILL BE EFFECTED AT MATURITY BUT ONLY UPON RECEIPT OF WRITTEN NOTIFICATION FROM THE BUYER STATING THAT GOODS HAVE PASSED CANADIAN AUTHORITIES INSPECTION. THE REMITTING BANK/ NEGOTIATING BANK MUST INDICATE ON THEIR COVERING LETTER TO SCOTIABANK THAT ALL DOCUMENTS MUST BE DELIVERED TO THE APPLI-CANT AGAINST A TRUST RECEIPT IN ORDER TO OBTAIN CLEARANCE OF MERCHANDISE TO SECURE IN-SPECTION BY CANADIAN AUTHORITIES.

+ PAYMENT/ACCEPTANCE OF DRAFTS WILL ONLY BE MADE AFTER RECEIPT OF WRITTEN ADVICE FROM THE APPLICANT STATING THAT THE MERCHANDISE HAS PASSED INSPECTION AND HAS BEEN RELEASED FOR SALE IN CANADA BY THE CANADIAN AUTHORITIES.

+ IF THE GOODS DO NOT PASS INSPECTION, THEN NOTICE TO THIS EFFECT MUST BE GIVEN IN WRITING BY THE CANADIAN AUTHORITIES WHO MUST PRESENT SAME TO SCOTIABANK. UPON RECEIPT OF THE REJECTION NOTICE, THE NEGOTIATING BANK/REMITTING BANK WILL BE ADVISED ACCORDINGLY AND SCOTIABANK'S LIABILITY WILL BECOME NULL AND VOID.

+ PLEASE DIRECT ALL ENQUIRIES AND FORWARD DOCUMENTS IN ONE LOT (VIA COURIER) TO THE BANK OF NOVA SCOTIA, VANCOUVER INTERNATIONAL TRADE SERVICES, MALL LEVEL, 650 WEST GEOR-GIA STREET, VANCOUVER, B. C., CANADA V6B4P6.

+ A DISCREPANCY HANDLING FEE OF USD 45. 00 WILL BE ASSESSED BY THE BANK OF NOVA SCOTIA ON

EACH PRESENTATION OF DOCUMENTS NOT IN STRICT COMPLIANCE WITH THE TERMS AND CONDITIONS OF THE CREDIT.

THIS FEE IS FOR THE ACCOUNT OF THE BENEFICIARY AND WILL BE DEDUCTED FROM THE PROCEEDS WHEN PAYMENT IS EFFECTED, IN ADDITION TO ANY OUT OF POCKET EXPENSES INCURRED BY THE BANK OF NOVA SCOTIA IN THIS CONNECTION.

+THIS IS THE OPERATIVE INSTRUMENT.

+DRAFT(S) MUST INDICATE THE NUMBER AND DATE OF THIS CREDIT.

CHARGES 7IB:

ISSUING BANK CHARGES ARE FOR THE ACCOUNT OF THE APPLICANT. ALL OTHER BANK CHARGES INCLUDING REIMBURSEMENT BANK CHARGES ARE FOR THE BENEFICIARY'S ACCOUNT.

PERIOD FOR PRESENTATIONS 48:

DOCUMENTS MUST BE PRESENTED AT PLACE OF EXPIRATION WITHIN 15 DAYS OF ON BOARD DATE OF OCEAN BILL OF LADING AND WITHIN THE L/C VALIDITY

CONFIRMATION INSTRUCTION 49: WITHOUT

样例 3.7 SWIFT 信用证

	项目	项目性质(英文)	项目性质(中文)	具体内容
信用证本身说明	27	SEQUENCE OF TOTAL	电文页次	
	40A	FORM OF DOCUMENTARY CREDIT	跟单信用证形式	
	40E	APPLICABLE RULES	适用规则	
	20	DOCUMENTARY CREDIT NUMBER	信用证号码	
	31C	DATE OF ISSUE	开证日期	
	31D	DATE AND PLACE OF EXPIRY	信用证有效期和有效地点	
当事人	51A	APPLICANT BANK	信用证开证的银行	
	57A	ADVISE THROUGH BANK	通知行	
	50	APPLICANT	信用证开证申请人	
	59	BENEFICIARY	信用证的受益人	
金额	32B	CURRENCY CODE, AMOUNT	结算的货币和金额	
兑用	41D	AVAILABLE WITH...BY...	指定的有关银行及信用证兑付的方式	
汇票	42C	DRAFTS AT...	汇票付款日期	
	42D	DRAWEE	汇票付款人	
装运条款	43P	PARTIAL SHIPMENTS	分装条款	
	43T	TRANSSHIPMENT	转运条款	
	44E	PORT OF LOADING/AIRPORT OF DEPARTURE	装运港/出发机场	
	44F	PORT OF DISCHARGE/AIRPORT OF DESTINATION	卸货港/目的地机场	
	44C	LATEST DATE OF SHIPMENT	最后装船期	

	项目	项目性质(英文)	项目性质(中文)	具体内容
货物描述	45A	DESCRIPTION OF GOODS AND/OR SERVICES	货物描述	
单据条款	46A	DOCUMENTS REQUIRED	单据要求	
特殊条款	47A	ADDITIONAL CONDITIONS	附加条款	
交单	48	PERIOD FOR PRESENTATION	交单期限	
保兑	49	CONFIRMATION INSTRUCTIONS	保兑指示	
费用	71B	CHARGES	费用情况	

样例3.8　空白SWIFT信用证分析单

任务四　审核信用证

任务背景

王芳小姐在纺织品部工作一段时间后,接触到许多不同地区、不同开立方式的信用证。在师傅们的耐心指导下,再加上本人的不懈努力,王芳很快就熟悉了信用证的主要内容,并能够准确翻译信用证的主要条款,为审核信用证奠定了扎实的基础。

在对日本丸红株式会社开立的女童成衣夹克衫信用证进行分析的基础上,王芳小姐发现其中有个别条款与买卖双方签订的合同条款不符,由此进入到审核信用证工作环节。

【背景分析】

信用证是银行有条件的付款保证,银行只有在"相符交单"的情况下才履行付款义务。这就要求我们一定要把好审证关,否则货物出运后向银行交单议付货款时才发现信用证中的某些条款无法满足,不能提供符合信用证、符合《UCP600》、符合《ISBP》要求的单据,则为时已晚,会给安全收汇带来巨大的隐患。因此王芳小姐应该掌握和具备如下知识、技能和素质。

知识目标

①了解信用证付款方式的特点。

②了解信用证付款方式的作用。

技能目标

①掌握信用证审核技巧。

②正确填写信用证审核单。

③学会草拟信用证改证函。

素质目标

①养成严谨、细致的工作作风。

②学会处理工作的原则性和灵活性之间的关系。

一、审核信用证的基础知识

【信用证的特点】

1. 信用证是一种银行信用

信用证是银行以自己的信用作出的付款保证,所以在信用证付款方式下,银行承担第一性的付款责任。信用证以银行信用取代了商业信用,减少了由于进出口商间相互不信任而造成的付款不确定性,为进出口商双方提供了信用保障。

2. 信用证是一份独立的文件

信用证虽以贸易合同为基础,但它一经开立就成为独立于合同之外的一项契约。《UCP600》第4条a款规定:“就性质而言,信用证与可能作为其依据的销售合同或其他合同,是相互独立的交易。即使信用证中提及该合同,银行亦与该合同完全无关,且不受其约束。”由此可见,信用证的所有当事人仅凭信用证条款办事,以信用证为唯一的依据。如果出口商认真履行了合同,却未能提供与信用证相符的单据,便会遭到银行拒付。

3. 信用证业务是纯粹的单据交易

信用证业务是纯粹的单据买卖,银行只凭符合信用规定的单据予以议付或付款。依据《UCP600》规定,银行一不管合同、二不管商品、三不管单据真伪、四不管出口商是否履约交货,银行只看单据,不看货物。银行仅对相符交单(complying presentation)承诺付款。《UCP600》第5条规定:“银行处理的是单据(documents),而不是单据所涉及的货物、服务或履约行为。”

【信用证的作用】

信用证支付方式是随着国际贸易的发展,以及银行参与到国际贸易结算的过程中而逐步形成的。由于货款的支付以取得符合信用证规定的装运单据为条件,避免了预付货款的风险,因此信用证支付方式在很大程度上解决了进出口商双方在付款和交货问题上的矛盾。尽管近年来信用证支付方式在老客户间的交易中有下降趋势,但其仍不失为国际贸易中主要的付款方式之一。

对出口商而言,L/C的最大好处是提供了一个可靠的账房(付款人),这就是银行。如果出口商收到的L/C不符合买卖合约,要求进口商修改而遭拒绝,便可以终止合约,不付运货物;如果L/C符合买卖合约,且没有特别难以达到的要求,出口商按照合同约定将货物在合约期内出运,并在信用证规定的有效期和交单期内将代表货物的全套单据送交银行,在单内相符、单单相符和单证相符的情况下,必然能从银行收回货款。

对进口商而言,是货运抵后才付款。只要双方诚信交易,进口商并不会冒多大风险,因为出口商已把货物付运,进口商拿到了已装船提单(B/L)等于拿到了货物。

二、审核信用证的基本技能

【实训目的】

通过本项目实训,应掌握的基本技能如下。

①掌握信用证审核技巧。

②正确填写信用证审核单。

③学会草拟信用证改证函。

【操作前准备】

进行本项任务的实训前,应准备的内容如下。

①预习信用证有关基础知识。

②铅笔、水笔、橡皮等工具。

③相关合同及资料。

④空白的纸质信用证审核单或空白的电子版信用证审核单。

【操作程序】

①总体浏览信用证。

②逐部分仔细审核信用证的条款,对不能接受的条款用铅笔作出标注。

③填写信用证审核单。

④对照信用证检查审核单填写是否正确,检查是否有漏审核条款。

【操作规范】

表 4.1 信用证的主要内容及其审核重点

	信用证具体内容	信用证条款及其对应的合同条款	审核的重点
信用证本身说明	(1)信用证页次 Pages/Sequence of total		①页码是否齐全 ②信用证所涉及的附件是否锁好
	(2)信用证种类 Kinds of credit		《UCP600》已取消可撤销信用证
	(3)信用证证号 Credit No.		每份证应该有唯一证号
	(4)金额 Amount	对应合同中的总金额	①金额与合同是否相符 ②币种与合同是否相同 ③如有大小写是否一致 ④佣金、折扣是否包含在总金额中 ⑤溢短装是否适用金额中
	(5)开证日期和地点 Date and place of issue		是否按照合同约定的期限开出信用证
	(6)装运期 Latest shipment date	对应合同中的装运期	①装运期是否与合同规定相符 ②如提前视具体情况考虑接受与否 ③如推迟(最晚……)无须改证
	(7)有效期和到期地点 Place and date of expiry	参照合同中的装运期	①一般比装运期晚 10 ~ 15 天为宜 ②原则上不接受在国外到期
	(8)交单期 Period of presentation		一般装船后 10 ~ 15 天为宜
	(9)兑用方式 Available with	对应合同中的支付条款	①议付信用证为好 ②最好不是付款信用证
	(10)有效性 Effectiveness		①是否有有效期 ②是否是有条件生效 ③是否有软条款 ④信开/电开证是否印鉴/密押相符
信用证当事人	(11)开证申请人 Applicant	对应合同中的买方	公司名称和地址都要核对
	(12)受益人 Beneficiary	对应合同中的卖方	公司名称和地址都要核对
	(13)通知行 Advising bank		通知行最好与受益人在同一地点
	(14)议付行 Negotiating bank		如议付行与受益人不在同一城市又限制议付,需考虑时间上的可行性

续表

	信用证具体内容	信用证条款及其对应的合同条款	审核的重点
汇票条款	(15)出票人 Drawer	对应合同中的卖方	
	(16)收款人 Payee	对应合同中的卖方或议付行	
	(17)付款人 Drawee	对应信用证中的开证行或指定的付款行	付款人不能是开证申请人
	(18)付款期限 Tenor	对应合同中的支付条款	汇票的付款期限是否与合同中的付款期限相符
	(19)出票依据 Drawn under		通常包括开证行、证号和开证日期
货物描述	(20)商品名称 Commodity name	对应合同中的品名条款	品名是否有拼写错误
	(21)规格/货号 Specification/Art No.	对应合同中的品质条款	须仔细审核,特别注意规格中最高、最多、最低、最少等描述是否与合同相符,货号完全正确与否
	(22)数量 Quantity	对应合同中的数量条款	①数量是否与合同相符 ②是否有溢短装
	(23)单价 Unit price	对应合同中的价格条款	①单价是否正确 ②币别是否相同 ③计量单位是否相符 ④贸易术语是否一致
	(24)唛头 Shipping marks	对应合同中的唛头	①若不一致视具体情况考虑接受与否 ②若已经备妥货物,原则上应要求改证 ③若没有备妥货物,按证中唛头刷唛
	(25)详细资料参照 Details as per...	对应合同号和合同日期	①引用的合同号是否与买卖双方签订的合同相符 ②引用的合同日期是否与实际合同相同
装运条款	(26)装运港 Port of loading	对应合同中的装运条款	①装运港是否与合同相同 ②如不同,不增加费用且能做到无须改证 ③来证笼统规定"CHINA MAIN PORTS"则无须改证
	(27)目的港 Port of destination	对应合同中的装运条款	①目的港是否与合同相同 ②如不同,不增加费用即无须改证 ③注意世界上重名港问题,其后应加国别
	(28)分批 Partial shipments	对应合同中的装运条款	若合同中规定禁分而来证允许,无须改证
	(29)转运 Transshipment	对应合同中的装运条款	若合同中规定禁转而来证允许,无须改证

续表

	信用证具体内容	信用证条款及其对应的合同条款	审核的重点
单据条款	(30)发票 Commercial invoice		若要求开证人会签需删除
单据条款	(31)装箱单 Packing list		若要求开证人会签需删除
单据条款	(32)提单 Bill of lading		①1/3 正本提单自寄需修改 ②运费支付情况与贸易术语矛盾需修改
单据条款	(33)保险单/凭证 Insurance policy/certificate	对应合同保险条款	①投保加成是否与合同规定相符 ②投保险别是否与合同相符 ③依据的保险条款及其版本年份是否一致 ④ICC 中的险别是否与 CIC 中的险别同时出现在保险条款中
单据条款	(34)原产地证 Certificate of origin		①签发单位能否接受 ②是否需要使领馆认证
单据条款	(35)检验证书 Inspection certificate	对应合同中的检验条款	①检验机构是否为对我友好的独立的第三方 ②是否为客检证,若是需修改
单据条款	(36)其他证明 Other certificate		所要求证明是否能够自行出具,如需第三方能否保证及时签发
单据条款	(37)特殊条款 Special terms	对应合同的备注	①特殊条款是否已单据化,若是是否能够保证及时签发 ②重点审核是否含有软条款
付款承诺	(38)开证行保证付款责任文句 Undertaking clause of opening bank		信开/电开证必须有银行保证付款的责任文句,否则信用证无效
适用惯例	(39)信用证所适用惯例 Credit is subject to...	THIS CREDIT IS SUBJECT TO... UCP 600	①信开/电开证必须适用于《UCP600》,否则信用证无效 ②升级后的 SWIFT 报文格式也增加了所适用的惯例

【信用证审核样例】

销 售 合 同

SALES CONTRACT

编号 No.: 08TF0858　　　　日期 Date :NOV. 05,2008

The sellers: TIFERT TRADING CO., LTD.

Add: NO. 86, ZHUJIANG ROAD, TIANJIN, CHINA　　　　Post code:300221

The buyers: MARUBENI CORP

Add: 5 -7, HOMMACHI, 2 -CHOME, CHUO-KU, OSAKA, JAPAN

Tel: 81 -1 -2124046　　　　Fax:81 -1 -2124055

兹确认售予你方下列货品,其成交条款如下:

We hereby confirm having sold to you the following goods on the terms and conditions as specified below:

(1)货物名称及规格 Name of commodity and specifications	(2)数量 Quantity	(3)单价 Unit price	(4)总值 Total amount
GIRL JACKET SYTLE NO. GJ234 SHELL: WOVEN TWILL 100% COTTON LINING: WOVEN 100% POLYESTER	5000PCS 10% MORE OR LESS ALLOWED	USD10.50/PC CIF TOKYO	USD52500.00

(5)包装:

Packing: 20PCS/CARTON, EACH CARTON SHOULD BE INDCIATED COMMODITY NAME, COLOR NO. AND STYLE NO. AND CARTON SIZE

(6)装运唛头:

Shipping mark: MARUBENI
S/C 08TF0858
TOKYO
CTN 1 – UP

(7)装运期限:

Time of shipment: APR. 30, 2008

(8)装运口岸: 目的地:

Port of shipment: TIANJIN Destination: TOKYO

WITH PARTIAL SHIPMENTS AND TRANSSHIPMENT ALLOWD

(9)付款条件:

Payment terms: BY SIGHT L/C WHICH REMAINS VALID IN CHINA FOR NEGOTIATION UNTIL 15 DAYS AFTER SHIPMENT.

(10)保险:卖方负责投保海运险按照 CIF 金额的 110% 投保一切险和战争险,如果发生索赔,在日本用美元赔偿。

Insurance: The seller shall arrange marine insurance covering All Risks and War Risk for 110% of CIF value. Claim, if any, payable in Japan, in currency of USD.

(11)检验:货物出运前应该由出入境检验检疫局进行施检,其签发的检验证书作为向银行议付货款的单据之一。

Inspection: The goods should be inspected by CIQ before shipment and the inspection certificate issued by CIQ will be one kind of documents to be presented for negotiation.

(12)买方须于2008 年2 月15 日前开出本批交易的信用证。否则,售方有权:不经通知取消本合同,或接受买方对本销售合同未执行的全部或部分,或对遭受的损失提出索赔。

The buyer shall establish the covering letter of credit before Feb. 15th, 2008. Failing which the seller reserves the right to rescind without further notice, or to accept whole or any part of this sales contract unfulfilled by the buyer, or to lodge a claim for direct losses sustained if any.

(13)凡以 CIF 条件成交的业务,保额为发票价的 110%,投保险别以本销售合同中所开列的为限,买方如要求增加保额或保险范围应于装船前经售方同意,因此而增加的保险费由买方负责。

For transactions concluded on C. I. F basis it is understood that the insurance amount will be for 110% of the invoice value against the risks specified in the sales contract, if additional insurance amount or coverage is required, the buyer must have the consent of the seller before shipment, and the additional premium is to be borne by the buyer.

(14)品质/数量异议:如买方提出索赔,凡属品质异议须于货到目的口岸之日起2个月内提出。凡属数量异议须于货到目的口岸之日起15天内提出,对所装货物所提任何异议属于保险公司,轮船公司及有关运输机构所负责者,售方不负任何责任。

Quality/Quantity discrepancy: In case of quality discrepancy, claim should be filed by the buyer within 2 months after the arrival of the goods at the port of destination while for quantity discrepancy claim should by filed by the buyer within 15 days after the arrival of the goods at the port of destination. It is understood that seller shall not be liable for any discrepancy of the goods shipped due to causes for which the insurance company, shipping company other transportation organization are liable.

(15)本合同内所述全部或部分商品,如因人力不可抗拒的原因,以致不能履约或延迟交货,售方概不负责。

The seller shall not be held liable for failure or delay in delivery of the entire lot or portion of the goods under this sales contract in consequence of any force maJeure incidents.

确认签署 Confirmed by

MARUBENI CORP.	TIFERT TRADING CO., LTD.
小泉太郎	王 宏
买方 (The buyers)	卖方 (The sellers)

样例4.1 女童夹克衫销售合同

中国银行 BANK OF CHINA 天津分行

信用证通知书

Notification of Documentary Credit

Address: 80, JIEFANG BEI LU, TIANJIN, CHINA

Cable: CHUNGKOU

Telex: 23233 TJBOC CN

Fax: 0086 22 23128900 Date: FEB. 19, 2008

To: 致 TIFERT TRADING CO., LTD. NO. 86, ZHUJIANG ROAD, TIANJIN, CHINA	When corresponding please quote our Ref No.
Issuing Bank 开证行 BANK OF CHINA, TOKYO BRANCH	Transmitted to us through 转递行
L/C No. 证号 A-08-0058 Dated 开证日期 FEB. 15, 2008	Amount 金额 USD52500.00
Expiry 效期 MAY 15, 2008 Tenor 远期	Charge 费用

Dear Sirs, 迳启者: We have pleasure in advising you that we have received from the a/m bank a(n) 兹通知贵司,我行收自上述银行 (　) telex issuing　电传开立　　　(　) ineffective　未生效 (　) pre-advising of　预先通知　　　(　) mail confirmation of　证实书 (×) original　正本　　　(　) duplicate　副本 letter of credit, contents of which are as per attached sheet(s). This advice and the attached sheet(s) must accompany the relative documents when presented for negotiation. 信用证一份,现随附通知,贵司交单时,请将本通知书及信用证一并提示。 (×) Please note that this advice does not constitute our confirmation of the above L/C nor does it convey any engagement or obligation on our part. 本通知书不构成我行对此信用证之保兑及其他任何责任。 (　) Please note that we have added our confirmation to the above L/C, negotiation is restricted to ourselves only. 上述信用证已由我行加具保兑,并限向我行交单。 Remark

This L/C consists of 2 sheet(s), including the covering letter and attachment(s).

本信用证连同面函及附件共 2 纸。

If you find any terms and conditions in the L/C which you are unable to comply with and or any error(s), it is suggested that you contact applicant directly for necessary amendment(s) so as to avoid any difficulties which may arise when documents are presented

如本信用证中有无法办到的条款及/或错误，请迳与开证申请人联系进行必要的修改，以排除交单时可能发生的问题。

Yours faithfully

for BANK OF CHINA

样例 4.2　信用证通知函

中国银行 BANK OF CHINA　东京分行

PAGE:1/1(1)

	IRREVOCABLE DOCUMENTARY CREDIT(2) NO. A-08-0058(3)
DATE AND PLACE OF ISSUE 08/2/15 IN TOKYO (5)	DATE AND PLACE OF EXPIRY 08/5/15 JAPAN (7) + (10)
APPLICANT (11) MARUBENI CORP. 5-7, HOMMACHI, 2-CHOME, CHUO-KU, OSAKA, JAPAN	BENEFICIARY (12) TIFERT TRADING CO., LTD. NO. 86, ZHUJIANG STREET, TIANJIN, CHINA

<table>
<tr><td>ADVISING BANK (13)
BANK OF CHINA, TIANJIN BRANCH</td><td>AMOUNT: USD52500.00 (4)
SAY: U. S. DOLLARS FIFTY-TWO THOUSAND FIVE HUNDRED ONLY.</td></tr>
<tr><td>LATEST SHIPMENT DATE 08/4/30 (6)
SHIPMENT FROM TIANJIN CHINA (26) TO TOKYO JAPAN(27)
PARTIAL SHIPMENT NOT ALLOWED (28)
TRANSHIPMENT NOT ALLOWED (29)</td><td>CREDIT AVAILABLE BY NEGOTIATION (9) AGAINST PRESENTATION OF THE DOC. DETAILED HEREIN AND OF YOUR(15) DRAFT AT 30 DAYS SIGHT(18) DRAWN ON APPLICANT(17) FOR FULL INVOICE VALUE (19) PAY TO TIFERT TRADING CO., LTD. ONLY (16) BEARING DRAWN UNDER L/C NO. A - 08 - 0058 ISSUED BY BANK OF CHINA TOKYO BRACH DATED 08/2/15 (19)</td></tr>
<tr><td colspan="2">LIST OF DOCUMENTS TO BE PRESENTED
1. SIGNED COMMERCIAL INVOICE IN TRIPLICATE CERTIFYING THE GOODS ARE OF CHINESE ORIGIN AND COUNTERSIGNED BY APPLICANT(30)
2. 2/3 SET OF CLEAN ON BOARD OCEAN BILL OF LADING MADE OUT TO ORDER AND BLANK ENDORSED NOTIFY APPLICANT WITH FULL NAME, ADDRESS AND TEL NO. 8745 9986 AND INDICATING THE NAME OF CARRYING VESSEL'S NAME AND TEL NO. AT THE PORT OF DESTINATION MARKED FREIGHT TO COLLECT. (32)
3. PACKING LIST IN DUPLICATE SHOWING THE GOODS HAVE BEEN PACKED IN CARTONS OF 20PCS EACH AND CERTIFYING EACH ITEM HAS BEEN MARKED THE LABEL "MADE IN CHINA". (31)
4. INSURANCE POLICY OR CERTIFICATE IN THE NAME OF APPLICANT FOR 120% OF INVOICE VALUE AGAINST ALL RISKS AND WAR RISK AS PER ICC DATED 1/1/1982 CLAIM, IF ANY, PAYABLE AT PORT OF DESTINATION. (33)
5. GSP CERTIFICATE OF ORIGIN FORM A ISSED BY CIQ INDICATING THE L/C NO AND SHOWING THE NAME OF MANUFACTURER (34)
6. BENEFICARY'S CERTIFICATE CERTIFYING THAT 1/3 ORIGINAL B/L AND ONE SET OF NON-NEGOTIABLE SHIPPING DOCUEMENTS TO BE SENT TO APPLICANT WITHIN 48 HOURS AFTER SHIPMENT. (36)
7. SHIPPING ADVICE SHOULD BE SENT TO APPLICANT WITHIN 2 DAYS AFTER SHIPMENT NOTIFYING THE VESSEL NAME, B/L NO. QUNTITY SHIPPED, TOTAL AMOUNT AND SHIPMENT DATE. (36)
8. SHIPPING COMPANY'S CERTIFICATE CERTIFYING THAT THE CARRYING VESSEL IS NOT OVER 15 YEARS OLD. (36)
9. INSPECITON CERTIFICATE IN DUPLICATE ISSUED AND SIGNED BY AUTHORIZED PERSON OF APPLICANT WHOSE SIGNATURE MUST COMPLY WITH THAT HELD IN OUR BANK'S RECORD. (10) + (35)</td></tr>
<tr><td colspan="2">COVERING SHIPMENT OF
5000PCS(22) OF GIRL JACKET(20) SYTLE NO. GJ234 SHELL: WOVEN TWILL 100% COTTON, LINING: WOVEN 100% POLYESTER(21) PACKING: 1PC TO A PLASTIC BAG, 20BAGS TO A CARTON
UNIT PRICE: USD10.50/PC CIF TOKYO(23) DETAILS AS PER S/C 08TF0858 (25)</td></tr>
<tr><td colspan="2">OTHER TERMS AND CONDITIONS</td></tr>
</table>

1. SHIPPING MARKS: MARUBENI
S/C 08TF0858
TOKYO
CTN 1 - UP (24)

信用证通知费已收
津 中 行

2. ALL BANKING CHARGES ARE FOR BENEFICIARY'S ACCOUNT.
3. DOCUMENTS MUST BE PRESENTED TO THE NEGOTIATING BANK WITHIN 7 DAYS AFTER SHIPMENT BUT WITHIN THE VALIDITY OF THE CREDIT. (8)
4. SHIPMENT MUST BE EFFECTED BY CONTAINER ONLY AND B/L SHOWING THE SAME. (37)
5. NEGOTIATION AND PRESENTATION OF THE DOCUMENTS UNDER THIS CREDIT IS RESTRICTED TO BANK OF CHINA TIANJIN BRANCH. (14)
6. NEGOTATING BANK IS KINDLY FORWARD ALL DOCUMENTS IN ONE LOT BY REGISTERED AIRMAIL IMMEDIATELY AFTER NEGOTIATION.
7. 10% MORE OR LESS BOTH IN QUANTITY AND AMOUNT ALLOWED. (22)
8. THE CREDIT WILL BECOME EFFECTIVE AFTER RECEIPT OF APPROVAL OF PRE-SHIPMENT SAMPLE FROM THE APPLICANT. (10)

WE HEREBY ENGAGE WITH DRAWERS, ENDORSERS AND/OR BONA FIDE HOLDERS THAT DRAFTS DRAWN AND NEGOTIATED ON PRESENTATION AND THAT DRAFTS ACCEPTED WITHIN THE TERMS OF THIS CREDIT WILL BE DULY HONORED AT MATURITY. (38)
THIS CREDIT IS SUBJECT TO UNIFORM AND CUSTOMARY PRACTICE 2007 REVERSION PUBLICATION NO. UCP600 (39)

YOURS FAITHFULLY,
FOR BANK OF CHINA HONGKONG BRANCH
周秀仪　　麦德强

印鉴核符

(10)

样例 4.3 女童夹克衫信用证

信用证审核记录

收证日期 FEB. 20,2008

信用证证号	A-08-0058	合同号	08TF0858	订单号	
开证行	Bank of China Tokyo Branch			开证日期	08/2/15
开证人	Marubeni Corp.				
受益人	Tifert Trading Co., Ltd.				
货物名称	Girl Jacket	数量	5000pcs	金额	USD52500.00
装运期	08/4/30	有效期	08/5/15	交单期	7 days
装运港	Tianjin	目的港	Tokyo	可否分批	Not allowed
贸易术语	CIF Tokyo	汇票期限	At 30 days sight	可否转运	Not allowed

<table>
<tr><td>特殊条款</td><td colspan="19">1. Shipment must be effected by container only and B/L showing the same.
2. Negotiation and presentation of the documents under this Credit is restricted to Bank of China Tianjin Branch.
3. The credit will become effective after receipt of approval of pre-shipment sample from the applicant.</td></tr>
<tr><td rowspan="2">单据种类及份数</td><td>汇票</td><td>发票</td><td>装箱单</td><td>重量单</td><td>尺码单</td><td>保险单</td><td>提单正本</td><td>提单副本</td><td>原产地证</td><td>GSP产地证</td><td>品质证</td><td>重量证</td><td>植检证</td><td>船行证明</td><td>寄单证明</td><td>寄样证明</td><td>受益人证明</td><td>邮包收据</td><td>其他</td></tr>
<tr><td>2</td><td>3</td><td>2</td><td></td><td></td><td>2</td><td>3</td><td></td><td></td><td>2</td><td>2</td><td></td><td></td><td></td><td>1</td><td></td><td></td><td></td><td></td></tr>
<tr><td rowspan="16">需要修改的内容</td><td colspan="10">来证条款内容</td><td colspan="9">应修改后条款内容</td></tr>
<tr><td colspan="10">1. 信用证到期地点 JAPAN</td><td colspan="9">应修改为 CHINA，原则上不接受国外到期</td></tr>
<tr><td colspan="10">2. 受益人地址 ZHUJIANG STREET</td><td colspan="9">应修改为 ZHUJIANG ROAD，地址不符</td></tr>
<tr><td colspan="10">3. 转运 NOT ALLOWED</td><td colspan="9">应修改为 ALLOWED，与合同不符</td></tr>
<tr><td colspan="10">4. 汇票付款期限 AT 30 DAYS SIGHT</td><td colspan="9">应修改为 AT SIGHT，与合同不符</td></tr>
<tr><td colspan="10">5. 汇票的付款人 DRAWN ON APPLICANT</td><td colspan="9">应修改为 DRAWN ON US，信用证为银行信用</td></tr>
<tr><td colspan="10">6. 发票中的 COUNTERSIGNED BY APPLICANT</td><td colspan="9">应该删除，否则无法保证在交单期内交单</td></tr>
<tr><td colspan="10">7. 提单中的 2/3 SET</td><td colspan="9">应修改为 3/3 SET，否则受益人无法控制物权</td></tr>
<tr><td colspan="10">8. 提单中的 FREIGHT TO COLLECT</td><td colspan="9">应修改为 FREIGHT PREPAID，与贸易术语不符</td></tr>
<tr><td colspan="10">9. 保险单中的投保加成 120%</td><td colspan="9">应修改为 110%，与合同不符</td></tr>
<tr><td colspan="10">10. 保险单中依据的保险条款和版本年份由 AS PER ICC DATED 1/1/1982</td><td colspan="9">应修改为 AS PER CIC DATED 1/1/1981，保险险别与依据的保险条款混淆</td></tr>
<tr><td colspan="10">11. 受益人证明函中的 1/3 ORIGINAL B/L</td><td colspan="9">应修改为 COPY OF B/L</td></tr>
<tr><td colspan="10">12. 检验证书的签发人 ISSUED AND SIGNED BY AUTHORIZED PERSON OF APPLICANT WHOSE SIGNATURE MUST COMPLY WITH THAT HELD IN OUR BANK'S RECORD</td><td colspan="9">应修改为 ISSUED BY CIQ，此系软条款</td></tr>
<tr><td colspan="10">13. 银行费用 ALL BANKINGCHARGES ARE FOR BENEFICIARY'S ACCOUNT</td><td colspan="9">应修改为 ALL BANKING CHARGES OUTSIDE JAPAN ARE FOR BENEFICIARY'S ACCOUNT，否则不合理</td></tr>
<tr><td colspan="10">14. 交单期 WITHIN 7 DAYS</td><td colspan="9">应修改为 WITHIN 15 DAYS，与合同不符</td></tr>
<tr><td colspan="10">15. 特殊条款中的第 8 条 THE CREDIT WILL BECOME EFFECTIVE AFTER RECEIPT OF APPROVAL OF PRE-SHIPMENT SAMPLE FROM THE APPLICANT</td><td colspan="9">应该删除，属于暂不生效条款</td></tr>
<tr><td>外销员签字</td><td colspan="10">陈 丽</td><td colspan="4">部门经理签字</td><td colspan="5">赵天明</td></tr>
</table>

样例 4.4 女童夹克衫信用证审核记录

中国银行 BANK OF CHINA 天津分行

修改通知书

Notification of Amendment

Address: 80, JIEFANG BEI LU, TIANJIN, CHINA

Cable: CHUNGKOU

Telex: 23233 TJBOC CN

Fax: 0086 22 23128900 Date: FEB. 27, 2008

To: 致 TIFERT TRADING CO., LTD. NO. 86, ZHUJIANG ROAD, TIANJIN, CHINA	When corresponding please quote our Ref No.
Issuing Bank 开证行 BANK OF CHINA, TOKYO BRANCH	Transmitted to us through 转递行
L/C No. 信用证号 A-08-0058	Amendment No 修改次数 1
L/C advised 信用证通知日期 FEB. 19, 2008	Amendment dated 修改日期 FEB. 25, 2008

Dear Sirs,

迳启者:

We have pleasure in advising you that we have received from the a/m bank a(n)

兹通知贵司,我行收自上述银行

(×) telex of 电传开立 ( ) ineffective 未生效

( ) original 正本 ( ) duplicate 副本

Amendment to the captioned L/C, contents of which are as per attached sheet(s).

内容见附件。

This amendment should be attached to the captioned L/C advised by us, otherwise, the beneficiary will be responsible for any consequences arising there from.

本修改须附于有关信用证,否则,贵公司须对因此产生的后果承担责任。

Remark 备注

This L/C consists of 2 sheet(s), including the covering letter and attachment(s).

本信用证连同面函及附件共2纸。

Yours faithfully

for BANK OF CHINA

样例4.5 女童夹克衫信用证修改通知书

FROM: BANK OF CHINA TOKYO BRANCH

TO: BANK OF CHINA TIANJIN BRANCH

80 JIEFANG BEI LU, TIANJIN

PEOPLE'S REP. OF CHINA

TEST: FOR USD52500.00 ON DATE 25/02/2008

PLEASE ADVICE BENEFICIARY OF THE FOLLOWING AMENDMENT TO L/C NO. A－08－0058 ISSUED BY US DATED 15/02/2008

DATE & NUMBER OF AMENDMENT：FIRST AMENDMENT ON FEB 25，2008 IN JAPAN

THE LETTER OF CREDIT HAS BEEN AMENDED AS FOLLOWS：

1. THE PLACE OF EXPIRY SHOULD BE IN CHINA INSTEAD OF IN JAPAN.

2. THE CORRECT ADDRESS OF BENEFICIARY IS NO. 86，ZHUJIANG ROAD，TIANJIN，CHINA.

3. TRANSHIPMENT SHOULD BE ALLOWED INSTEAD OF NOT ALLOWED.

4. BENEFICIARY'S DRAFT SHOULD BE AT SIGHT INSTEAD OF AT 30 DAYS SIGHT.

5. DRAFT SHOULD BE DRAWN ON OPENING BANK INSTEAD OF ON APPLICANT.

6. DELETE COMMERCIAL INVOICE COUNTERSIGNED BY APPLICANT.

7. B/L SHOULD BE FULL SET OF CLEAN ON BOARD INSTEAD OF 2/3 SET AND MARKED FREIGHT PREPAID NOT FREIGHT TO COLLECT.

8. INSURANCE VALUE SHOULD BE INVOICE VALUE OF GOODS PLUS 10% NOT 20% AND AS PER CIC DATED 1/1/1981 INSTEAD OF AS PER ICC DATED 1/1/1982.

9. BENEFICIARY'S CERTIFICATE SHOULD CERTITY THAT ONE COPY OF B/L INSTEAD OF 1/3 ORIGINAL B/L.

10. DELETE INSPECITON CERTIFICATE IN DUPLICATE ISSUED AND SIGNED BY AUTHORIZED PERSON OF APPLICANT WHOSE SIGNATURE MUST COMPLY WITH THAT HELD IN OUR BANK'S RECORD AND INSERT INSPECTION CERTIFICATE IN DUPLICATE ISSED BY CIQ.

11. ALL BANKING CHARGES ARE FOR BENEFICIARY'S ACCOUNT SHOULD CHANGE TO ALL BANKING-CHARGES OUTSIDE JAPAN ARE FOR BENEFICIARY'S ACCOUNT.

12. DOCUMENTS SHOULD BE PRESENTED FOR NEGOTIATION WITHIN 15 DAYS AFTER SHIPMENT INSTEAD OF 7 DAYS.

13. THE CREDIT WILL BECOME EFFECTIVE AFTER RECEIPT OF APPROVAL OF PRE-SHIPMENT SAMPLE FROM THE APPLICANT WHICH SHOULD BE DELETED.

OTHER TERMS AND CONDITIONS REMAIN UNCHANGED.

样例 4.6 女童夹克衫信用证修改

【操作注意事项】

①首先要注意审核信用证的“四性”，即：有效性、真实性、完整性和风险性。

②其次对照合同条款做到逐个条款审核，检查信用证中的所有条款是否能够满足。

③注意区分单据化条款和非单据化条款，对于单据化条款不能做到的一定坚持让进口商修改。

④对于信用证中的软条款要睁大眼睛仔细识别，及早剔除影响安全收汇的隐患。

⑤掌握信用证的修改原则，分清“必须修改”、“可改可不改”与“无须修改”的界限。

三、审核信用证的操作训练

【翻译语句】

①We hereby issue in your favor this irrevocable documentary credit which is available by payment against presentation of the following documents.

②Please notify Beneficiary and add your Bank's confirmation.

③We hereby add confirmation to this credit and we undertake that documents presented for payment in conformity with terms of this credit will be duly honored on presentation.

④Drafts drawn under this Credit are negotiable through ××× Bank.

⑤We hereby issue Irrevocable Documentary Credit in your favor which is available by negotiation of your draft at sight drawn on Issuing Bank.

⑥We are authorized to pay the face amount of your drafts upon presentation, discount charges being for account of Applicant.

⑦This credit is transferable in China only, and if it is totally transferred and negotiations restricted to Advising Bank.

⑧Drafts to be drawn at 30 days sight. Drafts drawn under this credit to be marked: "Drawn under ××× Bank L/C No.. . Dated (issuing date of credit. . . .)".

⑨Draft(s) drawn under this credit must be negotiated in China on or before August 12, 2008 after which date this credit expires.

⑩Signed commercial invoice in 6 copies, original of which must be certified by the Chamber of Commerce.

⑪Full set of 3/3 originals plus 3 non-negotiable copies clean on board ocean B/L, consigned to order and blank endorsed marked "Freight Prepaid" showing shipping agency at destination notify applicant and evidence the goods have been shipped by full container load.

⑫Insurance Policy/Certificate in 2 fold issued for 110% of the invoice value, covering Institute Cargo Clause A and War clause, stating claims payable in Holland by claims paying agent.

⑬Certificate of Origin issued by China Council for Promotion of International Trade showing consignee as "To whom it May Concern".

⑭Beneficiary's Certificate certifying that full set of non-negotiable copies of documents sent to applicant immediately after shipment.

⑮Please dispatch the first set of documents including five copies of commercial invoices direct to us by registered airmail and the second sent by following airmail.

【动脑思考】

①天津胜利制衣有限公司与法国家乐福采购商通过友好洽商就睡衣套达成一份出口合同，合同规定货物于2008年3月15日前从天津新港运往法国马赛港，而家乐福采购商通过法国巴黎银行开立的信用证规定："SHIPMENT FROM CHINESE MAIN PORTS"，你作为公司单证员认为有必要修改信用证吗？为什么？

②天津棉纺进出口公司拟出口全棉印花布约10 000米到南非的好望角港，当货物备妥出运前，业务员发现信用证货物描述的数量前没有"About"字样，因为国内染整厂设备临时出现故障，最后仅备齐9 600米面料，再推迟就要过装运期，要求客户修改信用证也为时已晚，此时业务员万分焦急，请你帮助他找出最好的解决方案。

③天津粮油进出口公司欲从泰国进口香米5 000公吨，合同约定从2007年12月至2008年4月每月供应我方1 000公吨大米，由泰国的曼谷港运至天津港。2007年12月泰国的供应商如期把货装到指定的载货船舶，我方中国银行在相符交单的情况下及时付清货款。但到2008年的1月份，泰国国内香米出现短缺情况，未能如期交运1月份的1 000公吨香米。泰国供应商费尽周折在2月份凑足2 000公吨香米一起发运至天津港，随后全套单据到达中国银行天津分行。请分析中行天津分行是否会如期付款？为什么？

④L/C 规定：Expiry 为 071111，Latest shipment date 为 071101，实际船期为071025，Period for presentation 为 10 days，作为业务员，你最迟应在哪天把全套单据交到银行议付货款？

⑤最近泰佛贸易公司收到一份美国花旗银行开来的信用证，单证员对该信用证进行了认真审核，没有发现与合同条款不符的内容，但整个信用证只有有效期，而信用证开立日期、最迟装运日期、交单期等都没有。单证员不知道该证是否有效，打电话向中行天津分行国际结算部进行了咨询。如果你是中行结算部的工作人员，你应该如何回答单证员的问题呢？

【动手操练】

实训操作一

泰佛贸易公司与日本通用贸易公司就出口"鸽牌"印花细布达成一出口合同，合同号为TJ080208(见样例4.7)，合同主要条款摘录如下。

合同号码：TJ080208

签订日期、地点：2008年12月11日于天津

卖方：泰佛贸易有限公司(Tifert Trading Co.，Ltd.)

买方：日本通用贸易公司（General Trading Company，Japan）

商品名称："鸽牌"印花细布（"Dove" brand printed shirting）

规格：30s ×36s 72 ×69 35/6″× 42 码

数量：67200 码

单价：CIF 大阪每码 3.00 日元

总值：210600.00 日元

装运期:2009 年 1 月 31 日前自中国港口至大阪,允许分批装运和转船。

付款条件:凭不可撤销即期信用证付款,于装运期前 1 个月开到卖方,并于上述装运期后 15 天内在中国议付有效。

保险:由卖方根据中国人民保险公司 1981 年 1 月 1 日中国保险条款按发票金额的 110% 投保一切险和战争险。

样例 4.7 合同

2008 年 12 月 28 日泰佛贸易公司收到日本通用贸易公司开来的第 L－1437 号不可撤销信用证(见样例 4.8),信用证主要条款摘录如下。

IRREVOCABLE DOCUMENTARY LETTER OF CREDIT

Date: Dec. 25, 2008

We hereby open our Irrevocable Letter of Credit No. L－1437 in favor of Tifert Trading Co., Ltd. for account of General Trading Company, Japan, up to an aggregate amount of JPY201, 600. 00(Say Japanese Yuan Two Hundred and One Thousand Six Hundred Only) CIFC 2% Osaka for 100% of the invoice value relative to the shipment of: 67,200 Pieces of Dove brand printed shirting 30s × 36s 72 × 69 35/6″ × 42 yards as per Contract No. TJ08028 dated Dec 11, 2008 from China port to Osaka, Japan.

Drafts to be drawn at 30 days after sight on our bank and accompanied by the following documents, marked "×":

(×) Signed Commercial Invoice in triplicate;

(×) Full set of CLEAN ON BOARD BILLS of LADING made out to our order quoting L/C NO. L－1437, marked FREIGHT PAID;

(×) One original Marine Insurance Policy or Certificate for 130% of invoice value covering ALL Risks and War Risk with claims payable in Japan in the currency of draft(s).

Partial shipments are permitted.

Transshipment is prohibited.

Shipment must be effected not later than January 31, 2009.

Draft(s) drawn under this credit must be negotiated in Japan on or before January 31, 2009.

样例 4.8 信用证

请认真审核该信用证并填写信用证的审核记录(见样例 4.9)。

信用证的审核记录

合同号	
信用证号	
审核结果	

样例 4.9　信用证审核记录

实训操作二

泰佛贸易公司通过香港中间商 ORCHID 贸易公司达成女士服装转口生意，货物最终目的港是德国汉堡，双方签订合同（见样例 4.10），并于 3 月 22 日收到通过香港 BANCA INTESA S. P. A. 银行开立的第 540370 号信用证（见样例 4.11）。请你认真审核信用证并填写信用证审核记录（见样例 4.12）。

SALES CONFIRMATION

No. HM08 - 1256
Date: 2008 - 3 - 5
Place: TIANJIN

The seller: TIFERT TRADING CO., LTD.
NO. 86, ZHUJIANG ROAD, TIANJIN, CHINA
The buyer: ORCHID TRADING LTD.
UNIT 513, CHINACHEM BLDG., 78 MODY ROAD, TST, KOWLOON, HONG KONG

After friendly negotiation, the seller agrees to sell and the buyer agrees to buy the following goods on the conditions stipulated below:

Style No.	P/O No.	Commodity	Quantity	Unit price	Amount
1484020	100020	LADIES WEARS ROUND NECK	1568PCS	CIF ROTTERDAM USD5. 40/PC	USD8467. 20
1484521	100021	JACKET	1568PCS	USD6. 20/PC	USD9721. 60
			3136PCS		USD18188. 80

Packing: IN CARTONS

Shipment: TO BE EFFECTED DURING APRIL, 2008 FROM TIANJIN TO HAMBURG WITH PARTIAL SHIPMENT AND TRANSHIPMENT ALLOWED.

Insurance: TO BE COVERED BY THE SELLER FOR 110% OF INVOICE VALUE AGAINGST ALL RISK AND WAR RISK AS PER CIC DATED 1/1/1981

Payment: BY SIGHT L/C TO REACH THE SELLER 15 DAYS BEFROE SHIPMENT AND REMAIN VALID IN CHINA 15DAYS AFTER SHIPMENT.

The seller	The buyer
王　宏	蔡林强

样例 4.10　合同

DOCUMENTARY LETTER OF CREDIT

ISSUING BANK: BANCA INTESA S. P. A. , HONG KONG

ADVISING BANK: BANK OF CHINA, TIANJIN BRANCH.

SEQUENCE OF TOTAL	27:	1/1
FORM OF DOC. CREDIT	40A:	IRREVOCABLE TRANSFERABLE
APPLICABLE RULES	40E:	UCP LATEST VERSION
DOC. CREDIT NUMBER	20:	540370
DATE OF ISSUE	31C:	080318
EXPIRY	31D:	DATE 080505 PLACE HONGKONG
APPLICANT	50:	ORCHID TRADING LTD. UNIT 513, CHINACHEM BLDG. , 78 MODY ROAD, TST, KOWLOON, HONG KONG
BENEFICIARY	59:	TIFERT TRADING CO. , LTD. NO. 86, ZHUJIANG ROAD, TIANJIN, CHINA
AMOUNT	32B:	CURRENCY USD AMOUNT 18188,80
POS. / NEG. TOL. (%)	39A:	05/05
AVAILABLE WITH/BY	41D:	ANY BANK BY NEGOTIATION
DRAFT AT ...	42C:	AT 30 DAYS SIGHT
DRAWEE	42D:	BANCA INTESA S. P. A. , HONG KONG
PARTIAL SHIPMENT	43P:	PERMITTED
TRANSSHIPMENT	43T:	PROHIBITED
LOADING IN CHARGE	44A:	SHANGHAI CHINA
FOR TRANSPORT TO....	44B:	ROTTERDAM
LATEST DATE OF SHIPMENT	44C:	080430
DESCRIPT. OF GOODS	45A:	

LADIES WEARS

STYLE NO.	P/O NO.	DESCRIPTION	QTY.	UNIT PRICE
1484020	100020	ROUND NECK	1568PCS	USD5. 40/PC
1484521	100021	JACKET	1586PCS	USD6. 20/PC

CIF ROTTERDAM INCOTERMS 2000

DOCUMENTS REQUIRED	46A:
	+ SIGNED COMMERCIAL INVOICE IN QUADRUPLICATE FOR CIF VALUE OF GOODS, SHOWING SEPARATELY THE L/C NO., P/O NO., STYLE NO., FREIGHT CHARGE AND INSURANCE PREMIUM.
	+ FULL SET OF CLEAN ON BOARD OCEAN BILL OF LADING MADE OUT TO OUR ORDER, MARKED FREIGHT PREPAID AND NOTIFY LERROS MODEN GMBH, IM TAUBENTAL 35, D-41468 NEUSS, GERMANY, FAX: 49-2131-3600999.
	+ PACKING LIST IN TRIPLICATE COUNTERSIGNED BY APPLICANT.
	+ G. S. P. CERTIFICATE OF FORM A IN ONE ORIGINAL.
	+ BENEFICIARY'S LETTER EVIDENCING THAT ONE SET OF N/N DOCUMENTS HAS BEEN DISPATCHED TO LERROS MODEN GMBH, IM TAUBENTAL 35, D-41468 NEUSS, GERMANY IMMEDIATELY AFTER SHIPMENT.
ADDITIONAL COND.	47A:
	+ DOCUMENTS PRESENTED WITH DISCREPANCY WHETHER INDICATED OR FOUND IS SUBJECT TO A HANDLING FEE FOR USD45.00 WHICH IS PAYABLE BY THE BENEFICIARY AND WILL BE DEDUCTED FROM PROCEEDS UPON NEGOTIATION.
	+ THIRD PARTY DOCUMENTS ARE ALLOWED.
	+ THIS L/C IS TRANSFERABLE AND L/C ADVISING BANK IS NOMINATED AS THE TRANSFERRING BANK.
	+ 5 PCT MORE OR LESS BOTH IN CREDIT AMOUNT AND QUANTITY ARE ACCEPTABLE.
DETAILS OF CHARGES	71B: ALL BANK CHARGES OUTSIDE HONGKONG ARE FOR THE ACCOUNT OF THE BENEFICIARY.
PRESENTATION PERIOD	48: WITHIN 5 DAYS AFTER THE DATE OF SHIPMENT BUT WITHIN THE VALIDITY OF THE CREDIT.
CONFIRMATION	*49: WITHOUT
INSTRUCTION	78: ON RECEIPT OF DOCUMENTS IN ORDER AT OUR COUNTER, WE SHALL REMIT IN ACCORDANCE WITH THE NEGOTIATING BANK'S INSTRUCTION IN THE SAME CURRENCY OF THE CREDIT.

样例 4.11　信用证

信用证审核记录

信用证号码		合同号码	
信用证通知号码		开证日期/地点	
信用证到期时间/地点		信用证种类	
开证行		通知行	
开证申请人		受益人	
汇票付款人		汇票期限	
议付行限制		收证日期	

<table>
<tr><td colspan="3">装运港</td><td colspan="4"></td><td colspan="2">目的港</td><td colspan="2"></td></tr>
<tr><td colspan="3">运输方式</td><td colspan="4"></td><td colspan="2">运费的支付方法</td><td colspan="2"></td></tr>
<tr><td colspan="3">可否分批</td><td colspan="4"></td><td colspan="2">可否转运</td><td colspan="2"></td></tr>
<tr><td colspan="3">装运日期</td><td colspan="4"></td><td colspan="2">交单天数</td><td colspan="2"></td></tr>
<tr><td rowspan="3">提单</td><td>抬头</td><td colspan="5"></td><td rowspan="3">保险</td><td>保险险别</td><td colspan="2"></td></tr>
<tr><td>托运人</td><td colspan="5">运费已付</td><td>保险加成</td><td colspan="2"></td></tr>
<tr><td>通知方</td><td colspan="5"></td><td>赔付地点/币种</td><td></td><td></td></tr>
<tr><td colspan="3">信用证金额</td><td colspan="4"></td><td colspan="2">溢短装</td><td colspan="2"></td></tr>
<tr><td rowspan="2">货物</td><td>品名</td><td></td><td>规格货号</td><td colspan="3"></td><td rowspan="2">唛头</td><td rowspan="2"></td><td>单价</td><td></td></tr>
<tr><td>数量</td><td></td><td>包装/件数</td><td colspan="3"></td><td>总值</td><td></td></tr>
<tr><td colspan="11">信用证要求的单据种类及份数</td></tr>
<tr><td></td><td>提单</td><td>发票</td><td>装箱单</td><td>保险单</td><td>原产地证</td><td>汇票</td><td>证明函</td><td colspan="3">其他所需单据及份数</td></tr>
<tr><td>份数</td><td></td><td></td><td></td><td></td><td></td><td></td><td></td><td colspan="3"></td></tr>
<tr><td>审证结果</td><td colspan="10"></td></tr>
<tr><td>审证员</td><td colspan="4"></td><td colspan="3">复核员</td><td colspan="3"></td></tr>
</table>

样例 4.12　信用证审核记录

实训操作三

The following are the contract（见样例 4.13）signed between Tifert Trading Co.，Ltd. & GB Posters Ltd. and the credit（见样例 4.14）opened through England Center Bank. Please check the credit according to the contract to see if the terms and conditions are in compliance with that of contract. If not, please use the letter paper（见样例 4.15）to write a mail in English to the buyer asking them to amend the credit accordingly.

SALES CONFIRMATION

No. 209511

Date JAN. 21,2008

The sellers: TIFERT TRADING CO., LTD.

Add: NO. 86, ZHUJIANG ROAD, TIANJIN, CHINA

The buyers: GB POSTERS LTD.

Add: 1 RUSSELL ST, SHEFFIELD, S3 8RW UNITED KINGDOM

Tel: +44 114 276 7454　　Fax: +44 114 278 7878

We hereby confirm having sold to you the following goods on the terms and conditions as specified below:

(1) Name of commodity and specifications	(2) Quantity	(3) Unit price	(4) Total amount
H_2SO_4	1350 KGS	GBP9.94/KG CIFC3 MANCHESTER	GBP13419.00
	—	TOTAL	GBP13419.00

(5) Packing: TO BE PACKED IN CARTONS OF 1KG EACH

(6) Shipping mark: AT THE SELLER'S OPTION

(7) Time of shipment: WITHIN 30 DAYS AFTER RECEIPT OF L/C ALLOWING TRANSSHIPMENT AND PARTIAL SHIPMENTS

(8) Port of shipment: TIANJIN　　Destination: MANCHESTER

(9) Terms of payment: By 100% confirmed, irrevocable, transferable and without recourse Letter of Credit to be available by sight draft and to remain valid for negotiation in China until the 15th day after the aforesaid time of shipment.

(10) Insurance: To be covered by the seller for 110% of total invoice value against All Risks and War Risk as per the ocean marine cargo clauses of the People's Insurance Company of China, dated Jan 1st 1981.

remarks:

(11) The buyer shall establish the covering Letter of Credit (or notify the import license number) before Feb. 5th,2008, failing which the seller reserves the right to rescind without further notice, or to accept whole or any part of this sales confirmation unfulfilled by the buyer, or to lodge a claim for direct losses sustained if any.

(12) For transactions concluded on C.I.F basis it is understood that the insurance amount will be for 110% of the invoice value against the risks specified in the sales confirmation. If additional insurance amount or coverage is required, the buyer must have the consent of the seller before shipment, and the additional premium be borne by the buyer.

(13) Quality/Quantity discrepancy: In case of quality discrepancy, claim should be filed by the buyer within 2 months after the arrival of the goods at the port of destination while for quantity discrepancy claim should be filed by the buyer within 15 days after the arrival of the goods at the port of destination. It is understood that seller shall not be liable for any discrepancy of the goods shipped due to causes for which the insurance company, shipping company other transportation organization are liable.

(14) The seller shall not be held liable for failure or delay in delivery of the entire lot or portion of the goods under this sales confirmation in consequence of any force majeure incidents.

confirmed by

GB POSTERS LTD.	TIFERT TRADING CO., LTD.
TOM SMITH	王 宏
The buyers	The sellers

样例4.13 合同

DOCUMENTARY LETTER OF CREDIT

FROM: ENGLAND CENTER BANK

OUR REF: NY980520004658001T01

TO: BANK OF CHINA TIANJIN BRANCH
80 JIEFANGBEI LU, TIANJIN
PEOPLE'S REP. OF CHINA

TEST: FOR GBP/13016,43 ON DATE 25/01/2008

PLEASE ADVISE BENEFICIARY OF THE FOLLOWING IRREVOCABLE LETTER OF CREDIT ISSUED BY US IN THEIR FAVOR SUBJECT TO UCP 600:

DOCUMENTARY CREDIT NUMBER: DRG-LDLC01

DATE AND PLACE OF EXPIRY: MAR 25 2008, IN LONDON.

APPLICANT: GB POSTERS LTD.
1 RUSSELL ST, SHEFFIELD, S3 8RW UNITED KINGDOM

BENEFICIARY: TIFERT TRADING CO., LTD.
NO. 86, ZHUJIANG STREET, TIANJIN, CHINA

AMOUNT: GBP13016,43

SAY GBP THIRTEEN THOUSAND AND SIXTEEN POINT FORTY-THREE ONLY

AVALIABLE WITH: ANY BANK

BY: NEGOTIATIN OF BENEFICIARY'S DRAFT (S) AT SIGHT DRAWN ON APPLICANT, ACCOMPANIED BY THE DOCUMENTS INDICATED HEREIN.

COVERING SHIPMENT OF:

COMMODITY	QUANTITY	UNIT PRICE
H2SO4	1305KGS	GBP9.49/KG

SHIPPING TERMS: CIF MANCHESTER

SHIPPING MARK: H_2SO_4/ENGLAND/C/NO. 1350/MADE IN CHINA

DOCUMENTS REQUIRED:

-3 COPIES OF COMMERCIAL INVOICE SHOWING VALUE IN GBP AND INDICATING L/C NO. AND CONTRACT NO.

-2 COPIES OF PACKING LIST SHOWING GROSS/NET WEIGHT AND MEASUREMENT OF EACH CARTON.

-CERTIFICATE OF ORIGIN IN TRIPLICATE ISSUED BY CHINA CHAMBER OF INTERNATIONAL COMMERCE.

-2 COPIES OF INSURANCE POLICY OR CERTIFICATE ENDORSED IN BLANK FOR THE INVOICE VALUE OF THE GOODS PLUS 120% COVERING ICC(A) AND WAR RISK AS PER AND SUBJECT TO INSTITUTE CARGO CLAUSES DATED 1/1/1982.

-2/3 SET AND ONE COPY OF CLEAN ON BOARD OCEAN BILLS OF LADING MADE OUT TO ORDER AND BLANK ENDORSED MARKED FREIGHT PREPAID AND NOTIFY APPLICANT.

PARTIAL SHIPMENTS: PERMITTED

TRANSSHIPMENTS: PERMITTED

SHIPMENT FROM: TIANJIN, CHINA

TO: MANCHESTER, ENGLAND

NOT LATER THAN: MAR. 15, 2008

DOCUMENTS MUST BE PRESENTED WITHIN 15 DAYS AFTER SHIPMENT, BUT WITHIN VALIDITY OF THE LETTER OF CREDIT.

INSTRUCTIONS TO THE PAYING/ACCEPTING /NEGOTIATING: BANK NEGOTIATING BANK IS TO FORWARD ALL DOCUMENTS IN ONE AIRMAIL TO ENGLAND CENTER BANK MELHAM ISLAND SHEFFIELD, 33 1RW, UNITED KINGDOM: LETTER OF CREDIT DEPARTMENT

END OF MESSAGE

34127 8B BOCSH CN

样例 4.14 信用证

TIFERT TRADING CO., LTD.

NO. 86, ZHUJIANG ROAD, TIANJIN, CHINA

TO: GB POSTERS LTD. DATE:

DEAR SIRS,

样例 4.15 信用证修改信函纸

3

缮制结汇单据

任务五 缮制商业发票

任务背景

王芳小姐收到中国银行天津分行通知的正式信用证修改书后，马上安排天津服装一厂加工该批女童夹克衫。生产期间，王芳经常与服装加工厂沟通了解生产进度，并与负责成衣检验人员（QC）一起下厂检查女童夹克衫的缝制工艺，保证该批服装的产品质量符合合同约定的品质要求。

当王芳小姐收到服装加工厂的传真，被告知该批夹克衫已基本备妥时，便进入到单据缮制的工作环节，王芳小姐开始着手缮制商业发票。

【背景分析】

商业发票是每笔出口业务中必不可少的结汇单据，是整笔业务中最基本的单据，也是全套单据中的核心单据，其他单据都要依据商业发票来缮制，故其作用非常重要。为了能够正确地缮制商业发票，王芳小姐应该掌握和具备如下知识、技能及素质。

知识目标

①了解发票的概念、种类及作用。

②看懂信用证中的发票条款。

技能目标

①准确翻译信用证中的发票条款及与发票相关条款。

②能够独立、正确缮制商业发票。

素质目标

①养成耐心、细致的工作作风。

②工作上要高标准、严要求,避免差错。

一、缮制商业发票的基础知识

【商业发票的概念】

商业发票(Commercial Invoice)简称发票(Invoice),是进出口贸易结算单据中最主要的单据之一,是出口商向进口商开立的发货价目清单,是装运货物的总说明。在单证缮制工作程序中,一般应首先缮制发票,再缮制其他单据。因此,发票可以说是整套单据的核心。

【发票的种类】

国际贸易结算中大多使用的是商业发票,除此之外还有以下几种发票。

1. 形式发票(Proforma Invoice)

在实际业务中,进口商有时会要求出口商提供一份有关出售货物的名称、规格、单价等内容的非正式的参考性发票,凭此向本国外管局或贸易管理局等申请进口许可证或批准给予支付外汇等,称这种发票为形式发票。形式发票虽然名为发票,但不是一种正式的发票,不能用于托收或议付,其所列的单价等内容,是出口商对某种商品的基本情况的一种估计,对双方无最终约束力,所以说形式发票只是一张估价单。正式成交后,还需另外缮制正式的商业发票作为结算凭证。

形式发票与商业发票在内容和格式上非常相似,且两者关系紧密。信用证在货物描述后常出现“按某年某月某日之形式发票”的条款,此时,出口商应按照形式发票来制单,在商业发票上加注“As per Proforma Invoice No. ××× dated ×××”即可;但若形式发票作为信用证的附件,缮制单据时出口商则要完全按形式发票的内容制单,银行也会按形式发票的要求审单。

2. 领事发票(Consular Invoice)

有些国家,例如拉丁美洲国家、菲律宾等规定,凡进口货物,必须领取进口国驻出口国的领事签证的发票,它是货物进口征收关税的前提条件。领事发票是一份官方签署的单据,有些国家制定了固定格式的领事发票,这种发票可以从出口国当地的进口国领事馆获得。在实际业务中,常常是某些国家来证规定由其领事在出口商的商业发票上认证,从而证实商品的实际产地。同时,领事发票的签发或认证,须收缴一定的签证或认证费用,作为领事馆的部分费用来源。出口商在对外报价时,不能遗漏这笔费用。在信用证支付方式下,应对领事发票签证或认证条款认真审核。

3. 厂商发票(Manufacturer's Invoice)

厂商发票是由制造厂商提供给出口商的销售货物的证明。它按照本国货币计算价格,以证明出口货物的出厂价格。来证要求提供厂商发票,主要是为了供进口国海关估价、核税,并检查出口商出口的商品是否涉及低价倾销,是否应征收反倾销税。厂商发票的签发人不是信用证的受益人,而是产品的实际生产制造者,其标明的货物价值应低于 FOB 价。

4. 证实发票(Certified Invoice)

证实发票指加注有证实发票内容真实无误等文句的商业发票。有的国外进口商在来证中要求受益人在商业发票上加注证明文句,以说明发票所列内容的真实性、正确性。例如在发票上注明"We hereby certify that the contents of invoice herein are true and correct"(兹证明此发票内容真实无误)。

5. 联合发票(Combined Invoice)

联合发票即将其他单据的内容混合出具在商业发票上,这些单据可以是装箱单、产地证和保险单等。联合发票的使用仅限于我国港、澳地区,现在已经很少使用。

6. 收讫发票(Receipt Invoice)

收讫发票指加注有收讫文句的商业发票。有的国外进口商在来证中要求受益人在商业发票上加注收讫文句,用来说明受益人已从出口地银行取得货款。收讫发票的缮制与商业发票基本相同,只需在商业发票的结尾部分加注下列类似文句"Payment received against credit No... dated... issued by... bank"。

7. 样品发票(Sample Invoice)

为了更好地让进口商了解商品的品质、价值等,使进口商对商品有更直观的印象,以便向市场推销,出口商往往在交易前先发送实样,供进口商选择,为此缮制的发票叫样品发票。它不同于商业发票,其目的主要是帮助进口商更好地向市场推销商品和报关取样。所提供的样品,若价值不大,多数是免费寄送的,但有时也可以收取部分款项,或是全额收取样品款,应视不同商品、不同贸易的具体情况而定。无论是以上何种情况,均应在发票上注明。

8. 海关发票(Customs Invoice)

海关发票是进口国(地区)海关制定的,由出口商填制,供进口商凭以报关用的一种特定格式的发票。它是一种特殊用途的发票,供进口国海关审查货物的原产地、成本价值以及统计定税之用。常见的有以下几种。

①美国 Special Customs Invoice。

②加拿大 Canada Customs Invoice。

③澳大利亚 Combined Certificate of Value and Origin。

④新西兰 Certificate of Origin for Exports to New Zealand Form 59。

⑤牙买加 Invoice and Declaration of Value Required for Shipments to Jamaica Form

C23。

⑥加勒比海共同体 Caricom(Caribbean Common Market)。

⑦赞比亚 Invoice and Certificate of Value for Exports to Zambia。

⑧东非 Combined Certificate of Value and Invoice in Respect of Goods for Importation into Kenya, Uganda and Tanzania。

⑨西非 Combined Certificate of Value and of Origin and Invoice of Goods for Exportation to West Africa Form C。

⑩尼日利亚 Combined Certificate of Value and of Origin and Invoice of Goods for Exportation to Federation of Nigeria。

【发票的作用】

商业发票的作用主要有以下几个方面。

①发票是整套出口单据的核心,也是缮制其他单据的依据。发票是出口商自行制作的单据,是装运货物的总说明,以帮助了解整笔交易的概况。其他单据应在商业发票缮制完成后,参照其和信用证进行缮制。

②便于进口商按照合同条款核对装运货物是否符合规定。发票记载了一笔交易的主要项目,包括装运货物的名称、规格、数量、重量、单价、总值等内容,它能帮助进口商了解出口商的履约情况,核查出口商是否按照合同规定的要求装运所需货物。因此,发票是出口商向进口商发送货物的凭证,它体现了合同的履约精神。

③作为出口商和进口商收付货款和记账的依据。发票是销售货物的凭证,进出口商双方均需按照发票记载的内容,逐笔登记入账。对出口商而言,通过发票可了解销售收入,核算盈亏,按不同的支付方式记好外汇账,及时对外催收外汇。对进口商而言,也应根据发票逐笔记账,及时履行付款义务。

④作为出口商和进口商在当地办理报关以及纳税的计算依据。货物出运前,出口商须向海关递交包括商业发票在内的一系列单据,凭以报关。而发票中有关货物的说明和记载的金额是海关确定税金、验关放行的凭据。在货物到达目的港后,进口商也需向当地海关提供发货人的发票通关,海关以此核定税金,使进口商能够清关提货。因此,发票必须制作准确、清楚。

⑤在不用汇票的情况下,发票替代汇票作为付款的依据。在国际贸易的 L/C 业务结算中,有时不要求使用跟单汇票,仅用发票就可代替汇票进行结算。

除以上几点外,商业发票还可在保险索赔时作为货物价值的证明,或作为统计的凭证等。

【不同国家对发票的要求】

1. 澳大利亚

发票内应加注发展中国家声明,可享受关税优惠待遇。声明文句为“Developing country declare that the final process of manufacture of the goods for which special rates are claimed has been performed in China and that not less than one half of the factory or works cost of the goods is represented by the value of the labor or materials of China and Australia"。

2. 墨西哥

发票必须手签。一般要求领事签证,也可由贸促会代签,并注明"There is no Mexican Consulate here"(本地没有墨西哥领事),在北京可由墨西哥驻华使馆签证。

3. 智利

发票内要注明运费、保险费和FOB价值。

4. 黎巴嫩

发票应加注证实其真实性的语句。如:"We hereby certify that the invoice is authentic, that it is the only one issued by us for the goods herein, that the value and price of the goods are correct without any deduction of payment in advance and its origin is exclusively China"。

5. 阿拉伯地区

一般要求发票注明货物原产地,并由贸促会签证,或者由贸促会出具产地证书。

6. 伊朗

发票内注明关税号。

7. 尼泊尔、印度

发票手签。

8. 巴拿马

可由我贸促会签证,但必须注明"此地无巴拿马领事"。

9. 巴林

发票内应加注货物原产地证明,并且手签。

10. 秘鲁

如果信用证要求领事签证,可由贸促会代签,货名应以西班牙文表示,同时列明运费和保险费等。

11. 科威特

发票内要注明厂商名称和船名,列明毛、净重并以千克表示。

二、缮制商业发票的基本技能

【实训目的】

通过本项目实训,应掌握的基本技能如下。

①熟悉并看懂相关信用证(合同)中有关发票的条款。

②掌握商业发票缮制的规范和技巧。

③学会独立缮制商业发票的技能。

【操作前准备】

进行本项任务的实训前,应准备的内容如下。

①生产厂家告知货已备妥的通知。

②计算器等计算工具。

③空白的纸质商业发票或电子版商业发票。

④信用证付款方式下有关信用证。

⑤销售合同或销售确认书。

【操作程序】

①仔细阅读信用证或合同中的发票条款以及与发票有关的特殊条款或附加指示,特别注意信用证特别要求加注的有关内容,如信用证证号要显示在所有单据上等。

②根据信用证或合同要求,认真缮制商业发票的各个栏目内容,做到准确、完整。

③对照信用证或合同中的发票条款,审核商业发票,检查是否做到单证(单同)相符。

【操作规范】

操作规范如表5.1所示。

表5.1 商业发票缮制规范

项目顺序号	填写内容	要点提示
(1)单据名称 Name of Doc	Commercial Invoice 或 Invoice	与信用证上规定的完全一致
(2)出单人 Issuer	签发发票的人	①信用证项下为受益人 ②托收和电汇项下为卖方 ③有些公司可能已印就,无须填写
(3)受单人 To	抬头人	①信用证项下为开证申请人 ②托收和电汇项下为合同买方
(4)运输详情 Transport details	启运港(地)、目的港(地)和运输方式	启运港(地)应明确具体,目的港(地)如有重名港后面要加国别
(5)发票号码 Invoice No.	此笔业务的发票号码	由卖方自行编制
(6)日期 Date	发票的出票日期	一般在信用证开证日期后,提单签发日前,且不能迟于信用证的交单期和有效期
(7)合同号 S/C No.	此笔业务的合同号码	应与信用证上引用的合同号保持一致
(8)信用证号 L/C No.	此笔业务的信用证号码	应与信用证上列明的证号保持一致,采用其他付款方式可留空
(9)付款方式 Terms of payment	此笔业务的付款方式	信用证方式填 By L/C,托收方式填 By D/P,电汇方式填 By T/T

续表

项目顺序号	填写内容	要点提示
(10)唛头 Marks and numbers	合同或信用证规定的唛头	信用证或合同有指定唛头必须严格按照规定制唛;信用证或合同没有规定唛头卖方可自行设计;没有唛头填 N/M
(11)货物描述 Number and kind of package, description of goods	包括货物的件数、货物名称、规格及包装情况等	必须与信用证上的货物描述完全一致,但并不要求如同镜子反射那样一致
(12)数量 Quantity	一般填写货物的实际出运数量	不要遗漏计量单位
(13)单价 Unit price	包括计价货币、计量单位、单位金额及贸易术语	填写要完整、正确,不能遗漏贸易术语
(14)总金额 Amount	单价与实际出运数量的乘积即发票总值	①一般不能超过信用证金额 ②有折扣或明佣的应在此扣除,计算出净值
(15)声明文句 Statement	来证要求的发票上加注各种费用金额、原产地、特定号码等声明文句	这些内容加注在发票货物描述以下的空白处
(16)签字 Signature	一般加盖签发人的英文名称加法人代表签字图章	①商业发票只能由 L/C 规定的受益人出具 ②无特殊规定,发票可以无须签署 ③若信用证要求手签,出单人要亲笔签署,不能以盖章代替

【商业发票样例】

<table>
<tr><td>Issuer (2)
TIFERT TRADING CO., LTD.
NO. 86, ZHUJIANG ROAD, TIANJIN, CHINA</td><td colspan="2">商 业 发 票 (1)
COMMERCIAL INVOICE</td></tr>
<tr><td rowspan="2">To (3)
MARUBENI CORP.
5 - 7, HOMMACHI, 2 - CHOME, CHUO-KU, OSAKA, JAPAN</td><td>No.: (5)
INVOICE NO. 123456</td><td>Date: (6)
APR. 15, 2008</td></tr>
<tr></tr>
<tr><td rowspan="2">Transport details (4)
SHIPMENT FROM TIANJIN TO TOKYO BY SEA</td><td>S/C No. (7)
08TF0858</td><td>L/C No. (8)
A - 08 - 0058</td></tr>
<tr><td colspan="2">Terms of payment (9)
L/C AT SIGHT</td></tr>
</table>

Marks and numbers	Number and kind of packages, description of goods	Quantity	Unit price	Amount
(10)	(11)	(12)	(13)	(14)
	250 CARTONS	5000PCS	USD10.50/PC	USD52500.00
MARUBENI			CIF TOKYO	
S/C 08TF0858	GIRL JACKET			
TOKYO	SYTLE NO. GJ234			
CTN 1 - 250	SHELL: WOVEN TWILL 100% COTTON			
	LINING: WOVEN 100% POLYESTER			
	PACKED IN CARTONS OF 20PCS EACH			

WE HEREBY CERTIFY THAT THE GOODS ARE OF CHINESE ORIGIN (15)

TIFERT TRADING CO., LTD.
泰佛贸易有限公司
*

(16) 王 宏

样例 5.1 商业发票

【操作注意事项】

1. 发票的种类

信用证要求"发票"但未作进一步的要求,则提交任何形式的发票都可以接受,如商业发票、海关发票、税务发票、最终发票、领事发票等。但是"形式发票"(Proforma Invoice)或类似的发票是不可接受的,除非信用证另有授权。当信用证要求提交商业发票时,标为"发票"的单据是可以接受的。

2. 发票的签发人

除可转让信用证外,发票必须表面看来由信用证中具名的受益人出具,地址中的电传或传真号码等内容无须提供,如果提供,也可不与信用证保持一致,但必须在同一国家内。

3. 发票抬头人

除信用证另有规定及可转让信用证外,发票必须以申请人为抬头。地址中的电传或传真号码等内容无须提供,如果提供,也可不与信用证保持一致。如果信用证有指定其他抬头人的,按来证规定缮制发票。如果该信用证已被转让,则银行也可接受由第二受益人提交的以第一受益人为抬头的发票。

4. 发票的签署

除非信用证要求,否则发票无须签字或标注日期。但是如信用证要求的证明文句加注在未要求签字的发票上，则该发票必须要签署。

5. 发票的货物描述

发票上的货物描述部分是发票的中心内容，必须反映实际装运的货物，且必须与信用证规定相符。如信用证规定了多种货物，应根据实际发货情况注明其中一种或几种，不可盲目照抄，发票也不能显示信用证未要求的货物（包括样品、广告材料等），即使注明免费。当信用证规定的货名并非英文文字（如中文或法文）时，发票应照原文显示出来。如出运的货物较多，信用证上标有统称时，发票上可在具体品名上按来证显示统称。如信用证只规定了货物的总称，发票除应照样显示外，还可加列详细的货名，但不得与总称矛盾。如信用证未规定货物的总称，但列举的货物名称很详细，则发票除显示详细的货物名称外，还可加注统称。

6. 发票的数量

发票必须如实反映实际装运货物的数量，尤其允许分批装运和允许溢短装的情况下更应该注意。如果信用证没有溢短装条款，则信用证要求的货物数量可以有5%的溢短装幅度。但如果信用证规定货物数量不得超额或减少，或信用证规定的货物数量是以包装单位或个数计算时，不适用此条款。货物数量在5%幅度内的溢装并不意味着允许支取的金额超过信用证金额。

7. 发票的总金额不能超过信用证的最高限额

发票中显示的单价和币种必须与信用证中的一致，且不能超过信用证的最高限额。发票必须显示信用证要求的折扣或扣减，发票还可显示信用证未规定的与预付款或佣金、折扣等有关的扣减额。

8. 发票的总金额允许比信用证少支取5%

如果信用证禁止分批装运，只要货物全部装运，且单价（如信用证有规定的话）没有减少，则发票金额有5%的减幅是可接受的。如果信用证未规定货物数量，发票的货物数量即可视为全部货物数量。

9. 发票的格式要求

如在一张发票中有多种货号的货物内容，要求在缮制发票时，格式整齐，每一货号的货物内容和总数排列有序。应做到横排是每一货号的货物内容，如货号、规格、数量、单价及该货号的金额。竖排应是各货号该列内容的总和，如数量、总金额。

10. 佣金和折扣

发票中对佣金和折扣等用词要正确。如果信用证或合同规定的单价含有“佣金”，发票决不可以“折扣”代替。如果信用证规定为“现金折扣”则也不能只写“折扣”或写成“贸易折扣”。总之，此类项目一个字不能错也不能省。如果信用证既有佣金也有折扣，一般是先扣除折扣，然后再计扣佣金，因为折扣部分是不应支付佣金的。

三、缮制商业发票的操作训练

【翻译语句】

①proforma invoice
②customs invoice
③manually signed commercial invoice
④terms of payment
⑤shipping marks
⑥transport details
⑦in 1 original and 2 copies
⑧certified invoice
⑨countersigned by applicant
⑩less excessive value for collection

⑪Signed commercial invoice in 6 copies indicating Invoice No. , Contract No. SCN36.

⑫Manually signed commercial invoice in duplicate issued by beneficiary made out in the name of TIFERT TRADING CO. , LTD.

⑬Commercial invoice in 4 – fold indicating S/C No. 1234 and certifying that the goods are of CHINESE origin.

⑭Signed commercial invoice in 1 original and 2 copies showing breakdown of freight charges and FOB value.

⑮Manually signed commercial invoice in triplicate showing less 5% commission from the total value.

【动脑思考】

①盛大贸易公司在一笔出口贸易中收到国外进口商开来的信用证,其显示如下。

Applicant: SEK Co. Ltd. ... All documents including commercial invoice must be in the name of ABC Co. Ltd.

请问:作为单证员,你在制作单据(包括商业发票)时应如何填写抬头人?

②泰佛贸易公司在一笔出口贸易中收到国外进口商开来的信用证,信用证金额为6 000 澳元,货物描述为:30M/T of Chinese Wheat at AUD200. 00/MT FOB Shanghai,出口商实际发货 30. 5M/T。请问:作为单证员你应如何填写发票金额,并在发票上作何种处理?

③泰佛贸易公司在一笔出口贸易中收到国外进口商开来的信用证,信用证金额为9 500 美元,货物描述为:100M/T of Northeast Soybean at USD100. 00/MT CIFC5% Hamburg,出口商实际发货 100M/T。请问:作为单证员你应如何填写发票金额,并在发票上作何种处理?

④天纺服装贸易公司把合同项下女式衬衫备妥,码单显示总共 5 000 件,每 10 件装一个纸箱。国外进口商开来信用证中有指定唛头为:TOP CORP/P. O. NO. 08F0018/BARCELONA/CTN NO. 1 – UP,作为单证员你在缮制商业发票时,应该如何填制唛头?

⑤天成贸易公司在一笔出口贸易中收到国外进口商开来的信用证,来证中规定:Commercial invoice in duplicate duly signed by beneficiary and contersigned by Mr. Jonson as applicant's legal representative,此条款要求单证员在缮制商业发票时要注意哪些事项?它对出口商安全、及时收汇有什么影响?

【动手操练】

实训操作一

泰佛贸易公司与日本 ITOCHU 公司经过友好洽商,就出口女式毛衫达成一份出口合同,数量 1 500 件,CIF KOBE,付款方式为即期信用证(L/C at sight)。作为制单员请你根据信用证有关条款和其他补充信息缮制商业发票。(空白商业发票见样例 5.2)

信用证中与发票相关的主要条款如下。

59: BENEFICIARY:	TIFERT TRADING CO., LTD.
	NO. 86, ZHUJIANG ROAD, TIANJIN, CHINA
50: APPLICANT:	ITOCHU CORP.
	88, RED SUN BUILDING, TOKYO, JAPAN
44E: PORT OF LOADING	TIANJIN
44F: PORT OF DISCHARGE	KOBE
45A: DESCRIPTION OF GOODS/SERVICE	
LADY'S SWEATER	ART NO. 123 700PCS USD10.00/PC CIF KOBE
	ART NO. 456 800PCS USD15.00/PC
	PACKING IN CARTONS OF 10PCS EACH
SHIPPING MARKS:	ITOCHU CORP.
	S/C NO. SC222
	KOBE
	NO. 1 - 150

46A: DOCUMENTS REQUIRED

+ SIGNED COMMERCIAL INVOICE IN 6 COPIES INDICATING S/C NO. SC222 AND L/C NO. LC333

其他补充信息如下。

发票号码为:INV. 1234

发票日期为:2008 年 2 月 20 日

Issuer	商 业 发 票 **COMMERCIAL INVOICE**	
To	No.:	Date:
Transport details	S/C No.	L/C No.
	Terms of payment	

Marks and numbers	Number and kind of packages, description of goods	Quantity	Unit price	Amount

样例 5.2　空白商业发票

实训操作二

天津金星贸易公司与埃塞俄比亚 AMENLI 公司经过友好洽商，就出口五金工具箱达成一份出口合同，数量 10 000 套，CIF ASEB，付款方式为电汇加托收（T/T + D/P AT SIGHT）。作为单证员请你根据贸易合同有关条款（合同见样例 5.3）及其他补充信息缮制商业发票（空白商业发票见样例 5.4）。

销 售 合 同
SALES CONTRACT

编号 No.：　SC080216　　　日期 Date：FEB. 16，2008

The sellers：　TIANJIN GOLDEN STAR TRADING CO.，LTD.

Add：　NO. 18 ZHUJIANG ROAD，TIANJIN，CHINA　　Post code：300221

The buyers：　AMENLI COMPANY，ETHIOPIA.

Add：　#5054 – 7 KING STREET，ETHIOPIA

Tel：　（+03）3434 7856

兹确认售予你方下列货品，其成交条款如下：

We hereby confirm having sold to you the following goods on the terms and conditions as specified below：

（1）货物名称及规格 Name of commodity and specifications	（2）数量 Quantity	（3）单价 Unit price	（4）总值 Total amount
Hardware Tools Case	CIF ASEB		
TC110	6000SETS	USD5. 00	USD30000. 00
TC120	4000SETS	USD4. 00	USD16000. 00
TOTAL：	10000SETS		USD46000. 00

（5）包装：

Packing：　PACKED IN CARTONS OF 100 SETS EACH

（6）装运唛头：

Shipping mark：　N/M

（7）装运期限：

Time of shipment：　NOT LATER THAN APRIL 10，2008

（8）装运口岸：　　　目的地：

Port of shipment：　TIANJIN　　　Destination：　ASEB

（9）付款条件：

Payment terms：　20% T/T IN ADVANCE，THE OTHERS 80% D/P AT SIGHT.

（10）保险：卖方负责投保海运险，按照 CIF 金额的 110% 投保一切险和战争险，如果发生索赔，在埃塞俄比亚用美元赔偿。

Insurance：

The seller shall arrange marine insurance covering All Risks and War Risk for 110% of CIF value. Claim，if any，payable in Ethiopia，in currency of USD.

（11）凡以 cif 条件成交的业务，保额为发票价的 110%，投保险别以本销售合同中所开列的为限，买方如要求增加保额或保险范围应在装船前经售方同意，因此而增加的保险费由买方负责。

For transactions concluded on C. I. F basis, it is understood that the insurance amount will be for 110% of the invoice value against the risks specified in the sales contract, if additional insurance amount or coverage is required, the buyer must have the consent of the seller before shipment, and the additional premium is to be borne by the buyer.

(12)品质/数量异议：如买方提出索赔，凡属品质异议须于货到目的口岸之日起2个月内提出，凡属数量异议须于货到目的口岸之日起15天内提出，对所装货物所提任何异议属于保险公司、轮船公司及期货有关运输机构所负责者，售方不负任何责任。

Quality/Quantity discrepancy: In case of quality discrepancy, claim should be filed by the buyer within 2 months after the arrival of the goods at the port of destination while for quantity discrepancy claim should by filed by the buyer within 15 days after the arrival of the goods at the port of destination it is understood that seller shall not be liable for any discrepancy of the goods shipped due to causes for which the insurance company shipping company other transportation organization are liable.

Confirmed by

AMENLI COMPANY, ETHIOPIA.	TIANJIN GOLDEN STAR TRADING CO., LTD.
Jonnie	王 义
买方（The buyers）	卖方（The sellers）

样例 5.3 合同

其他补充信息如下。

OUR BANK INFORMATION IS AS BELOW:

BENEFICIARY: TIANJIN GOLDEN STAR TRADING CO., LTD.

BENEFICIARY ADDRESS: No. 18 ZHUJIANG ROAD, TIANJIN, CHINA

BANK NAME: BANK OF CHINA TIANJIN BRANCH

ACCOUNT NO.: RMB64025013

BANK ADDRESS: NO. 80 JIEFANG ROAD, TIANJIN, CHINA

DOCUMENTS REQUIRED:

+SIGNED COMMERCIAL INVOICE IN DUPLICATE

+PACKING LIST IN DUPLICATE

+INSURANCE POLICY/CERTIFICATE IN DUPLICATE COVERING ALL RIAKS AND WAR RISK FOR 110% OF CIF VALUE. CLAIM, IF ANY, PAYABLE IN ETHIOPIA, IN CURRENCY OF USD

+FULL SET OF CLEAN ON BOARD BILL OF LADING IN TRIPLICATE MADE OUT TO ORDER OF SHIPPER AND NOTIFY THE BUYER WITH FULL NAME AND ADDRESS MARKED FREIGHT PREPAID.

发票号码为：INV. TDP 0802

发票日期为：2008年2月20日

天 津 金 星 贸 易 公 司

TIANJIN GOLDEN STAR TRADING CO. , LTD

商 业 发 票

COMMERCIAL INVOICE

To:

Invoice No: ____________

Date: ____________

L/C No: ____________

S/C No: ____________

From: ____________ To ____________

Marks & nos	Descriptions of goods	Quantities	Unit price	Amount

样例 5.4 空白商业发票

任务六 缮制包装单据

任务背景

王芳小姐依据信用证对发票的具体要求、信用证的货物描述及服装加工厂备货的一些具体情况顺利地完成了商业发票的缮制工作。在收到服装加工厂传真过来的详细装箱码单后,王芳小姐又开始着手缮制包装单据。

【背景分析】

包装单据是出口业务中常用的结汇单据之一,它是对商业发票的补充。由于商品的特性不同,买卖双方所关注的信息点也不同,因此包装单据可以冠以不同的单据名称。在缮制过程中没有统一的格式要求,非常灵活,在实际业务中,应不断总结经验。为了缮制好包装单据,王芳小姐应该掌握和具备如下知识、技能及素质。

知识目标

①了解包装单据的概念、种类及作用。

②看懂信用证中的包装条款。

技能目标

①准确翻译信用证中的包装条款及与包装相关条款。

②要具备一定的毛净重和尺码的计算能力。

③能够独立、正确缮制包装单据。

素质目标

①养成耐心、细致的工作作风。

②在枯燥的数字计算中做到耐心、精确。

一、缮制包装单据的基础知识

【包装单据的概念】

包装单据(Packing document)是指一切记载或描述商品包装情况的单据,列明了信用证(或合同)中买卖双方约定的有关包装事宜的细节,便于国外进口商在货物到达目的港时供海关检查和核对货物。通常可以将其有关内容加列在商业发票上,但是在信用证有明确要求时,就必须严格按信用证要求单独缮制包装单据。包装单据是商业发票的重要补充和主要结汇单据之一。包装单据主要用来说明出口商品的包装和内装货物的细节状况,便于有关方面对进出口货物的品种、花色、尺寸、规格及数量进行查验、检验及核实。

【包装单据的种类】

依据进出口商双方交易的商品特性的不同和进出口双方关注的信息不同,在实际业务中,包装单据可冠以不同的名称,主要有以下几种。

1. 装箱单(Packing List)

装箱单又称包装单或花色搭配码单(简称码单),是用以说明货物包装细节的清单。除散装和裸装货物外,一般进出口交易都要求提供装箱单,以便在货物到达目的港(地)后,供海关验货和收货人核对货物。装箱单主要载明货物装箱的详细情况,包括所装货物的名称、规格、数量及花色搭配等,尤其不定量包装的商品要逐件列明每批货物的逐件花色搭配。

2. 重量单(Weight List)

重量单又称磅码单(Weight Note/Memo),是用以说明货物重量细节的清单。重量单也是发票的补充单据,其作用在于作为进口商计价、计数或计算运费的依据,多见于以重量计量、计价的商品,有的还须增列皮重。按公量计量、计价的商品,则须列明公量及计算公量的有关数据,如棉花的出口。

3. 尺码单(Measurement List)

尺码单是用以说明单位包装的长、宽、高及总尺码细节的清单。其作用是便于进口商和承运人了解货物的尺码,以便合理安排运输、装卸及仓储,同时它也是计算运费的重要依据和包装件数的清单。

4. 规格单(Specification List)

规格单也称包装明细单,是用以说明包装规格细节的清单。规格单多用于规格、型号较多的货物,以便于进口商了解整批货物的详细情况和方便转售货物。规格单的内容与装箱单相似,但偏重于每件货物的包装规格,一般要求列明包装的方式及内含量。

【包装单据的作用】

包装单据是对发票的补充,通过对包装件数、规格及唛头等内容的缮制,阐明了商品的包装情况,列明了信用证(或合同)中进出口商双方约定的有关包装细节。便于进口商对商品包装及数量的了解和掌握,也便于进口商在货物到达目的港时,供海关检查和核对货物。包装单据的作用表现在以下几点。

①是出口商缮制商业发票及其他单据时计量、计价的基础资料。

②是进口商清点数量或重量以及销售货物的依据。

③是海关查验货物的凭证。

④是公证或商检机构查验货物的参考资料。

对大多商品交易来说,包装单据为不可缺少的文件。进口地海关验货、公证行检验及进口商核对货物时,通常以包装单据为依据。了解每个包装单位内具体的货物,以方便转售货物。

二、缮制包装单据的基本技能

【实训目的】

通过本项目实训,应掌握的基本技能如下。

①熟悉并看懂信用证(合同)中有关包装条款。

②掌握包装单据缮制的规范和技巧。

③学会独立缮制包装单据。

【操作前准备】

进行本项任务的实训前,应准备的内容如下。

①生产厂家提供的详细码单。

②计算器等计算工具。

③空白的纸质包装单或电子版包装单。

④已经缮制完成的商业发票。

⑤信用证付款方式的有关信用证。

⑥销售合同或销售确认书。

【操作程序】

①根据生产厂家提供的详细码单,准确计算拟出运货物的毛重、净重及尺码,并注意单位的换算和统一。

②仔细阅读信用证或合同中的包装条款及与包装有关的特殊条款,并注意信用证特别要求加注的有关内容,如信用证证号要显示在所有单据上等。

③根据信用证或合同要求,认真缮制包装单据的各个栏目内容,做到准确、完整。

④对照信用证或合同中的包装条款审核包装单据,检查是否做到单证(单同)相符。对照已缮制妥的商业发票,检查是否做到单单相符。

【操作规范】

表6.1 包装单据缮制规范

项目顺序号	填写内容	要点提示
(1)单据名称 Name of Doc	按照信用证规定的单据名称填写	与信用证规定的单据名称相一致
(2)出单人 Issuer	签发装箱单的人	①信用证项下为受益人 ②托收和电汇项下为卖方 ③有些公司可能已印就,无须填写

续表

项目顺序号	填写内容	要点提示
(3)受单人 To	抬头人	①信用证项下为开证申请人 ②托收和电汇项下为买方 ③信用证要求不显示抬头人时,可不填或填写"To whom it may concern"
(4)发票号 Invoice No.	此笔业务的发票号码	由卖方自行编制
(5)日期 Date	一般为发票日期	可略晚于发票日期,不能迟于信用证的有效期及提单日期
(6)运输标志 Marks and numbers	货物的唛头	①注意与信用证及合同规定的唛头完全一致 ②如合同和信用证无指定唛头,卖方可自行设计 ③如果没有唛头,填写"N/M"
(7)包装种类、件数及货物描述 Number and kind of packages, description of goods	包括货物的件数和货物描述	①可以用商品的统称 ②如果仅一种商品,便无须填写商品的规格
(8)毛重 Gross weight 净重 Net weight 尺码 Measurement	填写货物的毛重、净重和尺码	若信用证要求列出单件毛重、净重和尺码时,应按照货物的实际情况填写,并且要符合信用证的规定
(9)自由处理区 Additional condition	用于表达格式中其他栏目不能或不便表达的内容	符合信用证要求
(10)签署 Signature	一般加盖图章,通常图章上有公司的名称和法人代表的签字	①包装单据只能由 L/C 规定的受益人出具 ②无特殊规定,装箱单无须签署 ③若信用证要求手签,出单人必须亲笔签署,不能以盖章代替

【包装单据样例】

<table>
<tr><td colspan="2">Issuer (2)
TIFERT TRADING CO., LTD.
NO. 86, ZHUJIANG ROAD, TIANJIN, CHINA</td><td colspan="3">装箱单/ (1)
PACKING LIST</td></tr>
<tr><td colspan="2">To (3)
MARUBENI CORP.
5 - 7, HOMMACHI, 2 - CHOME, CHUO-KU, OSAKA, JAPAN</td><td colspan="2">Invoice No. (4)
INVOICE NO. 123456</td><td>Date (5)
APR. 15, 2008</td></tr>
<tr><td>Marks and numbers
(6)</td><td>Number and kind of package
Description of goods (7)</td><td>G. W
(8)</td><td>N. W
(8)</td><td>Meas.
(8)</td></tr>
</table>

MARUBENI S/C 08TF0858 TOKYO CTN 1 - 250	250 CARTONS GIRL JACKET SYTLE NO. GJ234 PACKED IN CARTONS OF 20PCS EACH	25992. 00KGS	24909. 00KGS	24. 548CBM
(9) WE HEREBY CERTIFY THAT EACH ITEM HAS BEEN MARKED THE LABEL"MADE IN CHINA". TIFERT TRADING CO., LTD. 泰佛贸易有限公司 * (10)				

样例 6.1 包装单据

【操作注意事项】

①如果信用证同时要求装箱单和重量单，受益人应分别出具两种单据，最好不要合二为一联合出具。如果受益人将两种单据名称印就在一起，而来证仅要求其中一种时，最好将另一种单据的名称删除。

②如果没有特别要求，包装单据可以不显示收货人。

③装箱单上的唛头应与发票上的规定一致。唛头中如果有"C/NO 1 - UP"，是指包装件号，应根据实际按序编写，这里的 UP 应理解为总箱数。缮制包装单据时，要具体化，标明总件数。

④装箱单中的货物描述，可以与发票相同。在与信用证中的货物描述不抵触的情况下，也可以只显示商品统称。

⑤包装单据中的毛重应注明每个包装件的毛重和此包装件内不同规格、品种及花色的货物各自的总毛重(Sub Total)，最后在合计栏处标注所有货物的总毛重。净重应注明每个包装件的净重和此包装件内不同规格、品种及花色的货物各自的总净重，最后在合计栏处标注所有货物总净重。尺码则要求注明每个包装件的尺寸和总尺码。

⑥包装单据一般不显示货物的单价和总价。进口商转售时，通常自制发票，只使用出口商提供的原始包装单据，以避免泄露其购买成本。

⑦货物如装托盘，尺码单上应同时标明托盘本身尺码和连同托盘的总尺码。

⑧包装单据应如实反映货物的实际包装情况，并且要符合信用证关于装箱的规定。如信用证规定货物装 25 公斤或 50 公斤的编织袋内，货物实际装在 25 公斤的编织袋内，包装单据应该缮制成"Packed in pp woven bags of 25 kgs net each."而不应该照抄信用证原句。不管信用证是笼统规定(Sea worthy packing 或 Standard export packing)，还是具体要求(Packed in woven bags)，均应准确显示在单据上。

⑨散装货物一般不须提供包装单据。

⑩如来证规定包装单以“Plain Paper”、“in Plain”或“in White Paper”等形式出具，则单据上不应显示进出口商双方的名称，也不可签章。

三、缮制包装单据的操作训练

【翻译语句】

①seaworthy packing

②customary packing

③insufficient packing

④warning mark

⑤indicative mark

⑥shipping mark

⑦bulk cargo

⑧nude cargo

⑨size assortment

⑩gross for net

⑪In iron drums of 185 ~ 190 kgs net each.

⑫In new gunny single bags of about 100 kgs each.

⑬In cartons of 48 pairs each and size assorted.

⑭Packed in colored cartons and packing charges included.

⑮Goods are in neutral packing and buyer's washing labels must reach the seller 45days before the month of shipment.

【动脑思考】

①大都服装厂把合同项下衬衫备妥，码单显示总共 1 000 箱，国外客户开来信用证中有指定唛头为：ABC CORP/P. O. NO. 08F0018/HAMBURG/CTN NO. 1 - UP。作为单证员，你在缮制包装单据时，唛头应该如何缮制？

②国外客户开来信用证中的货物描述如下。

COVERING SHIPMENT OF：

4 items terms of Chinese ceramic dinnerware including：

DS151130 - piece dinnerware and tea set, 544sets

DS220120 - piece dinnerware set, 800sets

DS450445 - piece dinnerware set, 443sets

DS512095 - piece dinnerware set, 245sets

Details in accordance with Sales Contract HSDS03027 dated Apr. 3, 2008.

作为单证员，你在缮制包装单据时，货物描述中的品名应该如何填写？

③如果信用证规定货物装在 25 公斤或 50 公斤的编织袋内（Packing in pp woven bags of 25 kgs or 50 kgs net each），实际货物装在 25 公斤的编织袋内。作为单证员，在缮制包装单据时，你为了做到单证相符，直接照抄原句“Packing in pp woven bags of 25 kgs or 50 kgs net each”，这样做是否可以？如果不可以，应该如何缮制？

④如若来证规定包装单据以“Plain paper”、“in Plain”或“in White Paper”等形式出具，作为单证员，你在缮制包装单据时该如何处理？

⑤信用证规定货物装在纸箱内，100 个纸箱装在一个托盘上，作为单证员，你在缮制包装单据时应该注意什么？

【动手操练】

实训操作一

信用证有关资料摘录如下。

SEQUENCE OF TOTAL	27：	1/1
FORM OF DOCUMENTARY CREDIT	40A：	IRREVOCABLE
APPLICABLE RULES	40E：	UCP LATEST VERSION
DOCUMENTARY CREDIT NUMBER	20 ：	00IM01413
DATE OF ISSUE	31C：	080731
DATE AND PLACE OF EXPIRY	31D：	080915 CHINA
APPLICANT	50：	NEW WORLD INTERNATIONAL INC 129 HAYWARD WAY CA 91733, USA
BENEFICIARY	59：	TIFERT TRADING CO., LTD NO. 86, ZHUJIANG ROAD, TIANJIN, CHINA
CURRENCY CODE, AMOUNT	32B：	USD30940,00
AVAILABLE WITH . . . BY	41D：	ANY BANK BY NEGOTIATION
DRAFTS AT	42C：	AT SIGHT FOR 100 PCT OF INVOICE VALUE
DRAWEE	42D：	CATHAY BANK LOS ANGELES, CA.
PORT OF LOADING	44E：	TIANJIN PORT, CHINA
PORT OF DISCHARGE	44F：	LOS ANGELES PORT, CA, USA
LATEST DATE OF SHIPMENT	44C：	080831
DESCRPT OF GOODS/SERVICES	45A：	2000PAIRS LADIES SLIPPERS FOB QINGDAO, CHINA
DOCUMENTS REQUIRED	46A：	

+SIGNED COMMERCIAL INVOICE IN 1 ORIGINAL AND 3 COPIES

+PACKING LIST IN 1 ORIGINAL AND 3 COPIES

补充信息如下。

①SIZE：EACH CARTON CONTAINING 37/10 38/10 39/10 40/10

②PACKING：IN CARTONS OF 40 PAIRS EACH

③MEASUREMENT：0.356M3/CTN

④GW：15KGS/CTN　NW：14KGS/CTN

⑤SHIPPING MARK：N/M

⑥INVOICE NO. LS628 DATED AUG 20, 2008

作为泰佛贸易公司的单证员，请根据以上信用证摘录信息及补充相关信息，利用空白装箱单（样例 6.2）独立缮制一份装箱单。

<table>
<tr><td colspan="3">Issuer</td><td colspan="4">装箱单
PACKING LIST</td></tr>
<tr><td colspan="3" rowspan="2">To</td><td colspan="2">Invoice No.</td><td colspan="2">Date</td></tr>
<tr><td colspan="2"></td><td colspan="2"></td></tr>
<tr><td>Marks and numbers</td><td>Number and kind of package, description of goods</td><td>Quantity</td><td>Package</td><td>G. W</td><td>N. W</td><td>Meas.</td></tr>
<tr><td></td><td></td><td></td><td></td><td></td><td></td><td></td></tr>
<tr><td colspan="7">TOTAL:

SAY TOTAL:</td></tr>
</table>

样例6.2　空白装箱单

实训操作二

泰佛贸易公司与日本五羊株式会社(GOYOO CO., LTD.)经过友好洽商就出口男士衬衫达成一份出口合同,数量5 000件,金额12 000美元,付款方式为即期付款交单(D/P at sight)。随后泰佛贸易公司与天津新华衬衣厂签订购货合同,委托其代为加工。新华衬衣厂如期把合同项下5 000件衬衫备妥,详见工厂传真过来的花色码单,请你根据买卖双方签订的销售确认书(见样例6.3)和加工厂提供的花色码单(见样例6.4)缮制包装单据(见样例6.5),以便办理出口报验工作。

Sales Confirmation

No. 08TF0010
Dated: Jan. 18, 2008

The seller: TIFERT TRADING CO., LTD.
NO. 86, ZHUJIANG ROAD, TIANJIN, CHINA
The buyer: GOYOO CO., LTD.
DAICHI BLOG 2-5-25, TOKYO, JAPAN

The undersigned sellers and buyers have agreed to close the following transaction according to the terms and conditions stipulated below:

Commodity & specification	Quantity	Unit price	Amount
100% COTTON MEN'S SHIRT STYLE No. A-118 B-116 SIZE: S M L XL COLOR: PINK BLUE GREEN	5000PCS	USD2.65/PC CIF TOKYO	USD13250.00

Remarks: With 5% more or less both in amount and quantity at the seller's option

Packing: In cartons and packing method as per P. O. No. GY0058 dated JAN. 15, 2008

Shipment: To be effected not later than Mar 15, 2008 from Tianjin to Yokohama allowing partial shipments and transshipment.

Insuranche: To be covered for 110 % of invoice value against All Risks and War Risk as per and subject to Ocean Marine Cargo Clauses of CIC dated 1/1/1981.

Payment: The buyer shall pay against documentary draft drawn by the seller at sight upon first presentation. The shipping documents are to be delivered against payment only.

The seller	The buyer
TIFERT TRADING CO., LTD.	GOYOO CO., LTD.
王 宏	三 井

样例6.3 销售确认书

天津新华衬衣厂

天津市海河东路118号

电话:24458896　传真:24458899

花色码单

商品名称:男士衬衣　　订单号:GY0058

款式号:A－118和B－116　　颜色:粉/蓝/绿

毛重:15公斤/箱　　净重:14公斤/箱

唛头:GOYOO　　尺码:45×35×30公分/箱

08TF0010

TOKYO

C/T NO. 1－139

C/NO 箱号	CTNS 箱数	STYLE 款式	COLOR 颜色	SIZE 尺码 ASSORTMENT				QTY/CTN 数量/箱	TTL QTY 总数量
				S	M	L	XL		
1－112	112	A－118	粉	1	1	6	4	36件	4 032件
			蓝	1	3	6	2		
			绿	2	1	6	3		
113－136	24	B－116	粉	1	1	6	4	36件	864件
			蓝	1	3	6	2		
			绿	2	1	6	3		
137	1	A－118	粉	2	1	8	3	36件	36件
			蓝		1	6	3		
			绿	1		6	5		
138	1	B－116	粉	2	2	4	4	34件	34件
			蓝	1	3	6	2		
			绿		1	6	3		
139	1	A－118	粉	2	2	4	4	34件	34件
			蓝	1	3	6	2		
		B－116	绿		1	6	3		
	139								5 000件

检验员:张丽丽　　日期:2008－3－10

样例6.4　花色码单

TIFERT TRADING CO., LTD.

NO. 86, ZHUJIANG ROAD, TIANJIN, CHINA

TEL: 0086-22-8566 5678 FAX: 0086-22-8566 5679

Packing List

INV NO. TF080310

DATE:

样例6.5 空白装箱单

任务七 缮制检验证书

任务背景

在王芳小姐具体负责女童夹克衫的进料加工业务过程中，买卖双方在签订合同时，明确规定出运前应委托中国出入境检验检疫局对货物实施检验，检验合格后方可出运，随后丸红株式会社通过中国银行东京分行修改的信用证也明确规定检验证书作为议付货款的单据之一。

于是王芳小姐将发票和装箱单缮制妥当后，提醒报检员和天津出入境检验检疫局办理报检手续，随时关注检验证书的签发进展情况，并对签发的检验证书进行认真核对，保证做到单证相符、单单相符。

【背景分析】

检验证书是出口业务中常用的结汇单据之一，是出口商是否按合同约定品质标准履行交货义务的具体体现，也是进口商非常关注的单据。通常检验证书都是由实施检验部门根据检测结果签发，但作为出口商也应掌握检验证书的缮制规范，这样才能保证做到相符交单。为此，王芳小姐应掌握和具备如下知识、技能及素质。

知识目标

①了解检验证书的概念、种类及作用。

②看懂信用证中的检验检疫条款。

技能目标

①准确翻译信用证中的检验检疫条款及与检验检疫相关条款。

②在掌握一般缮制规范的基础上，着重学会审核检验证书。

素质目标

①养成严谨、细致的工作作风。

②实事求是，塑造诚信形象。

一、缮制检验证书的基础知识

【检验证书的概念】

检验证书(Inspection Certificate)，是各种进出口商品检验证书、鉴定证书及其他证明书的统称，是进出口贸易有关各方履行契约义务、处理索赔争议、仲裁及诉讼中必需的具有法律依据的有效证件,也是海关验放、征收关税的必要证明。

【检验证书的签发机构】

检验分为法定检验和非法定检验。某些商品必须由出口国或进口国政府指定的机构检验才能出口或进口,这种检验是法定检验。凡非法定检验的商品,如进出口双方同意,也可采用由出口商的生产单位或进口商品的商业单位出具证明的形式。相应签发检验检疫证书的机构也有官方的、非官方的,还可以是生产商和进口商自身。

1. 官方检验机构

如国家质量监督检验检疫总局(General Administration of Quality Supervision Inspection and Quarantine of People's republic of China 简称 AQSIQ)及各地的出入境检验检疫局(Entry-Exit Inspection and Quarantine Bureau 简称 CIQ)。

2. 非官方检验机构

除政府设立的官方商品检验机构外,世界上许多国家中还有由商会、协会或同业公会设立的民间商品检验机构,负责国际贸易货物的检验和鉴定工作。由于民间商品检验机构承担的民事责任有别于官方商品检验机构承担的行政责任,所以在国际贸易中,民间商品检验机构更容易被进出口双方所接受。民间商品检验机构根据委托人的要求,以自己的技术、信誉及对国际贸易的熟悉,为国际贸易当事人提供灵活、及时、公正的检验鉴定服务,受到国际贸易当事人的共同信任。目前在国际上比较有名望、有权威的民间商品检验机构有瑞士通用公证行(SGS)、英国英之杰检验集团(ITS)及日本海事检定协会(NKKK)等。

3. 生产制造商

如果生产制造商具有一定的技术实力,并且具备完善的检验检疫设施,其出具的检验检疫证书是被进口商或产品的最终用户认可的。如有些信用证中明确规定"Inspection certificate issued by exporter/manufacturer acceptable"。

4. 用货单位和进口商

在实际进出口业务中,特别是纺织品、服装等产品的出口,往往在出运前进口商自己或派其代理前来验货,验货合格后签发一份检验证书作为出口商向银行议付货款的单据之一,即通常说的"客检证"。如信用证中明确规定"Inspection certificate signed by importer's nominee"。

【检验证书的签发流程】

检验证书的签发流程如图 7.1 所示。

1. 报验

报验是指报检单位向检验检疫机构申请检验。报验时,须填写"出境货物报验单",并提供出口合同或销售确认书、商业发票、装箱单、信用证复印件或有关往来信函;根据实际需要,有可能还需提供生产商出具的厂检结果单原件、检验检疫机构签发的"出境货物运输包装性能检验结果单"正本及其他相关的物品和材料,如成交小样，如果出境地和生产地不同，还需提供"出境货物换证凭单"正本或"出境货物换证凭条"等。

2. 抽样

商检机构接受报验之后，及时派员赴货物存放地点进行现场抽样。抽样时，要按照规定的方法和一定的比例，在货物的不同部位抽取一定数量的、能代表全批货物质量的样品供检验之用。

3. 检验

商检机构接受报验之后，认真研究申报的检验项目，确定检验内容，仔细审核合同和信用证中对品质、规格、包装的规定，弄清检验依据，确定检验标准和方法，然后进行抽样检验、仪器分析检验、物理检验、感官检验及微生物检验等。

4. 发证

凡列入"检验检疫商品目录"内的出口商品，经检验检疫合格后签发"出境货物通关单"。海关凭"出境货物通关单"放行货物，准予装船。凡合同或信用证规定由商检检疫部门检验出证的，或国外进口商要求检验证书的，则按合同或信用证要求签发检验检疫证书。

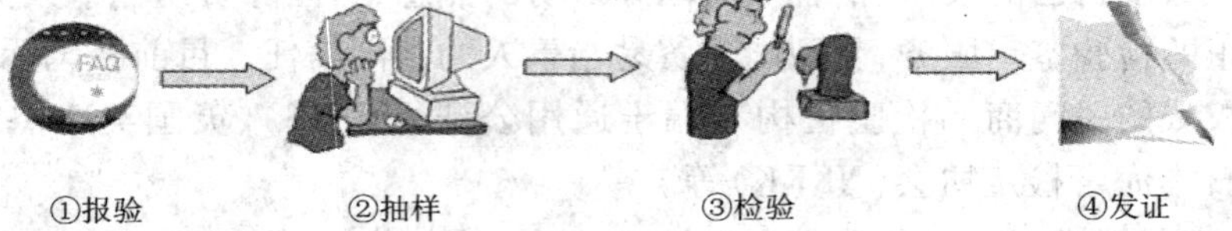

图7.1 检验证书签发流程图

【检验证书的种类】

目前，我国检验检疫机构签发的检验证书主要有以下几种。

①品质检验证书，是出口商品付运结汇和进口商品结算索赔的有效凭证，是法定检验商品的证书，是进出口商品报关、输出输入的合法凭证。进出境检验检疫局签发的通关单和在报关单上加盖的放行章有与商检证书同等的通关效力。

②重量或数量检验证书，是出口商品付运结汇、签发提单和进口商品结算索赔的有效凭证。出口商品的重量证书也是国外报关征税和计算运费、装卸费用的证件。

③兽医检验证书，是证明出口动物产品或食品经检疫合格的证件，是出口商品付运结汇和进口国通关输入的重要证件。此证书适用于冻畜肉、冻禽、禽畜罐头、冻兔、皮张、毛类、绒类、猪鬃等出口商品。

④卫生/健康证书，是证明可供人类食用的出口动物产品、食品等经过卫生检验或检疫合格的证件，是出口商品付运结汇和通关验放的有效证件。此证书适用于肠衣、罐头、冻鱼、冻虾、食品、蛋品、乳制品及蜂蜜等。

⑤消毒检验证书，是证明出口动物产品经过消毒处理，保证安全卫生的证件，是

出口商品付运结汇和国外进口通关验放的有效凭证。此证书适用于猪鬃、马尾、皮张、山羊毛、羽毛及人发等商品。

⑥熏蒸证书,适用于证明出口粮谷、油籽、豆类等商品,以及包装用木材与植物性填充物等已经过熏蒸灭虫的证书。

⑦残损检验证书,是证明进口商品残损情况的证件,是作为受货人向发货人或承运人或保险人等有关责任方索赔的有效证件。此证书适用于进口商品发生残、短、渍、毁等情况。

⑧积载鉴定证书,是证明船方和集装箱装货部门正确配载、积载货物及其履行运输契约义务的证件,可供货物交接或发生货损时处理争议之用。

⑨财产价值鉴定证书,是国际贸易当事人和司法、仲裁、验资等有关部门索赔、理赔、评估或裁判的重要依据。

⑩船舱检验证书,是证明承运出口商品的船舱清洁、密固、冷藏效能及其他技术条件是否符合标准,能否确保承载商品的质量和数量完整与安全的证书;也是作为承运人履行租船契约适载义务和国际贸易当事人进行货物交接及处理货损事故的依据。

⑪生丝品级及公量检验证书,是出口生丝的专用证书。其作用相当于品质检验证书和重量/数量检验证书。

⑫产地证明书,是出口商品在进口国通关输入、享受减免关税优惠待遇以及证明商品产地的凭证。

⑬舱口检视证书、监视装/卸载证书、舱口封识证书、油温空距证书、集装箱监装/拆证书,是作为证明承运人履行契约义务,明确责任界限,便于处理货损、货差责任事故的证明。

⑭价值证明书,是作为进口国管理外汇和征收关税的凭证。在发票上签盖检验检疫机构的价值证明章与价值证明书具有同等效力。

⑮货载衡量检验证书,是证明进出口商品的重量、体积吨位的证件,是作为计算运费和制订配载计划的依据。

【检验证书的作用】

在国际贸易中,检验证书主要起着公证证明的作用,具体表现如下。

①作为证明履约、交货接收的有效证件。货物经过长途运输后难免会出现质量变化或数量缺损、包装损坏等情况,从而引起进口商的争议。出口商为了免责,必须提供权威机构签发的检验检疫证书,凭以认定所交付的商品是合格的,证明其已履行交货义务。

②作为验收报关的有效凭证。许多国家为维护本国消费者利益,通常规定某些商品必须进行强制性检验检疫,如食品等。进口商必须出示出口地检验检疫机构签发的证明商品合格或符合国家进口标准的检验检疫证书才能通关,否则禁止进口。

③作为结算货款的依据。许多产品的定价取决于商品的等级,或某些主要成分

的含量。因此进出口合同中订有价格和金额的增减条款，以适应不同的检验检疫结果。在进口业务中，一般都根据检验检疫证书中标明的产品等级和主要成分含量，确定合适价格并计算出货值。

④作为议付货款的一种单据。进口商为了把好产品质量关，往往要求出口商提供权威机构出具的检验检疫证书，并把其作为向银行议付货款的单据之一，如果检验检疫证书中列明的项目或检验结果与信用证中的规定不符，开证行或付款行有权拒付货款。

⑤作为索赔、仲裁及诉讼的佐证文件。货物在抵达进口地后，一般都要进行复验，以确定收货时的质量、数量及状况等。这样既便于进口商转售商品，又可以在发现问题时拿出佐证。根据检验检疫结果，明确责任归属，提出赔偿要求。如要进行仲裁或诉讼，也必须提供检验检疫证书作为对货物缺陷、残损等事实的证明。

二、缮制检验证书的基本技能

【实训目的】

通过本项目实训，应掌握的基本技能如下。

①熟悉并看懂相关信用证（合同）中有关检验证书的条款。

②熟悉检验证书的不同格式及主要内容。

③掌握检验证书的缮制规范及缮制技巧。

【操作前准备】

进行本项任务的实训前，应准备的内容如下。

①出口商提供的合同、信用证副本、商业发票及装箱单。

②生产厂家提供的厂检结果。

③出口商填写的“出境货物报检单”。

【操作程序】

①仔细阅读信用证或合同中的检验条款及与检验相关方面的特殊要求，特别注意信用证特别要求加注的有关内容，如信用证证号要显示在所有单据上等。

②根据信用证或合同要求认真检查报检员缮制的出境货物报检单的各个栏目内容，做到准确、完整。

③对照信用证或合同中的检验条款审核检验证书，检查是否做到单证（单同）相符，对照已缮制妥的商业、装箱单等结汇单据，检查是否做到单单相符。

【操作规范】

表 7.1 检验证书缮制规范

项目顺序号	填写内容	要点提示
(1)签证机构 Issuer	官方机构或非官方机构	如信用证未规定具体单位,则由出口商决定
(2)检验证书的名称 Name of Certificate	填写证书名称	应与合同或信用证规定相符
(3)发货人 Consignor	出口商名称	一般只填写名称不填写地址
(4)收货人 Consignee	* * * * * *	不用填写具体的名称,中性单据可填写"To whom it may concern"
(5)货物描述 Description of goods	商品名称	可用统称
(6)报检的数量/重量 Quantity/weight declared	实际出运的数量或重量	应与装箱单和提单中的数量或重量一致
(7)包装的种类及数量 Number and kind of packages	货物的包装单位数量	应与包装单据和提单中的包装件数一致
(8)运输工具 Means of conveyance	海运 By sea freight 空运 By air freight 陆运 By rail/truck	
(9)标记及号码 Marks & No.	具体的唛头 没有唛头填 N/M	①此栏不能留空 ②应与其他单据的唛头保持一致
(10)检验结果 Result of inspection	所检验货物的实际现状	是检验证书中最重要的一项,应该与信用证或合同要求的品质标准相符,否则会遭到银行或进口商的拒付
(11)签证地点 Place of issue	此笔业务证书的签发地点	一般与货物装运港一致
(12)签证日期 Date of issue	此笔业务证书的签发日期	一般不迟于提单日期
(13)授权人签字 Authorized signature	证书签署人姓名的汉语拼音	
(14)签名 Signature	证书签署人亲笔签名	可用中文
(15)签章 Official stamp	签证机构的公章	

【检验证书样例】

中华人民共和国出入境检验检疫 (1) 正 本

ENTRY-EXIT INSPECTION AND QUARANTITE ORIGINAL

OF THE PEOPLE'S REPUBLIC OF CHINA

编号 No. :07CIQ1187

QUALITY CERTIFICATE (2)

发货人 (3)

Consignor TIFERT TRADING CO. , LTD.

收货人 (4)

Consignee * * * *

品名 (5) Description of goods GIRL JACKET	标记及号码 (9) Mark & No.
报检数量/重量 (6) Quantity/Weight declared 5000PCS	MARUBENI S/C 08TF0858
包装种类及数量 (7) Number and type of packages 250CARTONS	TOKYO CTN 1 - 250
运输工具 (8) Means of conveyance BY SEA FREIGHT	

检验结果 (10)

Result of inspection

SAMPLES WERE DRAWN AT RANDOM FROM THE WHOLE LOT OF GOODS AND INSPECTED STRICTLY ACCORDING TO THE S/C NO. 08TF0858

THE ABOVE RESULTS OF INSPECTION ARE IN CONFORMITY WITH THE REQUIREMENTS IN THE SAID CONTRACT.

(15) (11) (12)

印章: 签证地点 Place of issue TIANJIN 签证日期 Date of issue APR. 25, 2008

Official stamp (13) (14)

授权签字人 Authorized officer ***ZHANG CHI*** 签名 Signature 张驰

我们已尽所知和最大能力实施上述检验，不能因我们签发本证书而免除卖方或其他方面根据合同和法律所承担的产品质量责任和其他责任。

All inspection are carried out conscientiously to the best of our knowledge and ability. This certificate dose not in any respect absolve the seller and other related parties from his contractual and legal obligations especially when product quality is concerned.

样例 7.1 检验证书

【操作注意事项】

①如信用证对检验证书的签发机构有明确规定,则必须由该机构对商品实施检验检疫并出具相关检验证书。如没有具体规定,则可由任何机构包括出口商自己签发检验证书也可。

②检验证书是官方机构或由商会、协会、同业公会设立的民间商品检验机构签发的文件,进出口商不能擅自涂改,如要修改有关内容,必须向签证机关申请办理证书变更手续。

③检验证书的签发日期应早于运输单据的日期,因为出口商必须在出运前办理有关检验检疫手续,以证明其所交货物是否与合同约定的品质规格相符。

④检验证书的种类和证书内容应符合信用证的要求,并且应做到货证、事(货物的事实状态)证及证证(同一批货物各种证书之间)的"三相符"。

⑤检验证书所列明的货物规格、品质及数量等与发票一致。

⑥检验证书的更改除了在更正处加盖"更正"章外,还应加上"变更内容已经出单人授权"字样。

⑦信用证要求装运前检验证书(Pre-shipment Inspection Certificate)作为议付的单据之一时,其签发日期绝对不得晚于装运日期。如果信用证要求检验证书(Inspection Certificate)作为议付的单据之一,其签发日期最好不要迟于运输单据的签发日期,以说明装运前对货物实施的检验;一旦签发日期晚于运输单据的签发日期,最好通过标题或内容来表明检验发生在装运之前或装运当天,只是证书签发略晚些,以免遭信誉不好或挑剔的银行拒付。

⑧"商检软条款"是信用证中软条款最为集中的项目,对列有"由申请人或其授权人签发检验证书且其签字与银行留存签字样本一致"条款的信用证一般不宜接受,对不能或很难办到的商检条款应及时接洽进口商通过开证行改证,以保证安全收汇。

三、缮制检验证书的操作训练

【翻译语句】

①Inspection Certificate

②Certificate of Weight

③Fumigation Certificate

④Plant Quarantine Certificate

⑤Sanitary Certificate

⑥Health Certificate

⑦Analysis Certificate

⑧Tank Inspection Certificate

⑨Inspection Certificate of Packing

⑩Certificate of Value

⑪Certificate of Weight and Quality in triplicate

⑫Inspection Certificate issued by applicant and signed by Mr. Brown.

⑬Clean Report of Finding issued by Societe Generale de Surveillance(SGS), Hong Kong evidencing that quality, quantity and packing of goods in full compliance with the requirement of L/C.

⑭Sanitary Certificate in one original and 3 copies stating that skins are coming from alive animals slaughtered at least 4 months before shipment.

⑮Health Certificate issued by CIQ in triplicate stating that the lot of commodity has been treated under 140 degrees centigrade for 3 hours and this lot of product was delivered from health animals originating from safety and non-epidemic regions. Health Certificate must have hand-writing signature of chief veterinarian.

【动脑思考】

①请利用网络,查找我国的官方检验机构有哪些。

②请利用网络,查找国际上比较有名望、有权威的民间商品检验机构有哪些。

③请利用网络,查找换证凭单和换证凭条的相同点和不同点。

④中国光大贸易公司向德国出口一批商品,需用木制托盘,请问这种情况下出口商须提供哪些检验证书。

⑤中国昌盛贸易公司向西班牙出口一批羊皮,请问出口商须提供哪些检验证书?

【动手操练】

实训操作一

作为泰佛贸易公司的单证员,请你根据下面提供的信息,利用空白检验证书(见样例7.2)缮制一份品质检验证书。

①出口商: TIFERT TRADING CO., LTD
NO. 86, ZHUJIANG ROAD, TIANJIN, CHINA

②运输标志: BB CORP
S/C NO. HT222
LONDONG
NO. 1 – UP

③货物描述:

BEACH UMBRELLA ART NO. B68 200PCS USD10.00/PC
ART NO. B94 300PCS USD15.00/PC
CIF LONDON
PACKING IN CARTONS OF 10PCS EACH

④检验结果:SAMPLES WERE DRAWN AT RANDOM FROM THE WHOLE LOT OF GOODS AND INSPECTED STRICTLY ACCORDING TO THE S/C NO. HT222

THE ABOVE RESULTS OF INSPECTION ARE IN CONFORMITY WITH THE REQUIREMENTS IN THE SAID CONTRACT

⑤签发地点:TIANJIN

⑥签证时间:MAY 10,2008

⑦签证机关有权签字人:李丽

⑧证书号:08TJCIQ0526

中华人民共和国出入境检验检疫　　正　本

ENTRY-EXIT INSPECTION AND QUARANTITE　　ORIGINAL

OF THE PEOPLE'S REPUBLIC OF CHINA

编号 No.:

QUALITY CERTIFICATE

发货人
Consignor ______

收货人
Consignee ______

品名 Description of goods ______	标记及号码 Mark & No.
报检数量/重量 Quantity/Weight declared ______	
包装种类及数量 Number and type of packages ______	
运输工具 Means of conveyance ______	

检验结果
Result of inspection

印章:　　签证地点 Place of issue ______ 签证日期 Date of issue ______

Official stamp

授权签字人 Authorized officer ______ 签名 Signature ______

我们已尽所知和最大能力实施上述检验,不能因我们签发本证书而免除卖方或其他方面根据合同和法律所承担的产品质量责任和其他责任。

All inspection are carried out conscientiously to the best of our knowledge and ability. This certificate dose not in any respect absolve the seller and other related parties from his contractual and legal obligations especially when product quality is concerned.

样例 7.2　空白品质检验证书

实训操作二

信用证有关资料摘录如下。

27/ SEQUENCE OF TOTAL:	1/1
40A/ FORM OF DOCUMENTARY CREDIT:	IRREVOCABLE
40E/APPLICABLE RULES:	UCP LATEST VERSION
20/ DOCUMENTARY CREDIT NUMBER:	M19EBNU00018
31C/ DATE OF ISSUE:	080806 SEOUL
31D/ DATE AND PLACE OF EXPIRY:	081020 IN BENEFICIARY'S COUNTRY
50/ APPLICANT:	SMART TRADING CO. , LTD. 220 VTRA SEMARANG INDONESIA
59/ BENEFICIARY:	TIFERT TRADING CO. , LTD. NO. 86, ZHUJIANG ROAD, TIANJIN, CHINA.
32B/ CURRENCY CODE AMOUNT:	USD 24000.00
41D/ AVAILABLE WITH/BY:	ANY BANK BY NEGOTIATION
42C/ DRAFT AT:	30DAYS AFTER SIGHT
43P/ PARTIAL SHIPMENTS:	ALLOWED
43T/ TRANSHIPMENT:	PROHIBITED
44A/ ON BOARD/DISP/TAKING CHARGE:	CHINA PORT
44B/ FOR TRANSPORTATION TO:	KOREAN INCHON PORT
44C/ LATEST DATE OF SHIPMENT:	080930

45A/ DESCR GOODS AND/OR SERVICES:

200MT CHINESE SOYBEANS 2008 CROP AT USD120/MT FOB TIANJIN

PACKING IN GUNNY BAGS OF 50KGS NET EAHC DETAILS AS PER S/C NO.08RF0056

46A/ DOCUMENTS REQUIRED

+ SIGNED COMMERCIAL INVOICE IN TRIPLICATE

+ CERTIFICATE OF FUMIGATION ISSUED BY CIQ STATING THAT THE GOODS ARE FREE FROM LIVE WEEVIL.

补充信息资料如下。

①SHIPPING MARKS:

GA
06RF0056
INCHON
NO.1 - UP

②RESULT:

THE SOYBEANS HAVE BEEN FUMIGATED FOR 48HOURS BEFROE
SHIPMENT AND THE GOODS ARE FREE FROM LIVE WEEVIL.

③DATE OF ISSUE: SEPT 28, 2008

④PLAE OF ISSUE: TIANJIN

⑤AUTHORIZED SIGNATURE:陈立

作为泰佛贸易公司的单证员,请你根据以上信用证摘录信息及补充信息,利用空白熏蒸检验证书(样例7.3)独立填写一份熏蒸证。

中华人民共和国出入境检验检疫　　正　本

ENTRY-EXIT INSPECTION AND QUARANTITE　　ORIGINAL

OF THE PEOPLE'S REPUBLIC OF CHINA

编号 No.：

FUMIGATION CERTIFICATE

发货人
Consignor ______________________

收货人
Consignee ______________________

品名 Description of goods ______________	标记及号码 Mark & No.
报检数量/重量 Quantity/Weight declared ______________	
包装种类及数量 Number and type of packages ______________	
运输工具 Means of conveyance ______________	

检验结果
Result of inspection

印章：　　签证地点 Place of issue ________ 签证日期 Date of issue ________
Official stamp

授权签字人 Authorized officer ________ 签名 Signature ________

我们已尽所知和最大能力实施上述检验，不能因我们签发本证书而免除卖方或其他方面根据合同和法律所承担的产品质量责任和其他责任。

All inspection are carried out conscientiously to the best of our knowledge and ability. This certificate dose not in any respect absolve the seller and other related parties from his contractual and legal obligations especially when product quality is concerned.

样例 7.3　空白熏蒸检验证书

任务八 缮制原产地证书

任务背景

在由王芳小姐负责的女童夹克衫的进料加工业务中，该批夹克衫的面料为从日本进口的100%全棉的斜纹面料，100%涤的里料及其他所有辅料全部从国内采购。尽管面料从日本进口，但成品夹克衫成衣最终返销到日本，这样仍符合日本的原产地标准。为证明货物的国籍，以便在夹克衫到日本清关时享受优惠的进口关税税率，日本丸红株式会社通过银行开立的信用证中明确规定议付货款须提交由出入境检验检疫局签发的普惠制原产地证书作为结汇的单据之一。

王芳小姐提醒原产地证书的申领员与出入境检验检疫局办理原产地申领工作，由此进入缮制原产地证书的流程。

【背景分析】

原产地证书是货物的经济国籍，在国际贸易中扮演非常重要的角色，关系到货物通关所适用的进口关税税率，对提高我国出口产品的竞争力具有极其重要的作用。原产地证书也是出口业务中常用的结汇单据之一，在实际业务中，原产地证书通常是由出口商自行缮制，由出入境检验检疫局或贸促会签发。为能更好完成此项工作，王芳小姐应掌握和具备如下知识、技能及素质。

知识目标

①了解原产地证书的概念、种类、作用及申领程序。

②看懂信用证中的原产地证书的有关条款。

技能目标

①准确翻译信用证中的原产地证书的有关条款。

②学会独立、正确地缮制原产地证书。

素质目标

①关注与贸易相关的政策法规，以用于指导业务实践。

②学会利用各种有利因素扩大出口业务。

一、缮制原产地证书的基础知识

【原产地证书的概念】

原产地证书(Certificate of Origin)是一种证明货物原产地或制造地的证件,是出口商品在进口国通关和进口国海关核定进口货物应征税率的依据,是享受减免关税优惠待遇的凭证。

【原产地证书的种类】

1. 按照用途分类

(1)优惠原产地证书

这种证书包括普惠制原产地证书,亚太贸易协定及中国—东盟自由贸区、中国—智利自由贸区、中国—巴基斯坦自由贸区、中国—新西兰自由贸易区及中国—新加坡自由贸易区等区域性经济集团互惠原产地证书等。

(2)非优惠原产地证书

这种证书包括一般原产地证书和《金伯利进程国际证书》等。

2. 按照种类分类

(1)普惠制原产地证书

联合国贸发会议规定统一格式,根据普惠制给惠国的原产地规则和有关要求,由普惠制受惠国官方机构出具的具有法律效力的官方凭证。其作用是使受惠国的制成品和半制成品在给惠国享受在最惠国税率基础上的进一步减免进口关税,是普遍的、非歧视的、非互惠的。

享受普惠制优惠关税税率必须符合直接运输规则,如果由于地理原因必须经第三国或地区,必须签发未再加工证明。它是证明中国出口货物在途经第三个国家或地区时,未在中转地进行任何形式的加工或制作,符合给惠国直接运输规则的证明文件。

(2)一般原产地证书

这种证书是证明货物原产于某一特定国家或地区,享受进口国正常关税(最惠国)待遇的证明文件。其适用范围有征收关税、贸易统计、保障措施、歧视性数量限制、反倾销和反补贴、原产地标记及政府采购等方面。

(3)区域性经济集团互惠原产地证书

这种证书是订有区域性贸易协定的经济集团内的国家官方机构签发的享受互惠减让关税的凭证。包括如下几类。

①《<曼谷亚太贸易协定>优惠原产地证明书》:根据《曼谷亚太贸易协定》的要求签发的在协定成员国之间就特定产品享受互惠减免关税优惠待遇的具有法律效力的官方证明文件。

②《中国—东盟自由贸易区原产地证书》:根据中国—东盟自由贸易区货物贸易协定签发的在成员国之间就特定产品享受互惠减免关税优惠待遇的具有法律效力的官方证明文件。

③《中国—巴基斯坦自由贸易区原产地证书》:根据中国—巴基斯坦自由贸易协定签发的在成员国之间就特定产品享受互惠减免关税优惠待遇的具有法律效力的官方证明文件。

④《中国—智利自由贸易区原产地证书》:根据中国—智利自由贸易协定签发的在成员国之间就特定产品享受互惠减免关税优惠待遇的具有法律效力的官方证明文件。

⑤《中国—新西兰自由贸易协定原产地证书》:根据中国—新西兰自由贸易协定签发的在成员国之间就特定产品享受互惠减免关税优惠待遇的具有法律效力的官方证明文件。

⑥《中国—新加坡自由贸易区优惠税率原产地证书》:根据中国—新加坡自由贸易协定签发的在成员国之间就特定产品享受互惠减免关税优惠待遇的具有法律效力的官方证明文件。

(4)专用原产地证书

国际组织或国家根据政治和贸易措施的特殊需要,针对某一特殊行业的特定产品规定的原产地证书,这些产品应符合特定的原产地规则。包括如下几类。

①《输欧盟烟草真实性证书》:为使出口至欧盟的品目号 2401 项下部分烟草享受欧盟特定关税优惠待遇而签发的具有法律效力的官方证明文件。

②《输欧盟特定产品原产地名称证书》:为使出口至欧盟的葡萄、葡萄酒、奶酪、烟草及硝酸盐等特定产品享受欧盟特定关税优惠待遇而签发的具有法律效力的官方证明文件。

③《输欧盟农产品原产地名称证书》:为使出口至欧盟的蘑菇罐头等特定产品享受欧盟特定关税优惠待遇而签发的具有法律效力的官方证明文件。

④《输欧盟/美国纺织品原产地证书》:为使出口至欧盟和美国的纺织品顺利获得进口国海关的放行,对欧盟和美国出口纺织品时需提交该产地证,该证由地方外经贸委(厅)按照我国与欧盟和美国签订的纺织品贸易协议及相关规定颁发。

⑤《原产地标记证书》:证明货物符合《原产地标记管理规定》、《原产地标记管理规定实施办法》、《中华人民共和国进出口货物原产地条例》及《中华人民共和国非优惠原产地签证管理办法》,具有使用已注册原产地标记的资格的官方证明文件。

⑥《金伯利进程国际证书》:由参加金伯利进程国际证书制度的成员国签发的证明毛坯钻石合法来源地的官方证明文件。

另外,含进口成分的货物,经审核未达到原产地标准的,签发《加工装配证明书》或《转口证明书》。加工装配证明书是证明货物仅在中国境内加工装配而未取得中国原产资格的证明文件。转口证明书是证明非原产货物仅经中国转口的证明文件。

3. 按照签发者分类

(1)检验检疫机构出具的原产地证书

如中华人民共和国出入境检验检疫局(CIQ)出具的普惠制产地证格式A(GSP Form A)及一般原产地证书(Certificate of Origin)。

(2)商会或贸促会出具的原产地证书

如中国国际贸易促进委员会(CCPIT)出具的一般原产地证书,简称贸促会产地证书(CCPIT Certificate of Origin)。

(3)制造商或出口商出具的原产地证书

在国际贸易中,应该提供哪种原产地证明书,主要依据合同或信用证的要求。一般对于实行普惠制国家的出口货物,都要求出具普惠制原产地证明书。如果信用证并未明确规定产地证书的出具者,银行可接受任何一种原产地证明书,现在我国多数出口商习惯使用贸促会出具的证书。

【原产地证书的作用】

在国际贸易中,世界各国根据各自的对外贸易政策,普遍实行进口贸易管制,对进口商品实施差别关税和数量限制,并由海关执行统计。由于进口国要求出口国出具货物的原产地证明已成为国际惯例,因此一般原产地证书是进行国际贸易的一项重要证明文件。归纳起来,其具有以下几方面的作用。

①它是确定产品关税待遇,提高市场竞争力的重要工具。现在世界上大多数国家,对从不同国家进口的商品,均使用不同的税率,而关税方面的差别待遇是根据货物的原产地决定的,一般原产地证书则是各国海关据以征收关税和实施差别待遇的有效凭证。

如在进口国与出口国的政府之间订有关税协定,用条约形式规定了协定税率(Agreed Customs Rate),或两国间的条约上规定了最惠国条款(Most Favored Nation Clause)。进口商往往要求出口商提供有效的原产地证书,以证明进口货物的原产地确系缔约国才能获得相应的税率待遇。

②它是证明产品内在品质或结汇的依据。在国际贸易中,一般原产地证书还起到证明商品内在品质、提高商品竞争力的作用。如在国际市场上持有中国原产地证的丝绸比持有其他不产丝绸国家产地证的丝绸更能卖好价。此外,原产地证书有时还是贸易双方进行交接、结汇的必备单据。如买方在申请开立信用证(L/C)时常要求提供一般原产地证书以确保其自身利益,银行也常以产地证作为信用证(L/C)是否结付的重要凭证。

③它是进行贸易统计的依据。各国海关都承担对进出口货物进行统计的职责,原产地证书则是海关借以对进口货物进行统计的重要依据。

进入九十年代,国际贸易保护主义有所抬头,非关税壁垒形势日益严重,数量设限、反倾销等贸易摩擦不时出现,作好一般原产地证书签发工作对维护我国产品在国际贸易中的利益,缓解我国与有关国家的贸易摩擦具有重要作用。

④它是货物进口国实行有差别的数量控制,进行贸易管理的工具。世界各国根据其贸易政策,为保护本国工业生产和国际贸易竞争需要,往往对某些货物实行限制,制定一些进口货物数量控制措施,例如进口配额、许可证制度、反倾销及反补贴制度。为实行这些控制制度,首先须确定进口的货物是来自哪个国家,然后确定这批货物是否受到进口数量限制,是否须持有进口许可证,是否要冲销配额,及是否征收反倾销、反补贴税等等,原产地证书也就成为实施这些制度的重要工具。

【原产地证书的申请程序】

原产地证书的申请程序如图 8.1 所示。

1. 办理注册登记

凡符合规定的企业须办理原产地证书签证时,应先向企业所在地的签证机构办理注册登记手续。办理注册登记时,应提交的文件如下。

①政府主管部门授予企业进出口经营权的文件。

②企业营业执照副本。

③填妥规定格式的《注册登记表》(一式二份,向当地签证机构领取)。

④产品原材料来源的有关证明。

⑤规定的其他文件。

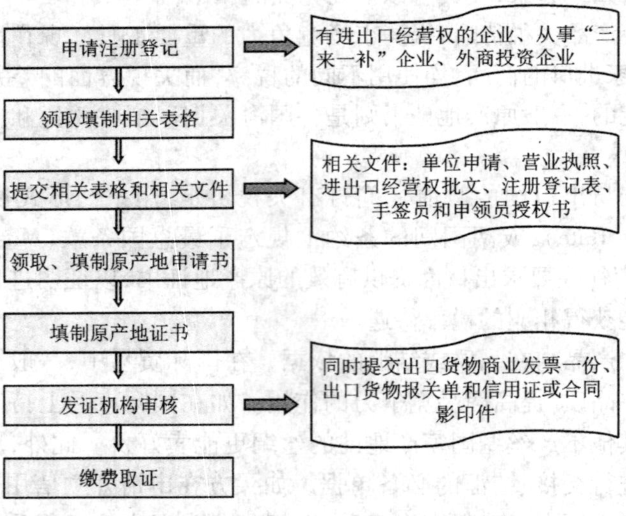

图 8.1 原产地证书申领程序

2. 下厂调查

签证机构受理申请后,将审核企业提供的文件材料。对于生产企业,签证机构还将派员到企业进行实地调查,核实该企业的生产加工情况,以便确定其产品是否分别符合有关给惠国的普惠制原产地标准和《中华人民共和国出口货物原产地规则》所规定的标准。

对审核合格的企业,签证机构给予注册登记。

3. 申请签发原产地证书

取得签证机构注册后,即可向该签证机构申请签发原产地证书。正常情况下申请单位最迟于货物报关出运前三天向签证机构提出申请,需缮制并提供的材料如下。

①规定格式的《申请书》一份。

②出口企业自行按标准缮制的普惠制原产地证书或一般原产地证书。

③出口商业发票一份。

④申请普惠制产地证的、含进口成分的产品,还需要提供《产品成本明细单》。

⑤签证机构认为必要的其他文件。

如果货物已经出口,须补办原产地证书时,除提供以上规定的材料外,还须提供以下材料。

①解释迟申请办证的函件。

②货物提单、航空提单或邮政收据。

除上述外,还有以下两种特殊情况。

更改证书:是指签证机构已经签出原产地证书,申请单位需要更改证书内容。对此,申请单位应书面申明理由,提交已更改的原产地证书,并退回原证书正本。

重发证书:是指已经签发的原产地证书遗失或损毁,申请单位按原证书内容重新申请一份原产地证书。对此,申请单位应书面说明遗失或损毁的原因,提交重新缮制的原产地证书及原证书副本或复印件。普惠制原产地证书申请重发证书,尚须在指定的报纸上声明原证书作废,方可重新签发。对于上述情况,签证机构审核有关材料后,将酌情处理。

一般规定,普惠制原产地证书为一正二副,一般原产地证书为一正三副。签证机构只在正本签名、盖章。

二、缮制原产地证书的基本技能

【实训目的】

通过本项目实训,应掌握的基本技能如下。

①熟悉并看懂相关信用证(合同)中有关原产地证书的条款。

②掌握一般原产地证书的缮制规范。

③掌握普惠制原产地证书的缮制规范。

【操作前准备】

进行本项任务的实训前,应准备的内容如下。

①出口商缮制妥的商业发票、装箱单。

②查明出口货物的海关编码。

③空白原产地证申请书。

④空白原产地证书。

【操作程序】

①仔细阅读信用证或合同对原产地证书的要求及相关附加指示,要注意信用证特别要求加注的有关内容,如在原产地证书上是否要注明生产厂家的名称、地址、进口许可证号码及信用证证号等。

②根据信用证或合同要求认真缮制原产地证书的各个栏目内容,做到准确、完整。

③对照信用证或合同中的有关要求,检查是否做到单证(单同)相符,对照已缮制妥的商业发票、装箱单等结汇单据,检查是否做到单单相符。

【操作规范】

表8.1 普惠制原产地证书缮制规范

项目顺序号	填写内容	要点提示
证书号码 Reference number	证书号码	符合签证机构证书号码的编排规则
(1)出口商名称、地址和国家 Goods consigned from	出口商的详细地址,包括街道名、门牌号码等	中国地名的英文译音应采用汉语拼音
(2)收货人名称、地址和国家 Goods consigned to	给惠国的最终收货人名称和详细地址	如果信用证未明确最终收货人,可以填写商业发票的抬头人,但不可填写中间商的名称
(3)所知航运方式和航线 Means of transport and route	具体的装货港、卸货港名称及运输方式,若经转运,还应注明转运地	对输往内陆给惠国的商品,如瑞士、奥地利,由于这些国家没有港口,因此如系海运,都须经第三国,再转运至该国,在填写时应注明转运地
(4)供官方使用 For official use	正常情况下留空	特殊情况,签证当局在此栏加注
(5)商品项目号 Item number	按不同品种分列	单项商品,此栏填"1",如果有两项以上,按顺序填写1、2、3……
(6)唛头及包装号 Marks and numbers of packages	与发票相同	①填写具体唛头,不可笼统填写成"As per Invoice No. ×××" ②没有唛头,应填写"NO MARK"(N/M),不能留空
(7)包装件数、包装种类及商品的名称 Number and kind of packages, description of goods	按发票填写,包括商品的件数和货物描述,并应加结束符	①包装件数必须用大小写同时表示 ②商品名称要填写具体,可以用统称,但不能过于笼统 ③如货物为散装,在商品名称后加注"In Bulk"字样 ④信用证有关产地证的特殊要求可以在此加列 ⑤不要遗落结束符(*　*　*),以防加添内容

续表

项目顺序号	填写内容	要点提示
(8)原产地标准 Origin criterion	如不含任何进口成分,此栏填写"P"	本栏是国外海关审核的核心项目。对含有进口成分的商品,应按照正本原产地证书背面的标准分不同情况填写
(9)毛重和其他数量 Gross weight or other quantity	商品的正常计量单位	以重量计算的填毛重,只有净重的,填净重即可,但要标上 N. W. (NET WEIGHT),以公斤为单位
(10)发票的日期和号码 Number and date of invoice	此笔业务的商业发票号码及日期	此栏不得留空,发票的日期和号码与申请签证时随附发票的发票号一致,为避免对月份、日期的误解,月份一律用英文表示(可用缩写)
(11)签证当局的证明 Certification	填写 CIQ 签证地点、日期。CIQ 签证人经审核后在此栏(正本)亲笔签名并盖签证印章	本栏日期不得早于发票日期(第 10 栏)和申报日期(第 12 栏)
(12)出口商声明 Declaration by the exporter	在生产国横线上填写"中国"(China)。进口国横线上填最终进口国,进口国必须与第 2 栏目的国别一致	申请单位应授权专人在此栏手签,标明申报地点、日期,并加盖申报单位中英文印章,手签人手迹必须在 CIQ 注册备案。此栏日期不得早于发票日期(第 10 栏)(最早是同日),盖章时应避免覆盖进口国名称和手签人姓名

【普惠制原产地证书样例】

1. Goods consigned from (Exporter's business name, address, country)
TIFERT TRADING CO., LTD.
NO. 86, ZHUJIANG ROAD, TIANJIN, CHINA

Reference No. 08A3－0808

GENERALIZED SYSTEM OF PREFERENCES
CERTIFICATE OF ORIGIN
(Combined declaration and certificate) FORM A

2. Goods consigned to (Consignee's name, address, country)
MARUBENI CORP.
5－7, HOMMACHI, 2－CHOME, CHUO-KU, OSAKA, JAPAN

Issued in THE PEOPLE'S REPUBLIC OF CHINA
(country)
See Notes overleaf

3. Means of transport and route (as far as known)
SHIPMENT FROM TIANJIN TO TOKYO BY SEA

4. For official use

5. Item number	6. Marks and numbers of packages	7. Number and kind of packages, description of goods	8. Origin criterion (see Notes overleaf)	9. Gross weight or other quantity	10. Number and date of invoices
1	MARUBENI S/C 08TF0858 TOKYO CTN 1－250	250(TWO HUNDRED AND FIFITY) CARTONS OF GIRL JACKET L/C NO. A－08－0058 NAME AND ADDRESS OF MANUFACTURER: NO. 1 GARMENT FACTORY 88, HONG XING ROAD, TIANJIN, CHINA * * * *	"P"	5000PCS	INV NO. 123456 APR. 15, 2008

11. Certification
It is hereby certified, on the basis of control carried out, that the declaration by the exporter is correct.

TIANJIN APR. 15, 2008

Place and date, signature and stamp of certifying authority

12. Declaration by the exporter
The undersigned hereby declares that the above details and statements are correct, that all the goods were

produced in CHINA
(country)

and that they comply with the origin requirements specified for those goods in the Generalized System of Preferences for goods exported to

JAPAN

TIANJIN APR. 15, 2008

Place and date, signature and stamp of authorized signatory

样例 8.1 普惠制原产地证书

表 8.2 一般原产地证书缮制规范

项目顺序号	填写内容	要点提示
证书号码 Certificate No.	证书号码	应符合签证机构证书号码的编排规则
(1)出口方 Exporter	此栏填写出口商的详细地址,包括街道名、门牌号码等	中国地名的英文译音应采用汉语拼音
(2)收货方 Consignee	最终收货人名称、地址和国家(地区)名。通常是出口合同中的买方或信用证上规定的提单通知人	如信用证规定所有单证收货人一栏留空,在这种情况下,此栏应加注"To Whom It May Concern"或"To Order",但此栏不得留空
(3)所知航运方式和航线 Means of transport and route	具体的装货港、卸货港名称及运输方式,若经转运,还应注明转运地	对输往内陆给惠国(如瑞士、奥地利)的商品,由于这些国家没有港口,因此如系海运,都须经第三国,再转运至该国,在填写时应注明转运地
(4)目的地国家(地区) Country/region of destination	目的地国家(地区)的名称	一般应与最终收货人的国别相一致,不能填写中间商国家名称
(5)签证机构用栏 For certifying authority use only	正常情况下证书申领单位应将此栏留空	由签证机构在签发后发证、补发证书或加注其他声明时使用
(6)运输标志 Marks and numbers	与发票相同	不可简单填写"按照发票"(As Per Invoice No ×××)或者"按照提单"(As Per B/L No ×××)。货物如无唛头,应填写"NO MARK"(N/M)字样,此栏不得空留
(7)包装数量及种类、商品描述 Number and kind of packages, description of goods	按发票填写,包括商品的件数和货物描述,并应加结束符	①包装件数必须用大小写同时表示 ②商品名称要填写具体,可以用统称,但不能过于笼统 ③如货物为散装,在商品名称后加注"In Bulk"字样 ④信用证有关产地证的特殊要求可以在此加列 ⑤不要遗落结束符(* * *),以防加添内容
(8)商品编码 H.S. Code	此笔业务的商品的海关编码,应与报关单一致	一般填写前4位,此栏不得空留
(9)数量 Quantity	出口商品的数量及计量单位	如果只有毛重时,则需填"G.W."
(10)发票号码及日期 Number and date of invoice	此笔业务的商业发票号码及日期	此栏不得留空,发票的日期和号码与申请签证时随附发票的发票号一致,为避免对月份、日期的误解,月份一律用英文表示(可用缩写)
(11)出口方声明 Declaration by the exporter	出口商所在地点及申报日期,由已在签证机构注册的人员签名并加盖中英文的印章	此栏日期不得早于发票日期(第10栏)(最早是同日),盖章时应避免覆盖进口国名称和手签人姓名
(12)由签证机构签字、盖章 Certification	签证地点、日期,签证机构签证人经审核后在此栏(正本)签名,并盖签证印章	本栏日期不得早于发票日期(第10栏)和申报日期(第11栏)

【一般原产地证书样例】

ORIGINAL

1. Exporter
TIFERT TRADING CO., LTD.
NO. 86, ZHUJIANG ROAD, TIANJIN, CHINA

Certificate No. 081210

CERTIFICATE OF ORIGIN OF
THE PEOPLE'S REPUBLIC OF CHINA

2. Consignee
MARUBENI CORP.
5 - 7, HOMMACHI, 2 - CHOME, CHUO-KU, OSAKA, JAPAN

3. Means of transport and route
SHIPMENT FROM TIANJIN TO TOKYO BY SEA

4. Country / region of destination
JAPAN

5. For certifying authority use only

6. Marks and numbers	7. Number and kind of packages, description of goods	8. H. S. Code	9. Quantity	10. Number and date of invoices
MARUBENI S/C 08TF0858 TOKYO CTN 1 - 250	250(TWO HUNDRED AND FIFITY) CARTONS OF GIRL JA KCET L/C NO. A - 08 - 0058 NAME AND ADDRESS OF MANUFACTURER: NO. 1 GARMENT FACTORY 88, HONG XING ROAD, TIANJIN, CHINA * * * *	6204	5000PCS	INVOICE NO. 123456 APR. 15, 2008

11. Declaration by the exporter

The undersigned hereby declares that the above details and statements are correct, that all the goods were produced in China and that they comply with the Rules of Origin of the People's Republic of China.

TIFERT TRADING CO., LTD.
泰佛贸易有限公司
*

王宏

TIANJIN APR. 15, 2008

Place and date, signature and stamp of authorized signatory

12. Certification

It is hereby certified that the declaration by the exporter is correct.

中国国际贸易促进委员会
天津分会

陈凯

TIANJIN APR. 15, 2008

Place and date, signature and stamp of certifying authority

样例8.2 一般原产地证书

【操作注意事项】

①如果信用证要求原产地证书做成第三方单据，原产地证书的出口商不能填写为合同中卖方或信用证的受益人，而应该填写为指明的一方。

②如果合同是通过中间商达成的，货物直运最终用户所在国，原产地证书的收货人应填写最终收货人的名称和地址。出于商业秘密中间商可能不会告知出口商真正的最终买主，这种情况下，可以填写成"To whom it may concern"或"To order"，而不能填写成中间商。

③唛头一定要严格参照发票或提单填写，并且要与发票或提单中的唛头保持一致，不能简单地填写成"As per invoice No. ××"、"As per B/L No. ××"或留空。

④目的地国家、地区应该填写为最终用户所在国或所在地区名称，不能填写中间商所在国或所在地区名称。

⑤货物名称应详尽到在海关税则中能找到对应的 H. S. Code，而不能太笼统。但无须填写商品的牌号、等级等内容。

⑥包装单位件数的大小写应该相符，最后不要漏写"ONLY"字样。

⑦信用证要求在原产地证书中加注一些内容，如信用证证号、许可证证号、制造商或生产商的名称和地址等时，应严格按要求填写，一般加注在货物描述后即可。

⑧货物描述最后不要漏打"* * *"以示结束。

⑨发票日期的月份应该用英文的缩写表示，不要用六位阿拉伯数字填写以免产生歧义。

⑩发票号应与申请原产地证书一起提供的发票相符，使签证机关能够看出二者之间的关联。

⑪出口货物的海关编码应能准确反映实际出运的货物。

⑫货物中如果含有进口成分（百分比），在原产地标准中应填写正确的原产地标准代码，不能笼统填写成"P"，申领原产地证书同时应提交进口成分明细表。

⑬注意原产地证书上几个日期的逻辑关系：申领日期不能早于发票日期，可略晚，最早可以与发票日期同一天；签发日期不能早于申领日期，可略晚，最早可以与申领日期相同，同时注意签发日期也不能晚于装运日期，否则被视为后发证。

⑭证书内容过多乃至有附页的情况下，附页要由签证机构签字盖章，同时也要盖骑缝章，以示其是证书的组成部分。

三、缮制原产地证书的操作训练

【翻译语句】

①C/O　　②G. S. P.

③CCPIT　　④Chamber of Commerce

⑤Origin Criterion ⑥H. S. Code

⑦Certificate of Processing ⑧Certificate of Re-Export

⑨item number ⑩for official use

⑪Certificate of Origin G. S. P. Form A one original and one copy, evidencing China as origin of goods.

⑫Certificate of China Origin issued by a relevant authority.

⑬Certificate of Origin in two copies indicating that goods are of Chinese Origin issued by Chamber of Commerce.

⑭Certificate of Origin issued by the Chamber of Commerce certifying that goods are of Chinese Origin in one original and one copy. The original legalized by the U. A. E. Representation in China.

⑮Certificate of Origin should state that the goods do not contain any component of an Israel Origin whatever the proportion of such component. The exporter or supplier has no direct or indirect connection whatsoever with Israel.

【动脑思考】

①泰佛贸易公司在完成一笔出口业务时,须在香港进行转口,转口商是香港大明公司(HongKong Daming Co., Ltd.)。请问,单证员在缮制一般原产地证书的出口商一栏时,应如何填写?

②泰佛贸易公司在一笔出口贸易中收到国外客户的信用证,证中规定"所有单证收货人一栏留空"。请问,业务员在缮制一般原产地证书的收货方一栏时应如何填写?

③泰佛贸易公司的业务员在缮制普惠制原产地证书时将运输标志一栏内填写"As Per Invoice No. 123"请问这样做是否可行?如填写"As Per B/L No. 123"是否可行?

④泰佛贸易公司的制单员在缮制一笔出口业务的普惠制产地证时出现了错误,遂在原证书上进行修改,并加盖了更正章,请问这样处理是否可行?

⑤泰佛贸易公司向瑞士出口一批商品,从天津出运。由于瑞士属于内陆国家,因此须经香港转船后运至德国,再运往瑞士。请问,单证员在填制普惠制原产地证书的所知航运方式和航线一栏时应如何填写?

【动手操练】

实训操作一

泰佛贸易公司与英国 BIG BEN 公司经过友好洽商就出口沙滩阳伞达成一份出口合同,数量 500 件,CIF LONDON,付款方式即期信用证(L/C at sight)。作为单证员,请你根据下列信息利用空白一般原产地证书(见样例 8.3),填制一般原产地证书。

信用证与提单相关的主要条款如下。

59: BENEFICIARY: TIFERT TRADING CO., LTD.
NO. 86, ZHUJIANG ROAD, TIANJIN, CHINA

50: APPLICANT: BIG BEN CORP
88, GREAT TOWER BUILDING, LONDON, U. K.

44E: PORT OF LOADING TIANJIN

44F: PORT OF DISCHARGE LONDON

44C: LATEST DATE OF SHIPMENT 080531

45A: DESCRIPTION OF GOODS/SERVICE

BEACH UMBRELLA ART NO. B68 200PCS USD10.00/PC
ART NO. B94 300PCS USD15.00/PC
CIF LONDON
PACKING IN CARTONS OF 10PCS EACH

SHIPPING MARKS: BB CORP
S/C NO. HT222
LONDONG
NO. 1 – UP

46A: DOCUMENTS REQUIRED

+CERTIFICATE OF ORIGIN ISSUED BY THE CHAMBER OF COMMERCE CERTIFYING THAT GOODS ARE OF CHINESE ORIGIN IN ONE ORIGINAL AND ONE COPY

补充信息如下。

发票号码: 45678

发票日期: 2008 年 5 月 5 日

毛重: 1000KGS

H. S. 编码: 6601

申请日期: 2008 列年 5 月 15 日

一般原产地证书编号:08EA7894

ORIGINAL

<table>
<tr><td>1. Exporter</td><td rowspan="2">Certificate No.

CERTIFICATE OF ORIGIN OF
THE PEOPLE'S REPUBLIC OF CHINA</td></tr>
<tr><td>2. Consignee</td></tr>
<tr><td>3. Means of transport and route</td><td rowspan="2">5. For certifying authority use only</td></tr>
<tr><td>4. Country / region of destination</td></tr>
</table>

6. Marks and numbers	7. Number and kind of packages, description of goods	8. H. S. Code	9. Quantity	10. Number and date of invoices

11. Declaration by the exporter	12. Certification
The undersigned hereby declares that the above details and statements are correct, that all the goods were produced in China and that they comply with the Rules of Origin of the People's Republic of China.	It is hereby certified that the declaration by the exporter is correct.
-- Place and date, signature and stamp of authorized signatory	-- Place and date, signature and stamp of certifying authority

样例 8.3　空白一般原产地证书

实训操作二

信用证有关资料摘录如下。

SEQUENCE OF TOTAL	27：	1/1
FORM OF DOCUMENTARY CREDIT	40A：	IRREVOCABLE
APPLICABLE RULES	40E：	UCP LATEST VERSION
DOCUMENTARY CREDIT NUMBE	20：	G/FO－7752807
DATE OF ISSUE：	31C：	080223
DATE AND PLACE OF EXPIRY	31D：	080610 TIANJIN CHINA
APPLICANT	50：	TOSHU CORPORATION OSALM 12－36，KYUTARO － MACHI 4 － CHOME CHUO － KU，OSAKA 561 － 8177 JAPAN
BENEFICIARY	59：	TIFERT TRADING CO.，LTD 86 ZHUJIANG ROAD，TIANJIN CHINA
CURRENCY CODE，AMOUNT	32B：	USD201780.00
AVAILABLE WITH ... BY ...	41D：	ANY BANK BY NEGOTIATION
PORT OF LOADING	44E：	TIANJIN
PORT OF DISCHARGE	44F：	YOKOHAMA
LATEST DATE OF SHIPMENT	44C：	080531
DESCRPT OF GOODS/SERVICES	45A：	CIF YOKOHAMA

MAN'S SHIRT(CONTRACT NO.08JA7031KL)

ST/NO.	Q'TY	UNIT PRICE
71 － 800	67200PCS	USD 1.43/PC
71 － 801	48000PCS	USD 1.46/PC
71 － 802	27600PCS	USD 1.29/PC

DOCUMENTS REQUIRED 46A：

+ COMMERCIAL INVOICE IN QUINTUPLICATE
+ PACKING LIST IN 3 COPIES
+ G S P CERTIFICATE OF ORIGIN FORM A IN 3 COPIES

补充信息资料如下。

①SHIPPING MARKS：

TOSHU
06JA7031KL
YOKOHAMA
MADE IN CHINA

②INVOICE NO. 08FZ008 DATED MAY20，2008

③PACKED IN CARTONS OF 50 PIECES EACH

作为泰佛贸易公司的单证员，请你根据以上信用证的摘录信息及补充相关信息，利用空白普惠制原产地证书(见样例8.4)填写一张普惠制原产地证书。

1. Goods consigned from (Exporter's business name, address, country)

Reference No.

GENERALIZED SYSTEM OF PREFERENCES

CERTIFICATE OF ORIGN

(Combined declaration and certificate) FORM A

2. Goods consigned to (Consignee's name, address, country)

Issued in ------------------------------

(country)

See Notes overleaf

3. Means of transport and route (as far as known)

4. For cofficial use

5. Item numbers	6. Marks and numbers of packages	7. Number and kind of packages, description of goods	8. Origin criterion (see Notes overleaf)	9. Gross weight or other quantity	10. Number and date of invoices

11. Certification

It is hereby certified, on the basis of control carried out, that the declaration by the exporter is correct.

Place and date, signature and stamp of authorized signatory

12. Declaration by the exporter

The undersigned hereby declares that the above details and statements are correct, that all the goods were

produced in ------------------------------

(country)

and that they comply with the origin requirements specified for those goods in the Generalized System of Preferences for goods exported to

----

Place and date, signature and stamp of certifying authority

样例8.4 空白普惠制原产地证书

任务九 缮制海运提单

任务背景

王芳小姐在负责女童夹克衫的进料加工业务过程中，货物备齐后，先后又进行了报检报验和申领原产地证书等工作。接下来要与船公司或货代公司办理租船订舱手续，以便在信用证规定的交货期内，如期履行卖方的交货义务。

王芳小姐按照部经理的指示与天津友通国际货运公司租妥了一个20尺货柜的舱位，随后王芳小姐就要着手缮制海运提单。

【背景分析】

海运提单是国际贸易中最重要的单据。在出口业务中，通常出口商以交单代替交货，进口商见单付款，之所以这样是因为提单是物权凭证，提单就代表货物，谁持有提单，谁就拥有提单项下的货物。为了能够完整、准确地缮制海运提单，王芳小姐应该掌握和具备如下知识、技能及素质。

知识目标

①了解提单的概念、种类及作用。

②看懂信用证中的提单条款。

技能目标

①准确翻译信用证中的提单条款及与提单相关条款。

②能够独立、正确缮制海运提单。

素质目标

①养成精打细算的工作作风，能节省的费用尽量节省。

②根据产品的特性，正确选择运输航线及货柜的种类，合理装柜减少不必要的亏舱。

一、缮制海运提单的基础知识

【海运提单的概念】

海运提单（Ocean Bill of Lading），简称提单，是指由船长或船公司或其代理人签发的，证明已收到特定货物，允诺将货物运到指定目的港并交付给收货人的凭证。海运提单也是收货人在目的港据以向船公司或其代理人提取货物的凭证。

【海运提单的种类】

海运提单可以从不同角度分类，在国际贸易中，其主要包括如下种类。

1. 按照签发提单时货物是否装船完毕分类

(1)已装船提单(Shipped or On Board B/L)

已装船提单是货物已经装在船上，由承运人签发的提单。这种提单使用最广泛。

(2)备运提单(Received for Shipment B/L)

备运提单又称“收讫待运提单”，是承运人已经收到待运的货物，但尚未装船时签发的提单，提单上有“收到备运……”或类似字句。此种提单于货物装船后可以加签“业已装船”或“已装某船”字样，从而形成已装船提单，但一般要求证明装船日期并签署。在国际贸易中，备运提单通常不能结汇。

2. 按照提单有无不良批注分类

(1)清洁提单(Clean B/L)

清洁提单是没有承运人对货物的表面状况或其他方面加注任何不良批注的提单。

(2)不清洁提单(Unclean or Foul B/L)

不清洁提单是承运人对货物表面状况或其他方面加注不良批注的提单，如包装破损等，银行拒绝接受不清洁提单。

3. 按照提单收货人抬头不同分类

(1)记名提单(Straight B/L)

记名提单是指提单的收货人栏内直接写明收货人名称的提单。记名提单只能由指定的收货人提货，不能流通转让。

(2)不记名提单(Bearer B/L)

不记名提单是指在提单的收货人栏内不填写收货人具体名称而填写“持有人(Bearer)”，任何人持有提单均可提货。该提单仅凭交付就可转让，流通性强，但风险较大，因为一旦提单遗失或被盗，货物容易被他人提走而引起纠纷，所以很少使用。

(3)指示提单(Order B/L)

指示提单是在提单收货人栏内注明“凭指定(To Order)”或“凭托运人指定(To order of shipper)”等字样的提单。指示提单可以通过背书的办法转让给他人。背书(Endorsement)有如下两种。

①空白背书。提单背书人(提单转让人)在提单背面签章，而不注明被背书人(提单受让人)名称。

②记名背书。背书人(提单转让人)在转让提单时除了在提单背面签章，还要注明被背书人(提单受让人)名称。

指示提单既可流通转让又相对安全，在国际贸易中使用较为广泛。目前我国出口贸易中，通常采用的是凭指定空白背书提单，俗称“空白抬头，空白背书提单”。

4. 按照运输方式不同分类

(1)直达提单(Direct B/L)

由承运人签发的由同一船只将货物由启运港直接运达目的港而不在其他中转港口转运的提单称为直达提单。

直达提单上不得有“转船”字样或“在某某港转船”字样,但如果提单条款内印有承运人有权转船的“自由转船条款”而无转船批注时,此提单被视为直达提单。

(2)转船提单(Transshipment B/L)

从启运港装运的船只不能将货物直接运到提单指定的目的港,而需要在中转港改换其他船只将货物续运至提单指定的目的港,在这种情况下签发的提单称转船提单。

(3)联运提单(Through B/L)

联运提单也称为全程提单。它与转船提单区别不大,但联运提单不只限于转船,还可在中途换装其他运输工具。联运提单是指经过海运和其他运输方式联合运输时由第一承运人在货物启运地签发的运往目的地的提单,并由第一承运人收取全程运费。对货物的风险,联运提单采取分段负责制,即承运人的责任仅限于其本身所承担的那一段运输。

5. 按照提单的效力分类

(1)正本提单(Original B/L)

正本提单是指有承运人、船长或代理人签名盖章并注明签发日期的提单。正本提单必须注明“正本(Original)”字样,正本提单一般一式两份或三份,凭其中任何一份提货后,其余各份均告作废。根据《UCP600》的规定,银行接受仅有一份的正本提单,如签发一份以上,应包括全套正本提单。

(2)副本提单(Copy B/L)

副本提单是没有承运人、船长以及代理人签名盖章的提单,副本提单仅供参考使用。

6. 其他种类提单

(1)过期提单(Stale B/L)

过期提单是指货已到而提单尚未到或错过交单日期提交的提单。前者在近洋航行中很容易出现,合同中一般注有“过期提单可以接受字样”,货到目的港,进口商依据“电放指令”提货;后者是指出口商超过提单日 21 天后提交的提单,根据《UCP600》的规定,除非另有规定,银行将拒绝接受此类提单。

(2)舱面提单(On Deck B/L)

舱面提单是承运人将货物装在甲板上所签发的提单,又称“甲板货提单”,此类提单上通常注明“装甲板(On Deck)”字样。货物装在甲板上容易出现货损,而根据《海牙规则》,承运人对甲板货不负责,所以进口商一般不愿意接受此类提单。根据《UCP600》的规定,除非另有规定,银行将拒绝接受此类提单。

(3)倒签提单(Anti-dated B/L)

倒签提单是指承运人签发提单时倒填日期的提单。提单签发日期应为货物装船完毕的日期,但如果由于各种原因,货物无法在合同或信用证规定的装运期内装船完毕,又来不及修改信用证,托运人会要求承运人倒填日期以顺利结汇。在托运人出具保函的情况下,承运人可能会出具此种提单。

(4)预借提单(Advanced B/L)

货物在装船前或装船完毕前,信用证结汇日期已到,托运人向承运人预先借用的提单为预借提单。预借提单比倒签提单风险更大,因为货物在装船前可能由于各种原因出现灭失、损坏或退关情况,而提单已经签发,这在法律上构成侵权。

倒签提单和预借提单都是违法的,如果进口商产生怀疑,很容易从航海日志中发现问题,因此承运人和托运人都冒很大风险。

【海运提单的性质和作用】

海运提单性质和作用主要表现在以下三个方面。

1. 货物收据(Receipt of the Goods)

海运提单是承运人或其代理人应托运人的要求所签发的货物收据。证明承运人已如数收到提单上所列货物。

2. 货物所有权凭证(Document of Title)

海运提单在法律上具有物权证书的作用。在载货船舶到达目的港交货之前,可进行转让,也可向银行办理抵押贷款,提单持有人可凭单提货。

3. 运输契约的证明(Evidence of the Contract of Carriage)

海运提单是承运人与托运人之间订立的运输契约的证明。明确了双方之间的权利、责任与豁免。

【海运提单的签发流程图】

海运提单签发流程如图 9.1 所示。

①出口商向船公司或货代公司提交订舱单(订舱委托书),英文为 Booking Note,简写 B/N,连同发票和装箱单办理租船订舱手续。

②船公司或货代公司确认舱位后签发配舱回单(装货单),英文为 Shipping Order,简写 S/O,给出口商。

③出口商自己或委托报关行凭下货纸向海关办理报关手续。

④海关在下货纸上盖"验讫章"放行货物。

⑤凭盖有海关"验讫章"的下货纸将货物装到指定船上。

⑥船长或大副收妥货物后签发大副收据(Mate's Receipt,简写为 M/R)给出口商。

⑦出口商提交大副收据给承运人用以换取提单。

⑧承运人签发提单给出口商。

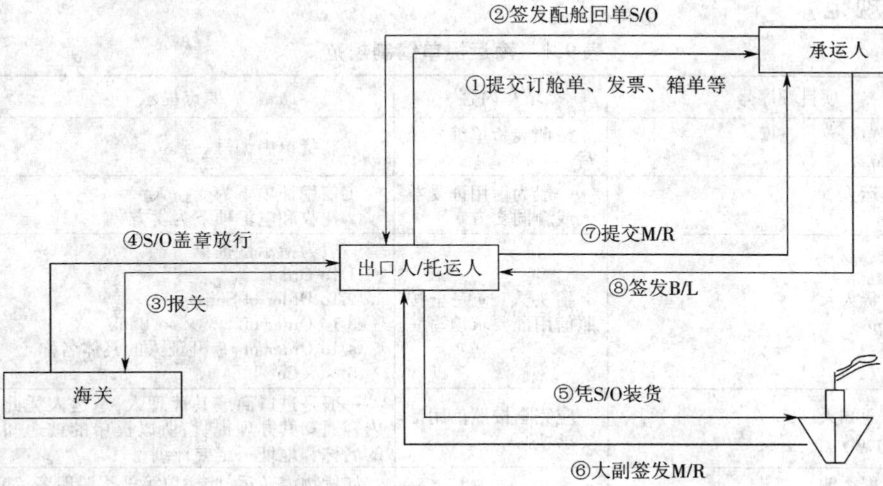

图9.1　海运提单签发流程图

二、缮制海运提单的基本技能

【实训目的】

通过本项目实训,应掌握的基本技能如下。

①熟悉并看懂相关信用证(合同)中有关提单的条款。

②掌握海运提单缮制的规范和技巧。

③学会独立缮制海运提单。

【操作前准备】

进行本项任务的实训前,应准备的内容如下。

①出口商提供的商业发票、装箱单。

②出口商提供的订舱委托书(Booking Note)。

③货代或船公司提供的配舱回单(Shipping Order)。

④所配舱位船公司或货代公司空白的提单。

【操作程序】

①浏览信用证对提单的要求及相关附加指示。

②仔细查看船公司或货代公司签发的下货纸。

③按照信用证、合同条款和下货纸认真填写提单的各个栏目,做到完整、准确。

④检查提单各个栏目填写是否与已缮制妥的发票、装箱单及原产地证书等结汇单据相符。

【操作规范】

表 9.1　海运提单缮制规范

项目顺序号	填写内容	要点提示
(1)提单号 B/L No.	按照装货单编号填写	与装货单中编号一致
(2)托运人 Shipper	一般为信用证受益人或合同卖方	①信用证项下为受益人 ②托收和电汇项下为卖方
(3)收货人 Consignee	抬头人,应完全按照信用证要求填写	一般为指示性提单 ①To Order ②To Order of Shipper ③To Order of ××× Bank ④To Order of + 开证人的具体名称 ⑤××Co, ltd.
(4)被通知人 Notify party	应完全按照信用证要求填写	一般是进口商或其代理人,承运人凭此栏内容通知其办理提货,所以提单的被通知人的名称和地址一定要详细
(5)前程运输 Pre-carriage by	前程运输方式	如货物需转运,此栏填第一程船船名;如不需转运,此栏留空
(6)装运港 Port of loading	装运港名称	按照信用证规定填写实际装运货物的港口
(7)船名 Vessel name	应填写货物所装船舶的船名及航次	如货物需转运,填写第二程船船名;如不需转运,填第一程船船名
(8)转运港 Port of transshipment	转运港名称	如不需转运,此栏留空
(9)卸货港 Port of discharge	货物实际卸下的港口名称	如有重名,在港口后面一定要加注国别
(10)最终目的地 Final destination	填最终目的地名称	如最终目的地就是目的港,此栏可留空
(11)集装箱号、铅封号及唛头 Container seal No. or marks & Nos.	此笔业务的集装箱号、铅封号及唛头	唛头应与商业发票、箱单上的一致
(12)包装的种类和数量 Number and kind of package	按照实际包装具体情况填写	总件数除小写外,还要用文字大写叙述,且大小写应一致
(13)货物名称 Description of goods	按照信用证规定填写,可用统称	要与其他单据如发票等保持一致
(14)毛重 Gross weight	填写总毛重	除非信用证另有规定,一般重量以公斤表示,保留两位小数
(15)尺码 Measurement	填写总尺码	除非信用证另有规定,一般体积以立方米表示,保留三位小数
(16)运费条款	按照信用证要求加注运费条款	应注意与使用的贸易术语一致
(17)装船批注的日期 On board notation	货物的装船完毕日期	此栏可与 18 栏日期相同,也可能略晚于提单的签发日期,但不能晚于信用证规定的最迟装运期
(18)提单签发地点及日期 Place and date of issue	提单的签发地点和签发日期	不能晚于信用证规定的最迟装运期
(19)正本提单签发份数 No. of original B/L	应按照信用证的规定提供要求的份数	此栏必须用英文大写数字表示
(20)承运人签章 Signed for the carrier	承运人或其代理人的签字	常见签署方式: ①承运人或其代理人签署 ②船长或其代理人签署

【海运提单样例】

<table>
<tr><td colspan="2">Shipper (2)
TIFERT TRADING CO. , LTD.
NO. 86, ZHUJIANG ROAD, TIANJIN, CHINA</td><td colspan="3" rowspan="6">B/L No. SINO081216 (1)
SINOTRANS
中国外运天津公司
SINOTRANS TIANJIN COMPANY
OCEAN BILL OF LADING
Shipped on board in apparent good order and condition (unless otherwise indicated) the goods or packages specified herein and to be discharged at the mentioned port of discharge or as near thereto as the vessel may safely get and be always afloat.
The weight, measure, marks and numbers, quality, contents and value, being particulars furnished by the Shipper, are not checked by the Carrier on loading.
The shipper, consignee and the Holder of this Bill of Lading hereby expressly accept and agree to all printed, written or stamped provisions, exceptions and conditions of this Bill of Lading, including those on the back hereof.
In witness whereof the number of original Bills of Lading stated below have been signed, one of which being accomplished the other(s) to be void.</td></tr>
<tr><td colspan="2">Consignee or order (3)
TO ORDER</td></tr>
<tr><td colspan="2">Notify address (4)
MARUBENI CORP.
5 – 7, HOMMACHI, 2 – CHOME, CHUO-KU, OSAKA, JAPAN
TEL NO. 8745 9986</td></tr>
<tr><td>Pre-carriage by (5)</td><td>Port of loading (6)
TIANJIN, CHINA</td></tr>
<tr><td>Vessel (7)
SHUNFENG V. 0827</td><td>Port of transshipment (8)</td></tr>
<tr><td>Port of discharge (9)
TOKYO, JAPAN</td><td>Final destination (10)</td></tr>
<tr><td>Container seal No. or marks and Nos. (11)</td><td>Number and kind of package (12)</td><td>Description of goods (13)</td><td>Gross weight (kgs.) (14)</td><td>Measurement (m^3) (15)</td></tr>
<tr><td>MARUBENI
S/C 08TF0858
TOKYO
CTN 1 – 250</td><td>250 CARTONS

SAY TWO HUNDRED AND
FIFTY CARTONS ONLY</td><td>GIRL JAKET

PREPAID FREIGHT
(16)</td><td>24909. 00KGS</td><td>24. 548CBM

ON BOARD DATE:
APR. 30, 2008
(17)</td></tr>
<tr><td colspan="3">Freight and charges</td><td colspan="2">REGARDING TRANSHIPMENT
INFORMATION PLEASE CONTACT</td></tr>
<tr><td rowspan="2">Ex. rate</td><td>Prepaid at</td><td>Freight payable at</td><td colspan="2">Place and date of issue (18)
TIANJIN, APR. 30, 2008</td></tr>
<tr><td>Total prepaid</td><td>Number of original Bs/L (19)
THREE</td><td colspan="2">Signed for or on behalf of the Carrier (20)
SINOTRANS TIANJIN COMPANY
张涛</td></tr>
</table>

样例9.1 海运提单

【操作注意事项】

①提单中的货物描述可只填写商品名称,无须填写规格或牌号等详情。如果涉及的商品较多,则可只填写商品的统称,但不得与信用证中货物的描述相抵触。

②提单上最好不要加注关于包装状况的描述,如“新袋”(New Bag)、旧箱(Old Carton)等词语。

③提单上的修正和变更必须经过证实。证实从形式上讲必须是由承运人、船长或其代理人所为(该代理人可以与出具或签署提单的代理人不同),只要表明其作为承运人或船长的代理人身份即可。

④对于正本提单上可能已做的任何修正或变更,无须在不可转让副本提单上做任何签字或证实。

⑤如果信用证要求提单注明运费已付或到目的港支付,则提单必须有相应标注。即使信用证对此未做具体规定,也应根据所采用的贸易术语,在运费支付栏填写“Freight to Collect”或“Freight Prepaid”。

三、缮制海运提单的操作训练

【翻译语句】

①shipped B/L ②received B/L

③consignee ④shipper

⑤notify party ⑥straight B/L

⑦order B/L ⑧freight prepaid

⑨freight to collect ⑩blank endorsed

⑪Full set of clean shipped on board bill(s) of lading marked “freight prepaid” made out to order of shipper endorsed to ××× bank, notifying buyers.

⑫Full set of clean on board marine bills of lading, made out to order of ABC company, Rotterdam, Netherlands, marked freight prepaid notify applicant.

⑬Full set of clean on board ocean bills of lading to order of ABC bank marked freight prepaid plus two non-negotiable copies notify applicant.

⑭Full set of clean shipped on board marine bill of lading, made out to our order, marked freight prepaid, notify opener, indicating LC No. and S/C No., received for shipment B/L not acceptable.

⑮Full set of not less than two clean on board marine bills of lading marked freight prepaid and made out to order and endorsed to us showing Blue Bird Trading Company as notifying party. Short form bills of lading are not acceptable. Bill of lading to state shipment has been effected in containers and container numbers.

【动脑思考】

①泰佛贸易公司在一笔出口贸易的提单中显示如下。

Shipper: ABC Co. Ltd.

Consignee: To Order

Notify Party: XYZ Co. Ltd.

请问:单证员在向银行交单时是否要做背书,如要做背书的话,第一背书人是谁?

②泰佛贸易公司在一笔出口贸易中收到国外进口商的信用证,证中规定如下。

Applicant: Nissho Iwia Corporation No. 12 Chome Mi Tokyo, Japan

Beneficiary: Tifert Trading Co., Ltd. No. 86 Zhujiang Road, Tianjin, China

Full set of clean on board marine bill of lading made out to order of shipper and blank endorsed and marked freight prepaid and notify applicant.

请问:单证员应如何填写提单中的托运人、收货人、通知人及运费支付方式?

③泰佛贸易公司在一笔出口贸易中收到国外进口商的信用证,证中规定如下。

Applicant: ABC Corporation No. 123 New Street New York, USA

Beneficiary: Tifert Trading Co., Ltd. No. 86 Zhujiang Road, Tianjin, China

Issuing Bank: Bank of China, New York Branch

Full set of clean on board B/L issued to our order, notifying applicant and marked freight prepaid and showing full name and address of the relative shipping agent in USA.

请问:单证员应如何填写提单中的托运人、收货人、通知人及运费支付方式?是否还有其他制单要求?

④泰佛贸易公司在一笔出口贸易中收到国外进口商的信用证,证中规定如下。

Applicant: ABC Corporation No. 123 New Street New York, USA

Beneficiary: Tifert Trading Co., Ltd. No. 86 Zhujiang Road, Tianjin, China

Issuing Bank: Bank of China, New York Branch

Full set clean on board ocean bill of lading, made out to order and blank endorsed, evidencing shipment from Tianjin to New York port not later than April 05 2008, marked freight prepaid and notify the applicant.

请问:单证员应如何填写提单中的托运人、收货人、通知人及运费支付方式?在交单结汇时提单应如何背书,由谁首次背书?提单的签发日期是否有限制?

⑤泰佛贸易公司在一笔出口贸易中收到国外进口商的信用证,证中规定如下。

Applicant: ABC Corporation No. 123 New Street New York, USA

Beneficiary: Tifert Trading Co., Ltd. No. 86 Zhujiang Road, Tianjin, China

Issuing Bank: Bank of China, New York Branch

Full set of clean shipped on board marine bill of lading, made out to our order, marked freight prepaid, notify opener, indicating LC No. and S/C No., received for shipment B/L not acceptable.

请问:单证员应如何填写提单中的发货人、收货人、通知人以及运费支付方式?是否还有其他制单要求?信用证对提单的种类是否有限制?

【动手操练】

实训操作一

泰佛贸易公司与英国 BIG BEN 公司经过友好洽商就出口沙滩阳伞达成一份出口合同,数量 500 件,CIF LONDON,付款方式即期信用证(L/C at sight)。随后泰佛贸易公司向中国外运天津公司订舱,提交订舱委托书。中国外运天津公司接受其订舱委托后,向泰佛公司出具了装货单。作为单证员,请你根据信用证有关条款、商业发票、装箱单及装货单中的信息,缮制海运提单(空白提单见样例 9.2)。

信用证中与提单相关的主要条款如下。

59: BENEFICIARY: TIFERT TRADING CO., LTD.
NO. 86, ZHUJIANG ROAD, TIANJIN, CHINA
50: APPLICANT: BIG BEN CORP.
88, GREAT TOWER BUILDING, LONDON, U.K.
44E: PORT OF LOADING TIANJIN
44F: PORT OF DISCHARGE LONDON
44C: LATEST DATE OF SHIPMENT: 080531
45A: DESCRIPTION OF GOODS/SERVICE
BEACH UMBRELLA ART NO. B68 200PCS USD10.00/PC
ART NO. B94 300PCS USD15.00/PC
CIF LONDON
PACKING IN CARTONS OF 10PCS EACH
SHIPPING MARKS: BB CORP.
S/C NO. HT222
LONDONG
NO. 1 - UP
46A: DOCUMENTS REQUIRED
+FULL SET CLEAN ON BOARD BILL OF LADING MADE OUT TO ORDER AND BLANK ECDORSED, MARKED FREIGHT PREPAID AND NOTIFY THE APPLICANT

发票、箱单和装货单中补充信息如下。

BL NO. : 08SBL050
装船日期 : MAY 20,2008
船名航次 : SHUNFENG V55
毛重 : 1000.00KGS
体积 : 15.00CBM

Shipper		B/L No.
Consignee or order		SINOTRANS 中国外运天津公司 SINOTRANS TIANJIN COMPANY OCEAN BILL OF LADING
Notify address		
Pre-carriage by	Port of loading	
Vessel	Port of transshipment	
Port of discharge	Final destination	

Container seal No. or marks and Nos.	Number and kind of package	Description of goods	Gross weight (kgs.)	Measurement (m^3)

Freight and charges			REGARDING TRANSHIPMENT INFORMATION PLEASE CONTACT
Ex. rate	Prepaid at	Freight payable at	Place and date of issue
	Total prepaid	Number of original Bs/L	Signed for or on behalf of the Carrier As Agent

样例9.2 空白提单

实训操作二

天津晚星贸易公司与印尼 SMART 公司经过友好洽商就出口工具达成一份出口合同,数量 100 000 件,CIF SEMARANG,付款方式为电汇加托收(T/T + D/P AT SIGHT)。随后天津晚星贸易公司向中国远洋运输公司订舱,提交订舱委托书。中国远洋运输公司接受其订舱委托后,向天津晚星贸易公司出具了装货单。作为单证员,请你根据销售合同有关条款(见样例 9.3)、商业发票、装箱单及装货单中的信息,缮制海运提单(空白提单见样例 9.4)。

销 售 合 同
SALES CONTRACT

编号 No.: 20081124　　日期 Date :MAY 16,2008

The sellers: TIANJIN EVENING STAR TRADING CO., LTD.

Add: NO. 18 ZHUJIANG ROAD, TIANJIN, CHINA　　Post code:300221

The buyers: SMART TRADING CO., LTD.

Add: 220 VTRA SABANG INDONESIA

Tel: 244 - 567896　　Fax:244 - 567898

兹确认售予你方下列货品,其成交条款如下:

We hereby confirm having sold to you the following goods on the terms and conditions as specified below:

(1)货物名称及规格 Name of commodity and specifications	(2)数量 Quantity	(3)单价 Unit price	(4)总值 Total amount
DOUBLE OPEN END SPANNER	CIF SABANG		
8 × 10 MM	60 000	USD0. 50	USD30000. 00
10 × 12 MM	40 000	USD0. 40	USD16000. 00
TOTAL:	100 000		USD46000. 00

(5)包装:

Packing: PACKED IN CARTONS OF 100 PCS EACH

(6)装运唛头:

Shipping mark: N/M

(7)装运期限:

Time of shipment: NOT LATER THAN MAY 10, 2008

(8)装运口岸:　　目的地:

Port of shipment: TIANJIN　　Destination: SABANG

(9)付款条件:

Payment terms: 30% T/T IN ADVANCE, THE OTHERS 70% D/P AT SIGHT.

(10)保险:卖方负责投保海运险按照 CIF 金额的 110% 投保一切险和战争险,如果发生索赔,在印尼用美元赔偿。

Insurance: The seller shall arrange marine insurance covering All Risks and War Risk for 110% of CIF value. Claim if any, payable in Indonesia, in currency of USD.

(11)凡以 cif 条件成交的业务,保额为发票价的 110%,投保险别以本销售合同中所开列的为限,买方如要求增加保额或保险范围应以装船前经售方同意,因此而增加的保险费由买方负责。

For transactions concluded on C. I. F basis, it is understood that the insurance amount will be for 110% of the invoice value against the risks specified in the sales contract, if additional insurance amount or coverage is required, the buyer must have the consent of the seller before shipment, and the additional premium is to be borne by the buyer.

(12)品质/数量异议:如买方提出索赔,凡属品质异议须于货到目的口岸之日起2个月内提出。凡属数量异议须于货到目的口岸之日起15天内提出,对所装货物所提任何异议属于保险公司、轮船公司及期货有关运输机构所负责者,售方不负任何责任。

Quality/Quantity discrepancy: In case of quality discrepancy, clam should be filed by the buyer within 2 months after the arrival of the goods at the port of destination while for quantity discrepancy claim should by filed by the buyer within 15 days after the arrival of the goods at the port of destination. It is understood that seller shall not be liable for any discrepancy of the goods shipped due to causes for which the insurance company, shipping company other transportation organization are liable.

(13)本合同内所述全部或部分商品,如因人力不可抗拒的原因,以致不能履约或延迟交货,售方概不负责。

The seller shall not be held liable for failure or delay in delivery of the entire lot or portion of the goods under this sales contract in consequence of any force maJeure incidents.

(14)需要的单据

Documents required:

+SIGNED COMMERCIAL INVOICE IN DUPLICATE

+PACKING LIST IN DUPLICATE

+INSURANCE POLICY/CERTIFICATE COVERING ALL RIAKS AND WAR RISK FOR 110% OF CIF VALUE. CLAIM, IF ANY, PAYABLE IN INDONESIA, IN CURRENCY OF USD

+FULL SET OF CLEAN ON BOARD BILL OF LADING IN TRIPLICATE. MADE OUT TO ORDER OF SHIPPER AND NOTIFY THE BUYER WITH FULL NAME AND ADDRESS MARKED FREIGHT PREPAID.

确认签署 Confirmed by

SMART TRADING CO., LTD.	TIANJIN EVENING STAR TRADING CO., LTD.
Bonnie	王宇
买方(The buyers)	卖方(The sellers)

样例9.3 销售合同

发票、箱单和装货单中补充的信息如下。

DOUBLE OPEN END SPANNER 1000CARTONS

SHIPPED IN ONE 20′ CONTAINER NO. CSU 820114

G. W. 2000KGS, MEAS. 20M3

提单号 : COSU200856

装船日期 : MAY 5, 2008

船名航次 : SHUNFENG V728

<table>
<tr><td colspan="2">Shipper</td><td colspan="2" rowspan="5">BILL OF LADING
B/L NO. :

CHINA OCEAN SHIPPING CO
中国远洋运输公司
ORIGINAL</td></tr>
<tr><td colspan="2">Consignee</td></tr>
<tr><td colspan="2">Notify party</td></tr>
<tr><td>Pre carriage by</td><td>* Place of receipt</td></tr>
<tr><td>Ocean Vessel Voy. No.</td><td>Port of Loading</td></tr>
<tr><td>Port of discharge</td><td>* Final destination</td><td>Freight payable at</td><td>Number original Bs/L</td></tr>
<tr><td>Marks and numbers</td><td>Number and kind of packages, description</td><td>Gross weight</td><td>Measurement m^3</td></tr>
<tr><td colspan="4">Total packages (in words)</td></tr>
<tr><td colspan="2" rowspan="2">Freight and charges</td><td colspan="2">Place and date of issue</td></tr>
<tr><td colspan="2">Signed for the carrier</td></tr>
<tr><td colspan="4">Applicable only when document used as a Through Bill of Loading</td></tr>
</table>

样例 9.4 空白提单

任务十 缮制保险单据

任务背景

在由王芳小姐负责的女童夹克衫的进料加工业务中，买卖双方签订合同时，采用的是 CIF 贸易术语。在此情况下，卖方负有与保险公司签订保险合约的义务，目的是转移运输途中的风险，同时，丸红株式会社通过中国银行东京分行开立的信用证也明确规定保险单据作为议付货款的单据之一。

于是王芳小姐与中国人民财产保险股份有限公司天津分公司办理投保手续，并且催促人保公司及时签发保险单据，以便及早向议付行交单办理结汇手续。

【背景分析】

保险单据也是出口业务中常用的结汇单据之一，特别在 CIF 和 CIP 贸易术语下，更是必备的结汇单据之一。国际贸易的特点是环节多，风险大，为了把运输途中的风险转嫁出去，出口商必须办理相关的投保手续。通常保险单据都是依据出口商提交的投保单由保险公司缮制并签发，但作为出口商也应掌握保险单据的缮制规范，这样才能保证做到相符交单。为此，王芳小姐应掌握和具备如下知识、技能及素质。

知识目标

①了解保险单据的概念、种类及作用。

②看懂信用证中的保险单据条款。

技能目标

①准确翻译信用证中的保险条款及与保险相关的条款。

②在掌握一般缮制规范的基础上，着重学会审核保险单据。

素质目标

①牢记风险无处不在，养成风险转移意识。

②在实际业务中注重贯彻保险业的最大诚信原则。

一、缮制保险单据的基础知识

【保险单据的概念】

保险单据(Insurance Document)，是指保险人(即保险公司)与被保险人(即投保人)之间订立正式保险合同的证明，其效力随着货物安全抵达目的地即告终止。保险合同反映了保险人与被保险人之间的权利和义务关系。当发生保险责任范围内的损失时，它是被保险人索赔的主要依据之一，也是保险人理赔的主要依据。在 CIF 或

CIP 交易中,它又是出口商必须向进口商提交的出口结汇单据之一。由卖方向保险公司递交投保单办理保险手续,保险公司依据投保单签发保险单给卖方。在 FOB 或 CFR 交易中,由买方向保险公司递交投保单办理保险手续,保险公司依据投保单签发保险单给买方。如图 10.1 所示。

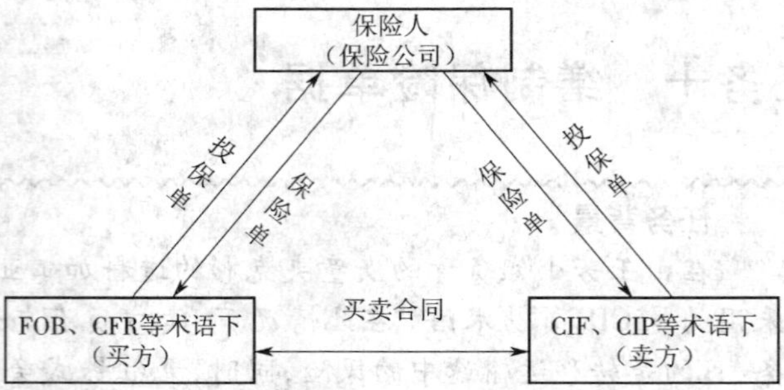

图 10.1 贸易术语与办理保险的责任归属

【保险单据的种类】

1. 投保单(Application)

它是指投保人向保险人申请订立保险合同的书面要约。

2. 保险单(Insurance Policy)

俗称大保单,是保险人与被保险人订立保险合同的正式书面证明,是目前我国进出口贸易中使用最广泛的一种正规的保险单据。

3. 保险凭证(Insurance Certificate)

俗称小保单,是一种简式的保险合同。其正面内容与保险单基本一致,但背面不载明保险人与被保险人之间的权利义务等条款。保险凭证与保险单具有同样的效力。近年来,随着单据要求的规范化,许多保险公司已逐步停止使用此类单据。

4. 联合保险凭证(Combined Insurance Certificate)

它是一种将发票和保险单相结合的,比保险凭证更为简化的保险单据。这种联合保险凭证不是专用单据,不能转让,仅适用于我国港、澳地区中资银行开来的信用证项下的业务,现已很少使用。

5. 预约保险单/总保险单(Open Cover/Open Policy)

又称预约保险合同。是被保险人(一般为进口人)与保险人之间订立的总合同。在实际业务中,预约保单适用于我国自国外进口的货物。凡属预约保单规定范围内的进口货物,一经启运,我国保险公司即自动按照预约保单所订立的条件承保。

6. 批单(Endorsement)

保险单出立后,投保人如要补充或变更其内容时,可根据保险公司的规定,向保险公司提出申请,经同意后即另出一种凭证,注明更改或补充的内容,这种凭证即为批单。

【保险单据的申办程序】

①选定投保方式(逐笔投保或预约保险)。

②选择保险险别。

③确定保险金额。

④填写投保单。

⑤交付保险费,领取保险单据。

【保险单据的作用】

保险单据是保险人接受投保人的投保申请并收取保险费后,向投保人签发的证明文件,具有以下作用。

①保险单据是保险人在其所负责期间和所负承保责任范围内,对保险单所列货物承担灭失和损害赔偿责任的凭证。

②保险单据是保险人与被保险人之间的一种契约,保险单据上的保险条款规定了保险人与被保险人的权利和义务。

③当保险单据上所列的被保险货物在保险人的责任范围内遭受灭失和损害时,保险单是被保险人或其合法持有人向保险公司要求赔偿的凭证。

④当保险单据上所列的被保险货物在保险人的责任范围内遭受灭失和损害时,保险单据是保险公司处理被保险人赔偿要求的主要理赔依据。

二、缮制保险单据的基本技能

【实训目的】

通过本项目实训,应掌握的基本技能如下。

①熟悉并看懂相关信用证(合同)中有关保险单据条款。

②掌握保险单据缮制的规范和技巧。

③学会独立缮制保险单据。

【操作前准备】

进行本项任务的实训前,应准备的内容如下。

①出口商提供的商业发票和装箱单。

②计算器等计算工具。

③确定投保金额和投保险别。

④出口商填写完整的投保单。

⑤所投保公司的空白保险单据。

【操作程序】

①浏览信用证(合同)中对保险单据的要求,如保险加成、保险险别、赔付地点及相关附加指示的规定等。

②根据保险加成,计算保险金额。

③浏览商业发票和装箱单,明确货描的基本内容,如品名、运输标志及总件数等。

④根据信用证(合同)要求缮制保险单据。

⑤按照信用证和合同条款认真仔细填写保险单据的各个栏目,做到完整、准确。

⑥检查保险单据各个栏目填写是否与已缮制妥的发票、装箱单、原产地证书及提单等结汇单据相符。

【操作规范】

表 10.1 保险单据缮制规范

项目顺序号	填写内容	要点提示
(1)保险公司名称 Name of insurance company	保险公司名称	一般在保险单据顶端已印好
(2)发票号 Invoice No.	本批投保货物所对应的发票号码	必须与所随附发票的发票号码一致
(3)保险单号 Policy No.	保险公司编制的保单号码	由保险公司统一编号
(4)保险单据名称 Insurance policy	由保险公司印好单据名称	应与信用证要求单据名称一致
(5)被保险人 Insured	投保人名称或称抬头人	一般填写信用证的受益人,即出口商的名称
(6)唛头 Marks & Nos.	具体唛头或填写 As per Invoice No. . . .	按照发票、提单上的唛头填写,如无唛头,可填写“N/M”
(7)保险货物项目 Description of goods	参照发票、提单填写,可用商品统称	应与提单、产地证的货物描述相一致
(8)数量 Quantity	参照发票、提单,填写最大外包装的总件数	散装货要注明“In Bulk”,再填写重量
(9)保险金额 Amount insured	发票毛值加上投保加成后的金额	此栏为小写金额,一般小数点后尾数一律进为整数,即保险金额不设辅币
(10)总保险金额 Total amount insured	保险金额的大写	计价货币也应填写全称,大写、小写金额必须保持一致
(11)承保险别 Conditions	本批投保货物投保的险别、依据的保险条款及版本年份	险别内容必须与信用证(合同)规定的保险条款保持一致
(12)保费 Premium	as arranged	保险公司已在此栏印好
(13)装载运输工具 Per conveyance S. S	运输工具名称及航次	应与提单上的运输工具的名称及航次相一致。若要转船,则应分别填写一程船名和二程船名,中间用“/”分开
(14)开航日期 Slg. on or about	As per B/L	不用填写实际开航日期
(15)运输起讫地 From . . . To. . .	提单的装运港和目的港	如要转运,则应加注转运港名称
(16)保险勘查代理人 Insurance survey agent	目的港保险代理人的名称、详细地址及联系方式	保险勘查代理人一般由保险公司自己选定,以便收货人在出险后通知其代理人联系有关查勘和索赔事宜
(17)赔付地点 Claim payable at. . .	应严格按照信用证规定,若没有具体规定,目的港为赔付地点	一般信用证规定在赔款偿付地点后要注明偿付所使用的货币名称
(18)保险单据签发日期和地点 Date and place of issue	此笔保险单据签发日期和签发地点	保险单据的签发日期应早于运输单据日期,以证明是在货物出运前办理的投保 ,签发地点一般为出口商所在地
(19)保险公司签章 Authorized signature	保险公司名称及签章	保险单据只有经保险公司或其代理签章后才生效

【保险单样例】

中保财产保险有限公司(1)

The People's Insurance (Property) Company of China, Ltd.

发票号码 保险单号次

Invoice No. INVOICE NO. 123456 (2) Policy No. PICC08526 (3)

海洋货物运输保险单 (4)

MARINE CARGO TRANSPORTATION INSURANCE POLICY

被保险人:

Insured: TIFERT TRADING CO., LTD. (5)

中保财产保险有限公司(以下简称本公司)根据被保险人的要求,及其所缴付约定的保险费,按照本保险单承担险别和背面所载条款与下列特别条款,承保下列货物运输保险,特签发本保险单。

This policy of Insurance witnesses that the People's Insurance (Property) Company of China, Ltd. (hereinafter called "The Company"), at the request of the Insured and in consideration of the agreed premium paid by the Insured, undertakes to insure the under mentioned goods in transportation subject to conditions of the Policy as per the Clauses printed overleaf and other special clauses attached hereon.

唛头 (6) Shipping marks	保险货物项目 (7) Descriptions of goods	数量 (8) Quantity	保险金额 (9) Amount insured
AS PER INV. NO. 123456	GIRL JACKET	250 CARTONS	USD57750.00

总保险金额: (10)

Total amount insured: U.S. DOLLARS FIFTY-SEVEN THOUSAND SEVEN HUNDRED AND FIFTY ONLY

承保险别 (11)

Conditions

COVERING ALL RISKS AND WAR RISK AS PER OCEAN MARINE CARGO TRANSPORTATION CLAUSES OF C.I.C. DATEED 1/1/1981.

保费 载运输工具 SHUNFENG 开航日期

Premium as arranged (12) Per conveyance S.S V.0827 (13) Slg. on or abt AS PER B/L (14)

起运港 目的港

Form TIANJIN (15) To TOKYO

所保货物,如发生本保险单项下可能引起索赔的损失或损坏,应立即通知本公司下述代理人查勘。如有索赔,应向本公司提交保险单正本(本保险单共有2份正本)及有关文件。如一份正本已用于索赔,其余正本则自动失效。(16)

In the event of loss or damage which may result in a claim under this Policy, immediate notice must be given to the Company's Agent as mentioned hereunder. Claims, if any, one of the Original Policy which has been issued in 2 original (s) together with the relevant documents shall be surrendered to the Company. If one of the Original Policy has been accomplished, the others to be void.

PICC TOKYO BRANCH
RM101, 10TH FLOOR SUPER BUILDING, TOKYO, JAPAN
TEL: 0081-61-2458 7531

赔款偿付地点

Claim payable at TOKYO IN USD (17)

日期 在

Date APR. 28, 2008 (18) At TIANJIN

THE PEOPLE'S INSURANCE (PROPERTY) COMPANY OF CHINA, LTD.

蒋彩石

地址:

Address: NO.16, REN BAO BUILDING, TIANJIN, CHINA (19)

样例10.1 保险单

【操作注意事项】

①保险单据的转让无须取得保险人的同意,也无须通知保险人。

②保险单据的出单日期不得迟于运输单据所列货物装船或发运或承运人接受监管的日期。因此,办理投保手续的日期也不得迟于货物装运日期。

③保险单据必须在表面上看来是由保险公司或其代理人出具并签署,银行不接受由保险经纪人签发的暂保单。

④中国人保公司可以按照 CIC 条款签发保险单,也可以按照 ICC 条款签发保险单,但两者不能混用,即不允许在一份保单内部分险别是依据 CIC 条款,而部分险别又是依据 ICC 条款。

三、缮制保险单据的操作训练

【翻译语句】

①insurer ②insured

③insurance agent ④insurance broker

⑤survey agent ⑥application

⑦FPA ⑧insured amount

⑨WPA ⑩all risks

⑪Insurance policies or certificates in two fold payable to the order of Commercial Bank of London Ltd. covering marine institute cargo clauses A, institute strike clauses, institute war clauses for invoice value plus 10% including warehouse to warehouse up to the final destination at Switzerland, marked premium paid, showing claims if any, payable in Germany, naming settling agent in Germany.

⑫Marine insurance policy or certificate in duplicate, endorsed in blank, for full invoice value plus 10 percent stating claim payable in Thailand covering FPA as per ocean marine cargo clause of the People's Insurance Company of China dated 1/1/1981, including T. P. N. D. loss and/or damage caused by heat, ship's sweat and odor, hoop-rust, breakage of packing.

⑬Insurance policies or certificates in duplicate endorsed in blank of 110% of invoice value covering all risks and war risk as per CIC with claims payable at Singapore in the currency of draft (irrespective of percentage), including 60 days after discharges of the goods at port of destination (or at station of destination) subject to CIC.

⑭Marine insurance policies or certificates in negotiable form, for 110% full CIF invoice covering the risks of war & W. A. as per the People's Insurance Co. of China dated 1/1/1981 with extended cover up to Kuala Lumpur with claims payable in Kuala Lumpur in the currency of draft (irrespective of percentage).

⑮Insurance policy or certificate covering W. A. (or F. P. A.) and war risk as per ocean marine cargo clause and ocean marine cargo war risk clause of the People's Insurance Company of China dated 1/1/1981.

【动脑思考】

①泰佛贸易公司在一笔出口贸易的发票中显示如下。

TOTAL AMOUNT: USD12356.00

请问:业务员在向保险公司投保时,保险金额一栏应如何填写?

②泰佛贸易公司在一笔出口贸易的结汇单据中保险单与提单的签发日期相同,请问这一做法是否可行?交单时银行是否会提出异议?

③泰佛贸易公司在一笔CIF出口贸易中收到国外进口商的信用证,证中未规定保险单是否需背书。请问:业务员在向银行交单时,是否应对保险单据进行背书?

④泰佛贸易公司在一笔出口贸易中收到国外进口商的信用证,证中没有明确规定保险险别,合同中也未对保险险别进行说明。请问:在办理保险时应如何选择险别?

⑤泰佛贸易公司在一笔出口纺织品到加拿大的贸易中,采用了联合保险凭证(Combined Insurance Certificate)来代替保险单,请问这一做法是否可行?

【动手操练】

实训操作一

泰佛贸易公司与英国BIG BEN公司经过友好洽商就出口沙滩阳伞达成一份出口合同,数量500件,CIF LONDON,付款方式即期信用证(L/C at sight)。随后泰佛贸易公司向中国人民保险公司进行投保,提交投保单。中国人民保险公司向泰佛贸易公司出具了保险单。作为单证员,请你根据信用证有关条款、商业发票、装箱单及投保单中的信息缮制保险单(空白保险单见样例10.2)。

信用证中与提单相关的主要条款如下。

59: BENEFICIARY: TIFERT TRADING CO., LTD.
NO.86, ZHUJIANG ROAD, TIANJIN, CHINA

50: APPLICANT: BIG BEN CORP
88, GREAT TOWER BUILDING, LONDON, U.K.

44A: LOADING ON BOARD/DISPATCH/TAKING IN CHARGE AT/FROM... TIANJIN

44B: FOR TRANSPORTATION TO LONDON

44C: NOT LATER THAN 31ST MAY, 2008

45A: DESCRIPTION OF GOODS/SERVICE

BEACH UMBRELLA ART NO. B68 200PCS USD10.00/PC
ART NO. B94 300PCS USD15.00/PC
CIF LONDON
PACKING IN CARTONS OF 10PCS EACH

SHIPPING MARKS: BB CORP
S/C NO. HT222
LONDONG
NO. 1 – UP

46A: DOCUMENTS REQUIRED

+ MARINE INSURANCE POLICY OF CERTIFICATE IN DUPLICATE, ENDORSED IN BLANK, FOR 110% OF THE INVOICE COST INCLUDING OCEAN MARINE CARGO CLAUSES (ALL RISKS), OCEAN MARINE CARGO WAR RISK CLAUSES AND OCEAN MARINE CARGO STRIKES RISKS AND CIVIL COMMOTIONS CLAUSES OF THE PEOPLE'S INSURANCE COMPANY OF CHINA INCLUDING WAREHOUSE TO WAREHOUSE CLAUSE, CLAIMS PAYABLE IN LONDON IN CURRENCY OF DRAFTS.

发票、箱单和装货单中补充信息如下。

INV. NO. : TJ8526
POLICY NO. : PICC8526
投保日期 : MAY15,2008
船名航次 : SHUNFENG V55
保险代理人 : LONDON INSURANCE CO LTD
12, DONG JIN STREET, LONDON, U.K.
TEL: 0044 2 3789 4598
ATN: MR MARAY

中保财产保险有限公司

The People's Insurance (Property) Company of China, Ltd.

发票号码 保险单号次

Invoice No. Policy No.

海洋货物运输保险单

MARINE CARGO TRANSPORTATION INSURANCE POLICY

被保险人：

Insured：

中保财产保险有限公司(以下简称本公司)根据被保险人的要求，及其所缴付约定的保险费，按照本保险单承担险别和背面所载条款与下列特别条款承保下列货物运输保险，特签发本保险单。

This policy of Insurance witnesses that the People's Insurance (Property) Company of China, Ltd. (hereinafter called "The Company"), at the request of the Insured and in consideration of the agreed premium paid by the Insured, undertakes to insure the under mentioned goods in transportation subject to conditions of the Policy as per the Clauses printed overleaf and other special clauses attached hereon.

唛头 Shipping marks	保险货物项目 Descriptions of goods	数量 Quantity	保险金额 Amount insured

总保险金额：

Total amount insured：

承保险别

Conditions

保费 载运输工具 开航日期

Premium ________ Per conveyance S. S ________ Slg. on or abt ________

起运港 目的港

Form ________ To ________

所保货物，如发生本保险单项下可能引起索赔的损失或损坏，应立即通知本公司下述代理人查勘。如有索赔，应向本公司提交保险单正本(本保险单共有 份正本)及有关文件。如一份正本已用于索赔，其余正本则自动失效。

In the event of loss or damage which may result in a claim under this Policy, immediate notice must be given to the Company's Agent as mentioned hereunder. Claims, if any, one of the Original Policy which has been issued in original(s) together with the relevant documents shall be surrendered to the Company. If one of the Original Policy has been accomplished, the others to be void.

赔款偿付地点

Claim payable at

日期 在

Date ________ at ________

地址：

Address：________

样例 10.2 空白保险单

实训操作二

上海电动工具制造有限公司与韩国大宇进出口贸易公司经过友好洽商就出口双向扳手达成一份出口合同,数量 5 600 件,CIF PUSAN,付款方式为电汇加托收(T/T + D/P AT SIGHT)。其后上海电动工具制造有限公司向中国平安保险公司投保,提交投保单。中国平安保险公司接受其投保后,向上海电动工具制造有限公司出具了保险单。作为单证员,请你根据合同 TT6321(样例 10.3)及以下信息缮制保险单(空白保险单见样例 10.4)。

发票号 : ES2008502
保险单号 : PA200856
提单日期 : NOV. 28, 2008
船名航次 : SHUNFENG V728
保险代理人: PING AN INSURANCE COMPANY OF CHINA LTD. PUSAN BRANCH
8, SUN-DONG, NAM-KU PUSAN KOREA

SALES CONTRACT

S/C No.: TT6321
Date: OCT. 18, 2008

The Seller: SHANGHAI POWER TOOLS MANUFACTURE CO., LTD.
Add: 3188 JINJIANG ROAD, SHANGHAI, CHINA
The Buyer: DAYU IMPORT & EXPORT TRADE CORPORATION
Add: 564-8, SUNAN-DONG, NAM-KU ULSAN KOREA
The seller agrees to sell and the buyer agrees to buy the under mentioned goods on the terms and conditions stated below:

(1) Marks & Nos.	(2) Name of commodity specifications	(3) Quantity (piece)	(4) Unit price (USD)	(5) Total amount (USD)
DAYU TT6321 PUSAN No. 1-100	DOUBLE OPEN AND SPANNER	5600PCS	USD2.43/PC CIF PUSAN	USD13608.00

Total value: THIRTEEN THOUSAND SIX HUNDRED AND EIGHT ONLY.

(6) Time of shipment: DURING NOV., 2008
(7) Port of loading: SHANGHAI, CHINA
(8) Port of destination: PUSAN, KOREA
(9) Insurance: TO BE COVERED BY THE SELLER FOR 110% OF CIF VALUE COVERING ALL RISKS AND WAR RISK AS PER OCEAN MARIN CARGO CLAUSES OF PICC DATED 1/1/1981.
(10) Terms of payment: 30% BY T/T IN ADVANCE, 70% BY D/P AT SIGHT
(11) Packing: 56PCS TO A CARTON
(12) Remarks: 5% MORE OR LESS BOTH IN QUANTITY AND AMOUNT ALLOWED.

Seller(signature): 王强　　　　Buyer(signature): 金大忠

样例 10.3 销售合同

中国平安保险股份有限公司

PING AN INSURANCE COMPANY OF CHINA LTD.

货物运输保险单

CARGO TRANSPORTATION INSURANCE POLICY

被保险人:

Insured:

中国平安保险股份有限公司根据被保险人的要求及其所缴付约定的保险费,按照本保险单背面所载条款与下列特款,承保下述货物运输保险,特立本保险单。

This Policy of Insurance witnesses that PING AN INSURANCE COMPANY OF CHINA, LTD., at the request of the Insured and in consideration of the agreed premium paid by the Insured, undertakes to insure the under mentioned goods in transportation subject to the conditions of Policy as per the clauses printed overleaf and other special clauses attached hereon.

保单号
Policy No. ______ 赔款偿付地点
Claim payable at

发票或提单号
Invoice No. or B/L No. ______ ______

运输工具
Per conveyance S. S. ______ 查勘代理人
Survey by:

起运日期 自 至
Slg. on or abt. From To

保险金额
Amount insured

保险货物项目、标记、数量及包装:
Description, marks, quantity & packing of goods:

承保条件
Condition:

签单日期
Date:

For and on behalf of
PING AN INSURANCE COMPANY OF CHINA, LTD.

______
Authorized signature

复核: 制单

地址及电话
Address & Tel.

注:未加盖本公司保单专用章,保单无效。

样例 10.4 空白保险单

任务十一　缮制其他单据

任务背景

一段时间来的单据工作经验告诉王芳小姐,国际贸易中除了商业发票、装箱单、提单及保险单等主要单据外,还会有许许多多其他单据,如受益人的寄样证明及寄单证明、船公司的船龄证明及航线证明等。在女童夹克衫业务中,日本丸红株式会社通过中行东京分行开立的信用证中明确规定议付货款须提交受益人证明函作为结汇的单据之一。

王芳小姐在等待货代公司签发提单期间,就着手开始缮制受益人证明函等单据,为拿到提单后赶在第一时间将全套结汇单据送银行议付货款做好充分准备。

【背景分析】

其他单据是出口业务中常用的结汇单据之一,依据证明的内容不同,可冠以不同的单据名称。如证明受益人已将一套单据邮寄给开证申请人的,叫受益人寄单证明;证明载货船舶的船龄不超过15年的,叫船公司出具的船龄证明。这些都是有关方面履行合同或信用证规定义务的证明,种类繁多,需要单证员在实际业务中不断总结经验,灵活应对,做到既履行规定义务又满足结汇需要。为此,王芳小姐应掌握和具备如下知识、技能及素质。

知识技能

①了解其他单据的概念、种类及作用。

②看懂信用证中的其他单据条款。

操作技能

①准确翻译信用证中的其他单据条款及其他单据相关条款。

②学会独立、正确缮制常见的其他单据。

职业素质

①养成终身学习的好习惯。

②应对各种挑战,不断提高自身的业务水平。

一、缮制其他单据的基础知识

【装运通知的概念和作用】

装运通知(Shipping Advice)是货物装船后,由出口商发送给进口商,通知后者一定数量的货物已经启运的通知文件。在 FOB 或 CFR 条件下,进口商需要根据装运通知来为进口货物办理保险手续,因此一般要求出口商在货物离开启运地后两个工作日内向进口商发出装运通知。

装运通知是在采用租船运输大宗进出口货物的情况下,在合同中加以约定的条款。规定这个条款的目的在于明确买卖双方责任,促使进出口双方互相合作,共同做好船货衔接工作。货物装船后,出口商应及时向国外进口商发出装运通知,以便对方准备付款、赎单,及办理进口报关和接货手续。

【船公司证明的概念和种类】

船公司证明(Shipping Company's Certificate),是船长或其代理人出具的单据,用来证明船籍、航程、船龄、船级、集装箱船及运费等,由受益人向船公司或其代理人索取。

1. 船舶本身的证明文件

(1)集装箱船只证明(Certificate of Container Vessel)

进口商或银行在合同或信用证中规定货物须装集装箱船并出具相应证明的,若信用证没有约定具体签发人,可由受益人自行缮制并加盖出口商图章,也可在运输单据上加以注明。但信用证如果规定具体的签发人,则必须依照信用证要求办理。

(2)船龄证明(Certificate of Vessel's Age)

有些国家或地区来证规定装载货物的船舶船龄不得超过 15 年,受益人必须要求船代或船公司出具载货船只的船龄证明书(Certificate to evidence the ship is not over 15 years old 或 is under 15 years of age),这样的要求主要目的在于禁止使用老龄船,确保货物运输安全。

(3)船籍证明(Certificate of Registry)

有些国家或地区来证规定货物必须装载某国籍的船舶或禁止装载某国籍的船舶时,受益人在租船订舱时就必须考虑此要求,同时要求船公司或船代出具载货船舶所属国籍的证明以满足信用证要求,确保安全收汇。

(4) 船级证明(Confirmation of Class)

有的信用证规定提供英国劳合社船级证明,如"Class certificate certifying that the shipment is made by a seaworthy vessel which are classified 100 A1 issued by Lloyds or equivalent classification society"。劳合社的船级符号为 LR,标志 100A1,100A 表示该船的船体和机器设备是根据劳氏规范和规定建造的,1 表示船舶的装备如船锚、锚链

及绳索等处于良好和有效的状态，对这样的要求我们通常应尽可能予以满足。国际上著名的船级社有英国劳合社、德国船级社（GL）、挪威船级社（DNV）、法国船级社（BV）、日本海事协会（NK）及美国船级社（ABS）等。

2. 运输和航行证明

（1）航程证明（Certificate of Itinerary）

主要说明航程中船舶停靠的港口。一些阿拉伯国家开来的信用证中，往往要求在提单上随附声明一份，明确船籍、船名、船东及途中所经港口顺序。出口商须请求船公司或船代按要求签发此类证明，并按证明中所述行程行驶和操作船舶。

（2）转船证明书（Certificate of Transshipment）

出口商要求船公司或船代出具转船证明书，说明出口货物将在中途转船且已联系妥当，并由托运人负责将有关转船事项通知收货人。

（3）货装具名船舶证明（Certificate of named carrying vessel）

如信用证要求"A certificate from the shipping company or its agent stating that goods are shipped by APL"，意思是要求出口商提供由船公司或其代理出具的货装美国总统轮船公司的证明。

（4）船长收据（Captain's Receipt）

有的信用证规定，样品或单据副本交载货船舶的船长代交进口商，并提供船长收据，如委托船长带去而未取得船长收据将影响出口商收汇。船长收据常见于近洋运输。

此外，船证还包括进港证明、运费已交收据、港口费用单（port charges documents）、装卸准备就绪通知书（NOR）及装卸时间事实记录等。由于政治原因，巴基斯坦和印度互不允许悬挂对方国旗的船舶靠岸，巴基斯坦港口还不接受来自南非、韩国、以色列及中国台湾的船舶，如要求出具相应证明的，出口商必须提供。

3. 航运组织和公约证明

（1）班轮公会证明（Conference Line Certificate）

信用证规定货物须装班轮公会船舶时，向银行所交单据中应包括船公司或船代出具的证明。

例1：信用证要求"A certificate issued by the carrier, shipping Co or their agents certifying that shipment has been effected by conference line and/or regular line vessels only covered by institute classification clause to accompany the documents"，其意思是由承运人、船公司或他们的代理签发证明，证实货物业已装运在符合伦敦协会船级条款的班轮公会船舶或定期船上，该船证随单据提交。

例2：信用证要求"Shipping company's certificate stating that the carrying vessel has entered P&I Club and should be attached with the original documents"，其意思是要求船证应明确载货船舶系船东保赔协会成员并应随附正本证明。

(2)黑名单证明(Certificate of Black List)

典型的是阿拉伯国家所要求的抵制以色列证明(Certificate of Boycott Israeli)。其通常规定为"The vessel carrying the goods is not Israeli and will not call on any Israeli ports while carrying the goods and that the vessel is not banned entry to the port of the Arab States for any reasons whatever under law and the laws and regulations of such Sates allowed",意思是船上所装货物为非以色列原产,以及船舶不经停任何以色列港口的情况下,该船舶可依法自由进入阿拉伯国家法律和规则所允许进出的港口。

(3)SMC、DOC 及 SOLAS

这几个缩略语近年来常出现在信用证的要求中。SMC(Safety Management Certificate 船舶安全管理证书)和 DOC(Document of Compliance 安全符合证书,也有人称其为船/港保安符合证书)是按照国际安全管理规则(ISM)的规定,载货船舶应在船上拥有的必要证书。我国海事局按 ISM 的规章发给船公司 DOC,船舶则可获 SMC,如船公司没有相应证书,那么就没有办法按信用证要求出具此类证明。信用证中的一般要求是"The carrying vessel should comply with the provisions of the (ISM) Code which necessitates that such vessel must have on board, copies of the two (SMC and DOC) valid Certificates and copies of such certificate must be presented with the original documents."也可体现为"Certificate issued, signed and stamped by the owner/carrier/master of the carrying vessel holds valid ISM certificate and ISPS (International Shipping And Port Security Safety Code《国际船舶和港口设施保安规则》)"。SOLAS 指的是《1974 年国际海上人命安全公约》(简称 SOLAS 公约)。"9·11"事件后国际海事组织于 2002 年 12 月召开缔约国大会通过对 SOLAS 公约的修正案,并在 2004 年 7 月 1 日起开始实施。按上述有关规定,船舶应持有"安全管理证书"正本,其船名与国籍证书一致,所载公司名称与"符合证书"中的公司名称相一致。

【受益人证明的概念、种类及作用】

受益人证明通常是指信用证受益人根据信用证的要求出具的证明受益人已经履行了合同或信用证规定义务的证明,是信用证付款方式下要求的常见单据之一。

受益人证明主要有寄单证明、寄样证明及包装证明几种。

受益人证明的主要作用包括如下几点。

①向有关方面证实某件事实。

②证明已经履行某种义务或完成某项工作。

③作为议付单据之一。

二、缮制其他单据的基本技能

【实训目的】

通过本项目实训,应掌握的基本技能如下。

①熟悉并看懂相关信用证(合同)中有关装运通知、船公司证明或受益人证明的条款。

②掌握装运通知、船公司证明及受益人证明的缮制规范和技巧。

③学会独立缮制装运通知、船公司证明及受益人证明。

【操作前准备】

进行本项任务的实训前,应准备的内容如下。

①出口商提供的合同和信用证。

②空白的纸质单据或空白单据的电子模板。

【操作程序】

①浏览信用证对装运通知、船公司证明或受益人证明的要求及相关附加指示。

②缮制装运通知、船公司证明及受益人证明等各种证明。

③审核所缮制装运通知、船公司证明及受益人证明是否正确。

【操作规范及单据样例】

表 11.1 装运通知缮制规范

项目顺序号	填写内容	要点提示
(1)单据名称 Name of Doc.	Shipping advice	应与信用证要求的单据名称一致
(2)日期 Date	发送装运通知的时间	一般与提单日期相同或略晚于提单日期
(3)通知对象 To	开证人或其他	按信用证要求填写
(4)声明或证明文句 Statement	声明货物已出运	按信用证要求填写
(5)通知内容 Contents	合同号、信用证号、品名、数量、运输工具、开航日期、装运港、目的港及提单号等详细内容	按信用证要求填写
(6)激励性文句 Encourage sentence	希望对方满意的文句	不是必需的部分
(7)签署 Signature	受益人签章	一般可以不签署

TIANJIN TIFERT TRADING CO., LTD.

NO. 86, ZHUJIANG ROAD, TIANJIN, CHINA

SHIPPING ADVICE (1)

TO: MARUBENI CORP. (3) DATE: APR. 30, 2008 (2)

DEAR SIR,

WE ARE PLEASED TO INFORM YOU THAT THE FOLLOWING MENTIONED GOODS HAS BEEN SHIPPED OUT, FULL DETAILS AS FOLLOWS: (4)

1. COMMODITY: GIRL JACKET
2. QUANTITY: 250 CARTONS
3. BILL OF LADING NO.: SINO081216
4. OCEAN VESSEL: SHUNFENG V.0827
5. PORT OF LOADING: TIANJIN, CHINA
6. DATE OF SHIPPMENT: APR. 30, 2008
7. PORT OF DESTINATION: TOKYO, JANPAN
8. TOTAL AMOUNT: USD52500.00
9. MARKS AND NUMBER ON B/L: MARUBENI
   S/C 08TF0858
   TOKYO
   CTN 1-250

(5)

WE HOPE YOU ARE SATISFIED WITH THE QUALITY OF OUR GOODS AND LOOK FORWARD TO RECEIVING YOUR REPEAT ORDER SOON. (6)

TIFERT TRADING CO., LTD.
泰佛贸易有限公司
*

(7)

王 宏

样例 11.1 装运通知

表 11.2 船公司证明缮制规范

项目顺序号	填写内容	要点提示
(1)单据名称 Name of Doc.	Certificate	单据名称应与信用证一致
(2)日期 Date	证明的日期	一般与提单日期相同
(3)抬头人 To	To whom it may concern	不填实际当事人
(4)证明文句 Contents	需证明的内容	按照信用证要求并结合实际情况做出证明
(5)签署 Signature	船公司或货代公司签章	应该与提单签单人一致

CERTIFICATE OF VESSEL'S AGE (1) TIANJIN, APR. 30, 2008 (2) TO: WHOM IT MAY CONCERN (3) THIS IS TO CERTIFY THAT THE M. S. /S. S. SHUNFENG V. 0827 WAS BUILT IN YEAR 1998 AND HAS THEREFORE NOT BEEN IN OPERATION FOR MORE THAN 15 YEARS AT TIME OF CARGO LOADING. (4) SINOTRANS TIANJIN COMPANY 张 涛 (5)

样例 11.2 船龄证明

表 11.3 受益人证明函缮制规范

项目顺序号	填写内容	要点提示
(1)单据名称 Name of Doc.	Certificate	单据名称应与信用证一致
(2)日期 Date	证明日期	应符合信用证规定
(3)发票号 Invoice No.	发票号码	
(4)抬头人 To	To whom it may concern	不填实际当事人
(5)证明文句 Contents	需证明的内容	应符合信用证规定,注意人称、时态及语态的变化
(6)签署 Signature	受益人签章	证明函无论信用证是否要求签署必须要签署

TIANJIN TIFERT TRADING CO., LTD.

NO. 86, ZHUJIANG ROAD, TIANJIN, CHINA

CERTIFICATE (1)

DATE: APR. 30, 2008 (2)

INVOICE NO.: 123456 (3)

TO: WHOM IT MAY CONCERN (4)

WE CERTIFY THAT 1/3 ORIGINAL B/L AND ONE SET OF NON-NEGOTIABLE SHIPPING DOCUEMENTS HAVE BEEN SENT TO MARUBENI CORP. WITHIN 48 HOURS AFTER SHIPMENT.

(5)

TIFERT TRADING CO., LTD.
泰佛贸易有限公司
*

(6)

样例 11.3 受益人证明函

【操作注意事项】

①出口商应及时缮制装运通知，并严格按合同或信用证要求的时间发送装运通知。

②装运通知应详尽、充分，以便买方或保险公司及时办理保险手续。信用证要求通知的内容必须一一列出，可以比信用证详尽，但不能与其他单据相应的信息发生矛盾。

③不能完全照抄信用证条款内容，应具体化，并在人称和时态等方面做相应变化。

④证明函本身的性质决定该单据需要由受益人签署。

三、缮制其他单据的操作训练

【翻译语句】

①shipping advice ②estimated time of arrival

③insurance declaration ④ETD

⑤ship's age certificate ⑥ship's nationality certificate

⑦ship's classification certificate ⑧black list certificate

⑨beneficiary's certificate ⑩freight note

⑪Original fax from beneficiary to applicant evidencing B/L No. , name of vessel, shipment date, quantity and value of goods.

⑫Shipment advice with full details including shipping marks, CTN numbers, vessel's name, B/L number, value and quantity of goods must be sent on the date of shipment to us.

⑬Copy of letter from beneficiary to applicant evidencing non negotiable B/L together with copy of other documents were sent directly to them after one day from shipment date.

⑭A statement from the beneficiary evidencing that packing effected in 25 kgs/ctn.

⑮Certificate from the shipping agents issued at the port of shipment stating that cargo are carried by a mechanically self propelled seaworthy vessel classified under Lloyd's register of shipping as 100A1 or equivalent provided such vessels are not over fifteen years of age or over fifteen years but not over twenty five years of age and have established and maintained a regular pattern of trading on an advertised schedule to load and unload at specific ports or equivalent.

【动脑思考】

①请举例说明为何有的进口商要求出口商提供船龄证明。

②请举例说明为何有的进口商要求出口商提供船旗或船籍证明。

③请举例说明为何有的进口商要求出口商提供黑名单证明。

④请分析在 FOB、CFR 及 CIF 术语下装运通知的具体作用。

⑤请列举常见的受益人证明。

【动手操练】

实训操作一

泰佛贸易公司与英国 BIG BEN 公司经过友好洽商就出口沙滩阳伞达成一份出口合同,数量 500 件,CIF LONDON,付款方式即期信用证(L/C at sight)。

信用证中的主要条款如下。

59: BENEFICIARY: TIFERT TRADING CO. , LTD.
NO. 86, ZHUJIANG ROAD, TIANJIN, CHINA

50: APPLICANT: BIG BEN CORP
88, GREAT TOWER BUILDING, LONDON, U. K.

44A: LOADING ON BOARD/DISPATCH/TAKING IN CHARGE AT/FROM... TIANJIN

44B: FOR TRANSPORTATION TO LONDON

44C: NOT LATER THAN 31ST MAY, 2008

45A: DESCRIPTION OF GOODS/SERVICE

BEACH UMBRELLA	ART NO. B68	200PCS	USD10. 00/PC
	ART NO. B94	300PCS	USD15. 00/PC
	CIF LONDON		

PACKING IN CARTONS OF 10PCS EACH

SHIPPING MARKS： BB CORP

S/C NO. HT222

LONDONG

NO.1 – UP

46A：DOCUMENTS REQUIRED

+BENEFICIARY'S CERTIFICATE CERTIFIES THAT FULL SET OF NON-NEGOTIABLE SHIPPING DOCUMENTS ARE TO BE ATTACHED TO THE GOODS.

+ SHIPMENT ADVICE WITH FULL DETAILS INCLUDING SHIPPING MARKS, CTN NUMBERS, VESSEL'S NAME, B/L NUMBER, VALUE AND QUANTITY OF GOODS MUST BE SENT ON THE DATE OF SHIPMENT TO US.

请根据以上内容完成装运通知(见样例 11.4)及受益人证明(见样例 11.5)。

SHIPPING ADVICE

DATE：

TO：

DEAR SIR,

WE ARE PLEASED TO INFORM YOU THAT THE FOLLOWING MENTIONED GOODS HAS BEEN SHIPPED OUT,FULL DETAILS FOLLOWS：

1. COMMODITY：
2. QUANTITY：
3. BILL OF LADING NO.：
4. OCEAN VESSEL：
5. PORT OF LOADING：
6. DATE OF SHIPPMENT：
7. PORT OF DESTINATION：
8. MARKS AND NUMBER ON B/L：

WE HOPE YOU ARE SATISFIED WITH THE QUALITY OF OUR GOODS AND LOOK FORWARD TO RECEIVING YOUR REPEAT ORDER SOON.

....

Authorized Signature

样例 11.4 装运通知

CERTIFICATE
DATE：
INVOICE NO：
....
Authorized Signature

样例 11.5 受益人证明函

实训操作二

泰佛贸易公司与科威特一贸易商就出口毛毯达成一出口合同，信用证规定货物需装中国籍船舶，并列举经停的港口且这些港口非属阿拉伯黑名单，作为公司单证员，请你按照信用证中的条款要求缮制船公司证明（见样例 11.6）。

46A： DOCUMENTS REQUIRED

+ SHIPPING COMPANY'S CERTIFICATE EVDENCING THAT THE CARRYING VESSEL FLYING THE FLAG OF P. R OF CHINA, FROM TIANJIN TO KUWAIT CALLING AT FOLLOWING PORTS DURING THIS PRESENT VOYAGE ACCORDING TO THE SCHEDULE, AND THAT THE VESSEL IS NOT BLACK LISTED BY THE ARABIAN.

(1) HONGKONG
(2) DAMMAM
(3) BANGKOK
(4) SINGAPORE
(5) KARACHI
(6) DUBAI

CERTIFICATE

Date:

To whom it may concern:

....

Authorized Signature

样例 11.6 船公司证明函

任务十二 缮制汇票

任务背景

由王芳小姐负责的女童夹克衫进料加工业务中，该批夹克衫已于日前由“顺风”轮从天津港装运出海驶往日本的东京港，并且王芳小姐已经拿到友通货运公司签发的已装船清洁提单，接下来就可以缮制汇票连同全套装运单据送中国银行天津分行议付货款。

于是王芳小姐抓紧时间缮制该票业务项下的商业汇票，然后送单证部审核全套装运单据，保证单单相符、单证相符，争取尽早安全收回货款。

【背景分析】

汇票是无条件的支付命令，是国际贸易中使用最多的支付工具。它具有流通性和无因性等特点，是一种金融单据，为了不影响其流通转让，汇票的缮制质量要高，在实际业务中一般不允许有涂改的痕迹。因此为了能够正确缮制商业汇票，王芳小姐应该掌握和具备如下知识、技能及素质。

知识技能

①了解汇票的概念、当事人及种类。

②看懂信用证中的汇票条款。

操作技能

①准确翻译信用证中的汇票条款。

②学会独立、正确缮制汇票。

职业素质

①养成认真细致的工作作风。

②工作上要一丝不苟、精益求精。

一、缮制汇票的基础知识

【汇票的概念】

汇票(Bill of Exchange 简称 Bill 或 Draft)是由一个人向另一个人签发的无条件的书面支付命令,要求对方立即或在将来的固定时间或可以确定的时间支付一定金额给特定的人或其指定的人或持票人。汇票是一种要式的有价证券,是出口贸易结汇中的重要和基本的单据之一,是出口商凭以向进口商要求付款的收款工具,也是进口商付款的重要凭证。如果汇票缮制有误,开证行有权以"单证不符"为由拒付货款。

一般汇票有两张正本 First Exchange 和 Second Exchange ,两张正本汇票具有同等效力,付款人付一不付二,付二不付一,先到先付,后到无效。

【汇票的当事人】

汇票的当事人主要有以下相关人。

1. 出票人(Drawer)

这是指出具汇票的人。在信用证和托收业务中,通常是出口商。

2. 付款人(Drawee)

这是指支付票款的人。在出口贸易中通常是进口商或开证行。

3. 收款人(Payee)

这是指收取票款的人或称抬头人。收款人是票面上的债权人,他有权要求付款人付款,如遭拒付,可以向出票人追索票款。在出口贸易中,收款人应该是受益人,但在实际业务中,也有议付行代为收款的情况。

4. 背书人(Endorser)

这是指收款人或持票人在汇票背面签字,将收款权利转让他人的人。

5. 承兑人(Acceptor)

远期汇票付款人办理了承兑手续即成为承兑人。在实际业务中承兑人可能是开证申请人、开证行或其指定的付款行。

6. 持票人(Holder)

这是指持有汇票有权收款的人。其中,善意持票人是持票人的一种,即汇票的合法持有者。他善意地支付了全部票款的代价,取得了一张表面完整、合格、不过期的票据,他未发现这张汇票曾被退票,也未发现其前手在权利方面有任何缺陷。例如,在信用证业务中,议付行押汇后就处于善意持票人的地位。善意持票人的权利优于其前手,如果其前手以不当手段获得汇票,善意持票人的权利并不因此而受到影响,他可以向汇票的所有责任方要求付款。

【汇票的种类】

1. 按照付款期限划分

(1)即期汇票(Sight Bill 或 Demand Draft)

在提示或见票时付款人立即付款的汇票。一般情况下,即期交易应出即期汇票。

(2)远期汇票 (Time Bill 或 Usance Bill)

按约定的期限或日期付款的汇票。一般情况下,远期交易应出具远期汇票。也有的即期交易而信用证开成假远期,在这种情况下受益人应出具远期汇票。

2. 按照是否随附单据划分

(1)跟单汇票(Documentary Draft 或 Documentary Bill)

即跟随装运单据的汇票。这种汇票在国际贸易中经常使用,出口商交付货物后出具以进口商为付款人的汇票,收取货款。信用证规定的受益人汇票 (Beneficiary's Draft)就是这种汇票。

(2)光票(Clean Bill)

不跟随装运单据的汇票,仅凭汇票办理结算。这种汇票经常用于收取尾款、佣金或代垫费用。

3. 按照出票人划分

(1)银行汇票 (Banker's Draft)

出票人和付款人都是银行的汇票叫银行汇票,这种汇票用于银行汇款。在出口贸易中,国外进口商可用这种方式汇付货款,出口商也可用这种方式汇付佣金等。

(2)商业汇票(Trade Bill 或 Commercial Bill)

以进口商或商号为出票人,以进口商、商号或银行为付款人的汇票叫商业汇票。这种汇票用于收款,是信用证或托收项下经常使用的汇票,受益人或出口商可用这种方法向对方收取货款。

4. 按照承兑人划分

(1)银行承兑汇票(Banker's Acceptance Bill)

即由银行承兑并到期付款的远期汇票。这种汇票有银行信用作保证,人们愿意接受,容易在市场上流通。

(2)商业承兑汇票(Trader's Acceptance Bill)

即以商号或个人为付款人并由其承兑和到期付款的远期汇票。这种汇票是以商业信用作保证,不如银行承兑汇票容易在市场上流通。

二、缮制汇票的基本技能

【实训目的】

通过本项目实训,应掌握的基本技能如下。

①熟悉并看懂相关信用证(合同)中有关汇票的条款。

②掌握汇票缮制的规范和技巧。

③学会独立缮制汇票。

【操作前准备】

进行本项任务的实训前,应准备的内容如下。

①出口商提供的合同和信用证。

②出口商提供的商业发票。

【操作程序】

①浏览信用证对汇票的要求和相关附加指示。

②结合商业发票了解发票号和金额等内容。

【操作规范】

表 12.1　汇票缮制规范

项目顺序号	填写内容	要点提示
(1)单据名称 Name of Doc	Bill of exchange, Exchange 或 Draft	一般已印妥
(2)汇票编号 No.	此笔业务的发票号	与商业发票上的编号保持一致
(3)日期和地点 Place and date	汇票的出票地点和日期	①出票地点一般为议付行和出票人所在地点 ②出票日期应在提单日之后,信用证有效期和交单期之前
(4)小写金额 Amount in figure	由支付货币名称缩写和阿拉伯数字构成	不得超过信用证最高限额
(5)付款期限 Tenor	①即期付款,在 At 和 sight 之间填写 * * * 或 - - - ②远期付款,在 At 和 sight 之间填写具体的期限	远期付款的几种表示方法: ①见票后××天付款 ②出票后××天付款 ③提单日后××天付款 ④指定日期付款

续表

项目顺序号	填写内容	要点提示
(6)收款人 Payee	①限制性抬头 ②指示性抬头,指示性抬头便于流通转让 ③来人抬头	
(7)大写金额 Amount in words	用文字叙述支付货币名称和支付的金额	①习惯上,在货币名称前加"say",在大写金额后加"only"字样 ②大小写金额保持一致
(8)出票依据 Drawn under	信用证方式下包括开证行名称、信用证号及开证日期	①信用证有规定的文句照抄即可 ②托收项下,填写 For collection
(9)付款人 Drawee	一般为开证行或信用证指定的付款行	托收项下,填写进口商
(10)出票人 Drawer	受益人或合同中出口商	①加盖受益人签章 ②如果要求手签,则必须亲笔签名

【汇票样例】

BILL OF EXCHANGE (1)

No. INV NO. 123456 (2) Tianjin, China. MAY 5, 2008 (3)

Exchange for USD52500.00 (4)

At * * * (5) sight of this FIRST of Exchange(Section of exchange being unpaid), pay to the order of

TIFERT TRADING CO., LTD ONLY (6) the sum of

U.S. DOLLARS FIFTY-TWO THOUSAND FIVE HUNDRED ONLY (7)

Drawn under BANK OF CHINA TOKYO BRANCH (8)

L/C No. A-08-0058

Date MAY 20, 2008

To: BANK OF CHINA TOKYO BRANCH (9)

TIFERT TRADING CO., LTD 泰佛贸易有限公司

(10)

样例 12.1 汇票

【操作注意事项】

①票面必须整洁、干净及清楚,金额不得涂改,不得加注与汇票无关的内容。

②为防备单据在邮寄途中遗失,一般远洋单据都分两次邮寄,所以汇票都应制成一式两联,"付一不付二"或"付二不付一",两联具有同等效力。港、澳地区一次寄单,可只出一联。

③一般情况下,汇票的金额与发票的金额一致,除非信用证另有规定。

④汇票必须由受益人或卖方出具。

⑤在信用证方式下汇票的收款人从票据法的角度看应该为受益人,受益人向银

行交单时通过背书把收款权利转让给议付行,但在实际业务中也有直接做成议付行为收款人的情况。在托收方式下汇票的收款人一般为托收行。

三、缮制汇票的操作训练

【翻译语句】

①sight bill or demand draft ②time bill or usance bill

③drawn under ④drawee

⑤drawer ⑥amount in figure

⑦amount in words ⑧sight draft drawn on the Issuing Bank

⑨negotiation against beneficiary's draft at 30 days after sight

⑩sight draft for full invoice value

⑪We hereby open our irrevocable letter of credit in your favor which is available by negotiation of your drafts at sight for full invoice value on us.

⑫This credit is available with any bank by negotiation of your draft at 20 days' sight for 95pct of the invoice value.

⑬We issue irrevocable documentary credit for a sum not exceeding HKD980000.00 (say HongKong Dollars Nine Hundred And Eighty Thousand Only.) available by the beneficiary's draft(s) at 30 days sight drawn on us bearing the clause "drawn under Nan Yang Commercial Bank Ltd., HongKong, documentary credit No. 34985 dated 1st May, 2008."

⑭All drafts should be marked "drawn under the Citi Bank, New York LC No. 1234 dated 2008/04/10".

⑮This L/C is available with us by payment at 45 days after receipt of full set of documents at our counters.

【动脑思考】

①盛大贸易公司在一笔出口贸易中收到国外进口商的信用证,该证显示如下。

This L/C is available with us by negotiation at 30 days after receipt of full set of documents at our counters.

请问:这是什么性质的信用证?作为单证员,你在缮制汇票时付款期限应如何处理?汇票的付款人是谁?

②泰佛贸易公司在一笔出口贸易中收到国外进口商的信用证,信用证金额为6 000澳元,货描为"30M/T of Chinese Wheat at AUD200.00/MT FOB Shanghai"。出口商实际发货30.5 M/T。

如双方同意将货款超过信用证金额的部分采用托收方式付款,请问:作为单证员,你应如何缮制汇票？需要做几套汇票？信用证项下的汇票金额如何填写？

③泰佛贸易公司在一笔出口贸易中收到国外进口商的信用证,证中规定如下。

Drafts to be drawn as follows：AUD30 000. 00—Drafts to be drawn at sight on National Australia Bank Ltd. , Brisbane, Australia. AUD20 000. 00—Drafts to be drawn at 45 Days' sight on National Australia Bank Ltd. , Brisbane, Australia.

请问:作为制单员,你应出具几套汇票？汇票的内容有哪些区别？

④天纺服装贸易公司把合同项下女式衬衫备妥,并按合同和信用证规定的装船期限于2008年4月5日装船并制作提单。信用证规定的交单议付期限为提单日后15天。请问:作为单证员,你在缮制汇票时,应该如何填制出票日期？

⑤天成贸易公司在一笔出口贸易中收到国外客户的信用证,证中规定如下。

All drafts should be marked "drawn under the Citi Bank, New York L/C No. 1234 dated 2008/04/10".

请问:此条款要求单证员在缮制汇票的出票依据时要注意什么？

【动手操练】

实训操作一

泰佛贸易公司与日本ITOCHU公司经过友好洽商就出口女式针织衫达成一出口合同,数量1 500件,CIF KOBE,付款方式即期信用证(L/C at sight)。请你作为单证员根据信用证有关条款和其他补充信息缮制汇票(空白汇票见样例12.2)。

信用证中与汇票相关的主要条款如下。

59：BENEFICIARY：	TIFERT TRADING CO. , LTD NO. 86, ZHUJIANG ROAD, TIANJIN, CHINA
50：APPLICANT：	ITOCHU CORP 88, RED SUN BUILDING, TOKYO, JAPAN.
41D：AVAILABLE WITH/BY：	BANK OF CHINA , TIANJIN BRANCH BY NEGOTIATION
42C：DRAFT(S) AT：	DRAFT(S) AT SIGHT FOR FULL INVOICE VALUE
42D：DRAWEE：	MIZUHO CORPORATE BANK, LTD. , HEAD OFFICE
44C：LATEST DATE OF SHIP. :080305	

其他补充信息如下。

ISSUING BANK：MIZUHO CORPORATE BANK, LTD. , HEAD OFFICE, TOKYO

L/C NO. LC333 DATED 2008-01-05

发票号码为:INV. 1234

发票日期为:2008年2月20日

发票金额为:USD19,000.00

提单日期为:2008年3月5日

汇票日期为:2008年3月6日

No.______________	Tianjin,China.______________
Exchange for	
At______sight of this FIRST of Exchange(Section of exchange being unpaid),pay to the order of	
______________________________ the sum of	
Drawn under______________	
L/C No.______________	
Date______________	
To:______________	
______________	______________

样例 12.2 空白汇票

实训操作二

天津金星贸易公司与埃塞俄比亚 AMENLI 公司经过友好洽商就出口五金工具箱达成一份出口合同,数量 10 000 套,CIF ASEB,付款方式为电汇加托收(T/T + D/P AT SIGHT)。作为单证员,请你根据贸易合同有关条款(见样例 12.3)及其他补充信息缮制托收项下汇票(空白汇票见样例 12.4)。

SALES CONTRACT

编号 No.: SC080216　　日期 Date :FEB. 16,2008

The sellers:TIANJIN GOLDEN STAR TRADING CO., LTD.

Add: NO. 18 ZHUJIANG ROAD, TIANJIN,CHINA　　Post code:300221

The buyers:AMENLI COMPANY, ETHIOPIA.

Add: #5054 - 7 KING STREET, ETHIOPIA

Tel: (+03)3434 - 5869

兹确认售予你方下列货品,其成交条款如下:

We hereby confirm having sold to you the following goods on the terms and conditions as specified below:

(1)货物名称及规格 Name of commodity and specifications	(2)数量 Quantity	(3)单价 Unit price	(4)总值 Total amount
Hardware tools case	CIF ASEB		
TC110	6000SETS	USD5. 00	USD30000. 00
TC120	4000SETS	USD4. 00	USD16000. 00
TOTAL:	10000SETS		USD46000. 00

(5)包装:

Packing: PACKED IN CARTONS OF 100 SETS EACH

(6)装运唛头:

Shipping mark: N/M

(7)装运期限:

Time of shipment: NOT LATER THAN APRIL 10, 2008

(8)装运口岸:　　目的地:

Port of shipment: TIANJIN Destination: ASEB

(9)付款条件:

Payment terms: 20% T/T IN ADVANCE, THE OTHERS 80% D/P AT SIGHT.

(10)保险:卖方负责投保海运险,按照 CIF 金额的 110% 投保一切险和战争险,如果发生索赔,在埃塞俄比亚用美元赔偿。

Insurance: The seller shall arrange marine insurance covering All Risks and War Risk for 110% of CIF value. Claim, if any, payable in Etiopia, in currency of USD.

确认签署 Confirmed by

AMENLI COMPANY, ETHIOPIA.	TIANJIN GOLDEN STAR TRADING CO., LTD
Jonnie	王义
买方(The buyers)	卖方(The sellers)

样例 12.3 销售合同

其他补充信息如下。

发票号码为:INV. DP0803

发票日期为:2008 年 3 月 4 日

托收项下汇票日期为:2008 年 4 月 11 日

OUR BANK INFORMATION IS AS BELOW:

BENEFICIARY: TIANJIN GOLDEN STAR TRADING CO., LTD.

BENEFICIARY ADDRESS: No. 18 ZHUJIANG ROAD, TIANJIN, CHINA

BANK NAME: BANK OF CHINA TIANJIN BRANCH

ACCOUNT NO.: RMB64025013

BANK ADDRESS: NO. 80 JIEFANG ROAD, TIANJIN, CHINA

BILL OF EXCHANGE

凭 不可撤销信用证
Drawn Under Irrevocable L/C No.

日期
Date 支取 Payable With interest @ % 按 息 付款

号码 汇票金额 天津
No. Exchange for Tianjin

见票 ------ 日后(本汇票之副本未付)付交
at sight of this FIRST of Exchange (Second of exchange being unpaid) pay to the order of

金额
the sum of

此致 For and on behalf of
To

样例 12.4 空白汇票

4 审核结汇单据

任务十三　审核单据

任务背景

经过辛勤工作，王芳小姐顺利地将女童夹克衫出运并完成了全套结汇单据的缮制任务，随后将全套单据送到公司单证部。踏进单证部王芳不由产生一种回家的感觉，她把单据交给单证部负责终审的庞师傅。庞师傅对她交来的全套单据进行了认真审核，总体来讲对王芳的工作相当满意，同时也指出了一些需要修改的地方。王芳小姐按照庞师傅的指示进行了认真细致地修改。其后，全套单据被单证部送交中行天津分行议付货款，此时王芳小姐心里或多或少地有了几分成就感。

【背景分析】

依据《UCP600》的解释，信用证是一项约定。该约定要求受益人以单据的形式向银行证明自己已履行了合同义务，银行即向其支付货款。同时信用证又是一种银行有条件的付款承诺，这里的条件是指由受益人提交符合信用证要求的单据。在国际贸易中，单据是当事人或第三方出具的履约证书，只有提交符合信用证要求的单据，做到单内相符、单单相符及单证相符，银行才履行付款义务，因此在实际业务中审单的环节是不可或缺的。因此王芳小姐应该掌握和具备如下知识、技能和素质。

知识技能

①了解审单的概念、方法及作用。

②积累和掌握不同地区对结汇单据的特殊要求。

操作技能

①准确理解信用证中的主要条款。

②掌握各种结汇单据缮制的规范。

③能够快速、准确地审核出单据中存在的不符点,并作出相应的修改。

职业素质

①养成耐心、细致的工作作风。

②牢记细节决定成败,把单据的差错率降到最低。

一、审核单据的基础知识

【审单的基本要求】

单据审核是根据信用证(信用证付款方式下)或合同(非信用证付款方式下)的有关条款内容,对已经缮制备妥的单据进行及时检查、核对及改正,从而保证安全及时收汇。按照审核人不同,具体分为企业审单和银行审单。其中,银行审单主要遵循表面一致性原则侧重从政策方面审核。在此,主要介绍企业审单的基本要求。

1. 及时性

及时审核单据可以第一时间发现并更正单据的错误,避免不及时审单给各项工作带来的被动和收汇风险。

2. 全面性

企业应当充分认识到审单工作对全面履行合同和安全收汇的至关重要性。企业在审单过程中,要做到按照信用证和合同认真审核每一份单证,不忽略任何一个瑕疵,同时在处理所发现问题时,应加强与各有关部门的联系和衔接,从而全面、妥善地处理好所发现的问题。

3. 单证相符

企业在审单过程中要做到与信用证条款、《UCP600》及《ISBP》一致。“单证相符”是安全收汇的前提和基础,信用证没有提到的内容应以跟单信用证统一惯例《UCP600》和国际标准银行实务《ISBP》为准。所提交的单据中存在的任何不符即使是微小的瑕疵都会造成难以挽回的损失。

【企业审单的基本方法】

为了保证审单工作的质量,除了要求单证人员在思想上高度重视和集中外,还要讲究工作方法。下面以信用证业务为例,介绍企业审单的方法。

1. 纵向审核法

纵向审核法是以信用证或合同为基础，对所要求的单据进行逐一审核，要求每个单据的内容与信用证条款严格相符，做到“单证相符”。

2. 横向审核法

横向审核法是在纵向审核的基础上，以商业发票为核心审核其他要求的单据，做到“单单相符”。

在审单过程中，如果发现单据的数据比较集中，可以先将各种单据的所有数据，如单价、数量、毛净重、尺码及包装件数等进行全面的复核，然后采用纵横审单法对其他内容进行审核。

二、审核单据的基本技能

【实训目的】

通过本项目实训，应掌握的基本技能如下。

①掌握审核单据的技巧。

②掌握处理单据瑕疵的技巧。

【操作前准备】

进行本项任务的实训前，应准备的内容如下。

①出口商提供的合同或信用证。

②信用证修改书。

③已经缮制好的全套单据。

④计算器等计算工具。

⑤审单记录表。

【操作程序】

①拿到信用证和单据后，先查看有无信用证修改书。如有信用证修改书，将修改内容在原信用证条款上作好相应记录，确保信用证条款内容完整和正确。

②按照信用证先后顺序对单据进行逐一审核，条款中涉及哪些单据就找出来进行审核。审核完毕，将这种单据放在固定和便于查阅的位置。

③核对单据内容与信用证条款是否一致，如有不一致应随手记录在审单记录表上。还要注意单据有些内容虽然信用证没有明确规定，但如与其他单据有联系的，要保证“单单相符”。

④全部单据审核完毕后，将发现的所有瑕疵一并与相关的业务部门沟通，落实具体解决办法。

【操作规范】

表 13.1 单据常见差错

单据种类	常见差错
商业发票 Commercial invoice	①发票名称与信用证规定不符 ②发票的抬头人与信用证要求不符 ③发票上启运港或目的港与提单不一致 ④发票的货物描述与信用证的货物描述不符或拼写错误 ⑤发票中的数量、单价或金额没有如实反映所装运的货物 ⑥发票上的金额超过信用证规定的金额或不在允许增减的机动幅度内 ⑦对佣金和折扣的处理不符合信用证的规定 ⑧发票上遗漏信用证要求表明和证明的内容,或缮制发票时机械照搬信用证中的证明词,没有作相应的变更
包装单据 Packing list	①包装单据的名称不符合信用证规定 ②包装单据的各项内容与发票、提单内容不符 ③包装单据中误现单价和总金额,泄露了进口商的底价 ④包装单的日期填写不合理 ⑤包装单的内容与货物实际包装内容不完全相符 ⑥包装单据的具体缮制不符合信用证规定
检验证书 Inspection certificate	①检验证书的种类不符合信用证要求 ②检验证书的出证机构不符合信用证要求 ③检验证书的商品名称、数量与发票和提单等其他单据不符 ④唛头与信用证或其他单据不符 ⑤检验结果有瑕疵者不符合信用证或合同规定的要求 ⑥检验日期晚于提单日期,或鲜活、易腐易烂商品检验过早 ⑦遗漏授权人签署或检验部门签章 ⑧附页漏盖骑缝章 ⑨证书更改处漏"更改章"及授权人签字
原产地证书 Certificate of origin	①原产地证书的出证机构不符合信用证要求 ②原产地证书出口商不符合信用证要求 ③原产地证书收货人不符合信用证要求 ④原产地标准引用不正确 ⑤原产地证书上的日期顺序不合理 ⑥原产地证书中货物件数的大小写不符 ⑦原产地证书中货物描述太笼统,导致在海关编码中找不到对应的编码信息 ⑧遗漏信用证中对产地证的其他要求

续表

单据种类	常见差错
海运提单 Ocean bill of lading	①海运提单提交的种类与信用证要求不符 ②海运提单正本的份数与信用证要求不符或漏填海运提单正本的份数 ③运费支付批注不规范或漏注 ④收妥待运海运提单漏装船批注或批注内容不完整 ⑤海运提单上记载的包装件数与信用证或其他单据不符 ⑥海运提单上包装件数大小写不一致或漏填大写 ⑦海运提单没有按照信用证要求正确背书或遗漏背书 ⑧海运提单装船日超过信用证规定的装运期 ⑨托运人与信用证规定不符 ⑩收货人与信用证规定不符 ⑪被通知人与信用证规定不符或填写不完整 ⑫正本提单漏注签发日期和签发地点
保险单 Insurance policy	①保险单的种类与信用证要求不符 ②保险单抬头人填写有误 ③保险金额不符合信用证规定 ④保险金额大小写不一致或大写金额不正确 ⑤保险金额所使用货币与信用证金额所使用货币不一致 ⑥保险单的投保险别与信用证规定险别不符或有遗漏 ⑦保险单上的船名与发票或提单上的船名不相符 ⑧保险单的出单日期晚于提单日期 ⑨漏注赔付地点或赔付货币 ⑩遗漏背书或背书错误
其他单据 Other documents	①单据的名称与信用证要求不符 ②单据的内容不详尽 ③单据的出单日期不符合信用证或惯例规定 ④证明文句的内容照抄信用证原句 ⑤遗漏签署
汇票 Bill of exchange	①汇票的金额与发票或信用证规定不符 ②汇票上金额大小写不一致或大写金额填写不正确、不规范 ③汇票上货币币别与信用证上货币币别不相符 ④汇票上付款期限不符合信用证或合同规定，或即期、远期的填写不规范 ⑤汇票漏出票人签署 ⑥汇票的出票条款内容与信用证不符 ⑦汇票的付款人与信用证规定不符 ⑧汇票提交的份数不正确

【审单样例】

IRREVOCABLE DOCUMENTARY CREDIT

TO：BANK OF CHINA

DEAR SIR,

IN ACCORDANCE WITH THE TERMS OF UCP 600 WE ADVISE HAVING RECEIVED THE FOLLOWING TELE-TRANSMISSION FROM CENTRAL BANK OF SPAIN.

(SWIFT ADDRESS：SPBSCATTMON)

27 SEQ OF TOTAL：
1/1
40A FORM OF DC：
IRREVOCABLE
40E APPLICABLE RULES
UCP LATEST VERSION
20 DC NO：
LCN038
31C DATE OF ISSUE：
NOV. 23, 2008
31D EXPIRY DATE AND PLACE：
DEC. 31, 2008 IN BENEFICIARY'S COUNTRY
50 APPLICANT：
SKY INTERNATIONAL I/E LTD.
1000 ALGECIRAS ST., SPAIN
59 BENEFICIARY：
TIFERT TRADING CORP LTD.
NO. 86, ZHUJIANG RD., TIANJIN, CHINA
32B DC AMT：
USD131512,30
41D AVAILABLE WITH /BY：
ANY BANK BY NEGOTIATION
42C DRAFTS AT：
SIGHT FOR FULL INVOICE VALUE
43P PARTIAL SHIPMENTS：
ALLOWED
43T TRANSHIPMENT：
ALLOWED
44C LATEST DATE OF SHIPMENT
DEC. 16, 2008
44A LOADING/DISPATCH AT/FORM：
TIANJIN, CHINA

44B FOR TRANSPORTION TO:

BARCELONA, SPAIN

45A DESCRIPTION OF GOODS AND/OR SERVICES:

NAPKIN

MATERIAL: 50% COTTON, 50% POLYESTER

SIZE: 18 * 18CM

PACKING: 100PCS/CARTON

46A DOCUMENTS REQUIRED

+ SIGNED COMMERCIAL INVOICE IN 6 COPIES INDICATING INVOICE NO., CONTRACT NO. SCN036

+ FULL SET OF CLEAN ON BOARD OCEAN BILLS OF LADING MADE OUT TO ORDER AND BLANK ENDORSED, MARKED PREPAID FREIGHT AND NOTIFYING THE APPLICANT

+ INSURANCE POLICY/CERTIFICATE IN 3 COPIES FOR 110 % OF THE INVOICE VALUE SHOWING CLAIMS PAYABLE IN SPAIN IN CURRENCY OF THE DRAFT, BLANK ENDORSED, COVERING ALL RISKS AND WAR RISK

+ PACKING LIST/WEIGHT MEMO IN 3 COPIES CERTIFYING THAT EACH ITEM HAS BEEN MARKED THE LABEL"MADE IN CHINA"

+ CERTIFICATE OF QUALITY IN 3 COPIES ISSUED BY CIQ INDICATING DETAILED AND DEFINITE INSPECTION RESULTS.

+ CERTIFICATE OF ORIGIN IN DUPLICATE ISSUED BY CCPIT SHOWING THE GOODS ARE WHOLLY PRODUCED IN CHINA

+ BENEFICIARY'S CERTIFICATE CERTIFYING THAT ONE FULL SET OF NON NEGOTIABLE DOCUMENTS HAVE BEEN SENT TO APPLICANT DIRECTLY WITHIN 48 HOURS AFTER SHIPMENT

47A ADDITIONAL CONDITIONS:

+ ALL BANKING CHARGES OUTSIDE THE OPENING BANK ARE FOR BENEFICIARY'S ACCOUNT.

+ DOCUMENTS MUST BE PRESENTED WITH 21 DAYS AFTER THE DATE OF ISSUANCE OF THE TRANSPORT DOCUMENTS BUT WITHIN THE VALIDITY OF THIS CREDIT.

THIS ADVICE CONSTITUTES A DOCUMENTARY CREDIT ISSUED BY THE ABOVE
BANK AND SHOULD BE PRESENTED WITH THE DOCUMENTS/DRAFTS FOR NEGOTIATION /PAYMENT /ACCEPTANCE, AS APPLICABLE.

ACCOUNT NO:88586 - 89778

BANK OF SPAIN

1000 MAIN STREET, ALGECIR SPAIN

TEL: 34 - 4 - 2125001

样例 13.1 信用证

Issuer TIFERT TRADING CO., LTD. NO. 86, ZHUJIANG ROAD, TIANJIN, CHINA	商 业 发 票 **COMMERCIAL INVOICE**	
To SKY INTERNATIONAL I/E LTD. 1000 ALGECIRAS STREET, SPAIN	No.: INV NO. 08FZ018	Date: NOV. 28, 2008
Transport details FROM TIANJIN TO BARCELONA BY SEA	S/C No. SCN036	L/C No. LCN038
	Terms of payment L/C AT SIGHT	

Marks and numbers	Number and kind of packages, description of goods	Quantity (PCS)	Unit price	Amount
NAPKIN	NAPKIN			
BARCELONA	MATERIAL:	72200	USD1.8215	USD131512.30
C/NO. 1 - 722	50% COTTON,			
MADE IN CHINA	50% POLYESTER			
	SIZE: 18 * 18CM			
	PACKING: 100PCS/CARTON			
	TOTAL:	72200PCS		USD131512.30

WE HEREBY CERTIFY THAT THE GOODS ARE OF CHINESE ORIGIN.

样例 13.2 发票

Shipper TIFERT TRADING CO., LTD NO. 86, ZHUJIANG ROAD, TIANJIN, CHINA	B/L No. SINO081216 中国外运天津公司 SINOTRANS TIANJIN COMPANY OCEAN BILL OF LADING
Consignee or order TO ORDER OF SHIPPER	
Notify address APPLICANT	

Pre-carriage by	Port of loading TIANJIN, CHINA
Vessel SHUNFENG V.0827	Port of loading
Port of discharge BARCELONA, SPAIN	Final destination

Container. seal No. or marks and Nos.	Number and kind of package	Description of goods	Gross weight (kgs.)	Measurement (m^3)
NAPKIN BARCELONA C/NO. 1 – 722 MADE IN CHINA	722 CARTONS SAY SEVEN HUNDRED AND TWENTY – TWO CARTONS ONLY	NAPKIN PREPAID FREIGHT	25992.00KGS	24.548CBM

Freight and charges	REGARDING TRANSHIPMENT INFORMATION PLEASE CONTACT

Ex. rate	Prepaid at	Freight payable at	Place and date of issue TIANJIN, CHINA, DEC. 8, 2008
	Total prepaid	Number of original Bs/L THREE	Signed for or on behalf of the Carrier SINOTRANS TIANJIN COMPANY 张涛

样例 13.3 提单

中保财产保险有限公司

The People's Insurance (Property) Company of China, Ltd.

发票号码 Invoice No. INVOICE NO. 08FZ018 保险单号次 Policy No. PICC08526

海洋货物运输保险单

MARINE CARGO TRANSPORTATION INSURANCE POLICY

被保险人：

Insured: TIFERT TRADING CO., LTD.

中保财产保险有限公司(以下简称本公司)根据被保险人的要求,及其所缴付约定的保险费,按照本保险单承担险别和背面所载条款与下列特别条款承保下列货物运输保险,特签发本保险单。

This policy of Insurance witnesses that the People's Insurance (Property) Company of China, Ltd. (hereinafter called "The Company"), at the request of the Insured and in consideration of the agreed premium paid by the Insured, undertakes to insure the undermentioned goods in transportation subject to conditions of the Policy as per the Clauses printed overleaf and other special clauses attached hereon.

唛头(6) Shipping marks	保险货物项目(7) Descriptions of goods	数量(8) Quantity	保险金额(9) Amount insured
AS PER INV. NO. 123456	NAPKIN	722CARTONS (72200PCS)	USD144664.00

总保险金额：

Total amount insured: SAY U. S. DOLLARS ONE HUNDRED FORTY-FOUR THOUSAND SIX HUNDRED SIXTY-FOUR ONLY

承保险别

Conditions

COVERING ALL RISKS AND WAR RISK AS PER OCEAN MARINE CARGO TRANSPORTATION CLAUSES OF C. I. C. DATEED 1/1/1981.

保费(12) 载运输工具(13) 开航日期(14)

Premium as arranged Per conveyance S. S SHUNFENG V.0827 Slg. on or abt AS PER B/L

起运港(15) 目的港

Form TIANJIN, CHINA To BARCELONA, SPAIN

所保货物,如发生本保险单项下可能引起索赔的损失或损坏,应立即通知本公司下述代理人查勘。如有索赔,应向本公司提交保险单正本(本保险单共有 2 份正本)及有关文件。如一份正本已用于索赔,其余正本则自动失效。(16)

In the event of loss or damage which may result in a claim under this Policy, immediate notice must be given to the Company's Agent as mentioned hereunder. Claims, if any, one of the Original Policy which has been issued in 2 original (s) together with the relevant documents shall be surrendered to the Company. If one of the Original Policy has been accomplished, the others to be void.

PICC SPAIN BRANCH

RM101, 10TH FLOOR SUPER BUILDING, BARCELONA, SPAIN

TEL: 0034 - 61 - 2458 7531

赔款偿付地点

Claim payable at CHINA IN USD The People's Insurance (Property) Company of China, Ltd.

日期 在

Date(18) DEC. 9, 2008 At TIANJIN 蒋彩石

地址：

Address: No. 16, REN BAO BUILDING. TIANJIN, CHINA

样例 13.4 保险单

<table>
<tr><td colspan="2">Issuer
TIFERT TRADING CO. , LTD.
NO. 86, ZHUJIANG ROAD, TIANJIN, CHINA</td><td colspan="3">装 箱 单
PACKING LIST/WEIGHT MEMO</td></tr>
<tr><td colspan="2">To
SKY INTERNATIONAL I/E LTD.
1000 ALGECIRAS STREET, SPAIN</td><td colspan="2">Invoice No.
INV NO. 08FZ018</td><td>Date
NOV. 28, 2008</td></tr>
<tr><td>Marks and numbers</td><td>Number and kind of package, description of goods</td><td>G. W</td><td>N. W</td><td>Meas.</td></tr>
<tr><td>NAPKIN
BARCELONA
C/NO. 1 – 722
MADE IN CHINA</td><td>NAPKIN
MATERIAL:
50% COTTON,
50% POLYESTER
SIZE: 18 * 18CM

PACKED IN CARTONS OF 10PCS EACH</td><td>25992. 00KGS</td><td>24909. 00KGS</td><td>24. 548CBM</td></tr>
<tr><td colspan="5">WE HEREBY CERTIFY THAT EACH ITEM HAS BEEN MARKED THE LABEL "MADE IN CHINA"</td></tr>
</table>

样例 13.5 装箱单

CIQ

中华人民共和国出入境检验检疫 正 本

ENTRY-EXIT INSPECTION AND QUARANTITE OF THE PEOPLE'S REPUBLIC OF CHINA ORIGINAL

编号 No. :08CIQ1187

QUALITY CERTIFICATE

发货人
Consignor TIFERT TRADING CO. , LTD.

收货人
Consignee * * * *

品名 Description of goods NAPKIN	标记及号码(9) Mark & No.
报检数量/重量 Quantity/Weight declared 72200PCS	NAPKIN
包装种类及数量 Number and type of packages 722CARTONS	BARCELONA CTN 1 – 722
运输工具 Means of conveyance BY SEA FREIGHT	

检验结果 (10)
Result of inspection

SAMPLES WERE DRAWN AT RANDOM FROM THE WHOLE LOT OF GOODS AND INSPECTED STRICTLY ACCORDING TO THE S/C NO. SCN036

THE ABOVE RESULTS OF INSPECTION ARE IN CONFORMITY WITH THE REQUIREMENTS IN THE SAID CONTRACT.

印章: 签证地点 Place of issue TIANJIN 签证日期 Date of issue DEC. 9, 2008
Official stamp

授权签字人 Authorized officer ***ZHANG CHI*** 签名 Signature 张驰

我们已尽所知和最大能力实施上述检验，不能因我们签发本证书而免除卖方或其他方面根据合同和法律所承担的产品质量责任和其他责任。

All inspection are carried out conscientiously to the best of our knowledge and ability. This certificate dose not in any respect absolve the seller and other related parties from his contractual and legal obligations especially when product quality is concerned.

样例 13.6 检验证书

ORIGINAL

1. Exporter TIFERT TRADING CO., LTD. NO. 86, ZHUJIANG ROAD, TIANJIN, CHINA	Certificate No. 061210 CERTIFICATE OF ORIGIN OF THE PEOPLE'S REPUBLIC OF CHINA
2. Consignee SKY INTERNATIONAL I/E LTD. 100 ALGECIRAS ST., SPAIN	
3. Means of transport and route SHIPMENT FROM TIANJIN TO TOKYO BY SEA	5. For certifying authority use only
4. Country / region of destination SPAIN	

6. Marks and numbers	7. Number and kind of packages, description of goods	8. H. S. Code	9. Quantity	10. Number and date of invoices
NAPKIN BARCELONA C/NO. 1 – 722 MADE IN CHINA	722(SEVEN HUNDRED AND TWENTY-TWO) CARTONS OF NAPKIN	4202	72200PCS	INV NO. 08FZ018 NOV. 28, 2008

11. Declaration by the exporter The undersigned hereby declares that the above details and statements are correct, that all the goods were produced in China and that they comply with the Rules of Origin of the People's Republic of China. TIFERT TRADING CO., LTD. 泰佛贸易有限公司 * TIANJIN DEC. 7, 2008 王宏 Place and date, signature and stamp of authorized signatory	12. Certification It is hereby certified that the declaration by the exporter is correct. 中国国际贸易促进委员会 天津分会 TIANJIN DEC. 7, 2008 陈凯 Place and date, signature and stamp of certifying authority

样例 13.7 原产地证书

TIANJIN TIFERT TRADING CO., LTD.

NO. 86, ZHUJIANG ROAD, TIANJIN, CHINA

CERTIFICATE

DATE: DEC. 8, 2008

INVOICE NO: 08FZ018

TO: WHOM IT MAY CONCERN

WE CERTIFY THAT A SET OF NON-NEGOTIABLE DOCUMENT UNDER L/C NO. LCN038 INCLUDING A COPY OF B/L, A COPY OF INVOICE, A COPY OF PACKING LIST HAVE BEEN SENT TO THE SKY INTERNATIONAL I/E LTD. WITHIN 48 HOURS AFTER SHIPMENT.

TIFERT TRADING CO., LTD.
泰佛贸易有限公司
*

....

Authorized Signature

样例 13.8 受益人证明

BILL OF EXCHANGE

No. INV NO. 08FZ018   Tianjin, China. DEC. 17, 2008

Exchange for USD131512.30

At * * * sight of this FIRST of Exchange(Section of exchange being unpaid), pay to the order of OURSELVES the sum of

U.S. DOLLARS ONE HUNDRED AND THIRTY ONE THOUSAND FIVE HUNDRED AND TWENTY AND THIRTY CENTS ONLY

Drawn under CENTRAL BANK OF SPAIN

L/C No. LCN038

Date NOV.23, 2008

TIFERT TRADING CO., LTD.
泰佛贸易有限公司
*

To: BANK OF CHINA

样例 13.9 汇票

发票号 INV NO. 08FZ018	船名 SHUNFENG V.0827	提单号 SINO081216
开证行 CENTRAL BANK OF SPAIN		装期 DEC.16, 2008
信用证号 LCN038	结汇金额 USD 131512,30	效期 DEC.31, 2008 交单期 DEC. 29, 2008

单据名称	汇票	发票	装箱单	保险单	产地证	检验证	GSP产地证	海关发票	船行证明	受益人证明	电抄	提单	提单副本	其他
应交份数	2	6	3	3	2	3				1		3		

存在问题及处理意见

发票：

①单价和金额处漏写贸易术语 CIF BARCELONA，单价漏写计量单位 PER PC

②装运港和目的港后漏加注 CHINA 和 SPAIN 国别

③多加注了 WE HEREBY CERTIFY THAT THE GOODS ARE OF CHINESE ORIGIN，应删除

海运提单：

①提单抬头应制成 TO ORDER 而不是 TO ORDER OF SHIPPER

②被通知人 APPLICANT 应具体写成 SKY INTERNATIONAL I/E LTD. 1000 ALGECIRAS ST., SPAIN

保险单：

①赔付地点应是 SPAIN 而不是 CHINA

②保险单日期应在装船前，如 DEC.5, 2008，而不是 DEC.9, 2008

装箱单：

①包装应该是 100 条口布装一纸箱，而不是 10 条

②在加注了声明文句后应有出票人的签字

检验证书：

①其签证日期应该早于提单日，如 DEC. 5, 2008 而不是 DEC. 9, 2008

②漏签章

产地证：

①漏声明文句"THE GOODS ARE WHOLLY PRODUCED IN CHINA"

②货物描述最后漏填 * * * * * 以示结束

汇票：

①金额大写应该为 U.S. DOLLARS ONE HUNDRED AND THIRTY ONE THOUSAND FIVE HUNDRED AND TWELVE AND THIRTY CENTS ONLY

②付款人应为 CENTRAL BANK OF SPAIN

其他应注意事项：

单证员	审单员	银行复核	结汇日期
王芳	庞峻岭		

样例 13.10 审单记录表

三、审核单据的操作训练

【翻译语句】

①terms and conditions of the credit
②horizontal examination
③vertical examination
④discrepancy
⑤be in accordance with
⑥international standard banking practice
⑦uniform customs and practice
⑧reasonable time
⑨check list
⑩reimburse
⑪A document dated before the issuing date of letter of credit is not acceptable.

⑫Documents which appear on their face to be inconsistent with one another will be considered as not appearing on their face to be in compliance with the terms and conditions of the credit.

⑬If a letter of credit calls for "full set of clean on board ocean bills of lading", then it's acceptable if there is no "on board" notation but there's pre-printed wording that goods have been shipped on board.

⑭If a letter of credit requires an insurance policy, an insurance certificate can not satisfy the need.

⑮If beneficiary presents documents that are not stipulated in the letter of credit, negotiating bank needn't examine these documents and don't send them to the Issuing Bank.

【动脑思考】

①盛大贸易公司在一笔出口贸易中收到国外进口商的信用证,信用证中要求提交 Form A 原产地证书,同时要求提单必须制成指示性抬头"To order of Issuing Bank"。在这种情况下,单证员在制作 Form A 原产地证书时第二栏收货人栏填写了该开证行的名称。请问:你在审核该单据时,对此应如何判断和处理?

②泰佛贸易公司在一笔出口贸易中收到国外进口商的信用证,信用证中对汇票期限规定为"At 30 days after sight of draft",而单证员在缮制汇票时将汇票的付款期限写成"At 30 days after date of draft"。请问:你在审核该单据时,对此应如何判断和处理?这两种写法的区别在哪里?

③泰佛贸易公司在一笔出口贸易中收到国外进口商的信用证,证中规定"CIF FO HONGKONG",在审单时,发现单证员在缮制发票时写成"CIF HONGKONG"。请问:你对此应如何判断和处理?这两种写法的区别在哪里?

④天纺服装贸易公司在一笔出口贸易中收到国外进口商的信用证,证中规定"Packing List and Weight List Each in Duplicate",并且在附加条款中表示"Combined Documents Unacceptable"。而单证员在缮制装箱单时将名称写为"Packing List and

Weight List”,并制作了一式两份。请问:你在审核该单据时,对此应如何判断和处理?

⑤天成贸易公司在一笔出口贸易中收到国外进口商的信用证,证中规定提单的被通知人(NOTIFY)制作成“XYZ CORP. LTD. ONLY”。而单证员在缮制提单时,将被通知人项写为“XYZ CORP. LTD.”。请问:你在审核该单据时对此应如何判断和处理?

【动手操练】

泰佛贸易有限公司出口一批五金工具箱到埃塞俄比亚 AMENLI COMPANY(ETHIOPIA),采用 L/C + CIFC3 ASEB 方式达成交易。请你以泰佛贸易有限公司审单员的身份审核该信用证项下全套结汇单据(样例13.11~样例13.16),并完成审单记录表(空白审单记录表见样例13.17)。

SEQUENCE OF TOTAL	27:	1/1
FORM OF DOC. CREDIT	40A:	IRREVOCABLE
APPLICABLE RULES	40E:	UCP LATEST VERSION
DOC. CREDIT NUMBER	20:	LC-0720
DATE OF ISSUE	31C:	080720
EXPIRY	31D:	DATE 080915 PLACE BENEFICIARY'S COUNTRY
APPLICANT	50:	AMENLI COMPANY, ETHIOPIA. #5054-7 KING STREET, ETHIOPIA FAX:(+03)3436 5758 TELE:(+03)3434 5756
BENEFICIARY	59:	TIFERT TRADING CO., LTD. NO. 86, ZHUJIANG ROAD, TIANJIN, CHINA FAX:02285665678 TELE:02285665679
AMOUNT	32B:	CURRENCY USD AMOUNT 39,370.00
AVAILABLE WITH/BY	41D:	ANY BANK IN CHINA BY NEGOTIATION
DRAFTS AT ...	42C:	DRAFT AT SIGHT FOR FULL INVOICE VALUE
DRAWEE	42A:	COMMERCIAL BANK ETHIOPIA
PARTIAL SHIPMENTS	43P:	NOT ALLOWED
TRANSSHIPMENT	43T:	NOT ALLOWED
LOADING IN CHARGE	44A:	CHINA PORTS
FOR TRANSPORT TO ...	44B:	ASEB ETHIOPIA
LATEST DATE OF SHIP.	44C:	080831
DESCRIPT. OF GOODS	45A:	

TRADE TERM CIFC3 ASEB

HARDWARE TOOLS CASE	TC110 250SETS
	TC120 250SETS
	TC130 250SETS

TC140 250SETS

DOCUMENTS REQUIRED 46 A:

1. SIGNED COMMERCIAL INVOICE IN 1 ORIGINAL AND 5 COPIES

2. FULL SET (3/3) OF CLEAN ON BOARD MARINE BILL OF LADING MADE OUT TO ORDER OF THE OPENING BANK NOTIFY APPLICANT MARKED FREIGHT PREPAID

3. SIGNED PACKING LIST IN 1 ORIGINAL AND 3 COPIES

4. 2 COPIES OF INSURANCE POLICY OR CERTIFICATE ENDORSED IN BLANK FOR THE INVOICE VALUE OF THE GOODS PLUS 10% COVERING ALL RISKS AND WAR RISKS AS PER AND SUBJECT TO OCEAN MARINE CARGO CLAUSES OF THE PEOPLE'S INSURANCE COMPANY OF CHINA DATED 1/1/1981.

DETAILS OF CHARGES 71B:

ALL BANKING CHARGES OUT SIDE ETHIOPIA ARE FOR ACCOUNT OF THE BENEFICIARY

PRESENTATION PERIOD 48:

DOCUMENTS TO BE PRESENTED WITHIN 15 DAYS AFTER THE DATE OF SHIPMENTBUT WITHIN THE VALIDITY OF THE CREDIT

样例 13.11 信用证

<table>
<tr><td colspan="2">Issuer
TIANJIN TIFERT I/E CORP.
NO. 86, ZHUJIANG ROAD TIANJIN CHINA</td><td colspan="2">商 业 发 票
COMMERCIAL INVOICE</td></tr>
<tr><td colspan="2">To
AMENLI COMPANY, ETHIOPIA.
#5054 - 7 KING STREET, ETHIOPIA</td><td>No.:
INV0805</td><td>Date:
2008 - AUG - 05</td></tr>
<tr><td colspan="2" rowspan="2">Transport Details
FROM TIANJIN TO ASEB</td><td>S/C No.
SC - 070626</td><td>L/C No.
LC - 0720</td></tr>
<tr><td colspan="2">Terms of payment
L/C AT SIGHT</td></tr>
<tr><td colspan="4">
<table>
<tr><th>Marks and numbers</th><th>Number and kind of packages, description of goods</th><th></th><th>Quantity</th><th>Unit price</th><th>Amount</th></tr>
<tr><td></td><td colspan="3">HARDWARE TOOLS CASE</td><td></td><td></td></tr>
<tr><td>SC - 0706265</td><td>TC110</td><td>5WCS</td><td>250SETS</td><td>USD18. 07</td><td>USD4517. 50</td></tr>
<tr><td>AMENLY</td><td>TC120</td><td>5WCS</td><td>250SETS</td><td>USD32. 34</td><td>USD8085. 00</td></tr>
<tr><td>ASEB</td><td>TC130</td><td>5WCS</td><td>250SETS</td><td>USD46. 60</td><td>USD11650. 00</td></tr>
<tr><td>NO. 1 - 10</td><td>TC140</td><td>5WCS</td><td>250SETS</td><td>USD60. 47</td><td>USD15117. 50</td></tr>
<tr><td></td><td>TOTAL:</td><td>20WCS</td><td>1000SETS</td><td></td><td>USD39370. 00</td></tr>
</table>
PACKING: 50SETS IN ONE WOODEN CASE, 20 CASES IN ONE 20′ CONTAINER.</td></tr>
</table>

样例 13.12 商业发票

Issuer TIANJIN TIFERT I/E CORP. NO. 86, ZHUJIANG ROAD TIANJIN CHINA	装箱单 **PACKING LIST**
To AMENLI COMPANY, ETHIOPIA. #5054 –7 KING STREET, ETHIOPIA	No. INV0805 Date 2008 – AUG –05
Transport Details FROM TIANJIN TO ASEB	S/C No. SC –070626 L/C No. LC –0720 Terms of payment L/C AT SIGHT

Marks and Nos.	Number and kind of packages, description of goods			Net weight	Gross weight	Measurement
	HARDWARE TOOLS CASE					
SC –070626	TC110	5WCS	250SETS	1250KGS	1375KGS	5.000CBM
AMENLY	TC120	5WCS	250SETS	1500KGS	1625KGS	5.000CBM
ASEB	TC130	5WCS	250SETS	1750KGS	1875KGS	5.000CBM
NO. 1 –20	TC140	5WCS	250SETS	1875KGS	2000KGS	5.000CBM
	TOTAL:	20WCS	1000SETS	6375KGS	6875KGS	20.000CBM

PACKING: 50SETS IN ONE WOODEN CASE, 20 CASES IN ONE 20′ CONTAINER.

样例 13.13 装箱单

Shipper TIANJIN TIFERT I/E CORP., NO. 86, ZHUJIANG ROAD, TIANJIN, CHINA	B/L No. SINO081216
Consignee or order TO ORDER	中国外运天津公司 SINOTRANS TIANJIN COMPANY OCEAN BILL OF LADING
Notify address AMENLI COMPANY, ETHIOPIA. #5054 – 7 KING STREET, ETHIOPIA	Shipped on board in apparent good order and condition (unless otherwise indicated) the goods or packages specified herein and to be discharged at the mentioned port of discharge or as near thereto as the vessel may safely get and be always afloat. The weight, measure, marks and numbers, quality, contents and value, being particulars furnished by the Shipper, are not checked by the Carrier on loading. The Shipper, Consignee and the Holder of this Bill of Lading hereby expressly accept and agree to all printed, written or stamped provisions, exceptions and conditions of this Bill of Lading, including those on the back hereof. In witness whereof the number of original Bills of Lading stated below have been signed, one of which being accomplished the other(s) to be void.

Pre-carriage by	Port of loading TIANJIN, CHINA
Vessel DONGFENG V. 208	Port of transshipment
Port of discharge ASEB, ETHIOPIA	Final destination

Container. seal No. or marks and Nos.	Number and kind of package	Description of goods	Gross weight (kgs.)	Measurement (m^3)
SC – 070626 AMENLY ASEB NO. 1 – 20	20 WOODEN CASES SAY TWENTY WOODEN CASES ONLY FREIGHT TO COLLECT	HARDWARE TOOLS CASE	6875.00KGS ON BOARD DATE: 15 – AUG – 08	20.000CBM

Freight and charges			REGARDING TRANSHIPMENT INFORMATION PLEASE CONTACT
Ex. rate	Prepaid at	Freight payable at	Place and date of issue TIANJIN 15 – AUG – 08
	Total prepaid	Number of original Bs/L THREE	Signed for or on behalf of the Carrier As Agent

样例 13.14 海运提单

中国平安保险股份有限公司
PING AN INSURANCE COMPANY OF CHINA LTD.
货物运输保险单
CARGO TRANSPORTATION INSURANCE POLICY

被保险人

Insured: TIANJIN TIFERT I/E CORP.

中国平安保险股份有限公司根据被保险人的要求极其所交付约定的保险费,按照本保险单背面所载条款与下列特款,承保下述货物运输保险,特立本保险单。

This Policy of Insurance witnesses that PING AN INSURANCE COMPANY OF CHINA, LTD at the request of the Insured and in consideration of the agreed premium paid by the Insured, undertakes to insure the undermentioned goods in transportation subject to the conditions of Policy as per the clauses printed overleaf and other special clauses attached hereon.

保单号

Policy No. BD0785

赔款偿付地点

Claim payable at

发票或提单号

Invoice No. or B/L No. INV NO. INV0805

CHINA IN USD

运输工具

Per Conveyance S. S. DONGFENG V. 208

查勘代理人

Survey By:

GODWIN INSURANCE COMPANY

01 ONE ST. ASEB FAX: 125 – 393 – 8576

起运日期 Slg. on or abt. AS PER B/L 自 From TIANJIN 至 To ASEB

保险金额

Amount insured SAY US DOLLARS FORTY-THREE HUNDRED THREE HUNDRED AND SENEN ONLY

保险货物项目、标记、数量及包装:

Description, marks, quantity & packing of goods:

20 WCS (1000SETS) HARDWARE TOOLS

AS PER INV NO. INV0805

承保条件

Condition:

COVERING ALL RISKS AND WAR RISKS

AS PER CIC OF P. I. C. C. DATED 1/1/1981

签单日期

Date: 16 – AUG – 08

For and on behalf of

PING AN INSURANCE COMPANY OF CHINA, LTD.

李虹

Authorized Signature

复核: 田光军　　制单 陈丽

地址及电话

Address & Tel. 022 2331 4567

No. 75 NANJING ROAD TIANJIN CHINA

注:未加盖本公司保单专用章,保单无效。

样例 13.15 保险单

No. INV NO. 0805 Tianjin，China. AUG 20，2008

Exchange for USD 39370.00

At * * * sight of this FIRST of Exchange(Section of exchange being unpaid),pay to the order of

BANK OF CHINA TIANJIN BRANCH the sum of

U.S. DOLLARS THIRTY-NINE THOUSAND THREE HUNDRED AND SEVENTY ONLY

Drawn under COMMERCIAL BANK OF ETHIOPIA

L/C No. LC-0720

Date JUL 29，2008

TIANJIN TIFERT I/E CORP.

To: COMMERCIAL BANK OF ETHIOPIA

样例 13.16 汇票

审单记录表

发票号	船名	提单号
开证行		装期
		效期
信用证号	结汇金额	交单期

单据名称	汇票	发票	装箱单	保险单	产地证	检验证	GSP产地证	海关发票	船行证明	受益人证明	电抄	提单	提单副本	其他
应交份数														
预交份数														

存在问题及处理意见	

其他应注意事项：

制单员	审单员	银行复核	结汇日期

样例 13.17　空白审单记录

5

电子制单

任务十四　电子制单

任务背景

为了进一步提高单证的准确度，降低单证差错率，增进单证工作的效率，王芳小姐所在的天津泰佛（TIFERT）贸易公司特请隆威软件公司为其开发了一套ERP系统，从此公司所有的业务操作就必须借助ERP系统来完成。单证工作同样也不例外，即须进入ERP系统进行电子制单。这样单证上类同项目的内容只须输入一次，电脑就可以自动生成。只要一次输入正确，一份正确，份份正确，于是大大提高了单证工作的效率，也很好地解决了“单单一致”的问题。经过半个多月的摸索，王芳很快地就掌握了电子制单技巧。

【背景分析】

尽管国际商务单证种类多，单证的内容复杂，但其主要内容有很多是相同的，如不同单证的进出口商名称、商品名称、商品规格、商品数量、商品价格、发货人、收货人、装运港及目的港等，必须在每种单据上填写，还要反复核对，出错的概率很高，因此开发和使用电脑软件制单，利用现代技术为企业提供一个便捷的单证缮制平台至关重要。利用电脑软件缮制单据，单证上类同项目的内容只须输入一次，电脑就可以自动生成，很好地解决了“单单一致”问题。可一旦出错，则会招致业务的满盘皆输，因此电脑制单对单证人员的要求会更高。因此王芳小姐应该掌握和具备如下知识、技能及素质。

知识技能

①了解电子制单的概念及主要形式。

②熟悉电子制单软件的基本功能和特点。

操作技能

①了解并熟悉几个典型制单软件的功能和使用。

②掌握轻松制单和 EasyBoss 等软件的操作方法。

职业素质

①养成终身学习的意识。

②积极进取,永不满足。

一、电子制单的基础知识

【电子制单的概念】

所谓“电子制单”是指利用电子计算机这一现代化工具缮制和处理各种进出口单证。简单的电子制单仅指利用电子计算机缮制并打印各种进出口单据,送银行议付或寄给进口商。完整的电子制单则指与计算机网络连在一起,除了利用计算机缮制各种进出口单据,还要将它们通过计算机网络传输到银行、商检、海关及国外客户等的计算机中,实现电子报关、电子报检及电子结算等,实现真正的“无纸贸易”。

电子制单技术的出现与运营,为外经贸企业提高进出口制单工作的效率、减少进出口单据缮制中的许多重复性操作和差错、提高办事效率和经济效益等起到了极其重要的作用。近些年来,我国进出口贸易采用电子制单的业务环节越来越多,如进出口报关、报检、进出口收/付汇核销、出口退税、进出口许可证及产地证申领等。

【电子制单的主要方式】

目前,我国外经贸企业电子制单主要有两种方式。

1. 利用 Office 的编辑功能制单

(1)利用 Word 软件制单

Word 是最流行的文字编辑软件。不但对所录入信息可以方便地进行修改、复制、剪切及储存等操作,而且可以综合处理文字与表格,所以被较早使用在进出口单证业务中。Word 制单方法简单、直观、明了,能做到输入的资料所见即所得。但 Word 计算、统计功能较低,它只不过是利用计算机模仿了人工打字机功能,没有“智能”操作。尽管如此,仍有许多外经贸企业利用 Word 做成各种单据模板,以此制单。

(2)利用 Excel 软件制单

Excel 可预先设置好模板并有统计功能。每一个 sheet 可直接命名为商业发票、装箱单、原产地证书、提单、受益人证明、装运通知及汇票等,使用选择性粘贴,实现一次输入多单显示,操作直观、方便,并能提高效率。外经贸企业可根据自己的实际情况设置模板,不用支出任何额外成本,故在实际业务中运用最广。

2. 利用专业制单软件制单

专业制单软件是指利用新一代计算机语言(如 java,c + + 等)强大的数据库访问能力以及完善的远程通信功能,配合先进的数据库存储大量的表单数据,并通过软件制作数据输入接口和单证模板,所形成的功能完备的单证表格软件。此类软件操作非常简单并智能化,只要单证员按照提示输入软件所需信息、选择所需单据,它就可以将单证员所要的各个单据即刻制成并显示出来,供单证员审查、调整或打印。专业制单软件具有信息一次录入,多次使用,多单使用,以及单据自动生成、可视化即时修改、单据套打等多种功能。

二、电子制单的基本技能

【实训目的】

通过本项目实训,应掌握的基本技能如下。

①了解并熟悉几个典型制单软件的功能和使用方法。

②掌握轻松制单和 EasyBoss 等软件的操作方法。

③学会独立使用制单软件缮制单据。

【操作前准备】

进行本项任务的实训前,应准备的内容如下。

①为电脑系统安装 Office 办公软件,包括 Word 和 Excel 软件。

②从互联网上搜索有关电子制单的软件并安装到电脑系统中。

③购买有关的电子制单软件,或请软件公司为企业专门开发 ERP 系统。

【操作程序】

①在电脑上安装电子制单软件,并进行测试。

②仔细阅读信用证或合同中的相关条款,对各种要求做到心中有数。

③录入基本信息,做到准确、完整。

④录入特殊条款。

⑤生成各种单据,在预览状态下审核单据,有问题及时更改。

⑥打印全套结汇单据。

【操作规范】

目前国内通用的电子制单软件有如下几种。

1. 轻松制单

“轻松制单”是阿丙软件(ABINSOFT)有限公司(http://www.abin.com.cn/gsjj.htm)针对国内外经贸企业信息化、标准化流程管理开发的专业进出口单证软件。“轻松制单”自推出以来,因界面简洁、操作简单、功能齐全及适用性强等特点,深受外经贸企业的欢迎。

轻松制单有两个主要版本:“轻松制单 2.08”、“轻松制单 XP3.03”(免费下载地址:http://www.abin.com.cn/rjxz.htm),它们是阿丙软件公司 EASYTODO 系列产品的重要组成部分。除“轻松制单”、“轻松制单 XP”外,该公司还有“EASYTODO——外贸业务管理系统”、“外贸企业综合管理系统”等外贸专业软件。现以轻松制单 2.08 和 XP 版本为例,介绍其操作规范。

“轻松制单 2.08”软件操作流程如下。

(1)下载和安装

①在 IE 地址栏中输入“轻松制单 2.08”下载地址,并回车,如图 14.1 所示。

图 14.1　输入下载地址

②点击“轻松制单 2.08”下载按钮,下载该软件,如图 14.2 所示。

图 14.2　下载软件

③打开软件安装程序,连续点击“下一个”按钮,至安装结束,如图14.3所示。

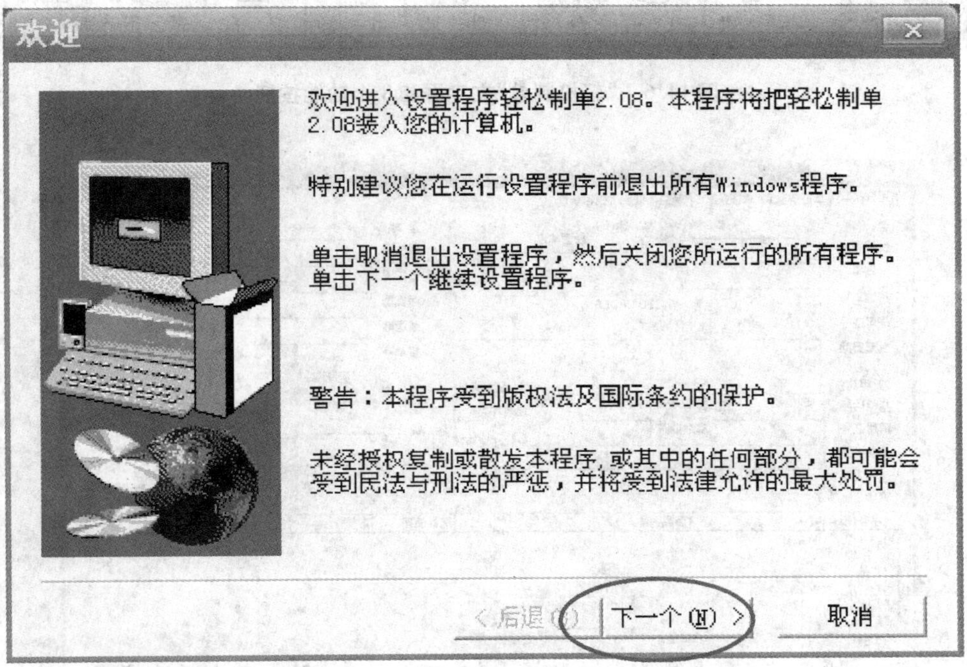

图14.3 安装软件

(2)进入操作界面

①点击“轻松制单”图标,如图14.4所示。

②在登录界面中输入用户名(QSZD)和口令(888),点击“确定”,如图14.5所示。

图14.4 快捷图标

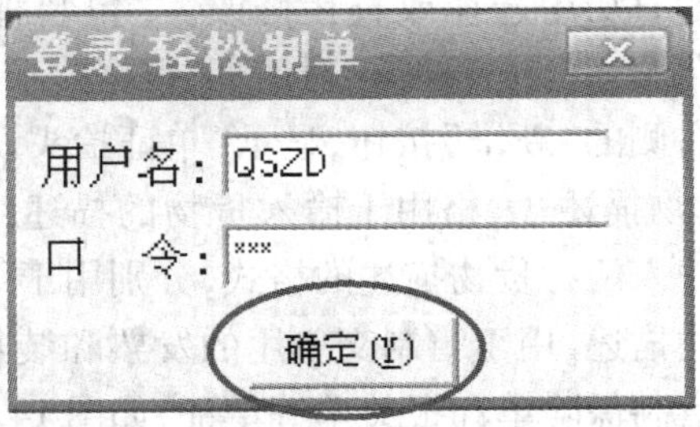

图14.5 输入用户名和口令

③屏幕左上角出现“轻松制单”滚动文字屏和8个功能按钮,如图14.6所示。

(3)创建并输入新的制单信息

①点击功能按钮中的“新建”,进入新的数据输入界面,如图14.7所示。

图 14.6 “轻松制单”文字屏和 8 个功能按钮

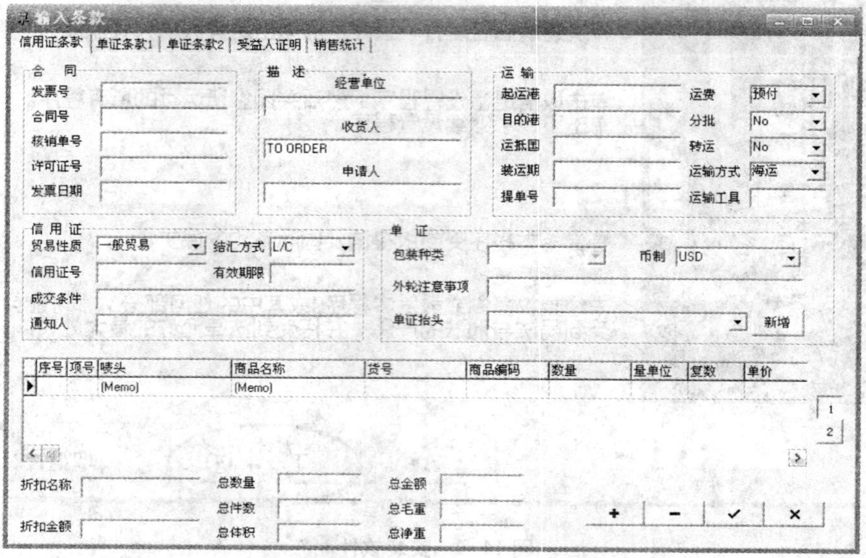

图 14.7 数据输入界面

②输入制单信息。

“信用证条款”中的数据是信用证条款中规定的数据，根据信用证的要求输入即可。“日期”缺省情况下，程序默认所有的日期为当天的日期，可以双击鼠标在显示出的日历中选择或直接修改。“包装种类”中如果没有可选的包装，可以选中“其他”，显示“包装种类”对话框，根据要求添加相应的包装种类。单击“单证抬头”输入框右侧的“新增”按钮，显示“单证抬头设置”对话框，其用于输入外经贸企业的资料。“货物描述”表格用于输入货物的描述细节，右侧有“1”、“2”两个选择按钮，可以分别输入两种货物描述的格式，分别用于缮制不同的单证。例如，在“1”中输入详细的货物描述，用于缮制交单用的发票和装箱单等，而在“2”中输入简单的综合描述，用于缮制保险单和报关单等单证，如图 14.8 所示。

“单证条款”主要用于输入每一个单证单独的特殊条款，如图 14.9 所示。

“受益人证明”用于输入信用证要求的受益人证明单证，如图 14.10 所示。

(4)预览和打印所需单据

①点击功能按钮中的“打印”，如图 14.11 所示，进入打印界面。

②选择发票号码及所需单据，点击“生成单证”，如图 14.12 所示。

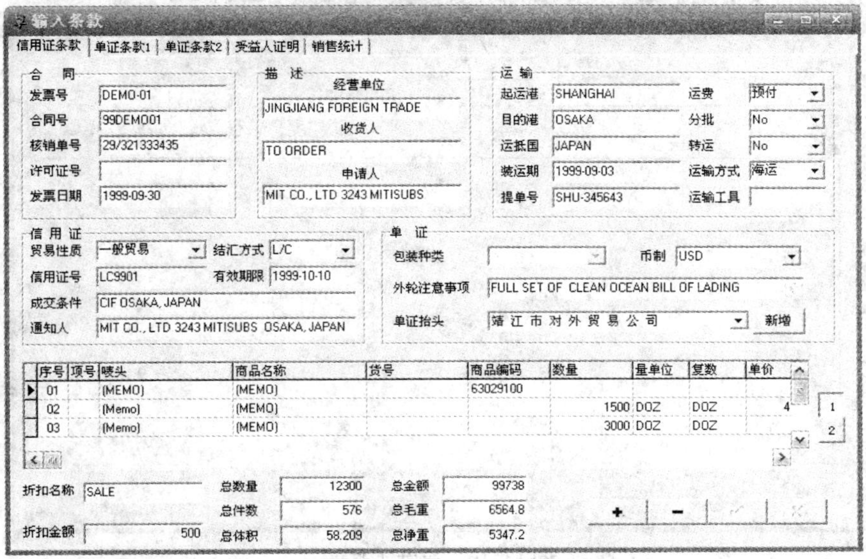

图 14.8 输入条款

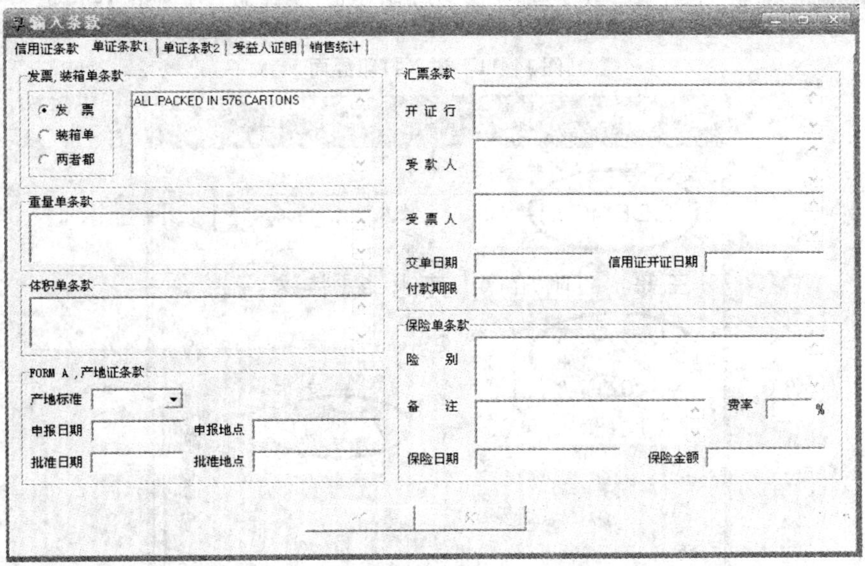

图 14.9 单证条款

③预览生成的单据,如图 14.13 所示。

④打印所需单据,如图 14.13 所示。

图 14.13 左上角的两个打印机图标分别用于打印全部单证和当前单证。每一种单证可以设置不同的打印份数,即使关闭预览窗口,该数值依然有效,直到改变发票

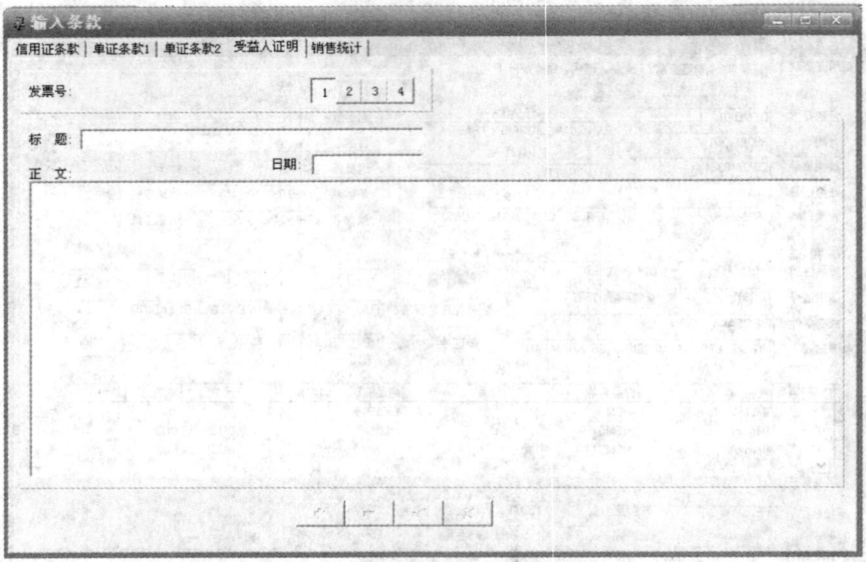

图 14.10 受益人证明

图 14.11 进入打印界面

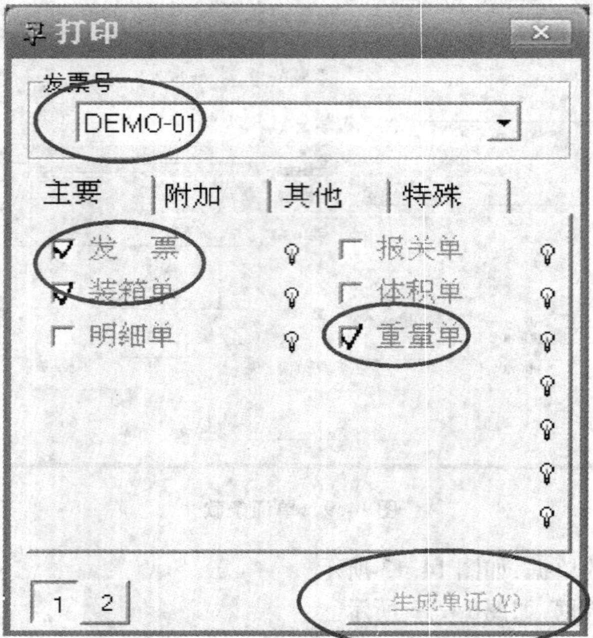

图 14.12 生成单证

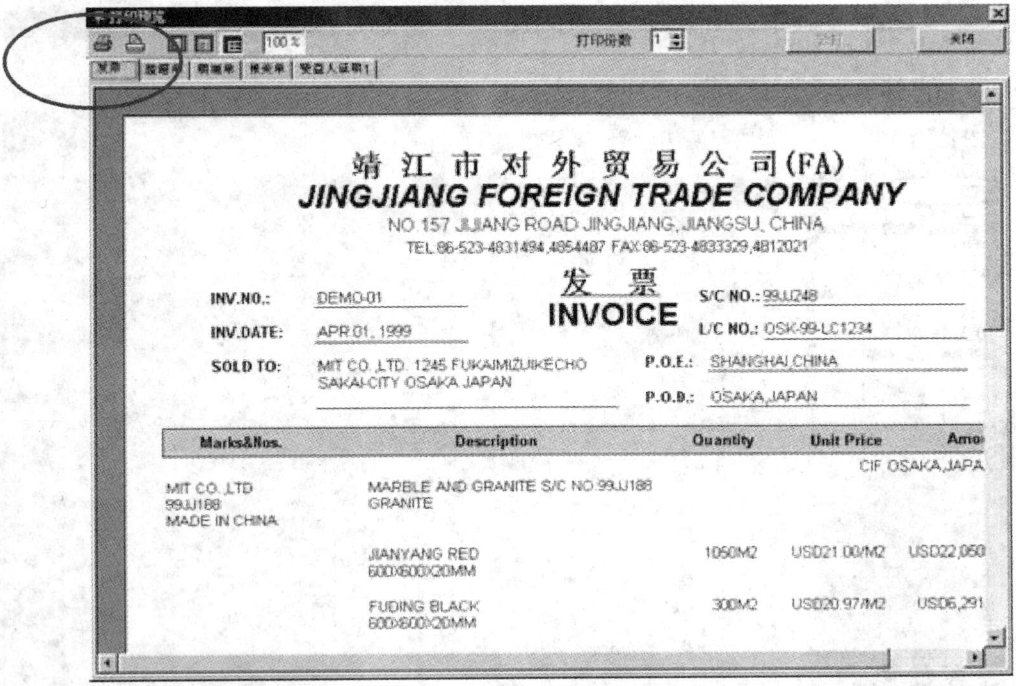

图 14.13 预览和打印单据

号。“套打”或者“取消套打”分别用于在已经印刷的格式单证上填充打印或在白纸上直接打印。

(5)其他功能

查找、帮助、退出等功能略。

“轻松制单 XP3.03”软件操作流程如下。

(1)下载和安装

方法同“轻松制单 2.08”。

(2)进入操作界面

①在登录对话框中输入用户名(QSZD)和口令,点击“确定”(888),如图 14.14 所示。

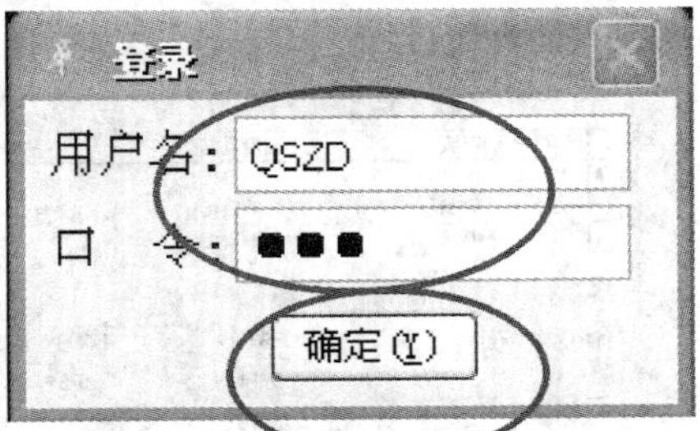

图 14.14 输入用户名和口令

②点击“轻松制单”操作平台中“新建单证”图标,进入“条款输入”界面,如图 14.15 所示。

(3)输入相关数据或信息

①在信用证条款界面中,输入合同和信用证信息,如图 14.16 所示。

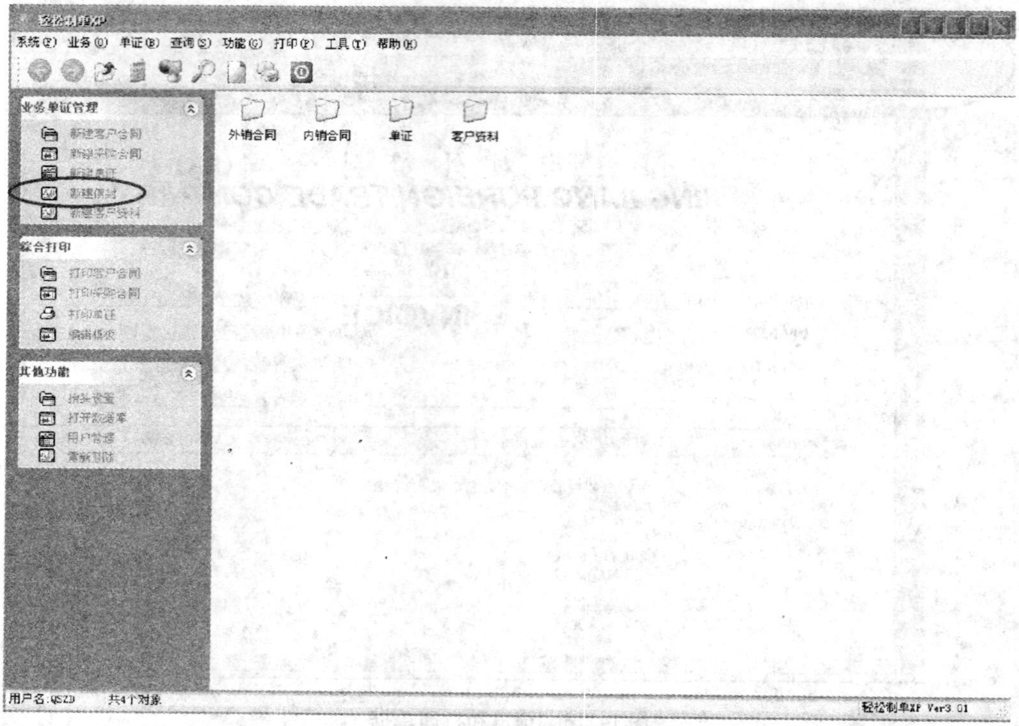

图 14.15 进入"条款输入"界面

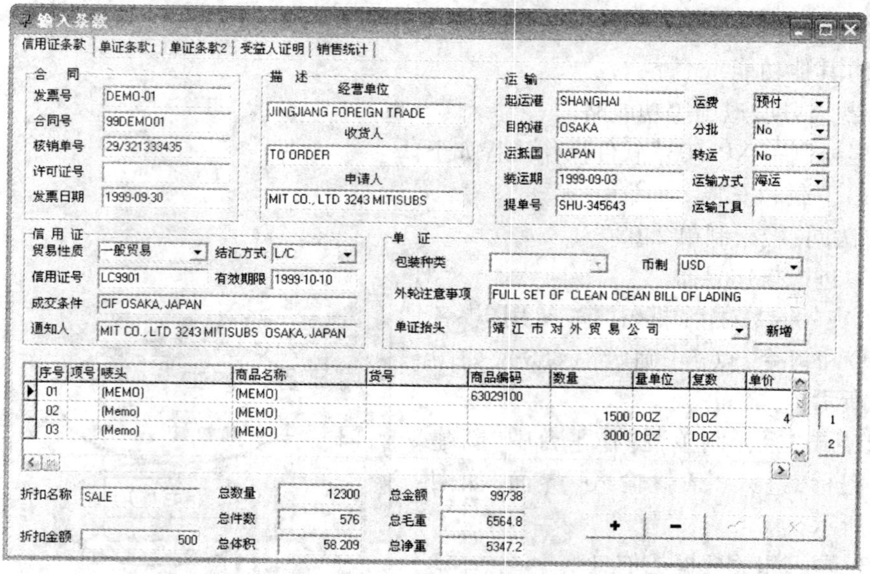

图 14.16 输入合同和信用证信息

②在单证条款1界面中，输入发票、汇票、保险单、产地证及包装单据缮制信息，如图14.17所示。

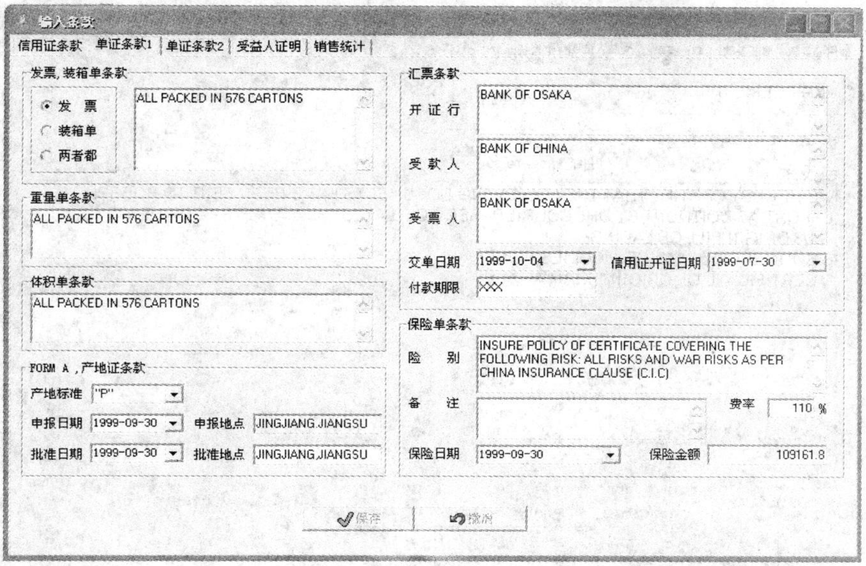

图14.17 输入发票、汇票、保险单、产地证及包装单据缮制信息

③在单证条款2界面中，输入运输单据(提单)缮制信息，如图14.18所示。

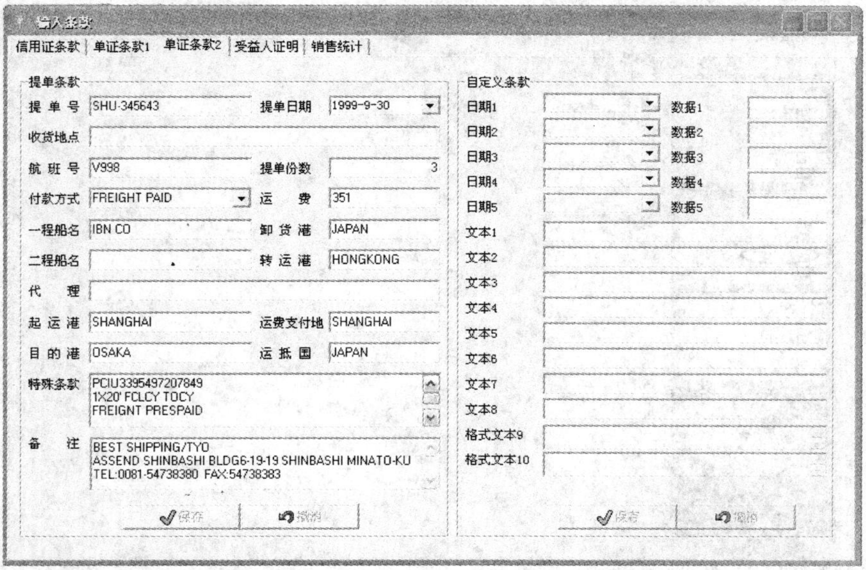

图14.18 输入运输单据(提单)缮制信息

④在受益人证明界面中,输入受益人证明缮制信息(受益人证明文句),如图 14.19 所示。

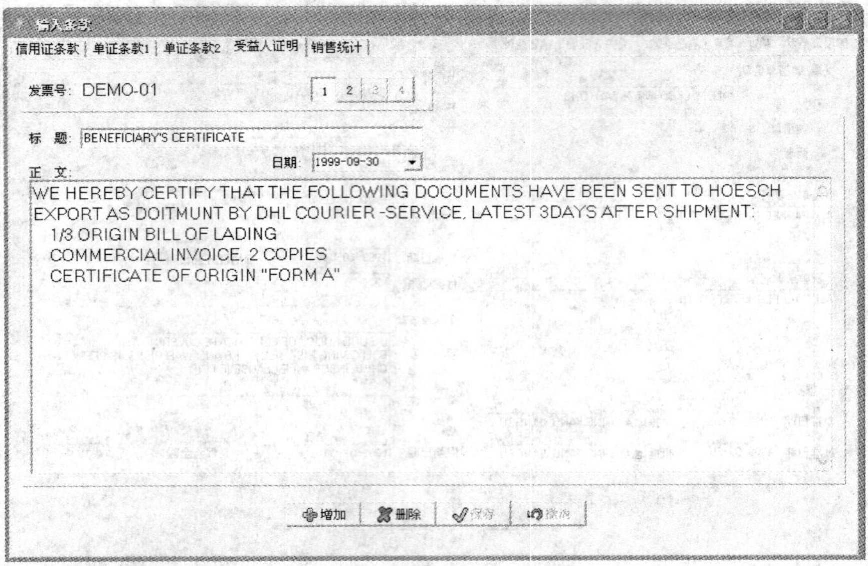

图 14.19 输入受益人证明缮制信息(受益人证明文句)

⑤点击操作平台中"打印单证"按钮,如图 14.20。调出打印界面,如图 14.21 所示。

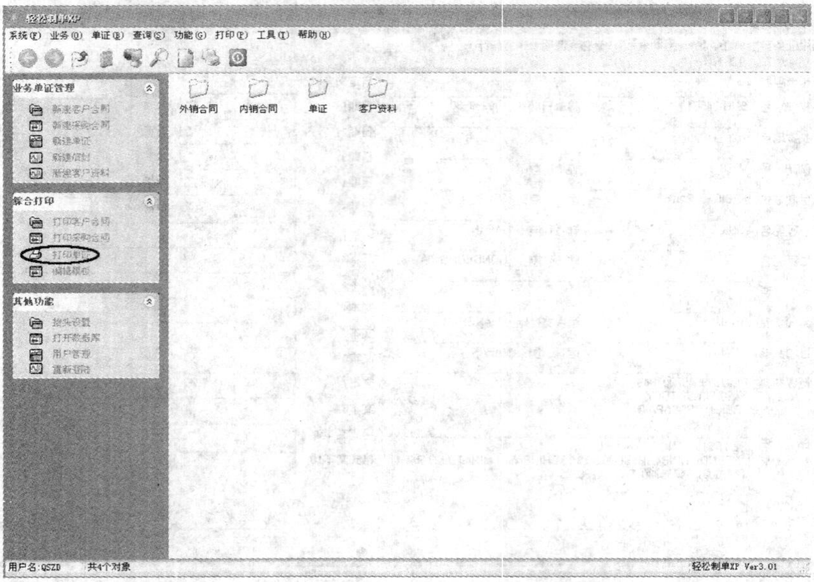

图 14.20 点击"打印单证"

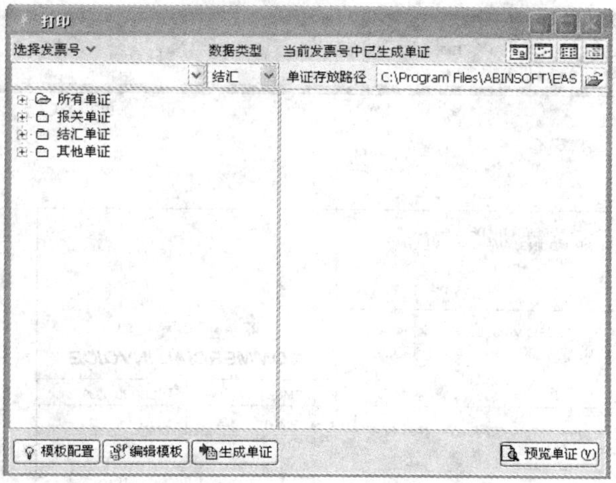

图 14.21 调出打印界面

⑥在打印界面中，选择发票号码、打印单据的种类及名称，点击“生成单证”按钮，如图 14.22 所示。

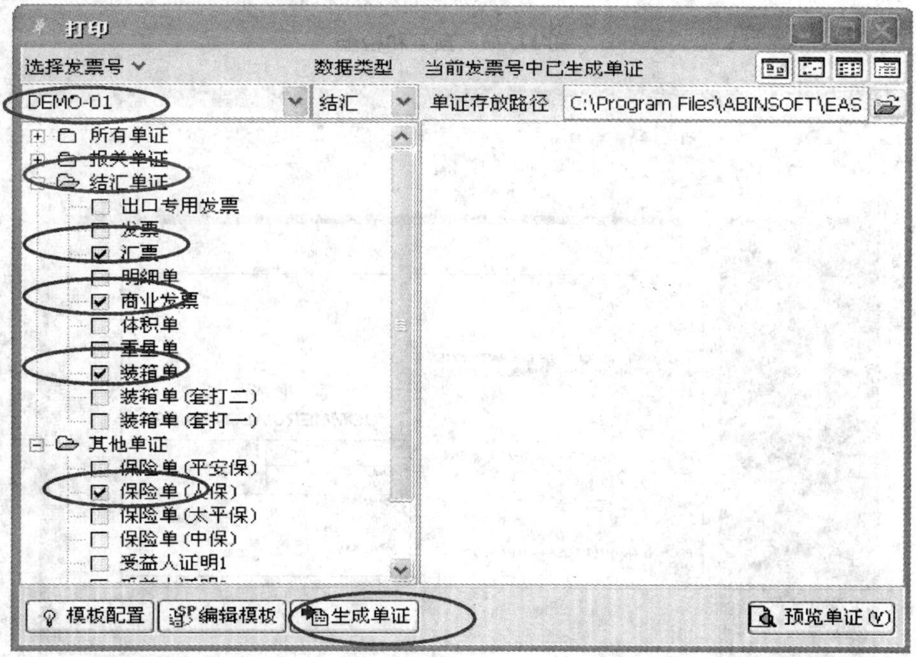

图 14.22 生成单证

⑦对生成的单据进行预览和检查，如图 14.23 所示。

⑧点击单据预览界面中的图标 ，打开单据编辑页面，如图 14.24 所示。

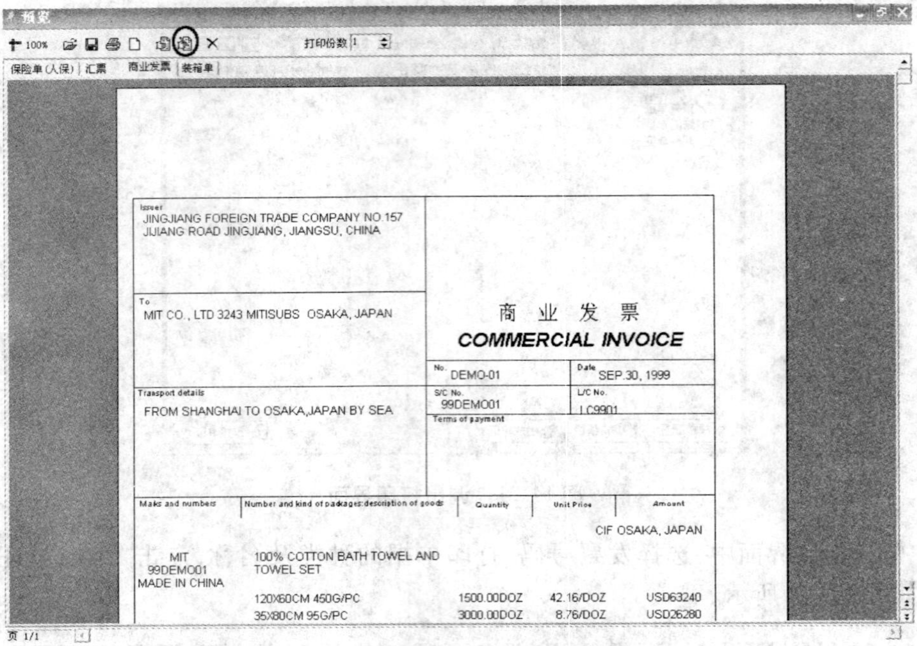

图 14.23 预览和检查

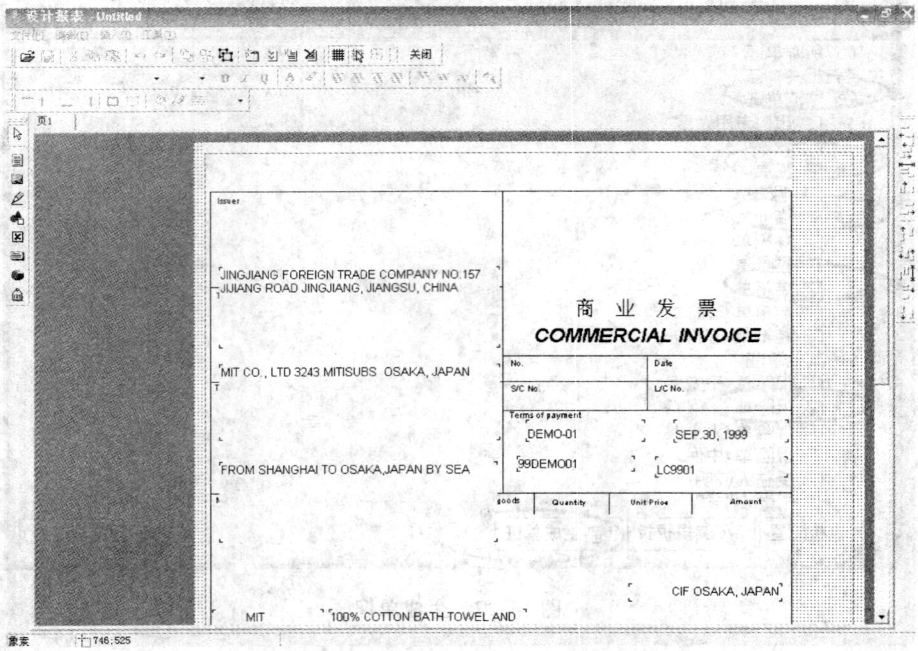

图 14.24 单据编辑页面

⑨双击要修改的内容,在文本编辑框中修改相关内容,如图 14.25 所示。

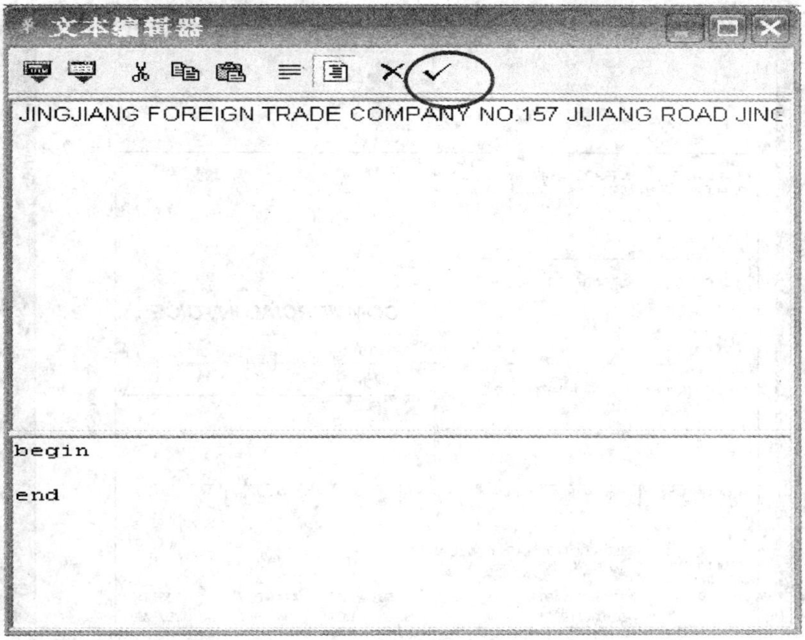

图 14.25 文本编辑框

⑩点击文本编辑页面中 ✓ “确定”,保存修改结果,如图 14.25 所示。

⑪点击单据预览页面中 “打印”,如图 14.26 所示。

⑫按照提示,完成单据打印,如图 14.27 所示。

2. EasyBoss(外贸业务管理平台)软件

EasyBoss 外贸业务管理平台是北京易商海泰克科技有限公司(http://www.aiecc.com/)推出的“让商务活动更容易”外贸系列软件之一,是国内第一套专为中小型及个人外贸企业量身打造的外贸管理软件。功能内容包括进出口函电、报价、合同、信用证、库存、单据、财务、配额、核销、退税及电子口岸业务管理。EasyBoss 以其优越的设计为用户提供全面而强大的外贸业务处理功能,并且它体贴用户,方便使用,具有很高的运行效率,因而赢得了广大用户的青睐。

除 EasyBoss 以外,针对外贸企业实际业务需要,该公司还开发有 EasyDoc(外贸单据管理)、EasyTrade(外贸 ERP 管理)和 EasyBusiness(外贸网站管理)等专业软件,并长期提供上述软件介绍、演示及下载。(产品中心地址:http://www.aiecc.com/cpzx.asp)

(1)EasyBoss 登录

①点击 EasyBoss 软件登录图标(如图 14.28),打开 EasyBoss 软件登录界面。

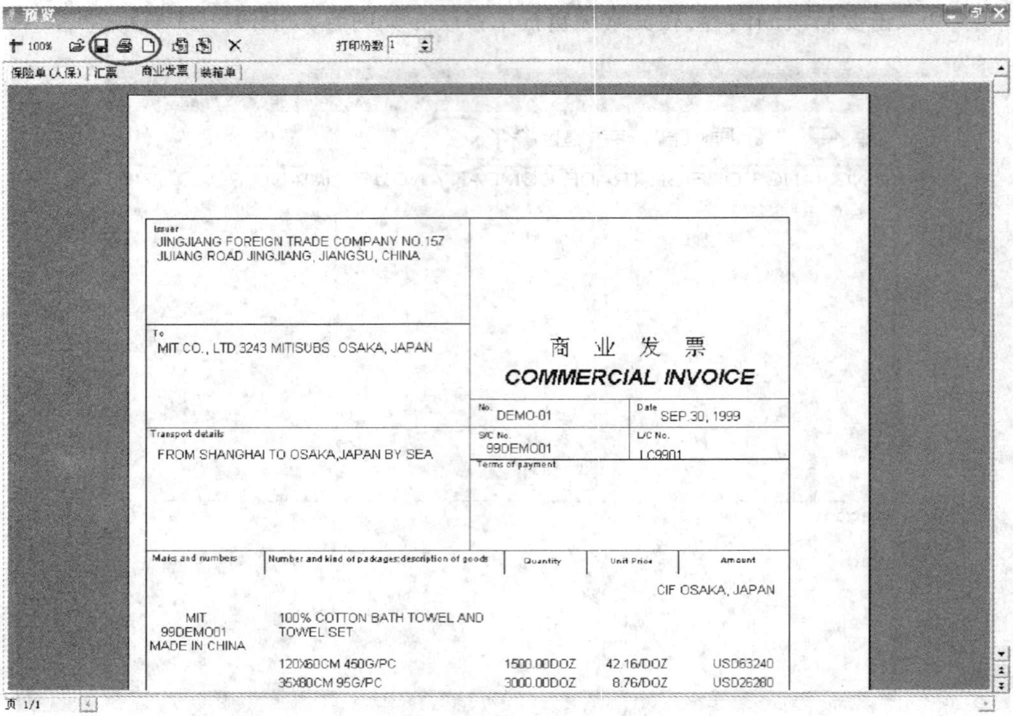

图 14.26 点击打印

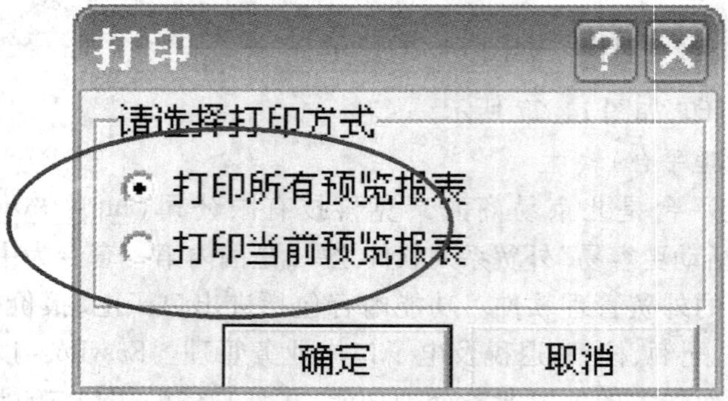

图 14.27 完成单据打印

图 14.28 Easy Boss 登录图标

②在 EasyBoss 登录界面中输入用户名(管理员)口令(0102),点击"确定",如图 14.29 所示。进入 EasyBoss 操作主界面如图 14.30 所示。在这里可以看到的软件功能包括基础信息、报价与合同、代理业务、业务案卷、函电、备货发运、库存、单证制作、财务管理、数据查询、核销退税及辅助业务等。

③点击界面右侧"进口业务"或"出口业务"图标,打开业务流程树,如图 14.31

所示,点击“树”上文字,可以打开相关业务模块,如“出口合同审核”,如图 14.32 所示。

图 14.29 EasyBoss 登录界面

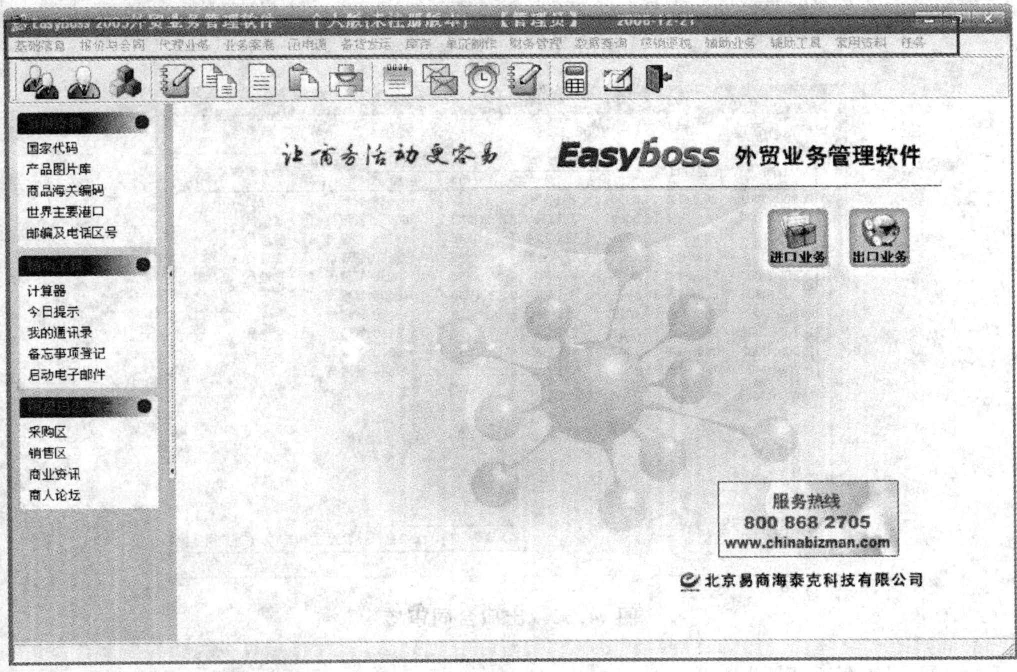

图 14.30 EasyBoss 操作界面

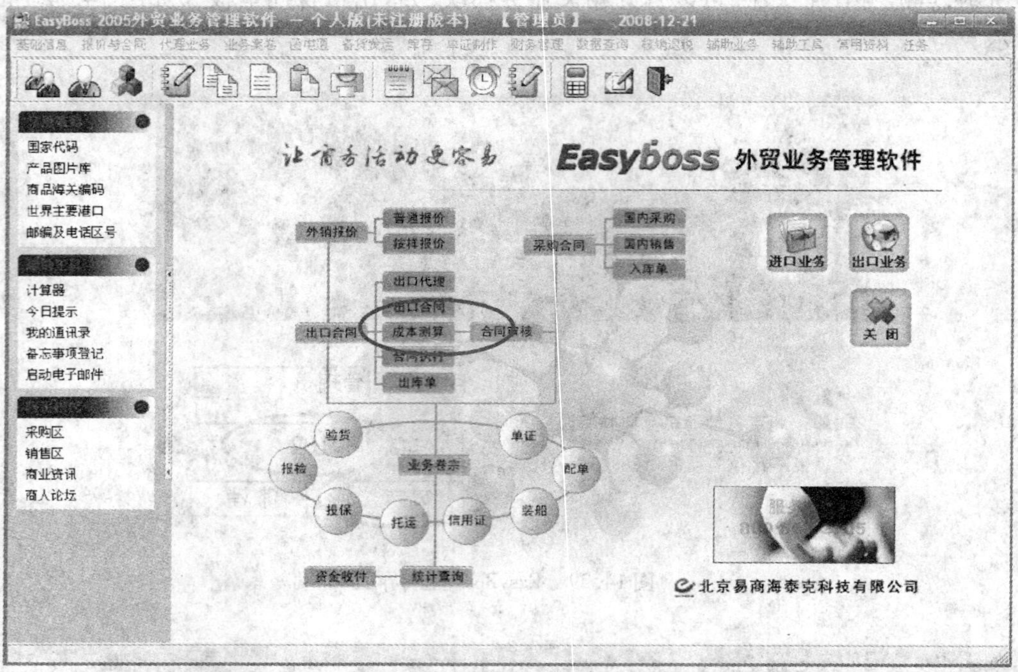

图 14.31 业务流程树

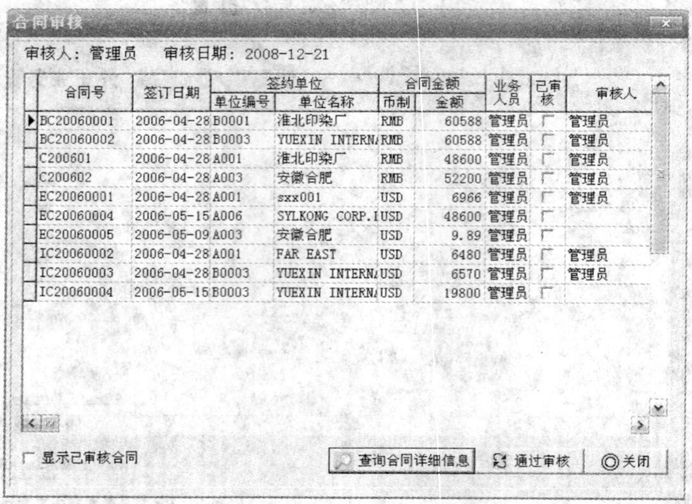

合同号	签订日期	签约单位		合同金额		业务人员	已审核	审核人
		单位编号	单位名称	币制	金额			
BC20060001	2006-04-28	B0001	淮北印染厂	RMB	60588	管理员		管理员
BC20060002	2006-04-28	B0003	YUEXIN INTERN/	RMB	60588	管理员		管理员
C200601	2006-04-28	A001	淮北印染厂	RMB	48600	管理员		管理员
C200602	2006-04-28	A003	安徽合肥	RMB	52200	管理员		管理员
EC20060001	2006-04-28	A001	sxx001	USD	6966	管理员		管理员
EC20060004	2006-05-15	A006	SYLKONG CORP.I	USD	48600	管理员		
EC20060005	2006-05-09	A003	安徽合肥	USD	9.89	管理员		
IC20060002	2006-04-28	A001	FAR EAST	USD	6480	管理员		管理员
IC20060003	2006-04-28	B0003	YUEXIN INTERN/	USD	6570	管理员		管理员
IC20060004	2006-05-15	B0003	YUEXIN INTERN/	USD	19800	管理员		

图 14.32 出口合同审核

(2)基础信息设置

①点击操作界面左上角“基础信息”，选择要设置的信息项目，如“我的单位”，如图 14.33 所示。

②在“我的单位”中输入我的单位信息，并保存，如图 14.34 所示。

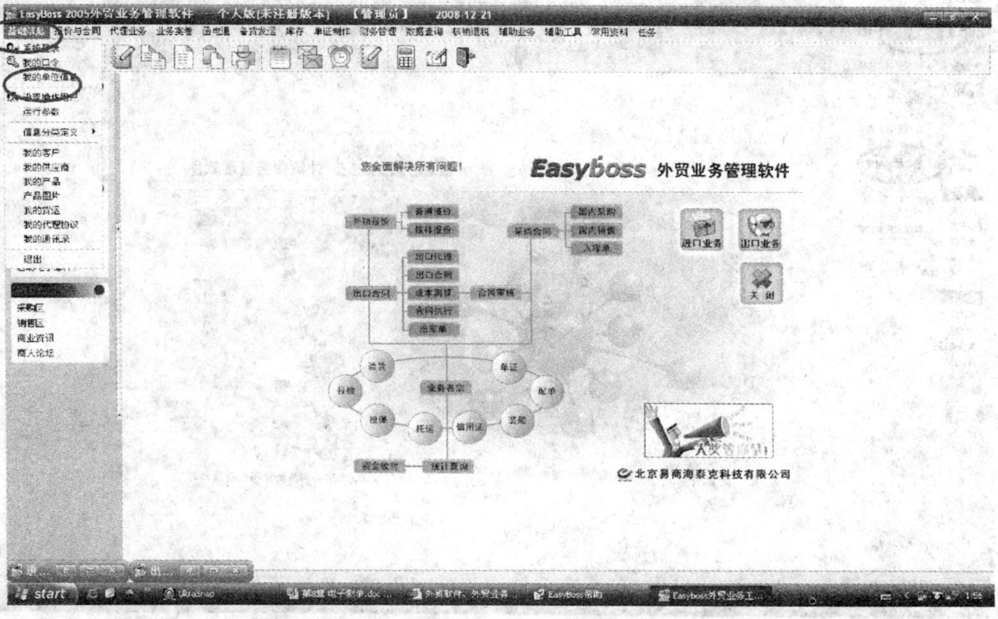

图 14.33 选择要设置的信息项目

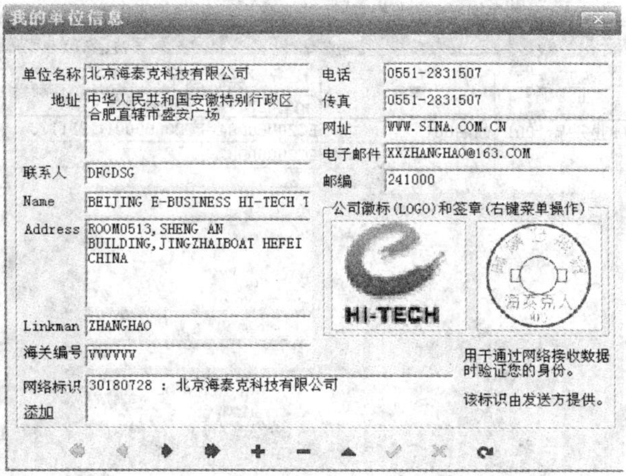

图 14.34 输入我的单位信息

(3)进出口报价与合同管理

①点击操作界面左上角“报价与合同”,选择要操作的对象,如“出口成本测算”,如图 14.35 所示。

②点击“成本测算单”页面中“新建”、“浏览”及“打印”等按钮,如图 14.36 所示。进行相关业务操作,如图 14.37 所示。

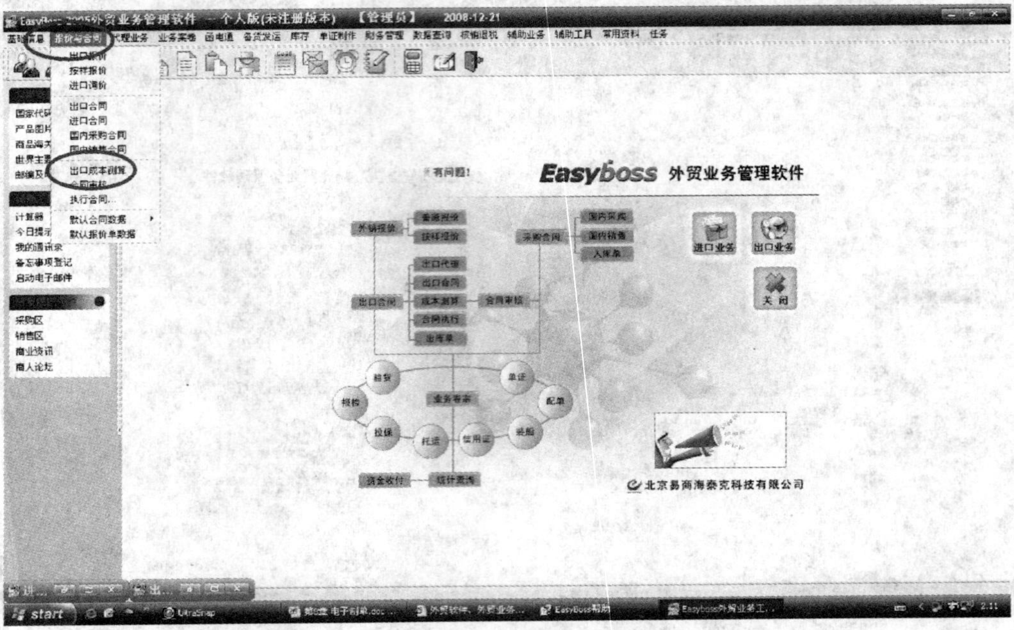

图 14.35 选择报价与合同的操作对象

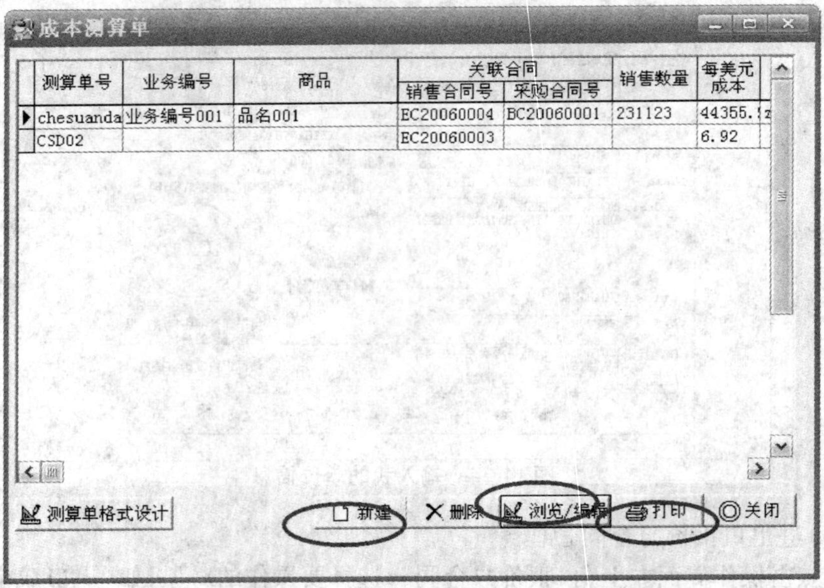

图 14.36 点击相关操作按钮

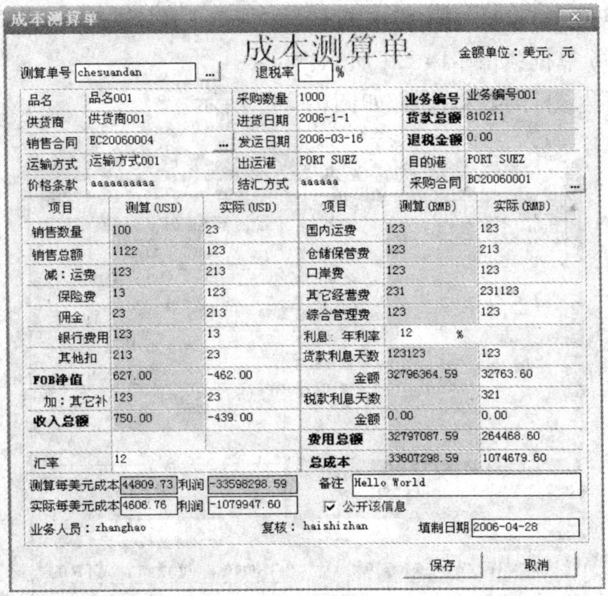

图 14.37　业务操作

(4)备货发运

①点击“备货发运”按钮，打开备货发运业务列表，如图 14.38 所示。

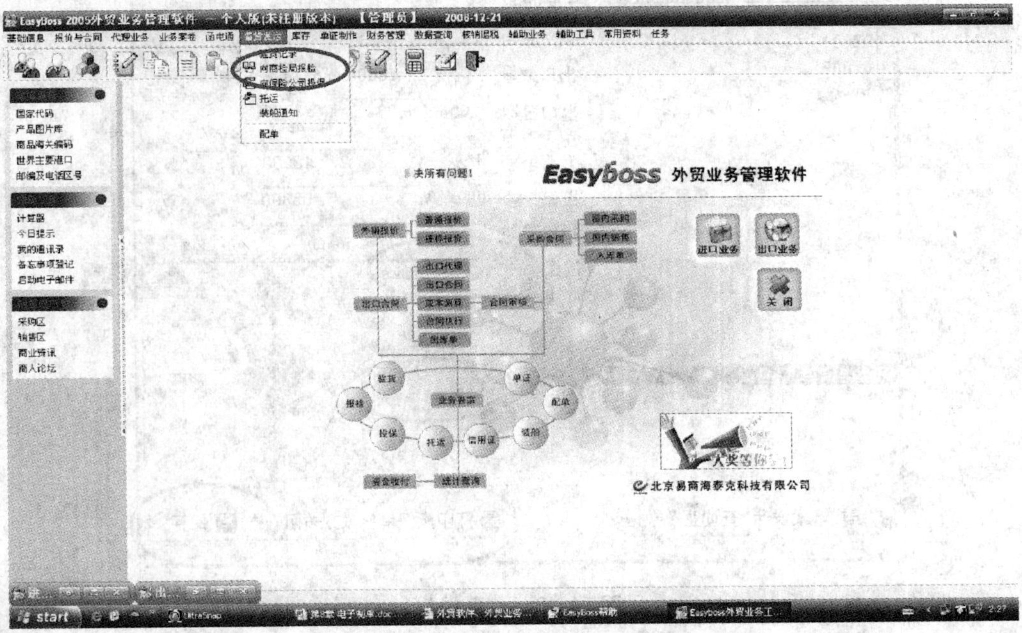

图 14.38　选择备货发运业务

②选择"业务功能",如"报检"、"投保"、"托运"及"装运通知"等,如图 14.38 所示。打开相关业务单据,如图 14.39 所示。

③编辑、保存及打印投保单据,如图 14.40 所示。

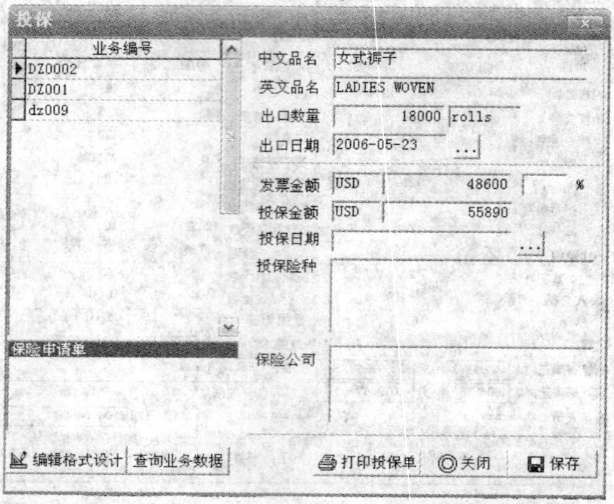

图 14.39 相关业务单据

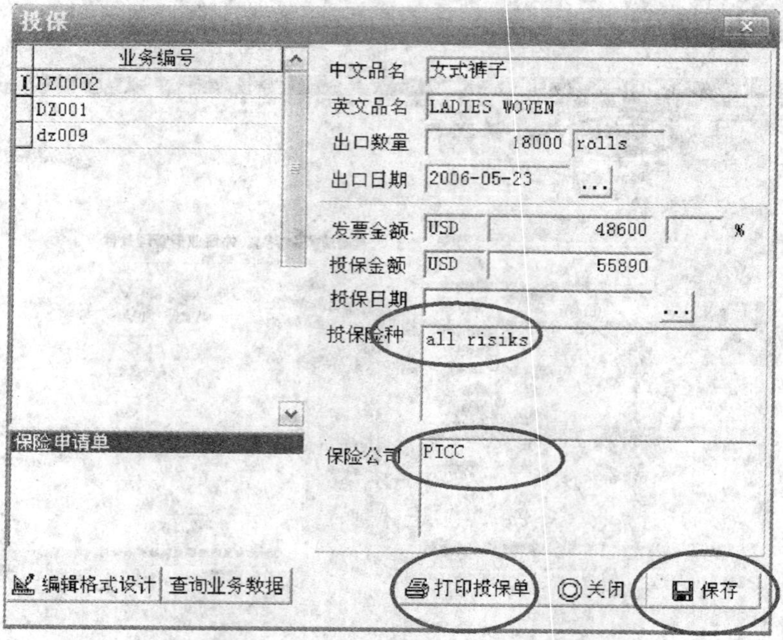

图 14.40 业务操作

(5)单证制作

①单击"单证制作"按钮,打开单据制作任务列表,如图14.41。

②点击单证制作具体任务("新建"、"修改"、"浏览"、"打印"及"审单签发"等),如图14.41所示。进行相关业务操作(如"查阅"、"通过"),如图14.42所示。

(6)核销退税

①单击"核销退税"按钮,打开核销退税任务列表,如图14.43所示。

②点击核销退税具体任务(如"核销"或"退税"),如图14.43所示。进行相关业务操作,如"申报退税",如图14.44所示。

(7)辅助业务

①单击"辅助业务"按钮,打开辅助业务任务列表,如图14.45所示。

②点击辅助业务具体任务(如"来证登记"和"进口开证申请"等),如图14.45所示,进行相关业务操作,如"进口开证申请",如图14.46所示。

(8)其他

略。

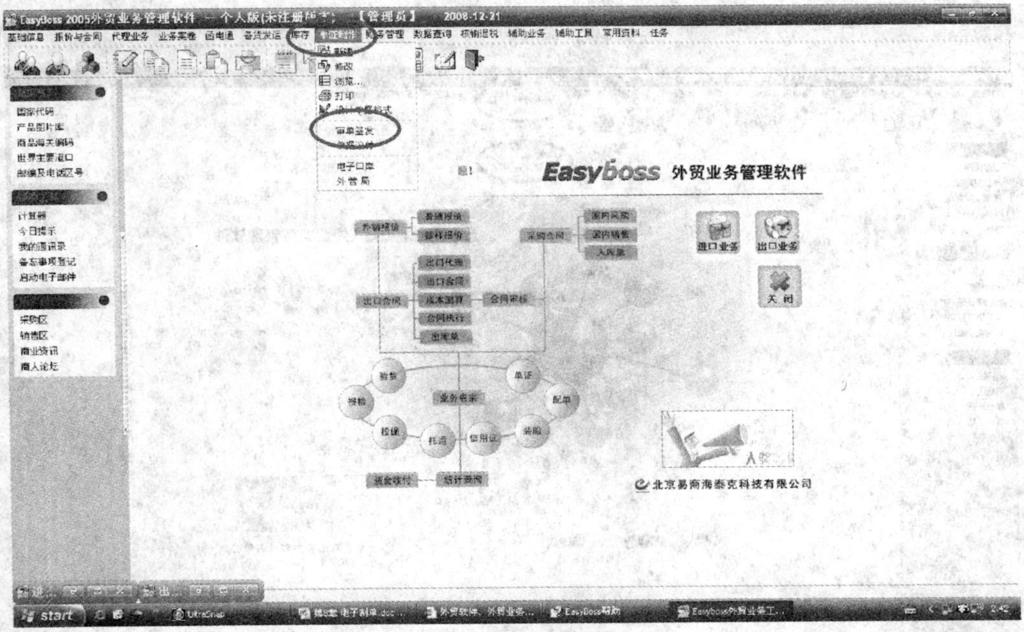

图14.41 选择单据制作任务

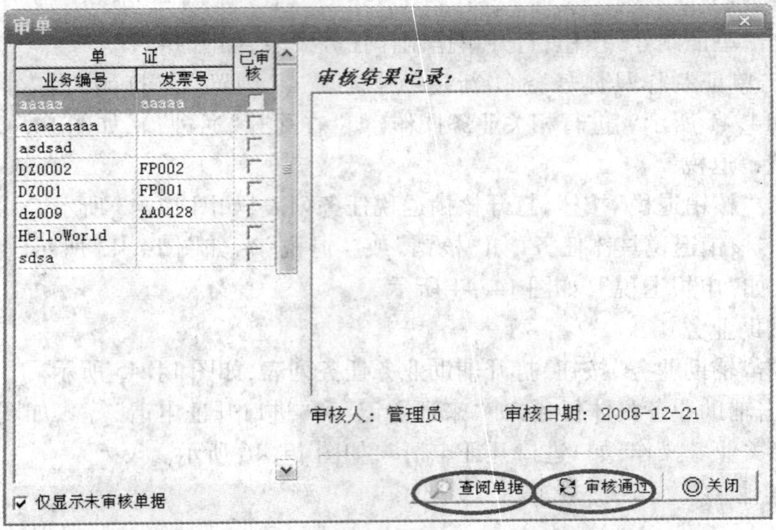

图 14.42　业务操作

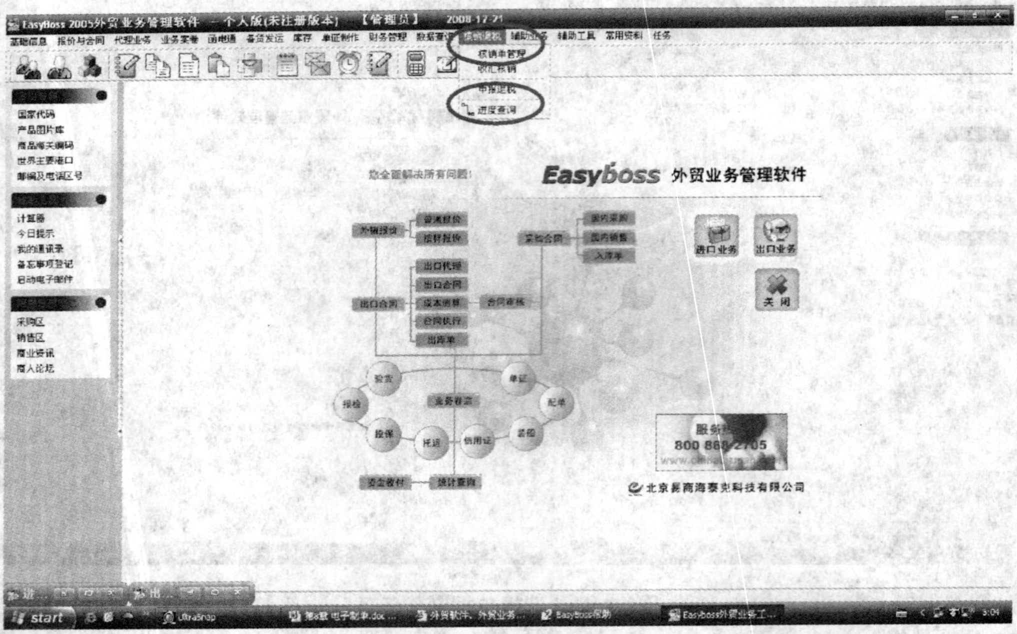

图 14.43　选择核销退税任务

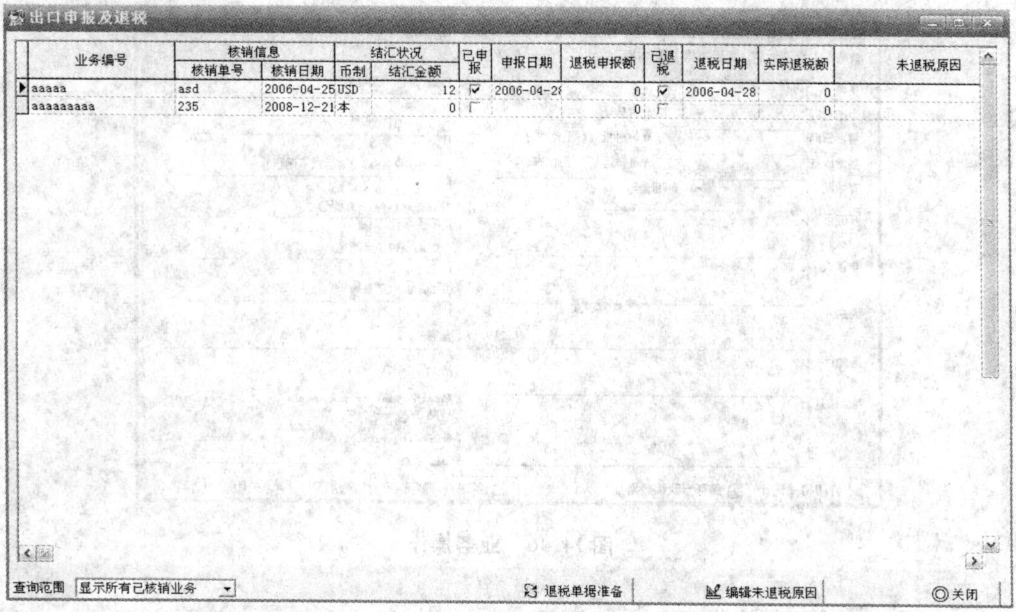

图 14.44 业务操作

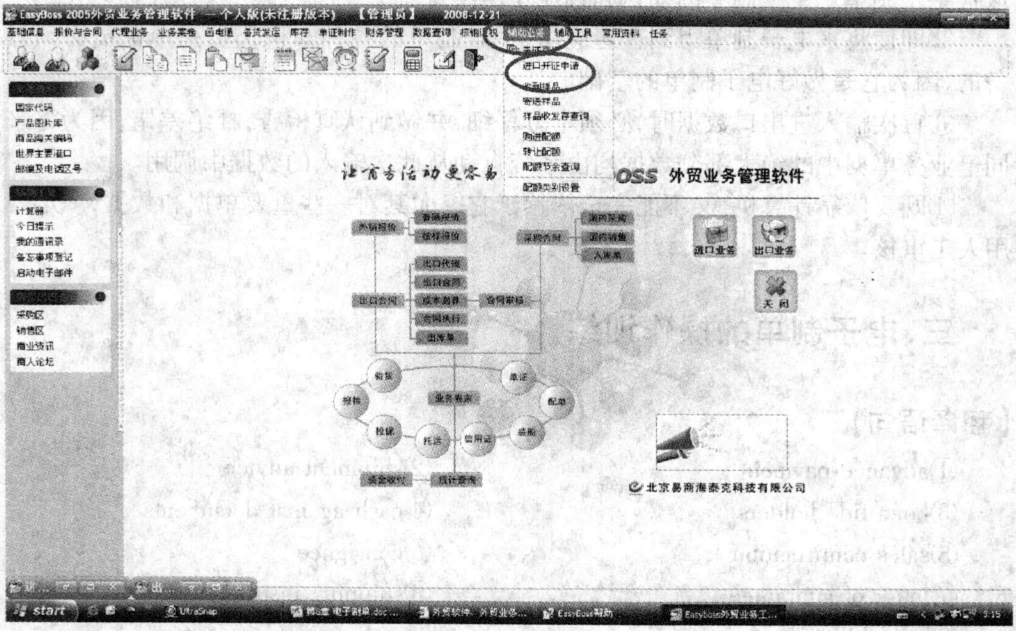

图 14.45 选择辅助业务

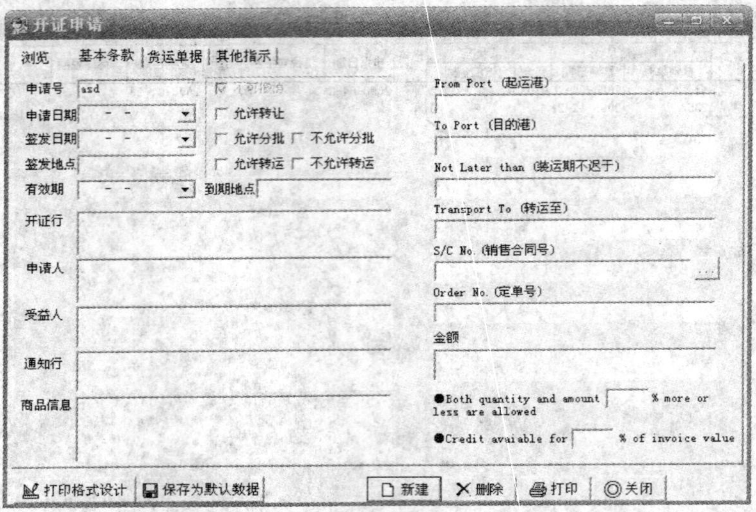

图 14.46　业务操作

【操作注意事项】

①尽管电子制单具有手工制单无法比拟的优势，但是电子制单目前还不能完全取代手工制单。手工制单的知识和技能还须具备。

②即使将来电子制单得到普遍应用，手工制单的各种知识仍然是单证员必须具备的，因为它是做好电子制单的基础。

③首次输入进出口数据时，必须十分仔细，并做到认真检查，杜绝差错，因为将来同笔业务单据中的绝大部分数据均由系统自动从此次输入的数据中调用。

④既要依靠计算机，又不能完全依赖于它。尤其对一些重要单据和数据，一定要用人工审核。

三、电子制单的操作训练

【翻译语句】

①advance payment
②shipment advice
③bona fide holders
④cash against documents
⑤sales confirmation
⑥consignee
⑦letter of guarantee
⑧shipping instruction
⑨sight bill of exchange
⑩with particular average
⑪most favored nation clause
⑫warehouse to warehouse clause
⑬errors and omissions excepted
⑭irrespective of percentage

⑮shipping agent

【动脑思考】

①什么是电子制单？电子制单的优点是什么？

②电子制单的方法有哪些？各有何特点？

③专业制单软件有哪些主要功能和特点？

④下载并安装几个外贸制单和外贸业务管理软件，比较并分析它们各自的功能和特点。

⑤访问中国电子口岸等网站，了解进出口网上托运、投保、报关、报检、认证、核销及退税等的操作规则和方法。

【动手操练】

实训操作一

天津联想电脑公司与伦敦电子公司就出口联想旭日125型的笔记本电脑达成一份出口合同，合同号AXY5728(见样例14.1)，买方将信用证(见样例14.2)及时开抵卖方，卖方备货的外箱尺码是55厘米×50厘米×45厘米，每箱毛重27公斤，净重25公斤，请利用轻松制单软件(或自己下载相关软件)缮制全套单据(没有提供的资料可自拟)。

销　售　合　同

SALES CONTRACT

编号 No.：AXY5728　　　　日期 Date：2008－11－20

The sellers：TIANJIN LENOVO COMPUTER COMPANY

Add：NO.25，XIANGGANG ROAD，TIANJIN　　　　Post code：300112

The buyers：LONDON ELECTRON COMPANY

Add：NO.52，VICTORY ROAD，LONDON

Tel：44－10－26561357　　　　Fax：44－10－26561237

兹确认售予你方下列货品，其成交条款如下：

We hereby confirm having sold to you the following goods on the terms and conditions as specified below：

(1)货物名称及规格 Name of commodity and specifications	(2)数量 Quantity	(3)单价 Unit price	(4)总值 Total amount
LENOVO COMPUTER MODEL NO. XURI－125	CIF LONDON		
	100UNITS	USD1000/UNIT	USD100000.00

(5)包装：

Packing：1UNIT/BOX，5BOXES/CARTON

(6)装运唛头：

Shipping mark：LENOVO COMPUTER
LONDON
C/NO.1－20

MADE IN CHINA

(7)装运期限:

Time of shipment: DEC. 30,2008

(8) 装运口岸:

Port of shipment: TIANJIN

目的地:

Destination: LONDON

(9)付款条件:

Payment: BY SIGHT L/C TO REACH THE SELLER NOT LATER THAN NOV. 5, 2008

(10)保险:

Insurance: The seller shall arrange marine insurance covering institute cargo clauses (A) and institute war clauses for 110% of CIF value. Claim, if any, payable in London in U. S. currency.

确认签署 Confirmed by

London Electron Company

Tianjin Lenovo Computer Company

JHON DAVID 章瀚

买方 (The buyers) 卖方 (The sellers)

样例 14.1 销售合同

LETTER OF CREDIT

FROM : LONDON BANK

TO: BANK OF TIANJIN

SEQUENCE OF TATAL	*27:	1/1
FORM OF DOC. CREDIT	*40A:	IRREVOCABLE
APPLICABLE RULES	40E:	UCP LATEST VERSION
DOC, CREDIT NUMBER	*20:	XYH2119
DATE OF ISSUE	31C:	081101
EXPIRY	*31D:	090115 IN CHINA
APPLICANT	*50:	LONDON ELECTRON COMPANY NO. 52, VICTORY ROAD, LONDON
BENEFICIARY	*59:	TIANJIN LENOVO COMPUTER COMPANY NO. 25, XIANGGANG ROAD, TIANJIN
AMOUNT	*32B:	USD100000,00
ANAILABLE WITH/BY	*41D:	BANK OF CHINA TIANJIN BRANCH BY NEGOTIATION
DRAFTS AT...	42C:	AT SIGHT
DRAWEE	42A:	LONDON BANK
PARIAL SHIPMENTS	43P:	NOT ALLOWED
TRANSHIPMENT	43T:	NOT ALLOWED
LOADING IN CHARGE	44A:	TIANJIN
FOR TRANSPORT TO	44B:	LONDON
LATEST DATE OF SHIP.	44C:	081230

DESCRIPTION OF GOODS AND/OR SERVICES 45A:

DESCRIPTION QUANTITY UNIT PRICE AMOUNT
LENOVO COMPUTER 100UNIT USD1000/UNIT USD100000
MODEL NO. XURI - 125
PRICE TERM: CIF LONDON
DOCUMENTS REQUIRED 46A:
+SIGNED COMMERCIAL INVOICE IN 6 COPIES INDICATING CONTRACT NO.
+FULL SET OF CLEAN ON BOARD OCEAN BILL OF LADING MADE OUT TO ORDER AND BLANK ENDORSED MARKED "FREIGHT PREPAID" AND NOTIFY APPLICANT
+INSURANCE POLICY/CERTIFICATE IN 3 COPIES FOR 110 % OF THE INVOIECE VALUE SHOWING CLAIMS PAYABLE IN LONDON IN CURRENCY OF THE DRAFT, BLANK ENDORSED, COVERING OCEAN MARINE TRANSPORTATION ALL RISKS, WAR RISK.
+BENEFICIARY'S CERTIFICATE STATING ONE SET OF NON-NEGOTIABLE SHPPING DOCUMENTS HAVE BEEN SENT DIRECTLY TO APPLICANT IMMEDIATELY AFTER SHIPMENT.
ADDITIONAL COND. 47A:
T. T. REIMBURSEMENT IS PROHIBITED.
DETAILS OF CHARGES *71B
ALL BANKING CHARGES OUTSIDE THE OPENING BANK ARE FOR BENEFICIARY'S ACCOUNT.
PRSENTATION PERIOD 48:
DOCUMENTS MUST BE PRESENTED WITHIN 15 DAYS AFTER DATE OF ISSUANCE OF THE TRANSPORT DOCUMENTS BUT WITHIN THE VALIDITY OF THIS CREDIT
INSTUCTIONS 78:
THE NEGOTIATION BANK MUST FORWARD THE DRAFTS AND ALL DOCUMENTS BY REGISTERED AIRMIL DIRECTLY TO US IN TWO CONSECUTIVE LOTS, UPON RECEIPT OF THE DRAFTS AND DOCUMENTS IN ORDER, WE WILL REMIT THE PROCEEDS AS INSTRUCTED BY THE NEGOTIATING BANK.

样例 14.2 信用证

实训操作二

天津服饰贸易公司与法国 BNP 公司就女士长裙出口业务达成一合同。法国客户及时通过银行开来信用证(见样例 14.3),天津服饰贸易公司也按照约定如期将货备好出运。载货船舶“星河”轮于 2008 年 10 月 30 日驶离天津港,提单号为 WY091208。作为公司单证人员,请你利用 EASYBOSS 软件,缮制全套结汇单据(其他单据编号自拟),并争取尽早将单据交银行议付货款。

27 :Sequence of total
1/1
40A : Form of Documentary Credit
IRREVOCABLE
40E : Applicable Rules
UCP LATEST VERSION
20 : Documentary Credit Number

00001LCC0603814

31C : Date of Issue
081015

31D : Date and Place of Expiry
081115 IN BENEFICIARY'S COUNTRY

51A : Applicant Bank
BNP PARIB AS
ZI DE LA PILATERIE
59442 WASQUEHAL FRANCE

50 : Applicant
DIRAMODE
3 RUE DU DUREMONT
BP 21, 59531 NEUVILLE MARSELLES FRANCE

59 : Beneficiary
TIANJIN APPREAL TRADING CO.
NO. 31 ZHONG SHAN ROAD TIANJIN. CHINA

32B : Currency Code, Amount
USD 80,000.00

39A : Percentage Credit Amount Tolerance
05/05

41D : Available With ... By ...
ANY BANK BY NEGOTIATION

42C : Draft at ...
SIGHT

42D : Drawee
BNP PARIB AS
ZI DE LA PILATERIE
59442 WASQUEHAL FRANCE

43P : Partial Shipment
NOT ALLOWED

43T : Transshipment
NOT ALLOWED

44A : Loading on Board/Dispatch/Taking in Charge at/from ...
TIANJIN CHINA

44B : For Transportation to ...
MARSELLES FRANCE

44C : Latest Date of Shipment
081030

45A : Description of Goods and/or Services
LADIES DRESS 10000 PCS AT USD8.00 CIF MARSELLES INCLUDING 3% COMMISSION AS PER ORDER NO. 113851

46A : Documents Required
+ COMMERCIAL INVOICE IN 4 FOLDS DULY SIGNED AND STAMPED, BEARING DOCUMENTARY CRED-

IT NUMBER.

+ PACKING LIST IN FIVE FOLD.
+ CERTIFICATE OF ORIGIN ISSUED BY CCPIT
+ 3/3 ORIGINAL BILL OF LADING MADE OUT TO ORDER OF SHIPPER AND ENDORSED IN BLANK NOTIFY EXPEDITORS INTERNATIONAL – ROUTE DES FAMARDS – 59818 MARSELLES FRANCE MARKED FREIGHT PREPAID.
+ INSURANCE POLICY/CERTIFICATE COVERING ALL RISKS AND WAR RISK FOR 110% OF INVOICE VALUE INCLUDING W/W CLAUSE CLAIMS AS PER CIC, IF ANY, PAYABLE AT PORT OF DESTINATION IN THE CURRENCY OF THE DRAFT.
+ SHIPPER MUST FAX ADVISING BUYER SHIPMENT PARTICULARS IN BRIEF
IMMEDIATELY AFTER SHIPMENT AND COPY OF FAX SHOULD BE PART OF NEGOTIATING DOCUMENTS.
+ ONE COPY OF SIGNED INVOICE AND ONE NON-NEGOTIABLE B/L TO BE SENT TO BUYER BY SPECIAL COURIER 5 DAYS BEFORE THE SHIPPING DATE. A CERTIFICATE TO THIS EFFECT SHOULD BE PRESENTED TO THE NEGOTIATING BANK AS PART OF DOCUMENTS NEEDED.

47A : Additional Conditions

+ ALL DOCUMENTS MUST MENTIONING THIS L/C NO. AND S/C NO.
+ 3% COMMISSION SHOULD BE DEDUCTED FROM TOTAL AMOUNT OF THE COMMERCIAL INVOICE.
+ MORE OR LESS 5 PERCENT IN QUANTITY AND CREDIT AMOUNT ACCEPTABLE
+ A FEE OF USD50.00 OR ITS EQUIVALENT WILL BE DEDUCTED FROM THE PROCEEDS OF EACH SET OF DISCREPANT DOCUMENTS, WHICH REQUIRE OUR OBTAINING ACCEPTANCE FROM APPLICANT.
+ AN EXTRA COPY OF INVOICE AND TRANSPORT DOCUMENTS, IF ANY, FOR L/C ISSUING BANK'S FILE ARE REQUIRED.

71B : Charges

ALL BANKING CHARGES OUTSIDE OPENING BANK ARE FOR THE
ACCOUNT OF BENEFICIARY.

48 : Period of Presentation

DOCUMENTS TO BE PRESENTED WITHIN 15 DAYS AFTER SHIPMENT DATE BUT WITHIN THE VALIDITY OF THE CREDIT.

49 : Confirmation Instructions

WITHOUT

78 : Instructions to the Paying/Accepting/Negotiating Bank

+ UPON RECEIPT OF DOCUMENTS CONFORMING TO THE TERMS AND CONDITIONS OF THIS CREDIT, WE SHALL PAY THE PROCEEDS AS DESIGNATED.
+ NEGOTIATING BANK MUST FORWARD ALL DOCUMENTS TO US IN ONE LOT BY COURIER SERVICE AT BENEFICIARY'S EXPENSES.

样例 14.3 信用证

6

综合训练

任务十五　综合训练

任务背景

王芳小姐经过近来单证工作中的具体操作,积累了一定的实际经验,但与周围的老师傅相比仍然感到自身差距很大。特别是随着业务的不断发展,她越来越发觉汇付和托收结汇方式呈现出不断上升的趋势,甚至有些业务采用混合付款方式,为此她利用业余时间进行大量的单证综合训练,使自己尽可能多地熟悉不同结汇方式下对单证的具体要求,从而更加熟练掌握单据的缮制技巧,提高单证工作质量,做到安全收汇,把好最重要的货款关。

【背景分析】

进出口单证工作是国际贸易中重要的基础性和技术性工作。外经贸企业的单证岗工作人员只有经过长期大量的工作实践和积累,才能成为一个真正合格的能胜任的单证员。每笔具体的进出口业务所涉及的交易国别和地区不同、所使用的贸易方式不同、所使用的贸易术语不同、所采用的结汇方式不同,对单证工作的具体要求就会有天壤之别,因此王芳小姐应该掌握和具备如下知识、技能及素质。

知识技能

①了解汇付的概念、当事人、种类及特点。

②了解托收的概念、当事人、种类及特点。

操作技能

①熟悉和掌握不同结汇方式下进出口单据缮制程序及技巧。

②进一步巩固信用证结汇方式下单证缮制的技巧,提高熟练程度。

职业素质

①不断学习,与时俱进,逐步提高工作质量。

②善于总结经验,提高业务的综合处理能力。

一、综合训练的基础知识

【基本概念】

在实际外贸工作中,有如下两种基本结汇方式。

1. 汇付(Remittance)

汇付又称汇款,指资金在不同国家或地区之间的转移,是付款人(进口商)委托银行将一定数额的款项(货款)转移至银行在国外的分行或代理行,并委托其付款给收款人(出口商)的一种结汇方式。

汇付方式由付款人向付款地银行填写汇付申请书,银行通过使用汇票、支付委托书及划账凭证等将货款转移至收款地银行付给收款人,实现货款的收付。采用这种方式时,进口商须主动按合同规定通过银行汇款给出口商。在汇付方式下,结算工具的流向与资金的流动方向相同,因此,被称作"顺汇"。国际贸易中,汇付方式主要用于预付货款或赊销。

2. 托收(Collection)

托收是出口商委托本国银行通过其在进口国的分行或代理行向进口商提示单据并收取货款的一种结汇方式。实际业务中,托收的一般做法是,出口商在货物装运后,开立以进口商为付款人的汇票,连同商业单据(主要是指提单、商业发票及保险单等)交给本国出口地银行,委托该行通过其在进口地的分行或代理行向进口商代收货款。

在托收方式下,结算工具的传递方向与资金流动的方向相反,被称为"逆汇"。托收是一种比较有利于进口商结汇的方式。近些年来,我国出口贸易采用托收方式进行货款结算的比例有上升的趋势。

【基本当事人】

汇付方式和汇收方式分别有如下基本当事人。

1. 汇付方式基本当事人

(1)汇款人(Remitter)

汇款人是将货款交给进口地银行,委托该银行向国外汇出资金的付款人或债务人。在国际贸易中,汇款人通常是指进口商。

(2)汇出行(Remitting Bank)

汇出行是接受汇款人的委托,将资金汇出国外,通过其在收款人所在地的分行或代理行,将货款付给收款人的银行。汇出行通常是指汇款人当地的开户银行。

(3)汇入行(Paying Bank)

汇入行也称解付行,通常是受汇出行委托,将货款解付给收款人的银行。汇入行通常是指汇出行在收款人所在地的分行或代理行。

(4)收款人(Payee or Beneficiary)

收款人是收取货款的债权人。在国际贸易中,收款人通常是指出口商。

2. 托收方式基本当事人

(1)委托人(Principal)

委托人是开出汇票,委托银行向国外付款人收取货款的人。在托收业务中,委托人通常为出口商。

(2)托收行(Remitting Bank)

托收行是接受委托人的委托,通过国外分行或代理行向国外付款人收取货款的人。在托收业务中,托收行通常为出口商所在地的开户银行。

(3)代收行(Collecting Bank)

代收行是接受托收行的委托,代为向付款人提示汇票并收取货款的银行。在托收业务中,代收行通常为进口商所在地银行。

(4)付款人(Payer 或 Drawee)

付款人即汇票受票人,是指根据托收指示进行付款的人。在托收业务中,付款人通常为进口商。

【基本种类】

1. 汇付方式分类

根据银行发出的委托付款指示的传递方式不同,汇付方式可分为信汇、电汇及票汇三种。

(1)信汇(Mail Transfer, M/T)

信汇是指汇出行应汇款人的申请,将信汇委托书以航空信方式寄给汇入行,授权解付一定金额给收款人的一种汇款方式。

信汇方式的特点是费用较为低廉,收款人收到汇款的时间较迟。

(2)电汇(Telegraphic Transfer T/T)

电汇是指汇出行应汇款人的申请,拍发加押电报、电传或 SWIFT 给在另一国家的分行或代理行(即汇入行),指示解付一定金额给收款人的一种汇款方式。

电汇方式是汇付业务中最常用的方式。特点是费用较高,收款人可迅速收到汇款。

(3)票汇(Remittance by Banker's Demand Draft, D/D)

票汇是指汇出行应汇款人的申请,代汇款人开立以其分行或代理行为解付行的银行即期汇票(Banker's Demand Draft),支付一定金额给收款人的一种汇款方式。

票汇与电汇、信汇的不同在于,票汇的汇入行无须通知收款人取款,而由收款人持票登门取款。这种汇票除有限制转让和流通的规定外,经收款人背书即可转让流通,而电汇、信汇的收款人则不能将收款权转让。

2. 托收方式分类

按汇票是否随附单据,托收方式可以分为光票托收和跟单托收两种。光票托收指出口商开具汇票而不随附商业单据(主要指货运单据)的托收;跟单托收指出口商开具汇票连同全套货运单据一起交银行并委托其代收货款。国际贸易一般把全套货运单据的交付和货款的支付当作对流条件,因此,国际贸易托收多采用跟单托收。

在跟单托收方式下,根据出口商对银行交单指示的不同,可将托收又分为付款交单和承兑交单两种方式。

(1)付款交单(Documents against Payment, D/P)

付款交单指出口商的交单以进口商的付款为条件,即出口商将汇票连同全套货运单据交银行托收时,指示银行只有在进口商付清货款时才能交出货运单据。如果进口商拒付,就不能从银行取得货运单据,也无法提取单据下的货物。付款交单按支付时间不同,又可分为即期付款交单和远期付款交单两种。

(2)承兑交单(Documents against Acceptance, D/A)

承兑交单指出口商的交单以进口商的承兑为条件。进口商承兑汇票后,即可向银行取得货运单据,并凭单据提货,待汇票到期日才付款。承兑交单只适用于远期汇票的托收。

【共同特点】

1. 商业信用

在汇付业务中,银行虽参与货款的拨付,但不垫付资金,不承担风险,不保证付款。出口商能否按期如数收回货款取决于进口商的信誉,进口商能否按质按量收到货物取决于出口商的信誉,银行只提供服务。同样,托收虽然也是通过银行办理,但银行只是按照出口商的指示办事,不承担付款的责任。在托收业务中,银行不过问单据的真伪,对已运到目的港(地)的货物也不负提货和看管责任。出口商交货后,能否收回货款完全取决于进口商的商业信誉,因此须承担一定的风险。因此,无论是汇付还是托收都属于商业信用。

2. 承担风险

汇付方式主要用于预付货款和赊销。对于预付货款的进口商和货到付款的出口商来说,一旦付款或者发货就失去了制约对方的手段,他们能否收到货或者收回款完全取决于对方的商业信用。如果对方的信用不好,很可能钱货两空,因此贸易本身存在较大风险。托收同样如此,特别是在承兑交单的情况下,如果进口商的信用不好,遇到市场行情发生剧烈波动的情况,出口商很容易落到货款两空的境地,承担风险较大。一般来讲,在信誉好的老客户之间才采取汇付或托收方式。

3. 手续简便、费用低

汇付方式手续最为简单、快捷，费用也最低。托收方式较信用证支付方式，也大大降低了费用。在进出口双方相互信任的情况下，汇付和托收不失为理想的支付方式，现在这两种结汇方式的使用率呈上升趋势。

二、综合训练的基本技能

【实训目的】

通过本项目实训，应掌握的基本技能如下。

①汇付结汇方式下单据缮制的具体要求。

②托收结汇方式下单据缮制的具体要求。

③混合付款结汇方式下单据缮制的具体要求。

【操作前准备】

进行本项任务的实训前，应准备的内容如下。

①预习有关不同付款方式的基础知识。

②熟悉合同中的主要条款，尤其要深刻理解付款条款。

③各种空白的纸质的单据或空白单据的电子模板。

【操作程序】

①仔细地逐条查看并理解合同条款。

②仔细阅读加工厂提供的具体码单，并与合同条款相比较，核查备货情况是否符合合同约定。

③缮制各种结汇单据。

④审核各种结汇单据。

⑤打印各种结汇单据。

⑥送议付行议付货款。

【操作规范及单据样例】

一般而言，托收和汇付结汇方式下所要求的单据较信用证项下所要求的单据简单，大部分单据的缮制规范与信用证项下的单据缮制规范基本相同，而较为显著的不同反映在汇票和发票上。就汇票而言，由于汇付属于顺汇，是进口商按照合同约定主动将款项通过银行划到出口商账户，故不需要汇票；托收属于逆汇，往往出口商将货物装船出运后，缮制汇票连同全套货运单据委托银行向进口商收款，故一般需要汇票（托收项下汇票缮制规范见表 15. 1，托收汇票见样例 15. 1）。就发票而言，在付款方式栏目和自由处理区略有不同（托收和汇付项下发票缮制规范见表 15. 2，托收商业发票见样例 15. 2）。

表 15.1 托收项下汇票缮制规范

项目顺序号	填写内容	要点提示
(1)单据名称 Name of Doc	Bill of exchange, Exchange 或 Draft	一般已印妥
(2)汇票编号 No.	此笔业务的发票号	
(3)日期和地点 Date and place	汇票的出票日期和出票地点	①出票日期应在提单日后,一般由银行代为填写 ②出票地点一般为议付行和出票人所在地点
(4)小写金额 Amount in figure	由支付的货币的名称缩写和阿拉伯数字构成	一般与发票金额相同
(5)付款期限 Tenor	即期付款 远期付款	在 At 前加注 D/P 字样,在 At 和 Sight 之间表示付款期限,如:即期填写 * * * 或 - - -,远期填写具体期限
(6)收款人 Payee	托收行名称	指示性抬头便于流通转让
(7)大写金额 Amount in words	用文字叙述支付货币名称和支付的金额	①习惯上,在货币名称前加"say",在大写金额后加"only"字样 ②大小写金额保持一致
(8)出票依据 Drawn under	货物名称、包装件数及合同号	也可以简单写成 For Collection
(9)付款人 Drawee	受票人	填写进口商的名称和地址
(10)出票人 Drawer	托收的委托人	①加盖出口商签章 ②如果要求手签,则必须亲笔签名

BILL OF EXCHANGE (1)

No. 123456 (2) Tianjin, China. APR. 30, 2008 (3)

Exchange for USD52500.00 (4)

D/P At * * * (5) sight of this FIRST of Exchange(Second of exchange being unpaid), pay to the order of

BANK OF CHINA (6) the sum of

U.S. DOLLARS EIGHT THOUSAND NINE HUNDRED AND SIXTY-SEVEN ONLY. (7)

Drawn under FOR COLLECTION (8)

1

To: MARUBENI CORP (9)
5-7, HOMMACHI, 2-CHOME,
CHUO-KU, OSAKA, JAPAN

TIFERT TRADING CO., LTD.
泰佛贸易有限公司

(10)

样例 15.1 托收汇票

表 15.2　托收和汇付项下发票缮制规范

项目顺序号	填写内容	要点提示
(1)单据名称 Name of Doc	COMMERCIAL INVOICE 或 INVOICE	与合同上的规定完全一致
(2)签发人 Issuer	合同中出口商	汇付项下也为合同中出口商
(3)抬头人 To	合同中进口商	汇付项下也为合同中进口商
(4)运输详情 Transport details	启运地、目的地及运输方式	启运港(地)应明确具体,目的港(地)如有重名港后面要加国别
(5)发票号码 Invoice No.	此笔业务的发票号码	由出口商自行编制
(6)日期 Date	发票的出票日期	一般在提单签发日前,是全套单据中最早的日期
(7)合同号 S/C No.	此笔业务的合同号码	
(8)信用证号 L/C No.	留空	托收和汇付无须填写
(9)付款方式 Terms of payment	此笔业务的付款方式	托收填写 By D/P,电汇填写 By T/T
(10)唛头 Marks and numbers	合同规定的唛头	合同有指定唛头,必须严格按照规定填写;合同未指定唛头,出口商可自行设计;没有唛头填写 N/M
(11)货物描述 Number and kind of package, description of goods	包括货物的件数、货物名称、规格及包装情况等	参照合同的规定结合实际情况进行填写
(12)数量 Quantity	一般填写货物的实际出运数量	不要遗漏计量单位
(13)单价 Unit price	包括计价货币、计量单位、单位金额及贸易术语	填写要完整、正确,不能遗漏贸易术语
(14)总金额 Amount	单价与实际出运数量的乘积,即发票总值	①一般不能超过合同总金额 ②有折扣或明佣的应在此扣除,计算出净值
(15)声明文句 Statement	加注进口国对发票的特殊要求,如各种费用金额、原产地、特定号码或标明特殊的付款方式等声明文句	这些内容加注在发票商品栏以下的空白处
(16)签字 Signature	签发人的签名或盖章	商业发票只能由合同中的出口商出具,但可以不签署

Issuer (2) TIFERT TRADING CO., LTD. NO. 86, ZHUJIANG ROAD, TIANJIN, CHINA	商　业　发　票 (1) **COMMERCIAL INVOICE**	
To (3) MARUBENI CORP 5－7, HOMMACHI, 2－CHOME, CHUO-KU, OSA-KA, JAPAN	No. (5) INVOICE NO. 123456	Date (6) APR. 15, 2008
Transport details (4) SHIPMENT FROM TIANJIN TO TOKYO BY SEA	S/C No. (7) 08TF0858	L/C No. (8)
	Terms of payment (9) D/P AT SIGHT (OR 50% BY T/T IN ADVANCE, 50% BY D/P)	

Marks and number (10)	Number and kind of packages, description of goods (11)	Quantity (12)	Unit price (13)	Amount (14)
MARUBENI S/C 08TF0858 TOKYO CTN 1－250	250 CARTONS GIRL JACKET SYTLE NO. GJ234 SHELL: WOVEN TWILL 100% COTTON LINING: WOVEN 100% POLYESTER PACKED IN CARTONS OF 20PCS EACH	5000PCS	CIF TOKYO USD10. 50/PC	USD52500. 00

WE HEREBY CERTIFY THAT THE GOODS ARE OF CHINESE ORIGIN (15)
(OR 50% OF TOTAL INVOICE AMOUNT RECEIVED IN ADVANCE)

TIFERT TRADING CO., LTD.
泰佛贸易有限公司
*

(16)

样例 15.2　托收商业发票

【操作注意事项】

在混合付款的结汇方式下，如果50%采用汇付，50%采用托收，则发票做成货款的100%，汇票金额只能做成50%的货款；如果50%采用托收，50%采用信用证，则发票做成货款的100%,汇票必须分别做两套,各为总金额的50%,信用证项下的汇票做成光票,托收项下的汇票做成跟单汇票,以确保安全收汇。

总之,要结合不同的结汇方式,来确定发票和汇票的金额。一般来说发票与汇票金额的关系有以下几种情况。

①汇票金额 = 发票金额,一般情况下发票金额等同汇票金额。

②汇票金额 = 两份发票金额之和,即两份发票合出一套汇票,但汇票要标明两份发票的发票号。

③汇票金额 = 部分发票金额,即发票的部分金额出一套汇票,部分不出具。如采用混合付款,部分为汇付,部分为托收或信用证,汇付部分不需要出具汇票。

④两套汇票金额 = 一份发票的金额,即一份发票出两套汇票,如采用混合付款时,50%托收,50%信用证,要分别出两套汇票,两套汇票金额之和等于发票金额。

§ 综合训练的操作训练

【翻译语句】

①cash against delivery
②combined transport documents
③overland common point
④container yard
⑤documents against acceptance
⑥uniform customs & practice
⑦European main ports
⑧estimated time of arrival(or departure)
⑨irrespective of percentage
⑩full container load
⑪China Council for Promotion of International Trade
⑫generalized system of preferences
⑬International Chamber of commerce
⑭International Rules for the Interpretation of Trade Terms
⑮International Standard Organization

【动脑思考】

①大田贸易公司在一笔出口贸易中收到国外进口商的信用证显示如下。

This L/C is available with us by mixed payment, 70% by L/C at 30 days after receipt of full set of documents, 30% by T/T in advance.

请问信用证要求的付款方式是什么?作为公司单证员,你须缮制几套汇票,每套汇票的金额各是多少?

②顺风纺织品公司与英国一客户就出口毛衫达成一份出口合同,合同中约定付款方式是50%即期信用证,50%即期付款交单。作为公司的单证员,你在制单时,应该缮制几套汇票?把全套单据备妥后向银行交单时,全套结汇单据随附在信用证项下汇票还是托收项下汇票?为什么?

③胜利服装有限公司收到国外进口商开来的信用证，其中41D具体描述为“Available with Bank of Tianjin by payment”。作为公司的单证员，你在缮制单据时，应注意什么？

④天虹日用品进出口公司通过中间商与一美国客户达成一餐具出口合同，收到的信用证在47A中规定“3% com will be deducted during negotiation”。作为公司单证员，你在缮制汇票时，具体金额应该打多少？为什么？

⑤翔宇化工进出口有限公司向中化日本公司出口染料孔雀蓝，合同规定30%采用前T/T，70%采用后T/T。作为公司单证员，你在制单时，是否应该缮制汇票？为什么？发票金额应该如何确定？付款方式如何填写？

【动手操练】

实训操练一

大连纺织品进出口公司与韩国大宇服饰有限公司于2008年3月8日就台布达成一份出口合同08DRA207（见样例15.3）。随后大连纺织品进出口有限公司抓紧按合同要求备货，并于2008年4月15日将48 000条台布全部备妥，在清河轮185航次订妥舱位，货代公司要求4月18日下午17点前把货送至大连指定仓库，下货纸号为BTB0810090。作为单证员，请你按照合同要求缮制发票、提单及保险单等结汇单据。（空白单据见样例15.4、15.5及15.6）

SALES CONFIRMATION

卖方　DALIAN TEXTILES IMPORT & EXPORT CORP.　　No.:08DRA207
Seller:　4 YING CHUN STREET, DALIAN, CHINA　　Date:MAR 8,2008
买方　DAWOO APPAREL CO. LTD.
Buyer:　C. P. O. BOX7155 SEOUL, KOREA
经买卖双方同意成交下列商品，订立条款如下：
This contract is made by and agreed between the buyer and seller, in accordance with the terms and conditions stipulated below.

唛头 Marks and numbers	名称及规格 Description of goods	数量 Quantity	单价 Unit price	金额 Amount
DAEHO 08DRA207 KOREA CTN 1－240	TABLE CLOTH 100% COTTON 120×120CM	48000PCS	CIF DALIAN USD12.00/PC	USD57600.00

总值 Total: U. S. DOLLARS FIFTY-SEVEN THOUSAND SIX HUNDRED ONLY.
Transshipment（转运）:
☐ Allowed（允许）　☒ Not allowed（不允许）
Partial shipments（分批装运）:
☐ Allowed（允许）　☒ Not allowed（不允许）

Shipment date（装运期）：

NOT LATER THAN 30TH JUNE, 2008

Packing（包装）：

1PC TO A PLASTIC BAG, 20BAGS TO A CARTON.

Insurance（保险）：

To be covered by the SELLER FOR 110% of the invoice value covering ALL RISKS AND WAR RISK from DALIAN to BUSAN .

Terms of payment（付款条件）：

The buyers shall pay 30% of the sales proceeds by T/T remittance to the seller not later than MAY 5, 2008. and 70% will be remitted to the sellers after the goods loaded on board.

The seller	The buyer
张天一	朴金焕

样例 15.3 合同

<table>
<tr><td>Issuer</td><td colspan="2" rowspan="2">商 业 发 票

COMMERCIAL INVOICE</td></tr>
<tr><td rowspan="2">To</td></tr>
<tr><td>No.</td><td>Date</td></tr>
<tr><td rowspan="2">Transport details</td><td>S/C No.</td><td>L/C No.</td></tr>
<tr><td colspan="2">Terms of payment</td></tr>
</table>

Marks and numbers	Number and kind of packages, description of goods	Quantity	Unit price	Amount

样例 15.4 空白发票

Shipper	**BILL OF LADING** **B/L NO. :** **CHINA OCEAN SHIPPING CO** 中国远洋运输公司 **ORIGINAL**
Consignee	
Notify party	

Pre carriage by	* Place of receipt		
Ocean Vessel Voy. No.	Port of loading		
Port of discharge	* Final destination	Freight payable at	Number original Bs/L

Marks and numbers	Number and kind of packages, description	Gross weight	Measurement m^3

Total packages(in words)

Freight and charges

Place and date of issue

Signed for the carrier

Applicable only when document used as a Through Bill of Loading

样例 15.5 空白提单

中保财产保险有限公司

The People's Insurance (Property) Company of China, Ltd.

发票号码
Invoice No.

保险单号次
Policy No.

海洋货物运输保险单

MARINE CARGO TRANSPORTATION INSURANCE POLICY

被保险人:
Insured:

中保财产保险有限公司(以下简称本公司)根据被保险人的要求,及其所缴付约定的保险费,按照本保险单承担险别和背面所载条款与下列特别条款承保下列货物运输保险,特签发本保险单。

This policy of Insurance witnesses that the People's Insurance (Property) Company of China, Ltd. (hereinafter called "The Company"), at the request of the Insured and in consideration of the agreed premium paid by the Insured, undertakes to insure the undermentioned goods in transportation subject to conditions of the Policy as per the Clauses printed overleaf and other special clauses attached hereon.

唛头 Shipping marks	保险货物项目 Descriptions of goods	数量 Quantity	保险金额 Amount insured

总保险金额:
Total amount insured:

承保险别
Conditions

保费
Premium ____________________

载运输工具
Per conveyance S. S ____________

开航日期
Slg. on or abt ____________

起运港
Form ____________________

目的港
To ____________________

所保货物,如发生本保险单项下可能引起索赔的损失或损坏,应立即通知本公司下述代理人查勘。如有索赔,应向本公司提交保险单正本(本保险单共有　　份正本)及有关文件。如一份正本已用于索赔,其余正本则自动失效。

In the event of loss or damage which may result in a claim under this Policy, immediate notice must be given to the Company's Agent as mentioned hereunder. Claims, if any, one of the Original Policy which has been issued in original (s) together with the relevant documents shall be surrendered to the Company. If one of the Original Policy has been accomplished, the others to be void.

赔款偿付地点
Claim payable at

日期
Date ____________________

在
at ____________________

地址:
Address: ____________________

样例 15.6　空白保险单

实训操练二

上海现代贸易有限公司与荷兰通尼产业公司就出口运动套装达成一纸合同（见样例 15.7），信用证规定付款方式为 50% 见票后 30 天付款交单，50% 提单日后 30 天信用证付款（见样例 15.8）。货物装“天河”轮 38 航次，提单号 08TH2345，保险单号 08TT123456，普惠制原产地证号 CIQ080622，运费 USD0.10/套，保险费率 1‰。作为公司单证员，请你缮制全套结汇单据，争取早日收回货款。空白单据见样例 15.9 ~ 样例 15.15，其他未给出的条件自拟。

售 货 合 同
SALES CONTRACT

The sellers: XIANDAI TRADING CO., LTD. S/C No. XD08008

Address: RM 2 - 8, 55 ZHEJIANG ROAD Date: MAR. 27, 2008

SHANGHAI, CHINA

Tel: (021)3478526 Fax: (021)3478525

E-mail: christina@163.com

The buyers: TONNY PRODUCTS PLC

Address: BERSTOFSGADE 48, ROTTERDAM, THE NETHERLAND

Tel: +(31)74 12 37 08 Fax: +(31)74 12 37 09

E-mail: chila@tvl.com

After friendly negotiation, the sellers agree to sell and the buyers agree to buy the undermentioned goods according to the terms and conditions stipulated below:

商品名称及规格 Name of commodity & specification	数量 Quantity	单价 Unit price	总 值 Total value
JOGGING SUIT（运动套装）		CIFC3% ROTTERDAM	
Art. No. KB7900	840SETS	EUR15.20/SET	EUR12,768.00
Art. No. KP6300	600SETS	EUR12.50/SET	EUR7,500.00
Art. No. KY5200	600SETS	EUR10.60/SET	EUR6,360.00
Total:	2040SETS		EUR26,628.00

Packing: PACKED IN CARTONS OF 12 SETS EACH

Shipping marks: TONNY/XD06008/ROTTERDAM/NO. 1 - UP

Port of shipment: SHANGHAI CHINA

Port of destination: ROTTERDAM NETHERLAND

Time of shipment: NOT LATER THAN MAY 31, 2008.

Terms of payment: 50% BY D/P AT 30 DAYS SIGHT;

50% BY L/C AT 30DAYS AFTER B/L DATE

The sellers:
XIANDAI TRADING CO., LTD.
SHANGHAI CHINA
李炜

The Buyers:
TONNY PRODUCTS PLC
ROTTERDAM NETHERLAND
STIVEN

样例 15.7 合同

MT:700	ISSUE OF A DOCUMENTARY CREDIT	
FROM: CITI-BANK ROTTERDAM, NETHERLAND		
SEQUENCE OF TOTAL:	*27:	1/1
FORM OF L/C	*40A:	IRREVOCABLE
APPLICABLE RULES	*40E:	UCP LATEST VERSION
L/C NO.	*20:	68IM6895
DATE OF ISSUE	*31C:	080415
EXPIRY DATE AND PLACE	*31D:	080615 CHINA
APPLICANT	*50:	TONNY PRODUCTS PLC. BERSTOFSGADE 48, ROTTERDAM, THE NETHERLAND
BENEFICIARY	*59:	XIANDAI TRADING CO., LTD RM 2-8, 55 ZHEJIANG ROAD SHANGHAI, CHINA
AMOUNT	*32B	EUR 13314, 00
AVAILABLE WITH BY	*41D:	WITH ANY BANK BY NEGOTIATION
DRAFTS AT	*42C:	AT 30DAYS AFTER B/L DATE
DRAWEE	*42D:	CITI-BANK LOS ANGELES, CA.
PARTIAL SHIPMENT	*43P:	NOT ALLOWED
TRANSHIPMENT	*43T:	NOT ALLOWED
LOADING FROM	*44A:	CHINA
FOR TRANSPORTATION TO	*44B:	ROTTERDAM, NETHERLAND
LATEST DATE OF SHIPMENT	*44C:	080531
DESCRIPTION OF GOODS/SERVICES	*45A:	

2040 SETS JOGGING SUIT DELIVERY CONDITION: CIF ROTTERDAM AS PER S/C XD08008

DOCUMENTS REQUIRED *46A:

+ SIGNED COMMERCIAL INVOICE IN 3 ORIGINAL AND 2 COPIES SHOWING FREIGHT CHARGES, INSURANCE PREMIUM AND FOB VALUE AND INDICATING THE ORIGIN OF GOODS IS CHINA.
+ PACKING LIST IN 3 FOLDS.
+ FULL SET OF CLEAN ON BOARD OCEAN BILLS OF LADING MADE OUT TO ORDER AND BLANK ENDORSED, MARKED "FREIGHT PREPAID" AND NOTIFYING APPLICANT.
+ INSURANCE POLICY IN DUPLICATE FOR 110% OF INVOICE VALUE COVERING ALL RISKS AND WAR RISK SUBJECT TO CIC DATED JAN. 1ST,1981.
+ GSP CERTIFICATE OF ORIGIN FORM A ISSUED BY CIQ
+ BENEFICIARY'S CERTIFICATE STATING THAT ONE SET OF NON-NEGOTIABLE SHIPPING DOCUMENTS HAVE BEEN SENT TO APPLICANT AFTER SHIPMENT.

ADDITIONAL CONDITIONS: *47A:

+ ALL DOCUMENTS MUST SHOW THIS L/C NO
+ A DISCREPANCY FEE OF USD 40.00 OR EQUIVALENT WILL BE DEDUCTED FROM THE PROCEEDS PAID UNDER ANY DRAWING WHERE DOCUMENTS PRESENTED ARE FOUND NOT TO BE IN STRICT CONFORMITY WITH THE TERMS OF THIS CREDIT.

CHARGES	*71B:	ALL BANKING CHARGES OUTSIDE OF OUR COUNTER ARE FOR ACCOUNT OF THE BENEFICIARY
PERIOD FOR PRESENTATION	*48:	WITHIN 15 DAYS FROM THE DATE OF B/L BUT NOT LATER THAN L/C EXPIRY DATE.
CONFIRMATION:	*49:	WITHOUT

MAC:A75A8689 CHK:39D0ADB5BC9A

样例 15.8 信用证

Issuer	商 业 发 票 COMMERCIAL INVOICE	
To	No.：	Date：
Transport details	S/C No.	L/C No.
	Terms of payment	

Marks and numbers	Number and kind of packages, description of goods	Quantity	Unit price	Amount

样例 15.9 空白发票

Issuer	装箱单 PACKING LIST					
To						
	Invoice No.			Date		
Marks and numbers	Number and kind of package, description of goods	Quantity	Package	G. W	N. W	Meas.
TOTAL: SAY TOTAL:						

样例 15.10 空白装箱单

Shipper

Consignee

Notify party

BILL OF LADING

B/L NO. :

CHINA OCEAN SHIPPING CO

中国远洋运输公司

ORIGINAL

Pre carriage by	* Place of receipt		
Ocean vessel Voy. No.	Port of loading		
Port of discharge	* Final destination	Freight payable at	Number original Bs/L

Marks and numbers	Number and kind of packages, description	Gross weight	Measurement m^3

Total packages(in words)

Freight and charges

Place and date of issue

Signed for the carrier

Applicable only when document used as a Through Bill of Loading

样例 15.11 空白提单

中保财产保险有限公司

The People's Insurance (Property) Company of China, Ltd.

发票号码　　　　　　　　　　　　　　　　　　　　　　保险单号次

Invoice No.　　　　　　　　　　　　　　　　　　　　　Policy No.

海洋货物运输保险单

MARINE CARGO TRANSPORTATION INSURANCE POLICY

被保险人：

Insured：

中保财产保险有限公司(以下简称本公司)根据被保险人的要求,及其所缴付约定的保险费,按照本保险单承担险别和背面所载条款与下列特别条款承保下列货物运输保险,特签发本保险单。

This policy of Insurance witnesses that the People's Insurance (Property) Company of China, Ltd. (hereinafter called "The Company"), at the request of the Insured and in consideration of the agreed premium paid by the Insured, undertakes to insure the undermentioned goods in transportation subject to conditions of the Policy as per the Clauses printed overleaf and other special clauses attached hereon.

唛头 Shipping marks	保险货物项目 Descriptions of goods	数量 Quantity	保险金额 Amount insured

总保险金额：

Total amount insured：

承保险别

Conditions

保费　　　　　　　　　　　　载运输工具　　　　　　　　　　开航日期

Premium ________　Per conveyance S. S ________　Slg. on or abt ________

起运港　　　　　　　　　　　　目的港

Form ________　To ________

所保货物,如发生本保险单项下可能引起索赔的损失或损坏,应立即通知本公司下述代理人查勘。如有索赔,应向本公司提交保险单正本(本保险单共有　　份正本)及有关文件。如一份正本已用于索赔,其余正本则自动失效。

In the event of loss or damage which may result in a claim under this Policy, immediate notice must be given to the Company's Agent as mentioned hereunder. Claims, if any, one of the Original Policy which has been issued in original (s) together with the relevant documents shall be surrendered to the Company. If one of the Original Policy has been accomplished, the others to be void.

赔款偿付地点

Claim payable at

日期　　　　　　　　　　　　在

Date ________　at ________

地址：

Address：________

样例 15.12　空白保险单

<table>
<tr><td colspan="3">1. Goods consigned from (Exporter's business name, address, country)</td><td colspan="3" rowspan="2">Reference No.
GENERALIZED SYSTEM OF PREFERENCES
CERTIFICATE OF ORIGIN
(Combined declaration and certificate) FORM A
Issued in <u>THE PEOPLE'S REPUBLIC OF CHINA</u>
(country)
See Notes overleaf</td></tr>
<tr><td colspan="3">2. Goods consigned to (Consignee's name, address, country)</td></tr>
<tr><td colspan="3">3 Means of transport and route (as far as known)</td><td colspan="3">4. For official use</td></tr>
<tr><td>5. Item number</td><td>6. Marks and numbers of packages</td><td>7. Number and kind of packages, description of goods</td><td>8. Origin criterion (see Notes overleaf)</td><td>9. Gross weight or other quantity</td><td>10. Number and date of invoices</td></tr>
<tr><td colspan="3">11. Certification
It is hereby certified, on the basis of control carried out, that the declaration by the exporter is correct.

Place and date, signature and stamp of certifying authority</td><td colspan="3">12. Declaration by the exporter
The undersigned hereby declares that the above details and statements are correct, that all the goods were
produced in THE PEOPLE'S REPUBLIC OF CHINA
(country)
and that they comply with the origin requirements specified for those goods in the Generalized System of Preferences for goods exported to
....
Place and date, signature and stamp of authorized signatory</td></tr>
</table>

样例 15.13 空白普惠制原产地证

BENEFICIARY'S CERTIFICATE

样例 15.14　空白受益人证明函

No.________________　　　　　　Tianjin, China.____________

Exchange for ________________

At__________sight of this FIRST of Exchange(Second of exchange being unpaid),pay to the order of

____the sum of

1

____

Drawn under____

____

To:________________________

No.________________　　　　　　Tianjin, China.____________

Exchange for ________________

At__________sight of this SECOND of Exchange(First of exchange being unpaid),pay to the order of

____the sum of

2

____

Drawn under____

____

To:________________________

____

样例 15.15　空白汇票

附录 1

世界主要港口一览表

（中英文对照）

港口名称	中译名	所属国家或地区	所属航线
以(A) 开头的世界港口			
Aarhus	奥尔胡斯	丹麦	西北欧
Abadan	阿巴丹	伊朗	波斯湾
Abidjan	阿比让	科特迪瓦	西非
Abu Dhabi	阿布扎比	阿联酋	波斯湾
Acajutla	阿卡胡特拉	萨尔瓦多	中南美
Acapulco	阿卡普尔科	墨西哥	中南美
Accra	阿克拉	加纳	西非
Adelaide	阿得雷德	澳大利亚	澳新
Aden	亚丁	也门	红海
Alexandria	亚历山大	埃及	地中海
Algiers	阿尔及尔	阿尔及利亚	地中海
Amsterdam	阿姆斯特丹	荷兰	西北欧
Ancona	安科纳	意大利	地中海
Annaba	安纳巴	阿尔及利亚	地中海
Antofagasta	安托法加斯塔	智利	中南美
Antwerp	安特卫普	比利时	西北欧
Apapa	阿帕帕	尼日利亚	西非

Apia	阿皮亚	西萨摩亚	澳新
Aqaba	亚喀巴	约旦	红海
Arica	阿里卡	智利	中南美
Assab	阿萨布	埃塞俄比亚	红海
Athens	雅典	希腊	地中海
Auckland	奥克兰	新西兰	澳新
Avonmouth	阿芬默思	英国	西北欧

以(B) 开头的世界港口

Bahia Blanca	布兰卡港	阿根廷	中南美
Bahrain	巴林	巴林	波斯湾
Baltimore	巴尔的摩	美国 (爱尔兰有同名港)	美国东岸
Banana	巴纳纳	扎伊尔	西非
Bandar Abbas	阿巴斯港	伊朗	波斯湾
Bandar Shahpour (Bandar Khomeini)	沙赫普尔港 (霍梅尼港)	伊朗	波斯湾
Bangkok	曼谷	泰国	泰国
Banjul (Bathurst)	班珠尔	冈比亚	西非
Barcelona	巴塞罗那	西班牙	地中海
Barranquilla	巴兰基利亚	哥伦比亚	中南美
Basra	巴士拉	伊拉克	波斯湾
Bassein	勃生	缅甸	孟加拉湾
Bata	巴塔	赤道几内亚	西非
Beira	贝拉	莫桑比克	东非
Beirut	帆鲁特	黎巴嫩	地中海
Belawan	勿拉沙璜湾	印尼	印尼
Belfast	贝尔法斯特	英国	西北欧
Belize	伯利兹	伯利兹	中南美
Benghazi	班加西	利比亚	地中海
Berbera	伯贝拉	索马里	东非
Bergen	卑尔根	挪威	西北欧
Bilbao	毕尔巴鄂	西班牙	西北欧
Birkenhead	伯肯黑德	英国	西北欧
Bissau	比绍	几内亚比绍	西非

Bizerta	比塞大	突尼斯	地中海
Boma	博马	扎伊尔	西非
Bombay	孟买	印度	波斯湾
Bordeaux	波尔多	法国	西北欧
Boston	波士顿	美国 （英国有同名港）	美国东岸
Bourgas （Burghaz 或 Burgas）	布尔加斯	保加利亚	地中海
Bremen	不来梅	德国	西北欧
Bremerhaven	不来梅哈芬	德国	西北欧
Brest	布雷斯特	法国	西北欧
Bridgetown	布里奇顿	巴巴多斯	中南美
Brighton	布赖顿	特立尼达和多巴哥 （英国有同名港）	中南美
Brindisi	布林迪西	意大利	地中海
Brisbane	布里斯班	澳大利亚	澳新
Bristol	布里斯托尔	英国	西北欧
Brunei （BandarSeri Begawan）	文莱 （斯里巴加湾）	文莱	北加里曼丹
Bruseels	布鲁塞尔	比利时	西北欧
Buenaventura	布埃纳文图拉	哥伦比亚	中南美
Buenos Aires	布宜诺斯艾利斯	阿根廷	中南美
Buffalo	布法罗	美国	美国岸
Bunbury	邦伯里	澳大利亚	澳新
Bushire	布什尔	伊朗	波斯湾
Butterworth	巴特沃思	马来西亚	新马

以（C）开头的世界港口

Cabinda	卡宾达	安哥拉	西非
Cadiz	加的斯	西班牙 （菲律宾有同名港）	西北欧
Caloutta	加尔各答	印度	孟加拉湾
Callao	卡亚俄	秘鲁	中南美
Cambrigde	坎布里奇	美国	美国东岸
Cape Town	开普敦	南非	西非
Casablanca	卡萨布兰卡	摩洛哥	西非

Charleston	查尔斯顿	美国	北美
Chiba	千叶	日本	日本
Chicago	芝加哥	美国	北美
Chittagong	吉大港	孟加拉	孟加拉湾
Colombo	科伦坡	斯里兰卡	孟加拉湾
Colon	科隆	巴拿马	中南美
Columbus	哥伦布	美国	北美
Copenhagen	哥本哈根	丹麦	西北欧
Cork	科克	爱尔兰	西北欧
Cotonou	科托努	贝宁	非洲
Cristobal	克里斯托巴尔	巴拿马	中南美

以(D)开头的世界港口

Dacca	达卡	孟加拉	孟加拉湾
Dakar	达喀尔	塞内加尔	西非
Damman	达曼	沙特阿拉伯	波斯湾
Da Nang	岘港	越南	越南
Dar es Salaam	达累斯萨拉姆	坦桑尼亚	东非
Darwin	达尔文	澳大利亚	澳新
Detroit	底特律	美国	美国东岸
Djakarta (Jakarta)	雅加达	印尼	印尼
Djibouti	吉布提	吉布提	红海
Doha	多哈	卡塔尔	波斯湾
Douala	杜阿拉	喀麦隆	西非
Dover	多佛尔	英国	西北欧
Dubai	迪拜	阿联酋	波斯湾
Dublin	都柏林	爱尔兰	西北欧
Dunedin	达尼丁	新西兰	澳新
Dunkirk	敦刻尔克	法国	西北欧
Durban	德班	南非	东非
Durres	都拉斯	阿尔巴尼亚	阿尔巴尼亚
Dusseldorf	杜塞尔多夫	德国	西北欧

以(E)开头的世界港口

East London	东伦敦	南非	东非

Ensenada	恩塞纳尔	墨西哥	中南美

以(F) 开头的世界港口

Felixstowe	费力克斯托	英国	西北欧
Fort de France	法兰西堡	马提尼克岛	中南美
Frankfurt	法兰克福	德国	西北欧
Freeport	弗里波特	巴哈马	联邦中南美
		(美国、百慕大群岛有同名港)	
Freetown	弗里敦	塞拉立昂	西非
Fremantle	弗里曼特尔	澳大利亚	澳新
Fukuo	福冈	日本	日本
Funafuti	富纳富提	图瓦卢	澳新
Funchal	丰沙尔	马德拉群岛	西非

以(G) 开头的世界港口

Gdansk	格但斯克	波兰	西北欧
Gdynia	格丁尼亚	波兰	西北欧
Gelaka	杰拉	意大利	地中海
Genoa	热那亚	意大利	地中海
Georgetown	乔治敦	圣文森特和格林纳丁斯	中南美
	(美国、加拿大、圭亚那、马来西亚均有同名港)		
Ghent	根特	比利时	西北欧
Gibraltar	直布罗陀	直布罗陀	西北欧
Glasgow	格拉斯哥	英国	西北欧
Gothenburg	哥德堡	瑞典	西北欧
Grangemouth	格兰杰默斯	英国	西北欧
Guayaquil	瓜亚基尔	厄瓜多尔	中南美
Gwadur	瓜达尔	巴基斯坦	波斯湾

以(H) 开头的世界港口

Haifa	海法	以色列	地中海
Haiphong	海防	越南	越南
Hakodate	函馆	日本	日本
Halifax	哈利法克斯	加拿大	加拿大东岸
Halmstad	哈尔姆斯塔	瑞典	西北欧
Hamburg	汉堡	德国	西北欧

Hamilton	哈密尔顿	百慕大群岛（加拿大有同名港）	中南美
Haugesund	豪格松	挪威	西北欧
Havana	哈瓦那	古巴	中南美
Helsingborg	赫尔辛堡	瑞典	西北欧
Helsingor	赫尔辛格	丹麦	西北欧
Helsinki	赫尔辛基	芬兰	西北欧
Hiroshima	广岛	日本	日本
Ho Chi Minh City	胡志明市（西贡）	越南	越南
Hobart	霍巴特	澳大利亚	澳新
Hodeida	荷台达	也门	红海
Hongay	鸿基	越南	越南
Hong Kong	香港	中国	港澳
Honiara	霍尼亚拉	所罗门群岛	澳新
Honolulu	火奴鲁鲁（檀香山）	美国	美国西岸
Horta	奥尔塔	亚速尔群岛（葡属）	西非
Houston	休斯敦	美国	美国东岸
Hull	赫尔	英国	西北欧

以（I）开头的世界港口

Immingham	伊明翰姆	英国	西北欧
Iquique	伊基克	智利	中南美
Iskenderun (Alexandretta)	伊斯肯德伦	土耳其	地中海
Istanbul	伊斯坦布尔	土耳其	地中海
Izmir	伊兹密尔	土耳其	地中海

以（J）开头的世界港口

Jamestown	詹姆斯顿	圣赫勒那岛	西非
Jidda(Jeddah)	吉达	沙特阿拉伯	红海
Jogjakarta	日惹	印尼	印尼
Johore Bahru	柔佛巴鲁（新山）	马来西亚	新马

以（K）开头的世界港口

Kaliningrad	加里宁格勒	俄罗斯	西北欧
Karachi	卡拉奇	巴基斯坦	波斯湾

Kavieng	卡维恩	巴布亚新几内亚	澳新
Kawasaki	川崎	日本	日本
Kholmsk	霍尔姆斯克	俄罗斯	俄罗斯
Khorramshahr	霍拉姆沙赫尔	伊朗	波斯湾
Kiel	基尔	德国	西北欧
Kieta	基埃塔	所罗门群岛	澳新
Kingston	金斯敦	牙买加	中南美
		(加拿大、中南美、澳大利亚有同名港)	
Kingstown	金斯敦	圣文森特和格林纳丁斯	中南美
Kismayu	基斯马尤	索马里	东非
Kobe	神户	日本	日本
Kompong Som	磅逊	柬埔寨	泰国
Kota Kinabalu	亚庇(哥打基纳巴卢)	马来西亚	北加里曼丹
Kotka	科特卡	芬兰	西北欧
Kuching	古晋	马来西亚	北加里曼丹
Kudat	库达特	马来西亚	北加里曼丹
Kure	吴港	日本	日本
Kuwait	科威特	科威特	波斯湾

以(L)开头的世界港口

Labuan	拉布安(纳闽)	马来西亚	北加里曼丹
Lae	莱城	巴布亚新几内亚	澳新
La Guaira	拉瓜伊拉	委内瑞拉	中南美
Lancaster	兰开斯特	英国	西北欧

以(M)开头的世界港口

Macao	澳门	中国	港澳
Madang	马丹	巴布亚新几内亚	澳新
Madras	马德拉斯	印度	孟加拉湾
Mahe	马埃	印度	波斯湾
Majunga	马任加	马达加斯加	东非
Makassar (Macassar)	望加锡	印尼	印尼
Malabo (SantaIsabel)	马拉博	赤道几内亚	西非
Malacca	马六甲	马来西亚	新马

Male	马累	马尔代夫	波斯湾
Malindi	马林迪	肯尼亚	东非
Malmo	马尔默	瑞典	西北欧
Malta	马耳他	马耳他	地中海
Manchester	曼彻斯特	英国	西北欧
Manila	马尼拉	菲律宾	菲律宾
Manzanillo	曼萨尼略	墨西哥 (古巴、多米尼加共和国有同名港)	中南美
Maracaibo	马拉开波	委内瑞拉	中南美

以(N)开头的世界港口

Nagasaki	长崎	日本	日本
Nagoya	名古屋	日本	日本
Nakhodka	纳霍德卡	俄罗斯	远东线
Nampo	南浦	朝鲜	朝鲜
Nantes	南特	法国	西北欧
Napier	纳皮尔	新西兰	澳新
Naples(Napoli)	那不勒斯(那波利)	意大利	地中海
Nassau	拿骚	巴哈马联邦	中南美
Nauru	瑙鲁	瑙鲁	澳新
New Amsterdam	新阿姆斯特丹	圭亚那	中南美
Newcastle	纽卡斯尔	英国 (美国、加拿大、澳大利亚有同名港)	西北欧
New Orleans	新奥尔良	美国	美国东岸

以(O)开头的世界港口

Oakland	奥克兰	美国	美国西岸
Odessa	敖德萨	乌克兰	地中海
Oran	奥兰	阿尔及利亚	地中海
Oranjestad	奥腊涅斯塔德	安的列斯(荷属)	中南美
Osaka	大阪	日本	日本
Oslo	奥斯陆	挪威	西北欧
Otaru	小樽	日本	日本
Owendo	奥文多	加蓬	西非

以(P)开头的世界港口

Padang	巴东	印尼	印尼
Pago Pago	帕果帕果	东萨摩亚(美属)	澳新
Palembang	巨港	印尼	印尼
Panama	巴拿马	巴拿马	中南美
Papeete	帕皮提	波利尼西亚(法属)	澳新
Paramaribo	帕拉马里博	苏里南	中南美
Paranagua	巴拉那瓜	巴西	中南美
Penang	槟城	马来西亚	新马
Perth	珀斯	澳大利亚 (美国有同名港)	澳新
Philadedlphia	费城	美国	美国东岸
Phom Penh	金边	柬埔寨	暹罗海
Piraeus	比雷埃夫斯	希腊	地中海
Plymouth	普列茅斯	蒙特塞拉特岛 (英国、美国、新西兰、特立尼达和多巴哥均有同名港)	中南美
Pointe-a-Pitre	皮特尔角	瓜德罗普岛	中南美
Pointe des Galets	加莱角	留尼汪岛(法属)	东非
Pointe Noire	黑角	刚果	西非
Ponce	蓬塞	波多黎各(美属)	中南美
Pondicherry	本地治里	印度	孟加拉湾
Pontianak	坤甸	印尼	印尼
Port Adelaide	阿德雷德	澳大利亚	澳新
Porau Prince	太子港	海地	中南美
Port Castries	卡斯特里港	圣卢西亚	中南美
Port Elizabeth	伊丽莎白港	南非	东非
Port Harcourt	哈科特港	尼日利亚	西非
Port Kelang	巴生港	马来西亚	新马
Port Kembla	肯布兰	澳大利亚	澳新
Portland(Maine 州)	波特兰	美国	美国东岸
Portland(Oregon 州)	波特兰	美国 (英国、澳大利亚有同名港)	美国西岸
Port Limon	利蒙港	哥斯达黎加	中南美
Port Louis	路易港	毛里求斯	东非
Port Moresby	莫尔兹比港	巴布亚新几内亚	澳新

Port of Spain	西班牙港	特立尼达和多巴哥	中南美
Porto Novo	波多诺伏	贝宁	西非
Port Said	塞得港	埃及	地中海
Portsmouth	朴次茅斯	英国 (美国有同名港)	西北欧
Port Stanley	斯坦利港	福克兰群岛	中南美
Port Sudan	苏丹港	苏丹	红海
Port Victoria	维多利亚港	塞舌尔群岛 (澳大利亚有同名港)	东非
Port Vila	维拉港	瓦努阿图	澳新
Priolo	辟利洛(普里奥洛)	意大利	地中海
Puerto Cabello	卡贝略港	委内瑞拉	中南美
Punta Arenas	彭塔阿雷纳斯	智利	中南美
Puntarenas	彭塔雷纳斯	哥斯达黎加	中南美
Pusan(Busan)	釜山	韩国	朝鲜

以(Q)开头的世界港口

Quebec	魁北克	加拿大	加拿大东岸

以(R)开头的世界港口

Rabat	拉巴特	摩洛哥	西非
Rabaul	拉包尔港	巴布亚新几内亚	澳新
Rangoon	仰光	缅甸	孟加拉湾
Rarotonga	拉罗汤加	库克群岛	澳新
Recife	累西菲	巴西	中南美
Reykjavik	雷克雅未克	冰岛	西北欧
Riga	里加	拉脱维亚	西北欧
Rijeka	里耶卡	克罗地亚	地中海
Rio de Janeiro	里约热内卢	巴西	中南美
Rio Grande	里奥格兰德	巴西	中南美
Rostock	罗斯托克	德国	西北欧
Rotterdam	鹿特丹	荷兰	西北欧

以(S)开头的世界港口

Sabang	沙璜	印尼	印尼
Sandakan	山打根	马来西亚	北加里曼丹

San Diego	圣迭戈	美国	美国西岸
San Fernando	圣费尔南多	特立尼达和多巴哥	中南美
		（西班牙、阿根廷、菲律宾有同名港）	
San Francisco	旧金山	美国	美国西岸
		（巴西有同名港）	
San Jose	圣何塞	危地马拉	中南美
San Juan	圣胡安	波多黎各	中南美
		（秘鲁、阿根廷有同名港）	
San Juan del Sur	南圣胡安	尼加拉瓜	中南美
San Lorenzo	圣洛伦索	阿根廷	中南美
Santa Cruz del Sur	圣克鲁斯蒂尔苏 古巴	中南美	
Santa Cruz	圣克鲁斯	加那利群岛	西非
		（亚速尔群岛、阿根廷、美国、菲律宾有同名港）	
Santiago	圣地亚哥	佛得角	西非
		（古巴有同名港）	
Santo	圣吐（桑托）	瓦努阿图	澳新
Santo Domingo	圣多明各	多米尼加共和国	中南美
Santos	圣多斯	巴西	中南美
San Tome	圣多美	圣多美和普林西北	西非
		（巴西有同名港）	
Savannah	萨凡纳	美国	美国东岸
Seattle	西雅图	美国	美国西岸
Semarang	三宝垄	印尼	印尼
Sete	塞特	法国	地中海
Sharjah	沙迦	阿联酋	波斯湾
Sibu	诗巫（泗务、西布）	马来西亚	北加里曼丹
Singapore	新加坡	新加坡	新马
Southampton	南安普敦	英国	西北欧
Split	斯普利特	波黑共和国	地中海
Stavanger	斯塔万格	挪威	西北欧
St. Denis	圣但尼	留尼汪岛	东非
St. Georges	圣乔治	百慕大群岛	中南美
		（加拿大、格林纳达有同名港）	
St. John	圣约翰	加拿大	加拿大东岸
St. Johns	圣约翰斯	安提瓜和巴布达	中南美
		（加拿大、南非有同名港）	

St. Lawrence	圣劳伦斯	加拿大 （澳大利亚有同名港）	加拿大东岸
Stockholm	斯德哥尔摩	瑞典	西北欧
St. Thomas	圣托马斯	维尔京群岛（美属）	中南美
Suez	苏伊士	埃及	红海
Sur	苏尔	黎巴嫩 （阿曼有同名港）	地中海
Surabaya	泗水	印尼	印尼
Suva	苏瓦	斐济	澳新
Swansea	斯旺西	英国	西北欧
Sydney	悉尼	澳大利亚 （加拿大有同名港）	澳新
Szczecin	什切青	波兰	西北欧

以（T）开头的世界港口

Tabaco	塔巴科	菲律宾	菲律宾
Takoradi	塔科拉迪	加纳	西非
Tallin	塔林	爱沙尼亚	西北欧
Tamatave	塔马塔夫	马达加斯加	东非
Tampico	坦皮科	墨西哥	中南美
Tandjungpriok	丹戎不碌	印尼	印尼
Tanga	坦噶	坦桑尼亚	东非
Tangier	丹吉尔	摩洛哥	西非
Tarawa	塔拉瓦	基里巴斯	澳新
Tawau	斗湖	马来西亚	北加里曼丹
Tel Aviv	特拉维夫	以色列	地中海
Tema	特马	加纳	西非
Tjirebon	井里汶	印尼	印尼
Tokyo	东京	日本	日本
Toronto	多伦多	加拿大	加拿大东岸
Toulon	土伦	法国	地中海
Trieste	的里雅斯特	意大利	地中海
Trincomalee	亭可马里	斯里兰卡	斯里兰卡
Tripoli	的黎波里	比亚 （黎巴嫩有同名港）	地中海
Trujillo	特鲁希略	洪都拉斯 （秘鲁有同名港）	中南美

Tumaco	图马科	哥伦比亚	中南美
Tunis	突尼斯	突尼斯	地中海
Turku	图尔库	芬兰	西北欧

以(U) 开头的世界港口

Umm Said	乌姆赛义德	卡塔尔	波斯湾

以(V) 开头的世界港口

Valletta	瓦莱塔	马耳他	地中海
Valona	发罗拉(法罗拉)	阿尔巴尼亚	阿尔巴尼亚
Valparaiso	瓦尔帕莱索	智利	中南美
Vancouver	温哥华	加拿大(美国有同名港)	加拿大西岸
Varna	戊尔纳	保加利亚	地中海
Vasa	瓦沙	芬兰	西北欧
Venice	威尼斯	意大利	地中海
Victoria	维多利亚	喀麦隆	西非
(澳大利亚、加拿大、马来西亚、几内亚、马耳他、塞舌尔群岛均有同名港)			
Vigo	维哥	西班牙	西北欧
Visby	维斯比	瑞典	西北欧
Vostochny	东方港	俄罗斯	远东线

以(W) 开头的世界港口

Walvis Bay	沃尔维斯湾	纳米比亚(西南非洲)	西非
Wellington	惠灵顿	新西兰	澳新
Wewak	威瓦克	巴布亚新几内亚	澳新
Willemstad	威廉斯塔德	安的列斯(荷属)(荷兰有同名港)	中南美
Wismar	维斯马	德国	西北欧

以(Y) 开头的世界港口

Yalta	雅尔塔	俄罗斯	地中海
Yokohama	横滨	日本	日本

以(Z) 开头的世界港口

Zanzibar	桑给巴尔	坦桑尼亚	东非

附录 2

世界各国货币一览表

（中英文对照）

亚洲	货币名称		货币符号		辅币进位制
	中文	英文	原有旧符号	标准符号	
中国香港	港元	HongKong Dollars	HK $	HKD	1HKD = 100cents（分）
中国澳门	澳门元	Macao Pataca	PAT.；P.	MOP	1MOP = 100avos（分）
中国	人民币元	Renminbi Yuan	RMB ¥	CNY	1CNY = 10 jiao（角） 1 jiao = 10 fen（分）
朝鲜	圆	Korean Won	₩	KPW	1KPW = 100 分
越南	越南盾	Vietnamese Dong	D.	VND	1VND = 10 角 = 100 分
日本	日圆	Japanese Yen	¥；J. ¥	JPY	1JPY = 100 sen（钱）
老挝	基普	Laotian Kip	K.	LAK	1LAK = 100 ats（阿特）
柬埔寨	瑞尔	Cambodian Riel	CR.；J Ri.	KHR	1KHR = 100 sen（仙）
菲律宾	菲律宾比索	Philippine Peso	Ph. Pes.；Phil. P.	PHP	1PHP = 100 centavos（分）
马来西亚	马元	Malaysian Dollar	M. $；Mal. $	MYR	1MYR = 100 cents（分）
新加坡	新加坡元	Singapore Dollar	S. $	SGD	1SGD = 100 cents（分）
泰国	泰铢	Thai Baht（Thai Tical）	BT.；Tc.	THP	1THP = 100 satang（萨当）
缅甸	缅元	Burmese Kyat	K.	BUK	1BUK = 100 pyas（分）
斯里兰卡	斯里兰卡卢比	Sri Lanka Rupee	S. Re. 复数：S. Rs.	LKR	1LKR = 100 cents（分）

续表

亚洲	货币名称		货币符号		辅币进位制
	中文	英文	原有旧符号	标准符号	
马尔代夫	马尔代夫卢比	Maldives Rupee	M. R. R; MAL. Rs.	MVR	1MVR = 100 larees(拉雷)
印度尼西亚	盾	Indonesian Rupiah	Rps.	IDR	1IDR = 100 cents(分)
巴基斯坦	巴基斯坦卢比	Pakistan Rupee	Pak. Re.; P. Re. 复数:P. Rs.	PRK	1PRK = 100 paisa(派萨)
印度	卢比	Indian Rupee	Re. 复数:Rs.	INR	1INR = 100 paise(派士)(单数:paisa)
尼泊尔	尼泊尔卢比	Nepalese Rupee	N. Re. 复数: N. Rs.	NPR	1 NPR = 100 paise(派司)
阿富汗	阿富汗尼	Afghani	Af.	AFA	1AFA = 100 puls(普尔)
伊朗	伊朗里亚尔	Iranian Rial	RI.	IRR	1Irr = 100 dinars(第纳尔)
伊拉克	伊拉克第纳尔	Iraqi Dinar	ID	IQD	1IQD = 1 000 fils(费尔)
叙利亚	叙利亚镑	Syrian Pound	£ . Syr.; £ . S.	SYP	1SYP = 100 piastres(皮阿斯特)
黎巴嫩	黎巴嫩镑	Lebanese Pound	£ L.	LBP	1LBP = 100 piastres(皮阿斯特)
约旦	约旦第纳尔	Jordanian Dinar	J. D.; J. Dr.	JOD	1JOD = 1 000 fils(费尔)
沙特阿拉伯	里亚尔	Saudi Arabian Riyal	S. A. Rls.; S. R.	SAR	1SAR = 100 halalas(哈拉拉)
科威特	科威特第纳尔	Kuwaiti Dinar	K. D.	KWD	1KWD = 1 000 fils(费尔)
巴林	巴林第纳尔	Bahrain Dinar	BD.	BHD	1BHD = 1 000 fils(费尔)
卡塔尔	卡塔尔里亚尔	Qatar Riyal	QR.	QAR	1QAR = 100 dirhams(迪拉姆)
阿曼	阿曼里亚尔	Oman Riyal	RO.	OMR	1OMR = 1 000 baiza(派沙)
阿拉伯也门	也门里亚尔	Yemeni Riyal	YRL.	YER	1YER = 100 fils(费尔)
民主也门	也门第纳尔	Yemeni Dinar	YD.	YDD	1YDD = 1 000 fils(费尔)
土耳其	土耳其镑	Turkish Pound (Turkish Lira)	£ T. (TL.)	TRL	1TRL = 100 kurus(库鲁)
塞浦路斯	塞浦路斯镑	Cyprus Pound	£ C.	CYP	1CYP = 1 000 mils(米尔)

大洋洲	货币名称		货币符号		辅币进位制
	中文	英文	原有旧符号	标准符号	
澳大利亚	澳大利亚元	Australian Dollar	$ A.	AUD	1AUD = 100 cents(分)
新西兰	新西兰元	New Zealand Dollar	$ NZ.	NZD	1 NZD = 100 cents(分)
斐济	斐济元	Fiji Dollar	F. $	FJD	1FJD = 100 cents(分)
所罗门群岛	所罗门元	Solomon Dollar	SL. $	SBD	1SBD = 100 cents(分)

欧洲	货币名称		货币符号		辅币进位制
	中文	英文	原有旧符号	标准符号	
欧洲货币联盟	欧元	Euro	EUR	EUR	1EUR = 100 euro cents(生丁)
冰岛	冰岛克朗	Icelandic Krona (复数:Kronur)	I. Kr.	ISK	1ISK = 100 aurar(奥拉)
丹麦	丹麦克朗	Danish Krona (复数:Kronur)	D. Kr.	DKK	1DKK = 100 ore(欧尔)
挪威	挪威克朗	Norwegian Krone (复数:Kronur)	N. Kr.	NOK	1 NOK = 100 ore(欧尔)
瑞典	瑞典克朗	Swedish Krona (复数:Kronor)	S. Kr.	SEK	1SEK = 100 ore(欧尔)
芬兰	芬兰马克	Finnish Markka (or Mark)	MK. ; FM. ; FK. ; FMK.	FIM	1FIM = 100 penni(盆尼)
俄罗斯	卢布	Russian Ruble (or Rouble)	Rbs. Rbl.	SUR	1SUR = 100 kopee(戈比)
波兰	兹罗提	Polish Zloty	ZL.	PLZ	1PLZ = 100 groszy(格罗希)
捷克和斯洛伐克	捷克克朗	Czech Koruna	Kcs. ; Cz. Kr.	CZK	1CZK = 100 Hellers(赫勒)
匈牙利	福林	Hungarian Forint	FT.	HUF	1HUF = 100 filler(菲勒)
德国	马克	Deutsche Mark	DM.	DEM	1DEM = 100 pfennig(芬尼)
奥地利	奥地利先令	Austrian Schilling	Sch.	ATS	1ATS = 100 Groschen(格罗申)
瑞士	瑞士法郎	Swiss Franc	SF. ;SFR.	CHF	1CHF = 100 centimes(分)
荷兰	荷兰盾	Dutch Guilder (or Florin)	Gs. ; Fl. ; Dfl. ; Hfl. ;fl.	NLG	1 NLG = 100 cents(分)
比利时	比利时法郎	Belgian Franc	Bi. ; B. Fr. ; B. Fc.	BEF	1BEF = 100 centimes(分)
卢森堡	卢森堡法郎	Luxembourg Franc	Lux. F.	LUF	1LUF = 100 centimes(分)
英国	英镑	Pound, Sterling	£ ;£ Stg.	GBP	1GBP = 100 new pence(新便士)

续表

欧洲	货币名称		货币符号		辅币进位制
	中文	英文	原有旧符号	标准符号	
爱尔兰	爱尔兰镑	Irish pound	£ . Ir.	IEP	1IEP = 100 new pence(新便士)
法国	法郎	French Franc	F. F. ; Fr. Fc. ; F. FR.	FRF	1FRF = 100 centimes(分)
西班牙	比塞塔	Spanish Peseta	Pts. ; Pes.	ESP	1ESP = 100 centimos(分)
葡萄牙	埃斯库多	Portuguese Escudo	ESC.	PTE	1PTE = 100 centavos(分)
意大利	里拉	Italian Lira	Lit.	ITL	1ITL = 100 centesimi(分)
马耳他	马耳他镑	Maltese Pound	£ . M.	MTP	1MTP = 100 cents(分) 1Cent = 10 mils(米尔)
南斯拉夫	南斯拉夫新第纳尔	Yugoslav Din	Din. Dr.	YUD	1YUD = 100 paras(帕拉)
罗马尼亚	列伊	Romanian Leu (复数:Leva)	L.	ROL	1ROL = 100 bani(巴尼)
保加利亚	列弗	Bulgarian Lev (复数:Lei)	Lev.	BGL	1BGL = 100 stotinki(斯托丁基)
阿尔巴尼亚	列克	Albanian Lek	Af.	ALL	1ALL = 100 quintars(昆塔)
希腊	德拉马克	Greek Drachma	Dr.	GRD	1GRD = 100 lepton(雷普顿) or lepta(雷普塔)

美洲	货币名称		货币符号		辅币进位制
	中文	英文	原有旧符号	标准符号	
加拿大	加元	Canadian Dollar	Can. $	CAD	1CAD = 100 cents(分)
美国	美元	U. S. Dollar	U. S. $	USD	1USD = 100 cent(分)
墨西哥	墨西哥比索	Mexican Peso	Mex. $	MXP	1MXP = 100 centavos(分)
危地马拉	格查尔	Guatemalan Quetzal	Q	GTQ	1GTQ = 100 centavos(分)
萨尔瓦多	萨尔瓦多科朗	Salvadoran Colon	¢	SVC	1SVC = 100 centavos(分)
洪都拉斯	伦皮拉	Honduran Lempira	L.	HNL	1HNL = 100 centavos(分)
尼加拉瓜	科多巴	Nicaraguan Cordoba	CS	NIC	1 NIC = 100 centavos(分)
哥斯达黎加	哥斯达黎加科朗	Costa Rican Colon	¢	CRC	1CRC = 100 centavos(分)
巴拿马	巴拿马巴波亚	Panamanian Balboa	B.	PAB	1PAB = 100 centesimos(分)
古巴	古巴比索	Cuban Peso	Cu. Pes.	CUP	1CUP = 100 centavos(分)

续表

美洲	货币名称		货币符号		辅币进位制
	中文	英文	原有旧符号	标准符号	
巴哈马联邦	巴哈马元	Bahaman Dollar	B. $	BSD	1BSD = 100 cents(分)
牙买加	牙买加元	Jamaican Dollars	$. J.	JMD	1JMD = 100 cents(分)
海地	古德	Haitian Gourde	G.;Gds.	HTG	1HTG = 100 centimes(分)
多米尼加	多米尼加比索	Dominican Peso	R. D. $	DOP	1DOP = 100 centavos(分)
特立尼达和多巴哥	特立尼达多巴哥元	Trinidad and Tobago Dollar	T. T. $	TTD	1TTD = 100 cents(分)
巴巴多斯	巴巴多斯元	Barbados Dollar	BDS. $	BBD	1BBD = 100 cents(分)
哥伦比亚	哥伦比亚比索	Colombian Peso	Col $	COP	1COP = 100 centavos(分)
委内瑞拉	博利瓦	Venezuelan Bolivar	B	VEB	1VEB = 100 centimos(分)
圭亚那	圭亚那元	Guyanan Dollar	G. $	GYD	1GYD = 100 cents(分)
苏里南	苏里南盾	Surinam Florin	S. Fl.	SRG	苏 1SRG = 100 分
秘鲁	新索尔	Peruvian Sol	S/.	PES	1PES = 100 centavos(分)
厄瓜多尔	苏克雷	Ecuadoran Sucre	S/.	ECS	1ECS = 100 centavos(分)
巴西	新克鲁赛罗	Brazilian New Cruzeiro	Gr. $	BRC	1BRC = 100 centavos(分)
玻利维亚	玻利维亚比索	Bolivian Peso	Bol. P.	BOP	1BOP = 100 centavos(分)
智利	智利比索	Chilean Peso	P.	CLP	1CLP = 100 centesimos(分)
阿根廷	阿根廷比索	Argentine Peso	Arg. P.	ARP	1ARP = 100 centavos(分)
巴拉圭	巴拉圭瓜拉尼	Paraguayan Guarani	Guars.	PYG	1PYG = 100 centimes(分)
乌拉圭	乌拉圭新比索	New Uruguayan Peso	N. $	UYP	1UYP = 100 centesimos(分)

非洲	货币名称		货币符号		辅币进位制
	中文	英文	原有旧符号	标准符号	
埃及	埃及镑	Egyptian Pound	£ E.;LF.	EGP	1EGP = 100 piastres(皮阿斯特) = 1 000 milliemes(米利姆)
利比亚	利比亚第纳尔	Libyan Dinar	LD.	LYD	1LYD = 100 piastres(皮阿斯特) = 1 000 milliemes(米利姆)

续表

非洲	货币名称		货币符号		辅币进位制
	中文	英文	原有旧符号	标准符号	
苏丹	苏丹镑	Sudanese Pound	£ S.	SDP	1SDP = 100 piastres(皮阿斯特) = 1 000 milliemes(米利姆)
突尼斯	突尼斯第纳尔	Tunisian Dinar	TD.	TND	1TND = 1 000 milliemes(米利姆)
阿尔及利亚	阿尔及利亚第纳尔	Algerian Dinar	AD.	DZD	1DZD = 100 centimes(分)
摩洛哥	摩洛哥迪拉姆	Moroccan Dirham	DH.	MAD	1MAD = 100 centimes(分)
毛里塔尼亚	乌吉亚	Mauritania Ouguiya	UM	MRO	1MRO = 5 khoums(库姆斯)
塞内加尔	非共体法郎	African Financial Community Franc	C. F. A. F.	XOF	1XOF = 100 centimes(分)
上沃尔特	非共体法郎	African Financial Community Franc	C. F. A. F.	XOF	1XOF = 100 centimes(分)
科特迪瓦	非共体法郎	African Financial Community Franc	C. F. A. F.	XOF	1XOF = 100 centimes(分)
多哥	非共体法郎	African Financial Community Franc	C. F. A. F.	XOF	1XOF = 100 centimes(分)
贝宁	非共体法郎	African Financial Community Franc	C. F. A. F.	XOF	1XOF = 100 centimes(分)
尼泊尔	非共体法郎	African Financial Community Franc	C. F. A. F.	XOF	1XOF = 100 centimes(分)
冈比亚	达拉斯	Gambian Dalasi	D. G.	GMD	1GMD = 100 bututses(分)
几内亚比绍	几内亚比索	Guine - Bissau peso	PG.	GWP	1GWP = 100 centavos(分)
几内亚	几内亚西里	Guinean Syli	GS.	GNS	辅币为科里 cauri,但 50 科里以下舍掉不表示;50 科里以上进为一西里
塞拉利昂	利昂	Sierra Leone Leone	Le.	SLL	1SLL = 100 cents(分)
利比里亚	利比里亚元	Liberian Dollar	L. $ £ ;Lib. $	LRD	1LRD = 100 cents(分)

续表

非洲	货币名称		货币符号		辅币进位制
	中文	英文	原有旧符号	标准符号	
加纳	塞地	Ghanaian Cedi	¢	GHC	1GHC = 100 pesewas(比塞瓦)
尼日利亚	奈拉	Nigerian Naira	N	NGN	1 NGN = 100 kobo(考包)
喀麦隆	中非金融合作法郎	Central African Finan-Coop Franc	CFAF	XAF	1XAF = 100 centimes(分)
乍得	中非金融合作法郎	Central African Finan-Coop Franc	CFAF	XAF	1XAF = 100 centimes(分)
刚果	中非金融合作法郎	Central African Finan-Coop Franc	CFAF	XAF	1XAF = 100 centimes(分)
加蓬	中非金融合作法郎	Central African Finan-Coop Franc	CFAF	XAF	1XAF = 100 centimes(分)
中非	中非金融合作法郎	Central African Finan-Coop Franc	CFAF	XAF	1XAF = 100 centimes(分)
赤道几内亚	赤道几内亚埃奎勒	Equatorial Guinea Ekuele	EK.	GQE	1GQE = 100 centimes(分)
南非	兰特	South African Rand	R.	ZAR	1ZAR = 100 cents(分)
吉布提	吉布提法郎	Djibouti Franc	DJ. FS;DF	DJF	1DJF = 100 centimes(分)
索马里	索马里先令	Somali Shilling	Sh. So.	SOS	1SOS = 100 cents(分)
肯尼亚	肯尼亚先令	Kenya Shilling	K. Sh	KES	1KES = 100 cents(分)
乌干达	乌干达先令	Uganda Shilling	U. Sh.	UGS	1UGS = 100 cents(分)
坦桑尼亚	坦桑尼亚先令	Tanzania Shilling	T. Sh.	TZS	1TZS = 100 cents(分)
卢旺达	卢旺达法郎	Rwanda Franc	RF.	RWF	1RWF = 100 cents(分)
布隆迪	布隆迪法郎	Burundi Franc	F. Bu	BIF	1BIF = 100 cents(分)
扎伊尔	扎伊尔	Zaire Rp Zaire	Z.	ZRZ	1ZRZ = 100 makuta(马库塔)
赞比亚	赞比亚克瓦查	Zambian Kwacha	KW.;K.	ZMK	1ZMK = 100 nywee(恩韦)
马达加斯加	马达加斯加法郎	Franc de Madagasca	F. Mg.	MCF	1MCF = 100 cents(分)
塞舌尔	塞舌尔卢比	Seychelles Rupee	S. RP(S)	SCR	1SCR = 100 cent(分)

续表

非洲	货币名称		货币符号		辅币进位制
	中文	英文	原有旧符号	标准符号	
毛里求斯	毛里求斯卢比	Mauritius Rupee	Maur. Rp.	MUR	1MUR = 100 centimes (分)
津巴布韦	津巴布韦元	Zimbabwe Dollar	ZIM. $	ZWD	1ZWD = 100 cents(分)
科摩罗	科摩罗法郎	Comoros Franc	Com. F.	KMF	1KMF = 100 tambala(坦巴拉)

附录 3

国际商务单证常用缩略语一览表

（中英文对照）

A

a(@)	at	按
A/B	Aktiebolaget	股份公司(瑞典文)
abt.	about	大约
A/C	for account of	代、代表
acct.	account	账(账户)
A. D.	Anno Domini(L)	公元(拉丁文)
ADB	Asia Development Bank	亚洲开发银行
add.	address	地址
Avdal	ad valorem	从值(从价)
A/G	Aktiengeselskabet	股份公司(德文)
a. m.	anno meridiem(L.)	上午
A/M	above mentioned	上述
amt.	amount	金额
A/O	account of...	入某人账户(由某人付账)
a. p. l.	as per list	按照表列
A. P. L.	American President Line	美国总统轮船公司
app.	appendix	附表
approx.	approximately	大约

续表

A. R	All Risks	一切险
art.	article	条款、货款
A/S	Aktieselskabet	股份公司(丹麦文)
	AktieseLskapet	股份公司(挪威文)
	Akzijn Sabeedriba	股份公司(芬兰文)
A/S	after sight = at sight	见票后(即付)
asst.	assortment	搭配
Asst	Assistant	助理
A. T. L.	actual total loss	实际全损
Att.	attached	附
Attn.	Attention	请洽
Aug.	August	八月
A. V.	Ad Valorem	从值(从价)
AV	Average	海损
Ave.	Avenue	路、大道
AWB	air way bill	航空运单

B

b/ -	bale, bag	包、装
BAF	bunker adjustment factor	燃油附加费
bal.	balance	余额、平衡
B. B. Clause	both to blame collision clause	船舶互撞条款
B/C	bill for collection	托收汇票
B. C.	before Christ	公元前
bdle.	bundle	把、捆
B/E	bill of exchange	汇票
BENELUX	Belgium, Netherland, Luxemburg	比利时、荷兰、卢森堡(三国)
b/f	brought forward	承前页
bg	bag	袋
Bk.	bank	银行
bkt	basket	篮、筐
bl.	bale	包
B/L	bill of lading	提单
bldg	building	大厦

续表

BOC	Bank of China	中国银行
B. O.	branch office	分公司
br	branch	分行、分支机构
brl	barrel	桶
Bros	brothers	兄弟(公司)
b/s	bales, bags	包、装(复数)
btl	bottle	瓶
BTN	Brussels Tariff Nomenclature	布鲁塞尔税则目录
bx(s)	box(es)	箱、盒

C

c/ –	case	箱
ca.	circa	大约
C/A	cable address	电挂
CAF	cost assurance freight	成本保险加运费价
CAF	currency adjustment factor	货币调整附加费
CAD	cash against delivery	货到付款
canc.	cancelled, cancellation	取消
Capt.	captain	船长
Caricom	Caribbean Community	加勒比海共同体
Cat.	catalogue	目录
	category	类别
C. C.	carbon copy	复写本
CCCN	Customs Co-operative Council Nomenclature	海关合作理事会税则目录
CCIB	China Commodity Inspection Bureau	中国商品检验局
CCIC	China Commodity Inspection Corporation	中国商品检验公司
CCPIT	China Council for Promotion of International Trade	中国国际贸易促进委员会
C. C. V. O	combined certificate of value and origin	价值、产地联合证明书(海关发票)
c/f	carried forward	续后页
C&F	cost and freight	成本加运费价
C&I	cost and insurance	成本加保险价
CFS	Container Freight Station	集装箱货物集散站
cft.	cubic feet	立方英尺
ch.	cheque	支票

续表

chg	charge	费用
Cia	Compania	公司(西班牙)
Cie	Compagnie	公司(法国)
C/I	certificate of inspection	检验证书
	certificate of insurance	保险凭证
CIC	China Insurance Clause	中国保险条款
CIF	cost, insurance, freight	成本、保险加运费价
CIFC	cost, insurance, freight, commission	成本保险运费加佣金价
C. I. O.	cash in order	订货时付款
CIP	freight of carriage & insurance paid to	运费保险费付至…价
CISS	Comprehensive Import Supervision Scheme	进口商品全面监督计划
ck.	check	支票
CPT	carriage paid to	运费付至…价
CL	container load	集装箱装载
CLP	container load plan	集装箱装箱单
cm	centimetre	公分、厘米
C. M. T	cutting, making and trimming	裁剪、缝制、整烫(整理)
C/N	credit note	贷项账单
CNFTTC	China National Foreign Trade Transportation Corp.	中国外贸运输公司
CNY	Chinese Yuan	中国元
Co.	Company	公司
C/O	certificate of origin	产地证书
	care of	转交
	cash order	本票
C. O. D	cash on delivery or collection on delivery	货到付款
comm.	commission	佣金
Cont.	contract	合同
contd.	continued	继续、未完
Co-op	co-operative	合作经营,合作社
Corp.	Corporation	公司
COSCO	China Ocean Shipping Company	中国远洋运输公司
C/P	charter party	租船方
c. q. d	customary quick dispatch	习惯快速装卸
Cr.	credit	贷方

续表

C/R	cargo receipt	货物承运收据
crt.	crate	板条箱
c/s	cases	箱
CTA	communicate to all address	分送电
C. T. B/L	combined transport bill of lading	联合运输提单
C. T. D	combined transport documents	联合运输单据
C. T. L	constructive total loss	推定全损
ctn.	carton	纸箱
C. T. O	combined transport operator	多式联运经营人
cu.	cubic	立方
c. u. ft.	cubic feet	立方英尺
c. u. m	cubic metre	立方公尺
cur.	currency	币制
C. V. C.	Chief value of cotton	主要成分是棉制
C. V. S.	Chief value of synthetic	主要成分是人造纤维
C. W. O.	cash with order	订货时付款
CWT	hundred weight	亨特威(英制 100 磅)
CY	container yard	集装箱堆场
CY to CY	container yard/container yard	集装箱堆场至集装箱堆场
C. Z.	canal zone	运河地带

D

d.	denarius(L.) = penny or pence	便士
D/A	documents against acceptance	承兑交单
D/A	documentary credit	跟单信用证
D/D	demand draft	即期汇票
dd.	dated	日期
Dec.	December	十二月
Dept.	department	部、处、科
D/F	dead freight	空舱费
DHL	DHL International Ltd.	敦豪公司(信使传递)
diam	diameter	直径
disc	discount	折扣、贴现息
D/N.	debit note	借项账单

续表

do.	ditto = the same	同上、同前
doc.	document	单据、单证
D/O,D. O.	delivery order	提货单
Dol.	dollar	元
Doz(Dz.)	dozen	打
D/P	documents against payment	付款交单
D/PT/P	documents against payment with trust receipt	付款交单可凭信托收据借贷
D. P. V.	duty paid value	完税价格
d/s	days	天数
Dr.	debit	借方
dup.	duplicate	副本

E

ea.	each	每
E. C. U	European Currency Unit	欧洲共同体货币单位
E/D	export declaration	出口申报书
E. E.	error excepted	错误当查
EEC	European Economic Community	欧洲经济共同体
e. g.	exempli gratia	例如
E/L	export license	出口许可证
EMP	European Main Ports	欧洲主要口岸
EMS	European Monetary System	欧洲共同市场货币体系
	Express Mail Service	特快专递
encl.	enclosure	附件
E. &. O. E	errors & omissions excepted	错漏当查
EPZ	export processing zone	出口加工区
equiv	equivalent	等于
Est	Establishment	机构、企业、商店
EAT	estimated time of arrival	预计到达时间
etc.	et cetera(and so on)	等等
ETCL	expected time of commencement of loading	预计开始装货时间
ETD	estimated time of departure	预计离港时间
ETFD	expected time of finishing discharging	预计卸完时间
ETFL	expected time of finishing	预计装完时间

续表

ea.	each	每
ex.	example	举例
exc.	excepted	除外
exch.	exchange	兑换,汇票
Ex. Facie	in accordance with the documents	按照单证
exp.	export	出口
EXQ	ex quay	码头交货价
EXS	ex ship	目的港船上交货价
EXW	ex work	工厂交货价

F

F. A. Q.	fair average quality	大路货
F. A. S.	Free alongside ship	船边交货
F. B.	freight bill	运费账单
F. B/L	FIATA combined transport B/L	国际运输商协会联合会联合运输提单
Feb.	February	二月
FC&S	free of capture & seizure clause	战争险不保条款
Fch.	franchise	免赔率
F. C. L.	full container load	整箱货
F. C. T. B/L	FIATA combined transport B/L	国际运输商协会联合会联合运输提单
FEFC	Far East Freight Conference	远东运费公会
FIATA	Federation Internationale des Associations de Transitaires et Assimiles	国际运输商协会联合会
F. I.	free in	船方不负担装货费用
F. I. O.	free in and out	船方不负担装卸费用
F. I. O. S.	free in and out and stowed	船方不负担装卸及积载费用
F. I. O. S. T.	free in and out and stowed and trimmed	船方不负担装卸及积载平舱费用
F. I. O. T.	free in and out and trimmed	船方不负担装卸及平舱费用
F. I. W.	free into wagons	车上交货
F. M. V.	fair market value	公平市场价
F. O.	free out	船方不负担卸货费用
F. O. B	free on board	离岸价
F. O. C	free on charge	免费
F. O. I	free on interest	免息

续表

F. A. Q.	fair average quality	大路货
F. O. P	free on plane	飞机上交货价
F. O. Q.	free on quay	码头交货价
F. O. R.	free on rail	铁路交货价
F. O. T	free on truck	车上交货价
F. O. W.	free on wagon	火车交货价
F. P. A.	free of particular average	平安险
Franco	franco rendu (free delivered)	免费送货到指定地点价
F. R. E. C.	fire risks extension clauses	火险扩展条款
Fri.	Friday	星期五
frt.	freight	运费
FRWD	fresh & Rain Water Damage	淡水雨淋险
F/T	freight ton	运费吨
Ft.	feet	英尺

G

GA	General Average	共同海损
gal.	gallon	加仑
GATT	General Agreement on Tariffs & Trade	关税及贸易总协定
gds.	goods	货物
Gent.	gentleman	先生、绅士
G. m. b. H	Gesellschaft mit beschrankter Haftung	有限公司
G. M. Q.	Good merchantable quality	上好可销品质
G. M. T.	Greenwich mean time	格林威治时间
G. P. O.	General Post Office	邮政总局
gr.	gross	罗
grm.	gram	克
G. R. T	gross registered tonnage	注册总吨
gr. wt.	gross weight	毛重
GSP	generalized system of preferences	普惠制
GSP C/O	generalized system of preferences certificate of origin	普惠制产地证
GSP Form A	generalized system of preferences Form A	普惠制格式 A

H

HAWB	house airway bill	航空分运单
H/H	house to house	集装箱门到门
H. O.	Head Office	总行
h. p.	horse power	马力
H/P	house to pier	从厂、库到码头
hrs.	hours	钟点
HSBC	Hongkong & Shanghai Banking Corporation	汇丰银行
ht.	height	高度
hund.	hundred	百

I

ICC	International Chamber of commerce	国际商会
	Institute Cargo Clause	伦敦保险学会条款
id	idem = the same	同前
I/D	import declaration	进口申请书
i. e.	id est(L.) = that is	即是
I/E	import/export	进口/出口
I/L	import license	进口许可证
In.	inch	英寸
Inc.	Incorporated	有限公司
ind.	indent	委托代购单
incl.	including, inclusive	包括
INCOTERMS	International Rules for the Interpretation of Trade Terms	国际贸易术语解释通则
Ins.	insurance	保险
inst.	instant	本月
inv.	invoice	发票
I/O	instead of	代替
I/P	import permit	进口许可证
	insurance policy	保险单
I. O. P.	irrespective of percentage	不计免赔率
I. Q.	idem quod(the same as)	同
	import quota	进口配额
I. O. U.	I owe you	借据
ISO	International Standard Organization	国际标准化组织

J

Jan.	January	一月
Jul.	July	七月
Jun.	June	六月
JWOB	jettison &/or washing overboard	抛掷、海水冲击险

K

Kg.	kilogram	公斤
K. Line	Kawasaki Kisem Kaisha Ltd.	川崎汽船株式会社
Km.	kilometer	千米、公里

L

LASH	lighter-aboard-ship	载驳船
lb(s)	pound(s)	磅
L/C	letter of credit	信用证
LCL	less(than)container	拼装集装箱货
ldg	loading	装载
L/G	letter of guarantee	保函
LIBOR	London Interbank Offer Rate	伦敦银行同业拆放利率
L/T	long ton	长吨、英吨
Ltd.	Limited(company)	有限公司
ltg.	lighterage	驳船费

M

Mar.	March	三月
MAWB	master airway bill	总航空运单
max.	maximum	最大量、最高额
M. D.	malicious damage	恶意行为损坏
mdse	merchandise	货物、商品
med.	medium	中等
memo	memorandum	备忘录
mfg	manufacturing	制造中,生产
MFN	most favored nation	最惠国
mfr	manufacturer	制造商

续表

min.	minimum	最小量
misc.	miscellaneous	其他
M. L. B.	Mini-Land-Bridge	小陆桥
M/L cls.	more or less clause	溢短装条款
mm.	millimeter	毫米
Mon.	Monday	星期一
M. P. H	miles per hour	时速...里
M/R	mate's receipt	大副收据
M/S	motor ship	内燃机轮
M/T	mail transfer	信汇
	metric ton	公吨
M. V.	motor vessel	内燃机轮
M. T. O.	multi-modal transport operation	多式联运
M/W	measurement/weight	体积或重量

N

N/A	not applicable	不适用
N. B.	nota bene = note below	注意
N. C. V.	no commercial value	无商业价值
N/M	no mark	无唛头
N. N. B/L	non-negotiable, not negotiable B/L	副本提单
No.	number	号码
non. d	not delivery	提货不着
N. O. E.	not otherwise enumerated	除非另有例举
N. O. P. F.	not otherwise provided for	除非另有规定
N. O. S.	not otherwise specified	除非另有指定
Nov.	November	十一月
N. P.	notary public	公证人
N/S	not sufficient	不足
N. Wt.	net weight	净重

O

O/A	on account of	代表
O/B	on behalf of	代表
O/C	open cover	预约承保书
OC	ocean	海洋
OCP	Overland Common Point	内陆运转点
Oct	October	十月
OG(I)L	Open General(Import)License	开放配额
OK	corrected ,approved	已获批准
OMCC	Ocean Marine Cargo Clause	海洋运输货物保险条款
O/O	(by) order of	送交
Orig.	original	正本
oz(s)	ounce(s)	英两、盎司
OSS	ourselves	我们自己

P

P. A.	particular average	单独海损
p. a	per annum	按年(计息)
P. & I. Club	Protection & Indemnity Club	保障赔偿协会
payt	payment	付款
p. c.	percent	百分之
P/C	polyester/cotton	涤/棉
pcs	pieces	件、个、只、块、张
pct.	percent	百分之
pd.	paid	付讫
p. d.	per day	按日(计息)
PICC	The People's Insurance Company of China	中国人民保险公司
pkg.	package	件、包
pls.	please	请
p. m.	post meridiem	下午
	per month	按月计息
P. O.	post office	邮局
	purchase order	邮货订单
P. O. B.	Post Office Box	邮政信箱

续表

P. O. D.	payment on delivery	付款交货
p. p.	per procuration	代表
pr(s)	pair(s)	双、付
pro rate	Proportionally	按比例
P. R. C	People's Republic of China	中华人民共和国
prem.	premium	保险费
prox.	proximo	下月
P. S.	postscript	附言
P. T. O	please turnover	请阅背面
pty	propriety	企业公司
Pte.	private	私人
P/V	polyester/viscose	涤/粘
P. V. C	polyvinyl chloride	聚氯乙烯

Q

qr.	quarter	四分之一
Q. V.	quod vide(which see)	请查阅
qnty.	quantity	数量
qlty	quality	品质

R

Re	reference	参考
Ref. No.	reference number	参考号
Reg.	registered	注册
retd.	returned	退回
R. F. W. D	rain &or fresh water damage	淡水雨淋险
Rm.	room	房间
RMB	Renminbi Yuan	人民币
R. S. V. P	repondez s'ill vous plait(Fr.)reply, if you please	请复
Ry.	railway	铁路

T

T.	tare, ton	皮重、吨
T/A	transshipment allowed	允许转运
	transshipment additional	转船附加费
	train/air	陆/空
TAT	train-air-truck	陆空陆
T/C	trueran/cotton	涤/棉
tdg.	trading	贸易
TEU	twenty equivalent of unit	相当于 20 英尺集装箱
Thur.	Thursday	星期四
Tlx	telex	电传
T. L. O.	total loss only	全损险
TM	telegram multiple	同文电
tonn	tonnage	吨位
T. P. N. D	theft, pilferage & non-delivery	盗窃提货不着险
tr. wt	tare weight	皮重
T/R	trust receipt	信托收据
T. Q.	tale quale or tel quel	现状条件
T/T	telegraphic transfer	电汇
TTL	total	总计
Tues.	Tuesday	星期二

U

U. A. E	United Arab Emirates	阿拉伯联合酋长国
UCP	uniform customs & practice	统一惯例
U. K. Ports	United Kingdom Ports	英国港口
ult	Ultimo	上月
U/T	unlimited transshipment	无限制转船
U/M	under-mentioned	下述

V

V.	vide	参阅
val.	value	价值
viz.	videlicet namely	即是

续表

voy.	voyage	航次
VV.	vice versa	反之亦然

W

W. A.	with average	水渍险
Wed.	Wednesday	星期三
whse	warehouse	仓库
W/M	weight/measurement	重量或体积
W. O.	washing overboard	冲失
W. P. A	with particular average	水渍险
W. R.	war risks	战争险
Wt.	weight	重量
W/T	with transshipment	转船
wtd.	warranted	保证
wty.	warranty	保证条款
W/W	warehouse to warehouse clause	仓至仓条款

X

XL	Extra large	特大
XP	express paid	快信
xs.	excess	超过

Y

Y. A. R	York-Antwerp Rule	约克-安特卫普规定（国际共同海损规则）

附录4

常用单位换算一览表

（中英文对照）

长度

1 千米(km) =0. 621 英里(mile)

1 米(m) =3. 281 英尺(ft) =1. 094 码(yd)

1 厘米(cm) =0. 394 英寸(in)

1 英里(mile) =1. 609 千米(km)

1 英尺(ft) =0. 304 8 米(m)

1 英寸(in) =2. 54 厘米(cm)

1 海里(n mile) =1. 852 千米(km)

1 码(yd) =0. 914 4 米(m)

1 英尺(ft) =12 英寸(in)

1 码(yd) =3 英尺(ft)

1 英里(mile) =5 280 英尺(ft)

1 海里(n mile) =1. 151 6 英里(mile)

质量

1 吨(ton) =1 000 千克(kg) =2 205 磅(lb)

=1. 102 短吨(short ton) =0. 934 长吨(long ton)

1 千克(kg) =2. 205 磅(lb)

1 短吨(short ton) =0. 907 吨(t) =2 000 磅(1b)

1 长吨(long ton) =1. 016 吨(t) =2 240(lb)

1 磅(lb) =0. 454 千克(kg)

1 盎司(oz) = 28. 350 克(g)

密度

1 千克/立方米(kg/m^3) = 0. 001 克/立方厘米(g/cm^3) = 0. 062 4 磅/立方英尺(lb/ft^3)

1 磅/立方英尺(lb/ft^3) = 16. 02 千克/立方米(kg/m^3)

1 磅/立方英寸(lb/in^3) = 27 679. 9 千克/立方米(kg/m^3)

1 磅/美加仑(lb/gal) = 119. 826 千克/立方米(kg/m^3)

1 磅/英加仑(lb/gal) = 99. 776 千克/立方米(kg/m^3)

1 磅/(石油)桶(lb/bbl) = 2. 853 千克/立方米(kg/m^3)

面积

1 平方公里(km^2) = 100 公顷(ha) = 247. 1 英亩(acre)
= 0. 386 平方英里($mile^2$)

1 平方米(m^2) = 10. 764 平方英尺(ft^2)

1 公亩(acre) = 100 平方米(m^2)

1 公顷(ha) = 10 000 平方米(m^2) = 2. 471 英亩(acre)

1 平方英里($mile^2$) = 2. 590 平方公里(km^2)

1 英亩(acre) = 0. 404 7 公顷(ha) = 40.47×10^{-4}平方公里(km^2)
= 4 047 平方米(m^2)

1 平方英尺(ft^2) = 0. 093 平方米(m^2)

1 平方英寸(in^2) = 6. 452 平方厘米(cm^2)

1 平方码(yd^2) = 0. 836 1 平方米(m^2)

体积

1 立方米(m^3) = 1 000 升(l) = 35. 315 立方英尺(ft^3) = 6. 290 桶(bbl)

1 立方英尺(ft^3) = 0. 028 3 立方米(m^3) = 28. 317 升(l)

1 千立方英尺(mcf) = 28. 317 立方米(m^3)

1 百万立方英尺(MMcf) = 2. 831 7 万立方米(m^3)

10 亿立方英尺(bcf) = 2831. 7 万立方米(m^3)

1 万亿立方英尺(tcf) = 283. 17 亿立方米(m^3)

1 立方英寸(in^3) = 16. 387 1 立方厘米(cm^3)

1 英亩 · 英尺 = 1 234 立方米(m^3)

1 桶(bbl) = 0. 159 立方米(m^3) = 42 美加仑(gal)

1 美加仑(gal) = 3. 785 升(l)

1 美夸脱(qt) = 0. 946 升(l)

1 美品脱(pt) = 0. 473 升(l)

1 美吉耳(gi) = 0. 118 升(l)

1 英加仑(gal) = 4. 546 升(l)

参 考 文 献

[1] ICC 跟单信用证统一惯例 UCP600[M]. 北京:中国民主法制出版社,2006.

[2] 杨金玲. 国际商务单证实务[M]. 北京:首都经济贸易大学出版社,2008.

[3] 童宏祥. 新编外贸单证实务[M]. 上海:华东理工大学出版社,2007.

[4] 林泽拯. 出口单证范本选[M]. 北京:中国对外经济贸易出版社,1997.

[5] 陈国武. 解读《跟单信用证统一惯例(2007 年修订本)》第 600 号出版物[M]. 天津:天津大学出版社,2007.

[6] 屈韬. 外贸单证处理技巧[M]. 广州:广东经济出版社,2000.

[7] [美]Edward G. Hinkelman. 国际贸易单证——进出口、运输和银行单证[M]. 董俊英,译. 北京:经济科学出版社,2002.

[8] 张军. 外贸单证实务[M]. 南京:东南大学出版社,2004.

[9] 张雪莹,刘昕蓉. 国际贸易实务单证大全[M]. 天津:天津大学出版社,2007.